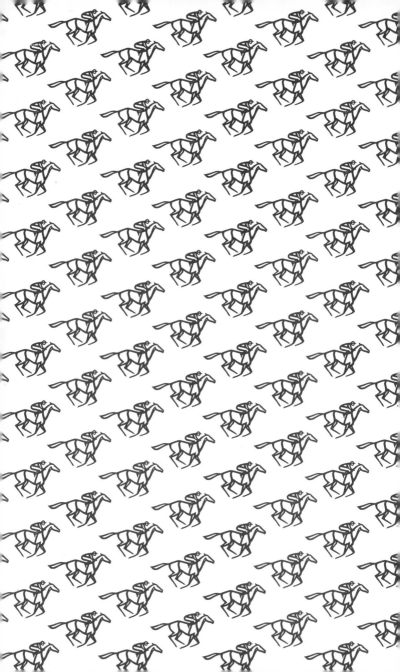

CHASERS & HURDLERS
1992/93
STATISTICAL COMPANION

A TIMEFORM PUBLICATION

Compiled and produced by

G. Greetham, B.A., G. F. Walton, Dip.A.D. (Directors), J. D. Newton, B.A. (Editor-in-Chief), E. K. Wilkinson (Editor), S. D. Rowlands, B.A. (Handicapper), R. J. C. Austen, B.A., G. Crowther, M. T. Greenwood, W. Hughes, G. M. Johnstone, D. Sheard, J. Willoughby and C. Wright, B.A.

© **Portway Press Limited 1993**

ISBN 0 900599 65 0

CONTENTS

4   Introduction

5   Promising Horses

11   Trainers Record

37   Sires of Winners

90   Trainers, Permit Holders, Jockeys,
        Conditional Jockeys and Amateur Riders

114   Big Races 1946-1993

179   Characteristics of Racecourses

INTRODUCTION

The objective of the 'Chasers & Hurdlers 1992/93 Statistical Companion' is to provide an authoritative source of useful statistical data and other information.

The statistical sections in the Companion are abstracted from the wealth of information contained in the main volume of 'Chasers & Hurdlers 1992/93'. Presenting the data in this way, adapted for easy reference and use, should prove invaluable.

Being able to identify those horses in a race with potential—those likely to improve or those which, for one reason or another, are capable of better than they have shown—is essential for the serious backer. All horses in Timeform publications which have a 'p' or a large 'P' attached to their ratings are worthy of special attention. These horses, all thought capable of noteworthy improvement, are highlighted in a section in the Companion which lists them under their trainers.

The Companion also provides a neatly-tabulated record for every trainer whose horses earned more than £25,000 in win prize money in Britain last season. For each of the trainers there is a list of his or her winning horses and their Timeform Ratings, an indication of the quality of the horses in the stable. Also provided are the courses at which each of the horse's victories was achieved (course specialists—equine and human—identified at a glance). There's also a month-by-month breakdown of the trainer's record of runners and winners.

There are as many misleading theories about sires as there are about trainers, and the sires section in the Companion should prove informative. Some of the ideas in common currency about the racing characteristics that are passed down from a particular sire to his progeny seem to enjoy the status of 'received wisdom'. Following ill-conceived theories on the lines of 'All horses by so-and-so need the mud' can, however, be costly for the backer.

The record of winners, sire by sire, in the Companion provides the Timeform Rating of each winner and the distance and going for each race it won. This section, which over the course of time will build into a definitive domestic picture of each stallion, should become a standard reference for anyone with an interest in the pedigrees of racehorses.

All the statistical sections in the Companion present information relating only to the 1992/93 jumping season in Britain. The abbreviations used are the same as in the main volume of 'Chasers & Hurdlers'.

Some reference material traditionally featured in 'Chasers & Hurdlers' now appears in the Companion, including the Characteristics of Racecourses section which has been expanded to include racecourse maps and trainers' records.

As its name implies, the 'Statistical Companion' is an integral part of 'Chasers & Hurdlers 1992/93'. We hope you will find it an informative and entertaining addition.

October 1993

The ability to identify potential for improvement in a horse can be priceless. It is one of the qualities for which Timeform is most famous. When a 'p'—denoting that the horse is likely to make more than normal progress—or, exceptionally, a large 'P'—indicating convincing evidence or a strong presumption that the horse is capable of much better form than it has so far displayed—is attached to a Timeform Rating you can be certain that the horse is worthy of special attention. All the horses in *Chasers & Hurdlers 1992/93* thought capable of noteworthy improvement are listed under their individual trainers.

J. AKEHURST
Carousel Music 6 b.m h87p

R. AKEHURST
Amazon Express 4 b.c h137p
Dancing Sen'tion (USA) 6 b.m h89 c—p
Sarazar (USA) 4 ch.g h80p

R. ALLAN
Tawafij (USA) 4 ch.c h85p

R. H. ALNER
High Baron 6 gr.g h136p

MRS R. ATKINSON
Country Spider 8 b.m c74p

K. C. BAILEY
Cariboo Gold (USA) 4 b.c h128p
Drumstick 7 ch.g h86 c110p
Killura (IRE) 5 b.g h91p
Louandy 9 b.g h—p
Noble Ben (NZ) 9 b.g h— c101p
Old Father Time 6 b.g h78p
Sacrosanct 9 b.g h109 c78p
Strong Medicine 6 b.g h109p
Top Brass (IRE) 5 ch.g h86p

G. B. BALDING
Coasting 7 b.g h— c—p
Flashthecash 7 b.g h95 c134p
Graham Gooch 7 b.g h87p
One More Run 6 ch.g h87p

I. A. BALDING
Knock Knock 8 ch.g h113p
Pay Homage 5 ch.g h—p
Spinning 6 b.g h151p

M. A. BARNES
Beaucadeau 7 b.g h107 c—p

D. H. BARONS
Fly Guard (NZ) 6 gr.g h87p

T. D. BARRON
Eurotwist 4 b.g h94p

P. BEAUMONT
Jodami 8 b.g h— c174p

R. BEWLEY
Creeshla 6 b.g c95p

MISS L. BLACKFORD
Great Gusto 7 b.g h— c88p

E. BOLGER, IRELAND
Elegant Lord (IRE) 5 ch.g c110P

M. BRADSTOCK
Never Let On (IRE) 5 ch.g h77p

MRS S. A. BRAMALL
Antonin (FR) 5 ch.g h— c135p

Beauchamp Grace 4 b.f h131p
Hurdy 6 ch.g h111p
Soul Agreement 6 b.g h92p

O. BRENNAN
Ottoman Empire 6 b.g h—p
Strath Royal 7 b.g h118p

R. BREWIS
Carnetto 6 b.m h71p
Vicaridge 6 b.g h72 c—p

K. S. BRIDGWATER
Shanakee 6 b.g h91p

H. DE BROMHEAD, IRELAND
Fissure Seal 7 ch.g h137p c131p

C. P. E. BROOKS
Black Humour 9 b.g h— c145p
Fieldridge 4 ch.g h—p
Mere Class 7 b.g h— c110p
Mr Flanagan 7 b.g h109p
Switch 7 ch.g h129 c90p
Winnowing (IRE) 5 b.m h—p

S. A. BROOKSHAW
Star Crossed (NZ) 8 b.g c—p

M. J. CAMACHO
Avro Anson 5 b.g h136p

I. CAMPBELL
Mill Burn 4 ch.g h76p

R. F. CASEY
Petrullo 8 b.h h—p

P. CAUDWELL
Exciting Prospect 9 ch.g h— c—p

MRS J. CECIL
Albemine (USA) 4 b.g h113p
Alderbrook 4 b.c h—P

J. N. CHEATLE
Electra Lad 7 ch.g c85p

P. CHEESBROUGH
Buckwheat Lad (IRE) 5 br.g h—p
Lynch Law (IRE) 5 b.h h112p
Mr Royal 7 b.g h69p
One Man (IRE) 5 gr.g h126p
Road By The River (IRE) 5 ch.g h—p

S. CHRISTIAN
David John 6 b.g h93p
Los Buccaneros 10 br.g h— c85p

H. T. COLE
Dubacilla 7 b.m h— c124p

K. O. CUNNINGHAM-BROWN
Dancing Paddy 5 b.h h132p

6

B. J. CURLEY
Chuck Curley (USA) 5 b.g h98p
Mullingar Con (IRE) 5 gr.g h73p
No Pain No Gain (IRE) 5 ch.g h85p

S. DOW
Sharptino 4 ch.c h—p

J. W. DUFOSEE
Sonofagipsy 9 b.g c80p

A. J. K. DUNN
Green Island (USA) 7 b.g h— c113p

M. H. EASTERBY
Dawson City 6 ch.g h— c123p

M. W. EASTERBY
Auburn Boy 6 ch.g h—p

J. A. C. EDWARDS
Monsieur Le Cure 7 b.g h123p
Wadeley 6 br.g h101p
Zanyman 7 b.g h90p

C. R. EGERTON
Admiral Villeneuve 5 b.g h75p

C. W. C. ELSEY
Best Gun 4 b.g h85p

D. R. C. ELSWORTH
Roll A Dollar 7 b.g h136p

P. D. EVANS
Kirkman's Kamp 8 b.g h82p

J. G. FITZGERALD
Bellton 5 gr.g h118p
Hazel Crest 6 b.g h73p
I'm Toby 6 b.g h104p
Just Molly 6 b.m h78p
Newlands-General 7 ch.g h— c90p
Rustic Air 6 ch.g h95 c90p
Sunkala Shine 5 ch.g h84p
Sunset Rock 6 b.g h93p
Uranus Collonges (FR) 7 b.g c103p

P. J. FLYNN, IRELAND
Montelado 6 b.g h150P

CAPT. T. A. FORSTER
Coonawara 7 b.g h130p
Dublin Flyer 7 b.g h— c118p

R. G. FROST
Irish Velvet 7 b.g h—p c88p

MISS S. L. GALLIE
Billy Boru 5 b.g h92p

D. R. GANDOLFO
Captain Dolford 6 ch.g h108p
Nadjati (USA) 4 ch.g h131p
Road To Fame 6 b.g h73p

N. A. GASELEE
Benjamin 5 b.g h103p
Divine Chance (IRE) 5 b.g h75p
Indian Quest 4 b.g h130p
Prize Match 4 ch.f h89p

J. T. GIFFORD
Armala 8 ch.g h— c97p
Book of Music (IRE) 5 b.g h111p
Brave Highlander (IRE) 5 b.g h95p
Duke of Aprolon 6 ch.g h99p
Fighting Words 7 ch.g h— c122p
Gandouge Glen 6 b.g h116p
Martin's Lamp 6 b.g h124p
Over The Pole 6 b.g h114p
Pilgrims Way (NZ) 6 ch.g h89p
Poors Wood 6 b.g h109p
Rose King 6 b.g h—p
Spuffington 5 b.g h95p
Truth Be Told 9 ch.g h125p c—

J. A. GLOVER
Kiveton Tycoon (IRE) 4 b.c h129p

MISS A. J. GREEN
My Nominee 5 b.g c—p

C. A. GREEN
Indian Knight 8 b.g c98p

M. D. HAMMOND
Tobin Bronze 6 b.g h—p

R. HANNON
General Dixie (USA) 4 b.g h—p

G. HARWOOD
Pontoon Bridge 6 ch.g h99p

M. J. HEATON-ELLIS
Elaine Tully (IRE) 5 b.m h—p

J. A. HELLENS
Preset 6 ch.g h— c—p

N. J. HENDERSON
Give Me An Answer 7 ch.m h89p
Le Piccolage 9 b.g h— c123p
Per Quod (USA) 8 b.g h98p
Propaganda 5 b.g h108p
Raymylette 6 ch.g h116p
Sorbiere 6 b.g h102p
Thumbs Up 7 b.g h128p
Travado 7 br.g h— c152p

MAJOR W. R. HERN
Moon Spin 4 b.f h—p

LADY HERRIES
Castle Courageous 6 b.g h130p

B. W. HILLS
Snow Board 4 gr.g h116p

P. J. HOBBS
Clerihue 4 br.f h—p
Cru Exceptionnel 5 b.g h—p
Elite Leo 8 b.g h75 c—p
Greenhill Raffles 7 ch.g h109p c—
Mulbank 7 b.g h105 c105p
Munka 7 b.g h96p

C. A. HORGAN
State of Affairs 6 b.g h96p

J. M. JEFFERSON
Dolikos 6 b.g h— c100p

J. R. JENKINS
Durshan (USA) 4 ch.c h—p

J. H. JOHNSON
Buck Owens 8 ch.g h— c95p

MRS M. A. JONES
Light Veneer 8 ch.g h? c113p

F. JORDAN
Majestic Gold 5 b.g h76p

J. S. KING
Inchcailloch (IRE) 4 b.c h79p

MISS H. C. KNIGHT
Factor Ten (IRE) 5 b.g h104p
Grouseman 7 gr.g h107 c—p
Oatis Regrets 5 b.g h110p

P. LEACH
Mardood 8 b.g h116p

F. H. LEE
I Perceive 6 b.g h—p

L. LUNGO
Attadale 5 b.g h120p
Handsome Gent 4 b.g h78p
It's The Pits 6 b.g h102p

D. LUXTON
Little Lemon 9 b.m c78p

J. F. C. MAXWELL, IRELAND
All For Luck 8 b.g h— c88p

D. MCCAIN
Chalie Richards 6 b.g h—p c93?

J. C. MCCONNOCHIE
Armateur (FR) 5 b.g h85p

G. M. MOORE
Bold Boss 4 b.g h140p
High Alltitude (IRE) 5 b.g h136p
Nouvelle Cuisine 5 b.m h87p
Raiseamillion 5 b.g h94p

K. A. MORGAN
Enigmatic (USA) 5 b.h h91p

M. F. MORRIS, IRELAND
Belvederian 6 b.g h143p

PATRICK MULLINS, IRELAND
Force Seven 6 b.m h— c123p

F. MURPHY
Bedfield (IRE) 5 b.g h—p
Sibton Abbey 8 b.g h— c161p
Simwell (IRE) 5 ch.g h79p

MRS A. M. MURRAY
Radical Views 8 b.g h— c120p

J. L. NEEDHAM
Leinthall Doe 7 b.m h71p

P. F. NICHOLLS
James The First 5 ch.g h108p
Warfield 6 b.g h—p

D. NICHOLSON
Barton Bank 7 br.g h— c142p
Hebridean 6 b.g h138p
Little-Nipper 8 ch.g h— c102p
Meleagris 9 b.g h114p
Sandybraes 8 ch.g h— c107p
Viking Flagship 6 b.g h— c144p
Winter Squall (IRE) 5 gr.g h136p

M. J. P. O'BRIEN, IRELAND
Shawiya (IRE) 4 b.f h141p

E. J. O'GRADY, IRELAND
Kerry Orchid 5 gr.g c116p

J. J. O'NEILL
Chic And Elite 6 b.m h94 c—p
Konvekta Control 6 ch.g h96p

J. G. M. O'SHEA
Killula Chief 6 b.g h99 c—p

R. J. O'SULLIVAN
El Volador 6 br.h h99p

W. D. OAKES
Lady Llanfair 7 b.m c93p

J. A. B. OLD
Barge Boy 9 b.g h122 c101p
Quadrireme 4 b.g h123p
Simpson 8 ch.g h136p

MRS L. PIGGOTT
Aude La Belle (FR) 5 ch.m h—p

S. PIKE
Synderborough Lad 7 ch.g c73p

MRS T. D. PILKINGTON
Coraco 6 br.g h99p

M. C. PIPE
Capability Brown 6 b.g h137 c137p

Dagobertin (FR) 7 ch.g h119 c119p
G'Ime A Buzz 5 ch.m h—p
Hawthorn Blaze 7 br.g h145p c126P
Heathfield Gale 6 b.m h106p
Lemon's Mill (USA) 4 b.f h132p
Lord Relic (NZ) 7 b.g h140p
Merlins Wish (USA) 4 ch.g h91p
Polar Hat 5 ch.g h92p
Rovulenka 5 b.g h107p
Saraville 6 ch.m h— c118p
Side of Hill 8 b.g h— c112p
Swahili Run 5 ch.g h103p

MRS J. PITMAN
Celtic Laird 5 ch.g h—p
Tammy's Friend 6 b.g h— c102p

W. G. REED
Master Sandy (USA) 6 b.g h85p

MRS J. R. RENFREE-BARONS
Riva (NZ) 6 ch.g h116p

MRS M. REVELEY
Bervie House (IRE) 5 br.g h74p
Brackenfield 7 ch.g h137p
Cab On Target 7 br.g h— c154p
Imhotep 6 gr.g h102p
Kayartis 4 b.f h94p
Lady Donoghue (USA) 4 b.f h68p
Majed (IRE) 5 b.h h135p
My Desire 5 ch.m h97p
Mythical Storm 6 b.m h96p
Notable Exception 4 b.g h96p
Taroudant 6 b.g h—p
Wellwotdouthink 7 b.m h92P
Young Ty 9 br.g h— c98p

W. K. RHEAD
Hill Royale 7 b.g c90p

G. RICHARDS
Bironi 4 b.g h—p
General Pershing 7 br.g h— c144p
Johns The Boy 7 b.g h—p
Mont Mirail 7 b.g h85p
Mr Five Wood (IRE) 5 ch.g h95p
Mutual Trust 9 ch.g h— c110p
Ninfa (IRE) 5 b.m h84P
Savoy 6 ch.g h85p
Tartan Tyrant 7 b.g c103p
The Whirlie Weevil 5 gr.m h—p
Whispering Steel 7 b.g h— c120P

R. ROWE
Baby Wizzard 4 b.f h82p
King of Zurich 6 b.g h—p

MISS B. SANDERS
Booth's Bouquet 5 b.g h—p

MISS C. SAUNDERS
Overheard 6 ch.g c109p

D. SHAW
Coleridge 5 gr.g h84p

O. SHERWOOD
Boll Weevil 7 b.g h99 c—p
Father Fortune 5 b.g h76p

S. E. SHERWOOD
Bank Place 6 ch.g h94p
Boycott 6 b.g h129p
Dusty Miller 7 b.g h— c124p
Midnight Caller 7 br.g h— c112p
Rocco 6 b.g h— c106p
Rubins Boy 7 ch.g h100 c—p

DENYS SMITH
Galloway Raider 9 br.g h— c78p

A. P. STRINGER
The Goofer 6 b.g h97p

G. J. TARRY
Lord Fawsley 8 b.g c83p

T. P. TATE
Hazlewood Glen 7 b.g h—p

H. THOMSON JONES
Jackson Flint 5 b.g h96p

N. TINKLER
Comstock 6 ch.g h88p
Puritan (CAN) 4 b.c h95p

M. H. TOMPKINS
Arany 6 b.g h93p
Glaisdale (IRE) 4 b.g h121p
Highbrook (USA) 5 b.m h111p

ANDREW TURNELL
Bathwick Bobbie 6 b.g h89p
Cogent 9 b.g h— c136p
Country Member 8 ch.g h— c143p
Giventime 5 ch.g h134p
Night Wind 6 b.g h94p
Storm Alert 7 b.g h— c143p
Washingtoncrossing 7 ch.g h— c117P

N. A. TWISTON-DAVIES
April's Model Lady 7 b.m h71 c78p
Bengazee (IRE) 5 b.g h—p
Dakyns Boy 8 ch.g h— c136p
Indian Tonic 7 br.g h— c110p
Knave of Clubs 6 ch.g h121p
Sausalito Boy 5 b.g h106p
Sohrab (IRE) 5 ch.g h107p

C. F. WALL
Corals Dream (IRE) 4 b.g h—p

9

W. J. WARNER
Sheer Jest 8 b.g c117p

C. WEEDON
Miracle Man 5 b.g h92p

D. K. WELD, IRELAND
Vintage Crop 6 ch.g h159p

H. WELLSTEAD
Roving Report 6 gr.g c85p

J. WHITE
Cultured 4 b.g h116p
Ostura 8 b.g h— c—p

R. C. WILKINS
Double Silk 9 b.g c122p

M. J. WILKINSON
Andrew's First 6 br.g h127p

M. WILLIAMS
Knock To Enter (USA) 5 b.g h—p

MRS S. D. WILLIAMS
Country Lad (IRE) 5 b.g h110p
Morgans Man 4 b.c h91p

D. A. WILSON
North Esk (USA) 4 ch.g h—p

S. WOODMAN
King Credo 8 b.g h161p

F. J. YARDLEY
Nevada Gold 7 ch.g h— c117p

Many misleading theories about trainers have become received wisdom. Acceptance of racing myths can be costly, even to the experienced backer. The 'Statistical Companion' provides a tabulated record for every trainer whose horses earned more then £25,000 in win prize money in 1992/93 in Britain. For each of these trainers there is a list of his or her winning horses and their Timeform Rating, an indication of the quality of the horses in the stable. Also provided are the courses at which each of the horse's victories was achieved (course specialists—equine and human —identified at a glance). There is also a month-by-month breakdown of the trainer's record of runners and winners.

Trainer & Winning Horses	Timeform Rating	Races Won	Value £	Course at which horse won
R. AKEHURST		**13**	**58,678**	
Amazon Express 4 b.c	h137	2	11,704	Fak Kem
Coe 7 b.g	c111	1	3,068	Lin
Dare To Dream (IRE) 4 b.g	h132	3	23,477	Plu Lin Chp
Green's Van Goyen (IRE) 5 b.g	h117	1	2,448	Plu
Here He Comes 7 b.g	h129	2	4,895	Lin Lin
Never Forgotten 8 ch.g	h104	2	2,682	Hun Fnt
Solidasarock 11 ch.g	c118	2	10,404	Nwb Wnc

Jy 0-0 Au 1-1 Se 1-2 Oc 2-14 No 1-20 De 3-11 Ja 1-17 Fe 1-11 Mr 2-11 Ap 0-4 My 1-11 Jn 0-2

K. C. BAILEY		**57**	**170,195**	
Beanley Brook 5 ch.m	h87	1	1,763	Exe
Briggs Lad (IRE) 4 ch.g	h98	2	3,669	Utt Her
Captain Frisk 10 bl.g	c114	2	9,896	Chl Utt
Cariboo Gold (USA) 4 b.c	h128	2	5,651	Utt Asc
Corrupt Committee 10 ch.g	c88	1	2,174	MRa
Docklands Express 11 b.g	c165	3	40,547	Liv War Fak
Drumstick 7 ch.g	c110	5	12,335	MRa Her Sou Hun Str
Far Senior 7 ch.g	c132	2	10,588	Kem San
Glenshane Lad 7 b.g	h108	1	1,954	Her
Killula Chief 6 b.g	h99	1	2,271	Ban
Le Metayer (FR) 5 b.g	h115	2	4,177	Lud Wnc
Mabthul (USA) 5 b.g	h81	1	1,595	Hun
Martomick 6 br.m	h122	1	2,233	Wnc
Nathan Blake 8 gr.g	c99	2	4,419	Her Lud
Native Pride 6 ch.g	c120	2	6,305	Chl Wnd
Noble Ben (NZ) 9 b.g	c101	1	2,252	Wol
Not So Soon 8 b.g	c95	1	2,348	Fak
Pardon Me Mum 8 ch.g	h119	3	5,905	NAb Lud Her
Richville 7 b.g	c101	1	3,028	Fnt
Sacrosanct 9 b.g	h109	2	5,380	Per Utt
San Lorenzo (USA) 5 b.g	h121	4	8,388	Exe Wol Hun Lud
Shahdjat (IRE) 5 ch.m	h101	2	4,253	Chp Nwb
Show The Flag 5 b.g	h85	1	1,822	Hun
Simple Arithmetic 5 ch.g		1	1,679	Utt
Storm Drum 4 ch.g	h100	2	3,343	Plu Lud
Strong Medicine 6 b.g	h109	3	5,041	Wnd Fnt Str
Stunning Stuff 8 b.g	c101	1	2,159	Exe
Tareesh 6 br.m	h94	1	2,738	Sou
The Master Gunner 9 ch.g	c103	1	4,163	Asc
Touch of Winter 7 b.g	h99	1	1,837	Lin
Unholy Alliance 6 b.g	h119	4	6,282	Fnt Wor Chl Chl

Jy 0-0 Au 0-3 Se 6-13 Oc 6-37 No 3-21 De 3-26 Ja 3-49 Fe 2-25 Mr 5-23 Ap 11-51 My 15-49 Jn 3-5

G. B. BALDING		**38**	**212,447**	
Ask Moss 8 ch.g	h125	1	2,290	Kel
Ask The Governor 7 b.g	h110	3	7,143	Fnt Wnc War
Beech Road 11 ch.g	c143	3	22,546	War Chl Str
Belmount Captain 8 ch.g	c137	2	11,031	Chp Chl
Boraceva 10 b.g	c137	3	10,800	War Per Tow
Doonloughan 8 b.g	c99	1	3,835	Chl
Farm Week 11 gr.g	c113	2	5,589	Wnc Wnd
Father Dowling 6 br.g	c93	1	1,856	Fnt
Flashthecash 7 b.g	c134	6	30,326	Fnt Str Chp Liv Chl War
Forest Sun 8 ch.g	c139	2	9,033	Chl San
Glove Puppet 8 ch.g	c97	1	2,726	San

La Cienaga 9 ch.g	c99	1	2,879	Ban
Major Bugler (IRE) 4 b.g	h135	2	8,886	Nwb Chl
Morley Street 9 ch.g	h169	2	52,858	Chl Liv
Obie's Train 7 ch.g	c105	1	2,824	Exe
Romany King 9 br.g	c149	1	3,420	Exe
Run Fast For Gold 6 ch.m	h81	1	1,805	Tau
Sea Buck 7 b.g	h112	1	2,843	San
Sirrah Jay 13 b.g	c112	3	26,965	NAb Lin Liv
Thats The Business 9 br.g	c89	1	2,792	Hun

Jy 0-0 Au 0-0 Se 0-11 Oc 6-35 No 6-49 De 2-37 Ja 4-40 Fe 3-32 Mr 6-34 Ap 6-33 My 5-19 Jn 0-1

I. A. BALDING   6   47,234

Fight To Win (USA) 5 b.g	c103	3	6,425	Wnd Plu Tau
Lunabelle 5 b.m	h95	1	1,604	Wnc
Spinning 6 b.g	h151	2	39,205	Liv Hay

Jy 0-0 Au 0-0 Se 0-1 Oc 0-7 No 0-2 De 1-5 Ja 0-9 Fe 0-5 Mr 1-12 Ap 3-3 My 1-2 Jn 0-0

D. H. BARONS   16   94,997

Casting Time (NZ) 9 br.g	c98	1	3,435	San
Colonel O'Kelly (NZ) 9 br.g	c89	1	2,616	Wol
Happy Horse (NZ) 6 ch.g	h92	1	1,480	Str
Innocent Princess (NZ) 6 ch.m	h103	2	3,817	NAb Str
Martell Boy (NZ) 6 b.g	h104	1	1,480	Wor
Mine's An Ace (NZ) 6 br.g	h95	2	3,249	NAb NAb
Musical Monarch (NZ) 7 ch.g	h112	2	5,423	Chp War
Rocktor (NZ) 8 b.g	c122	1	4,163	Lud
Royal Piper (NZ) 6 br.g	h111	1	2,411	Utt
Top Javalin (NZ) 6 ch.g	h129	2	4,507	Chp Wor
Topsham Bay 10 b.g	c148	2	62,416	Nwb San

Jy 0-0 Au 1-2 Se 2-11 Oc 0-27 No 0-27 De 3-35 Ja 0-14 Fe 2-21 Mr 7-36 Ap 1-32 My 0-6 Jn 0-0

P. BEAUMONT   19   162,642

Any Dream Would Do 4 b.f	h84	1	2,005	Wth
Barkisland 9 b.g	c91	2	3,962	Sou Edi
Choctaw 9 gr.g	c94	1	2,820	Sed
Decent Man 10 b.g	c102	3	14,124	Sed MRa Cat
Hudson Bay Trader (USA) 6 b.g	h125	4	8,023	MRa Nwc Nwc MRa
Hunmanby Gap 8 ch.g	h75	1	1,969	Sed
I'm Fine 8 b.m	h74	1	1,165	Cat
Jodami 8 b.g	c174	3	122,322	Nwb Hay Chl
Skircoat Green 8 ch.g	h101	2	3,647	Sed Wth
Tammy My Girl 10 ch.m	c87	1	2,605	MRa

Jy 0-0 Au 0-1 Se 0-4 Oc 2-8 No 0-18 De 3-13 Ja 3-13 Fe 4-11 Mr 2-13 Ap 3-14 My 2-11 Jn 0-0

MRS S. C. BRADBURNE   18   46,919

Charming Gale 6 b.m	c93	3	7,768	Kel Kel Crl
Classic Minstrel 9 br.g	c87	1	2,151	Edi
Dante's Inferno 7 ch.g	c116	4	10,054	Ayr Ayr Ayr Per
Forth And Tay 11 b.g	c94	2	6,172	Crl Per
Interim Lib 10 b.g	c115	1	1,848	Nwc
Native Crown (IRE) 5 b.g	h104	1	1,796	Nwc
Off The Bru 8 b.g	c104	1	4,327	Kel
On The Hooch 8 ch.m	c106	1	2,918	Crl
Sonsie Mo 8 b.g	c101	2	5,342	Edi Wth
Willie Sparkle 7 b.g	h115	2	4,543	Ayr Ayr

Jy 0-0 Au 0-2 Se 0-4 Oc 2-18 No 2-21 De 0-8 Ja 3-18 Fe 2-21 Mr 4-18 Ap 3-23 My 2-19 Jn 0-0

MRS S. A. BRAMALL   16   42,942

Able Player (USA) 6 b.g	h123	1	1,872	Edi
Antonin (FR) 5 ch.g	c135	4	15,556	Edi Hun Hun Asc

Battle Standard (CAN) 6 b.g	h90	2	2,588	Cat Ban
Clonroche Driller 8 b.g	c97	2	5,609	Lei Per
Inconclusive 6 b.g	c86	1	2,924	Wth
Piper O'Drummond 6 ch.g	c100	2	5,654	Kel Kel
Red Under The Bed 6 b.g	c103	1	1,865	Sed
Spy Hill 7 b.g	c90	1	2,801	Utt
Veleda II (FR) 6 ch.g	h90	1	1,480	Hun
Viva Bella (FR) 6 b.g	c94	1	2,593	Crl

Jy 0-0 Au 0-0 Se 0-0 Oc 2-16 No 0-20 De 2-9 Ja 1-14 Fe 4-19 Mr 5-21 Ap 1-14 My 0-6 Jn 1-1

O. BRENNAN — 25 56,429

Boston Rover 8 b.g	c109	4	12,305	MRa Tow Str Tow
Earlham 7 ch.g	h85	1	1,675	Sou
Foolish Affair 9 b.g	c94	1	1,358	Sou
Hallo Mam (IRE) 4 br.f	h86	3	5,812	Utt Wor Utt
Loxley Range (IRE) 5 ch.g	h80	1	2,043	Cat
Marsh's Law 6 br.g	h106	3	6,318	MRa MRa Tow
Strath Royal 7 b.g	h118	4	7,211	Not Not Tow Tow
This Nettle Danger 9 b.g	h96	2	4,012	Tow Hun
Threeoutoffour 8 b.g	c104	1	3,818	Wth
Vulrory's Clown 15 b.g	c90	3	6,949	MRa Cat Str
What If 9 ch.m	h98	2	4,928	Not Tow

Jy 0-0 Au 1-7 Se 1-7 Oc 1-13 No 2-14 De 0-12 Ja 2-13 Fe 1-10 Mr 4-19 Ap 3-13 My 9-23 Jn 1-2

C. D. BROAD — 17 37,885

Bell Staffboy (IRE) 4 b.g		1	1,795	Ban
Invite d'Honneur (NZ) 11 ch.g	h87	1	2,150	Crt
King's Shilling (USA) 6 b.g	h121	5	13,416	Her Her Str Wor Ban
Kissane 12 br.g	c110	1	1,996	Her
Knights (NZ) 7 br.g	h107	3	6,306	Sed Sed Utt
Landed Gentry (USA) 4 b.c	h108	1	1,305	Lei
Little Big 6 b.g	h85	1	1,411	Exe
Reltic 6 b.g	h78	1	1,847	Tau
Shu Fly (NZ) 9 ch.g	c128	2	6,372	Tau Exe
Super Sharp (NZ) 5 ch.g		1	1,287	Cat

Jy 0-0 Au 0-2 Se 1-5 Oc 1-12 No 2-13 De 0-5 Ja 0-11 Fe 0-10 Mr 5-12 Ap 5-22 My 3-13 Jn 0-1

C. P. E. BROOKS — 16 51,947

All Jeff (FR) 9 b.g	c127	1	4,663	Hay
Black Humour 9 b.g	c145	3	15,711	Wor War Liv
Couldnt Be Better 6 br.g	h106	1	1,870	Lin
Goodshot Rich 9 b.g	c115	2	6,733	NAb Lin
Le Ginno (FR) 6 ch.g		1	2,036	Utt
Mere Class 7 b.g	c110	2	7,309	Hay Str
Mr Flanagan 7 b.g	h109	1	2,460	Utt
Pintail Bay 7 b.g	c88	1	2,790	NAb
Roc Color (FR) 4 b.g	h102	2	2,955	Fnt Her
Roscoe Harvey 11 br.g	c108	1	2,600	Exe
Switch 7 ch.g	h129	1	2,820	Wor

Jy 0-0 Au 0-0 Se 1-2 Oc 1-9 No 2-10 De 4-16 Ja 2-27 Fe 0-5 Mr 1-10 Ap 4-13 My 1-6 Jn 0-2

R. H. BUCKLER — 12 25,434

Air Commander 8 br.g	c96	1	1,950	NAb
Carbonate 8 b.g	c111	3	9,383	Her Wor Asc
Galagames (USA) 6 ch.g	c85	1	2,411	Her
Haitham 6 b.h	h107	1	2,093	Fnt
Shimmering Scarlet (IRE) 5 b.m	h99	3	5,340	Lin Lin Tau
Sydney Barry (NZ) 8 b.g	h83	3	4,257	Her Her Her

Jy 0-0 Au 1-3 Se 1-6 Oc 1-5 No 0-10 De 0-8 Ja 3-13 Fe 1-6 Mr 0-6 Ap 1-7 My 4-12 Jn 0-1

14

D. BURCHELL   12   28,466

Acrow Line 8 b.g	h122	1	2,332	Crt
Auvillar (USA) 5 br.g	h84	1	1,604	Wol
Broom Isle 5 b.m	h96	1	3,590	Hay
Emrys 10 ch.g	c97	3	7,216	Wor Her Exe
Maamur (USA) 5 gr.g	h128	1	1,302	Her
Pims Gunner (IRE) 5 b.g	c101	2	6,966	Lud Chp
Pontynyswen 5 b.g	h127	2	3,556	Chp Sou
Prime Mover 5 b.g	h74	1	1,900	Utt

Jy 0-0 Au 0-6 Se 2-7 Oc 0-11 No 1-10 De 0-7 Ja 0-16 Fe 1-8 Mr 3-13 Ap 0-11 My 5-12 Jn 0-2

P. CHEESBROUGH   30   94,141

Break The Chain 8 b.g	c107	2	5,470	Sed Sed
Castle King 6 b.g	c116	3	10,614	Don Don Don
Dark Dawn 9 b.g	c116	3	5,314	Lei Per Utt
Fettuccine 9 ch.g	h126	1	2,390	Str
Gale Again 6 br.g	c137	2	13,242	Nwc Hay
Kidlaw 5 b.g	h94	1	2,024	Kel
Lynch Law (IRE) 5 b.h	h112	2	2,659	Hex Crl
Once Stung 7 br.g	c116	4	10,214	Nwb Kel Kel Utt
One Man (IRE) 5 gr.g	h126	2	3,921	Not Ayr
River House 11 ch.g	c105	1	6,938	Nwc
Shahmiraj 5 b.m	h73	1	1,800	Crl
Shelton Abbey 7 br.g	h106	2	5,451	Sed Wth
Southern Minstrel 10 ch.g	c116	1	4,143	Wth
Spree Cross 7 b.g	c110	1	4,143	Per
Stay On Tracks 11 gr.g	c118	1	5,248	Hay
Stepfaster 8 gr.m	c104	1	3,966	MRa
The Laughing Lord 7 b.g	c94	1	3,688	Hay
Wrekin Hill 11 b.g	c109	1	2,916	Ayr

Jy 0-0 Au 0-0 Se 0-0 Oc 0-0 No 0-0 De 3-17 Ja 2-21 Fe 6-36 Mr 9-34 Ap 7-41 My 2-12 Jn 1-3

W. CLAY   21   40,071

Admiralty Way 7 b.g	h118	3	6,310	Sou Her Ban
Band of Hope (USA) 6 ch.m	h88	2	4,059	Utt Ban
Court Circular 4 b.c	h107	4	6,494	Sou Sou Sou Str
Johnsted 7 ch.g	h94	4	9,870	Sou Sou Sou Her
Northern Nation 5 b.g	h102	3	5,808	Sou Sou Sou
Pollerton's Pride 6 b.m	h95	2	2,881	Not Str
Sayant 8 b.g	h91	1	1,756	Ban
Taurian Princess 4 b.f	h74	1	1,319	Not
Titus Gold 8 b.g	h107	1	1,574	Utt

Jy 0-2 Au 0-4 Se 0-10 Oc 1-12 No 3-11 De 1-12 Ja 4-16 Fe 2-17 Mr 6-21 Ap 1-13 My 2-22 Jn 1-3

R. CURTIS   14   52,277

Flying Ziad (CAN) 10 ch.g	c95	2	3,825	NAb Hun
Mister Ed 10 ch.g	c127	2	27,152	Fnt Utt
Petmer 6 b.g	h82	1	1,495	NAb
St Athans Lad 8 b.g	c121	9	19,805	Fnt Fnt Fnt Fnt Fnt Fnt Fnt Fnt Fnt

Jy 0-0 Au 3-10 Se 1-13 Oc 3-11 No 0-17 De 0-8 Ja 0-11 Fe 1-15 Mr 3-20 Ap 1-7 My 2-7 Jn 0-0

P. T. DALTON   11   26,066

Doolar (USA) 6 b.g	h118	2	5,231	Utt Utt
Rochestown Lass 7 b.m	h106	3	5,658	Utt Utt Tow
Tort 9 b.g	c103	1	1,520	Tow
Trimlough 8 b.g	c127	5	13,657	Ban Wol Cat Utt Wor

Jy 0-0 Au 0-0 Se 0-2 Oc 3-9 No 4-7 De 0-4 Ja 0-0 Fe 1-7 Mr 0-7 Ap 2-8 My 1-11 Jn 0-1

R. DICKIN   **15**   **37,256**

Dr Rocket 8 b.g	c113	3	8,080	Utt Tow Tow
Fairfields Cone 10 ch.m	h113	3	7,221	Chl NAb War
K C'S Dancer 8 ch.g	c98	2	4,167	Her Fnt
Miss Fern 8 b.m	c96	1	2,192	Her
Northern Jinks 10 b.m	c115	3	9,294	Wor Str Wor
Orchipedzo 8 ch.g	c80	1	1,580	Wor
Winabuck 10 ch.g	c114	2	4,722	Wor Utt

Jy 0-0 Au 2-6 Se 0-8 Oc 2-13 No 2-18 De 2-13 Ja 1-12 Fe 2-16 Mr 1-12 Ap 1-17 My 2-7 Jn 0-1

F. DOUMEN, FRANCE   **1**   **44,500**

The Fellow (FR) 8 b.g	c171	1	44,500	Kem

Jy 0-0 Au 0-0 Se 0-0 Oc 0-0 No 0-1 De 1-2 Ja 0-0 Fe 0-0 Mr 0-1 Ap 0-1 My 0-0 Jn 0-0

M. H. EASTERBY   **39**   **114,756**

Bollin Magdalene 5 b.m	h90	1	2,233	Wth
Bollin William 5 b.h	h140	3	8,445	Ban Chp Hay
Burgoyne 7 b.g	h158	1	7,845	Wth
Chain Shot 8 b.g	c107	2	5,795	MRa Per
Curtain Factory 4 ch.g	h86	1	1,811	Nwc
Dawson City 6 ch.g	c123	4	25,572	Not Liv Wth Nwc
Gymcrak Sovereign 5 b.g	h103	2	4,287	Not Sou
Gymcrak Stardom 7 gr.g	h127	2	5,331	Cat San
Habton Whin 7 b.g	c100:h100	2	3,750	MRa Sed
Icarus (USA) 7 b.g	c119	2	6,902	Edi Ban
Nishkina 5 b.g	h91	1	2,103	MRa
On Tap 9 ch.g	c106	1	3,143	Hay
Personal Hazard 4 ch.g	h104	2	4,606	Wth Wth
Seagull Hollow (IRE) 4 b.g	h103	3	7,579	Cat Wth MRa
Secret Castle 5 b.g	h95	1	935	Cat
Sheriff's Band 6 ch.g	c84	1	2,327	MRa
Stated Case 8 b.g	h113	5	9,907	Tow Sed Hex Crl Sed
Toogood To Be True 5 br.g	h99	2	4,022	Cat Sed
Who's Tef (IRE) 5 b.g	h106	2	4,020	MRa Hun
Young Benz 9 ch.g	c141	1	4,143	Hay

Jy 0-0 Au 0-6 Se 3-13 Oc 6-30 No 7-34 De 3-29 Ja 7-35 Fe 4-23 Mr 3-20 Ap 2-21 My 4-7 Jn 0-0

M. W. EASTERBY   **11**   **27,214**

Coulton 6 ch.g	h157	1	4,760	Not
Houghton 7 b.g	c97	1	2,559	Nwc
Knayton Prospect 5 br.g	h97	1	1,746	Nwc
Macarthur 8 b.g	c121	1	2,301	Cat
Merano (FR) 10 ch.g	c130	1	2,846	Nwc
Our Survivor 9 b.g	h80	1	1,572	Sou
Silver Stick 6 gr.g	h106	2	3,561	Sed Crl
Tresidder 11 b.g	c108	2	5,539	Wor Sed
Yaheeb (USA) 9 b.h	c98	1	2,330	Crl

Jy 0-0 Au 0-2 Se 1-2 Oc 1-12 No 1-10 De 2-15 Ja 0-21 Fe 2-24 Mr 4-20 Ap 0-3 My 0-4 Jn 0-0

J. A. C. EDWARDS   **29**   **77,414**

Ask For More 8 b.g	h98	1	1,484	Wol
Book of Runes 8 b.g	h96	2	4,187	Utt Her
Channels Gate 9 b.g	c104	2	3,781	Her NAb
Direct 10 b.g	c116	2	8,529	Chp War
Don't Light Up 7 b.g	h100	1	2,273	Lei
False Economy 8 ch.g	c111	1	3,493	Tow
Master William 9 b.g	h87	1	1,024	Sou
Monsieur Le Cure 7 b.g	h123	1	1,663	NAb
Muizenberg 6 b.g	h95	1	1,305	Str
Poulstone 6 ch.g		1	1,732	Exe

Proplus 11 ch.g	c107	3	7,352	Sou Sou Lud
Ross Venture 8 b.g	c129	1	3,340	Wnd
Rufus 7 ch.g	c105	2	3,893	NAb Hex
Ru Valentino 9 ch.g	c106	1	2,957	Lud
Saddler's Choice 8 b.g	c99	2	5,590	Lud Hun
Snitton Lane 7 b.m	c117	2	13,182	Lud Kem
Sooner Still 9 b.g	c105	1	2,719	Utt
Taramoss 6 b.g	h102	1	1,660	Hex
Tinas Lad 10 b.g	c105	2	5,766	Str Lud
Wadeley 6 br.g	h101	1	1,484	Wol

Jy 0-1 Au 2-7 Se 2-11 Oc 2-23 No 2-21 De 1-27 Ja 6-37 Fe 7-40 Mr 2-26 Ap 1-35 My 4-25 Jn 0-0

C. R. EGERTON		**15**	**36,118**	
Daphnis (USA) 4 b.c		1	1,570	MRa
Djebel Prince 6 b.g	h103	2	4,845	NAb NAb
Kabayil 4 b.f	h92	2	2,950	Plu Plu
Material Girl 7 b.m	c109	3	4,138	Not Wth Her
Scobie Boy (IRE) 5 ch.g		1	1,940	Not
Stirrup Cup 9 b.g	c123	6	20,675	Plu Plu Not NAb Not Utt

Jy 0-0 Au 0-0 Se 0-2 Oc 0-0 No 2-5 De 4-5 Ja 1-5 Fe 5-19 Mr 1-7 Ap 2-12 My 0-1 Jn 0-0

D. R. C. ELSWORTH		**18**	**133,170**	
Big Beat (USA) 5 br.g	h128	2	6,272	Flk San
Fit For Firing (FR) 9 b.m	c114	2	5,543	Wnc NAb
Fragrant Dawn 9 br.g	c134	2	7,587	Nwb Nwb
Givus A Buck 10 br.g	c147	3	35,292	Fnt Nwb Chl
Muse 6 ch.g	h165	3	49,638	Asc Wnd Chl
Rocket Launcher 7 b.g	c106	2	5,843	Plu Nwb
Roll A Dollar 7 b.g	h136	3	19,908	Nwb Kem Liv
The Glow (IRE) 5 b.g	h112	1	3,087	Asc

Jy 0-0 Au 0-0 Se 0-0 Oc 0-4 No 4-18 De 3-22 Ja 2-16 Fe 3-19 Mr 5-20 Ap 1-16 My 0-0 Jn 0-0

J. FFITCH-HEYES		**9**	**25,150**	
Baptismal Fire 9 ch.g	c126	1	1,520	Fnt
King of Normandy (IRE) 4 ch.g	h74	1	1,602	Fnt
Kisu Kali 6 ch.g	c84	3	16,298	Fnt NAb Lin
Manhattan Boy 11 b.g	h95	2	2,345	Plu Plu
Marzocco 5 ch.g	h88	1	1,954	Lin
Oco Royal 4 b.c	h78	1	1,431	Plu

Jy 0-0 Au 0-2-9 Se 2-6 Oc 0-7 No 1-11 De 1-5 Ja 1-9 Fe 1-12 Mr 1-12 Ap 0-6 My 0-2 Jn 0-0

J. G. FITZGERALD		**62**	**261,080**	
Aslan (IRE) 5 gr.g		3	6,890	Sed Crl Chp
Astings (FR) 5 b.g	h90	1	2,024	Crt
Bellton 5 gr.g	h118	2	4,128	Not Wth
Boutzdaroff 11 ch.g	c134	2	25,698	Sed Liv
Dara Melody (IRE) 4 b.g	h84	1	1,940	Sou
Dari Sound (IRE) 5 b.g	h113	1	2,611	MRa
Delpiombo 7 br.g	h98	1	1,822	Cat
Doradus 5 br.g	h98	2	3,569	Sed Sed
Fox Chapel 6 b.g	h114	1	3,002	War
Gaveko (USA) 4 b.g	h97	2	4,247	Nwc Cat
Gold Options 11 ch.g	c154	1	30,987	Hay
Greek Flutter 8 b.g	c116	1	3,056	Hay
Gris Et Violet (FR) 6 ch.g	h110	2	5,309	MRa Nwc
Heathview 6 b.g	h87	1	1,822	Sed
High Padre 7 b.g	c109	3	8,875	Wth Not Not
I'm Toby 6 b.g	h104	2	4,150	Don Utt
Lumberjack (USA) 9 b.g	c127	2	6,287	Str Wth
Native Field (IRE) 4 b.g		3	10,746	Don Don Liv

Nijmegen 5 b.g	h122	3	7,773	Utt Wth Hay
Otterburn House 9 b.g	c123	2	7,309	Utt Hay
Philharmonic (IRE) 5 b.g		1	1,984	Hay
Phils Pride 9 b.g	c115	2	4,614	Cat MRa
Polar Region 7 br.g	c112	5	15,208	Crl Sed Sed Per Sed
Rustic Air 6 ch.g	c90	1	4,325	MRa
Sandy's Beacon 8 b.g	c92	1	1,488	Sed
Sheep Stealer 5 gr.g	h88	1	1,764	Cat
Sunset Rock 6 b.g	h93	1	1,363	Cat
Sybillin 7 b.g	c156	5	55,116	Utt Asc Nwc Asc Not
Trainglot 6 ch.h	h129	4	24,454	Edi Not San War
Uncle Ernie 8 b.g		1	1,488	Wth
Uranus Collonges (FR) 7 b.g	c103	2	4,190	Don Cat
Vienna Woods 6 b.g		2	2,841	Cat MRa

Jy 0-0 Au 0-5 Se 0-4 Oc 3-22 No 11-35 De 8-36 Ja 9-44 Fe 14-46 Mr 9-33 Ap 6-33 My 2-9 Jn 0-0

P. J. FLYNN, IRELAND		**1**	**30,014**	
Montelado 6 b.g	h150	1	30,014	Chl

Jy 0-0 Au 0-0 Se 0-0 Oc 0-0 No 0-0 De 0-0 Ja 0-0 Fe 0-1 Mr 1-1 Ap 0-0 My 0-0 Jn 0-0

CAPT. T. A. FORSTER		**29**	**95,694**	
Amari King 9 b.g	c124	1	3,968	San
Buddington 8 b.g	c109	2	5,537	NAb Flk
Cherrykino 8 b.g	c145	4	14,816	Wor Utt Chp Wnc
Coonawara 7 b.g	h130	3	5,798	Lin Lin War
Crystal Bear (NZ) 8 b.g	h132	1	2,233	Chp
Dublin Flyer 7 b.g	c118	2	7,044	Don Utt
Glen Cherry 7 b.g	c104	1	1,956	Utt
Hearts Are Wild 6 ch.g	h97	1	1,737	Hun
Herlin 5 b.g		1	1,206	Her
Martha's Son 6 b.g	h128	3	13,799	Fnt Wnc Nwb
Nicklup 6 ch.m	h94	2	3,745	Hun Exe
Penultimate Hand 5 ch.m		1	1,751	Exe
Postman's Path 7 ch.g	c99	1	1,873	Utt
Rio Haina 8 ch.g	c109	1	3,716	War
Sun Surfer (FR) 5 ch.g	h127	4	24,149	Wnc Str Nwb San
What A To Do 9 b.g	c92	1	2,366	Fnt

Jy 0-0 Au 0-2 Se 0-2 Oc 6-27 No 6-43 De 3-24 Ja 7-34 Fe 2-27 Mr 3-17 Ap 2-33 My 0-8 Jn 0-0

R. G. FROST		**12**	**27,104**	
Bill Quill 9 ch.g	c94	1	1,738	Wor
Bold Choice 7 b.g	c87	1	2,120	Wor
Cabochon 6 b.g	h127	2	5,326	Asc Lud
Charly Pharly (FR) 6 b.g	h97	1	1,590	Fnt
Irish Velvet 7 b.g	c88	1	2,443	Wor
Lasting Memory 7 b.m	h104	1	2,075	Fnt
Ling (USA) 8 b.g	h98	1	2,385	Wor
Miramac 12 br.g	h93	1	1,806	NAb
Playpen 9 b.g	c101	2	4,869	NAb Lin
Play The Blues 6 gr.m	c84	1	2,752	Exe

Jy 0-0 Au 2-14 Se 2-24 Oc 0-15 No 1-17 De 0-16 Ja 2-28 Fe 1-20 Mr 0-20 Ap 2-23 My 2-20 Jn 0-3

D. R. GANDOLFO		**12**	**26,439**	
Ardcroney Chief 7 ch.g	c96	2	3,568	Tow Hun
Ballyroe Lady 7 ch.m	c103	2	4,691	Wnc Hun
Buckingham Gate 7 gr.g	c91	1	2,853	Lud
Fast Thoughts 6 b.g	h111	1	3,678	Wor
Father Ralph 7 ch.g	h89	1	1,485	Wnd
Gladtogetit 7 br.m	c98	1	3,152	Fak
Noble Eyre 12 br.g	c89	1	2,147	Wol

Playing Truant 5 b.g	h95	1	1,744	Wnc
Shannon Juliette 6 b.m	h79	1	1,646	Wnc
The Holy Golfer 6 br.g	h72	1	1,475	Her

Jy 0-1 Au 0-4 Se 0-10 Oc 3-21 No 4-26 De 1-10 Ja 1-20 Fe 2-17 Mr 0-19 Ap 0-16 My 1-3 Jn 0-0

N. A. GASELEE — 13 65,579

Come Home Alone 5 ch.g	h89	1	1,302	Lud
Easy Buck 6 b.g	h131	2	13,553	Asc War
Indian Quest 4 b.g	h130	2	4,276	Not Kem
Kentish Piper 8 br.g	c116	2	5,875	Str Lei
Mr Entertainer 10 gr.g	c129	1	3,908	Nwb
Party Politics 9 br.g	c156	1	27,018	Hay
Prince Tino 5 b.g	h101	1	1,858	Str
Prize Match 4 ch.f	h89	1	1,446	NAb
Rathmore 7 b.g	c101	2	6,343	Lin Flk

Jy 0-0 Au 0-0 Se 0-4 Oc 1-12 No 2-17 De 2-15 Ja 1-18 Fe 4-20 Mr 1-11 Ap 1-14 My 1-10 Jn 0-0

J. T. GIFFORD — 49 285,837

Annio Chilone 7 b.h	c117	3	14,976	Asc Flk San
Armala 8 ch.g	c97	2	5,217	Lin Hun
Bollinger 7 ch.g	h131	1	2,846	Wth
Bradbury Star 8 b.g	c151	1	13,420	Chl
Call Home (IRE) 5 b.g		2	3,880	Wnc Chl
Champagne Lad 7 ch.g	c116	3	9,030	Wnd Wnc Chp
City Kid 8 br.g	c97	2	4,134	Flk NAb
Cool And Easy 7 b.g	c99	1	3,485	Tau
Cythere 9 gr.g	c111	3	7,815	Fnt Tow Chp
Deep Sensation 8 ch.g	c148	3	135,054	Asc Chl Liv
Duke of Aprolon 6 ch.g	h99	1	2,898	San
Fantasy World 7 ch.m	h97	2	5,441	Fnt San
Fighting Words 7 ch.g	c122	3	10,206	Wth Wth San
Gandouge Glen 6 b.g	h116	3	4,425	Flk Fnt Fnt
Martin's Lamp 6 b.g	h124	2	4,063	Tow Tow
Mr Jamboree 7 b.g	c112	3	10,587	Kem Nwb San
Poors Wood 6 b.g	h109	2	4,259	Kem Flk
Retail Runner 8 b.g	c118	2	12,560	Asc Asc
Run Up The Flag 6 ch.g	h133	3	9,573	War Kem San
San Fernando 7 b.g	h123	1	5,345	Asc
Super Sense 8 b.g	h145	1	2,794	War
The Widget Man 7 b.g	c119	1	2,007	Fnt
Truth Be Told 9 ch.g	h125	1	3,517	Not
Vodka Fizz 8 ch.g	c92	1	2,063	Fnt
Yorkshire Gale 7 br.g	h115	2	6,242	Nwb Chl

Jy 0-0 Au 0-2 Se 0-0 Oc 5-29 No 10-57 De 3-34 Ja 5-55 Fe 10-48 Mr 11-38 Ap 5-29 My 0-8 Jn 0-0

D. M. GRISSELL — 18 35,021

Brightling Boy 8 ch.g	h94	2	3,905	Wnd Fnt
Captain Dolford 6 ch.g	h108	1	1,475	Fnt
Carrikins 6 b.m	h90	1	929	Plu
Early Man 6 b.g	h110	3	5,921	Flk Kem Plu
Ginger Tristan 7 ch.g	h100	1	1,475	Fnt
Handsome Ned 7 br.g	h95	2	3,982	Plu Flk
Hurricane Blake 5 b.g	h120	2	4,133	Wnd San
Le Chat Noir 10 br.g	c118	1	2,196	Flk
Mr Matt (IRE) 5 b.g	h111	2	4,222	Plu Lin
Soleil Dancer (IRE) 5 b.g	h107	1	2,343	Wnd
Tip Top Lad 6 b.g	h97	1	2,013	Lin
Yellow Spring 8 b.g	h131	1	2,427	Kem

Jy 0-0 Au 0-0 Se 0-1 Oc 2-11 No 4-8 De 1-6 Ja 1-10 Fe 5-14 Mr 3-12 Ap 2-7 My 0-1 Jn 0-0

M. D. HAMMOND   51 125,103

Horse				
As d'Eboli (FR) 6 b.g	h90	1	1,277	Hex
Burn Bridge (USA) 7 b.g	h98	1	1,351	Crt
Carousel Calypso 7 ch.g	c100	2	5,115	Nwc Cat
Carousel Rocket 10 ch.g	c103	3	8,662	Crl Crl Crl
Chiparopai (IRE) 5 b.m	h76	1	1,730	Ban
Clyde Ranger 6 b.g	h104	2	2,951	Nwc Hex
Colour Cost (IRE) 5 b.g	h87	1	2,038	Crl
Dominant Serenade 4 b.g	h130	4	20,903	Hex Kel Chl Ayr
Fingers Crossed 9 b.m	h94	2	2,515	Hex Crl
Fishki 7 b.m	c96	1	2,424	Ayr
Hamanaka (USA) 4 b.f	h97	1	2,478	Wth
Heliopsis 5 b.g	h113	2	2,734	Hay Wth
James My Boy 13 ch.g	c93	2	5,225	Ban Ban
Julietski 5 gr.m	h88	3	5,557	Per Per Utt
Kalko 4 b.c	h102	2	4,132	Kel Kel
King of Steel 7 b.g	h96	1	1,778	Cat
Liability Order 4 b.g	h104	2	3,469	Cat MRa
Miner Jackson 6 b.g	h97	1	828	Hex
Over The Stream 7 b.g	c92	1	2,862	Don
Palmrush 9 b.g	c103	3	8,472	Hex Wth War
Pink Gin 6 ch.g	c98	3	8,722	Crl Nwc Sou
Polishing 6 ch.g	h119	2	7,178	Wth Nwc
Reluctant Suitor 4 ch.g		1	1,700	Edi
Shoon Wind 10 b.g	c125	2	6,944	Nwc Ayr
Sir Peter Lely 6 b.g	c100	1	2,065	Hex
The Yank 7 b.g	c95	3	6,429	Edi Edi Edi
Valiant Warrior 5 br.g	h101	1	1,953	Wth
Wishing Gate (USA) 5 br.g	h104	2	3,611	Edi Nwc

Jy 0-0 Au 3-8 Se 2-14 Oc 3-27 No 8-39 De 10-38 Ja 5-40 Fe 7-30 Mr 7-32 Ap 2-22 My 4-23 Jn 0-0

G. HARWOOD   12 26,333

Horse				
Alkinor Rex 8 ch.g	c126	1	3,655	Tow
Ashfold Copse 7 ch.g	c124	3	7,798	Wnd Hun Kem
Fine Thyne (IRE) 4 ch.g		1	2,013	Chl
Hunting Ground 5 b.h	h102	2	2,853	Fnt Wor
Peace King 7 ch.g	h126	1	1,172	Fnt
Pontoon Bridge 6 ch.g	h99	1	2,968	San
Second Call 4 ch.f	h101	3	5,874	Flk San Fnt

Jy 0-0 Au 1-4 Se 2-5 Oc 0-8 No 2-5 De 2-5 Ja 0-6 Fe 1-3 Mr 2-6 Ap 1-3 My 1-1 Jn 0-0

P. R. HEDGER   8 28,128

Horse				
Avonburn (NZ) 9 ch.g	c112	2	6,752	Wnd Wnd
Kilcash (IRE) 5 b.g	h139	2	10,543	Chp San
Lyph (USA) 7 b.g	h85	1	1,660	Lin
Peace Officer 7 br.g	c114	1	4,202	Tau
The Nigelstan 12 b.g	c106	1	3,213	Str
Welsh Singer 7 ch.g	h95	1	1,758	Fnt

Jy 0-0 Au 0-1 Se 0-3 Oc 3-9 No 2-6 De 0-12 Ja 1-10 Fe 0-6 Mr 1-7 Ap 0-8 My 0-3 Jn 1-1

N. J. HENDERSON   53 243,210

Horse				
Acre Hill 9 gr.g	c124	1	3,454	Kem
Amtrak Express 6 ch.g	h115	4	16,419	Chl Tau Wnc Wnc
Arabian Bold (IRE) 5 br.g	h131	2	4,277	War Utt
Badrakhani (FR) 7 b.g	h126	1	1,988	Hun
Bally Clover 6 ch.g	h124	2	4,174	Fnt Chl
Billy Bathgate 7 ch.g	c125	2	5,255	Kem Her
Calabrese 8 ch.g	c123	1	2,234	Her
Carrigeen Lad 6 b.g	h104	2	3,254	Plu Str

Case Harden 6 ch.g	h104	1	2,367	War
Cooley's Valve (IRE) 5 b.g	h116	1	2,553	Nwb
Emerald Storm 6 br.g	h93	1	1,302	War
Flown 6 b.g	h165	1	5,222	Fnt
Freeline Finishing 9 b.g	c135	2	10,303	Exe Chp
Give Me An Answer 7 ch.m	h89	1	1,030	War
Golden Spinner 6 ch.g		1	1,702	Nwb
Grey Hussar (NZ) 7 gr.g	h90	1	1,822	Wnd
Home Counties (IRE) 4 ch.g	h117	1	1,730	NAb
Interpretation (NZ) 7 b.g	c102	1	2,398	Lud
Irish Bay 7 b.g	h108	2	? 301	Tow Fnt
Jopanini 8 b.g	h139	1	2,924	Chl
Le Piccolage 9 b.g	c123	2	11,025	Not Chl
Lucky Villain 8 b.g	c87	1	2,179	Tau
Parsons Green 9 b.g	c133	1	3,600	Nwb
Philip's Woody 5 b.g	h107	1	1,719	Lin
Propaganda 5 b.g	h108	1	2,532	Nwb
Remittance Man 9 b.g	c163	2	26,767	Wnc Hun
Sorbiere 6 b.g	h102	1	2,653	Nwb
Spectacular Dawn 4 gr.f	h109	1	1,473	War
Sweet George 6 b.g	h79	1	3,302	Nwb
Thinking Twice (USA) 4 ch.c	h123	1	11,450	Hay
Thumbs Up 7 b.g	h128	3	26,524	Chp Wor Chl
Tinryland 9 b.g	c141	1	7,180	Don
Travado 7 br.g	c152	4	50,918	Nwb Nwb Kem Chl
Vicompt de Valmont 8 b.g	c90	1	2,301	Plu
Whatever You Like 9 b.g	c124	1	3,563	War
Windy Ways 8 br.g	c124	1	4,143	Tow
Wont Be Gone Long 11 b.g	c128	1	4,172	San

Jy 0-0 Au 0-0 Se 0-1 Oc 8-33 No 11-40 De 4-33 Ja 4-44 Fe 9-40 Mr 9-49 Ap 3-37 My 5-21 Jn 0-0

P. J. HOBBS		37	90,077	
Aal El Aal 6 br.h		1	1,998	Per
Bankroll 6 b.g	h111	1	2,448	Wnc
Bill Quill 9 ch.g	c94	1	2,094	NAb
Chapel of Barras (IRE) 4 b.g		1	1,684	Wnd
Chiaroscuro 7 b.g	h85	1	1,632	Her
Clever Shepherd 8 b.g	c107	1	3,259	Exe
Connaught Crusader 5 b.g		1	2,400	Asc
Dextra Dove 6 gr.g	h119	2	5,947	Wnc Chp
Fort Noel 10 br.g	c106	1	2,310	Chp
Gold Cap (FR) 8 ch.g	c111	1	2,334	Fnt
Greenhill Raffles 7 ch.g	h109	2	3,660	Wor NAb
Guiburn's Nephew 11 ch.g	c125	3	13,252	NAb Chp Asc
Kittinger 12 b.g	c101	1	2,710	Tau
Kiwi Velocity (NZ) 6 b.m	h112	2	5,129	Wor Wnc
Miami Splash 6 ch.g	h121	3	7,069	Wnc Exe Wnc
Mulbank 7 b.g	c105	1	2,445	Chp
Munka 7 b.g	h96	1	3,179	Nwb
Myhamet 6 b.g	h98	3	5,032	Exe Fnt Tau
Real Progress (IRE) 5 ch.g	h102	1	1,305	Wnd
Sea Barn 10 ch.g	h91	2	3,276	NAb Her
Uncle Eli 10 br.g	c123	1	2,898	Kem
Up-A-Point 8 gr.g	c105	1	4,240	Chl
Warner Forpleasure 7 b.g	h81	1	1,940	Wor
Warner For Winners 7 b.g	c91	2	4,747	Plu War
Wide Boy 11 b.g	c120	1	2,085	Wor
Wingcommander Eats 8 b.g	h95	1	1,004	Wor

Jy 0-1 Au 1-15 Se 3-18 Oc 2-34 No 5-36 De 3-22 Ja 2-31 Fe 7-33 Mr 9-51 Ap 4-40 My 1-23 Jn 0-1

R. J. HODGES   **32**   **90,962**

Came Down 10 gr.g	c96	1	2,989	Chp
Commanchero 6 gr.g	h75	1	2,072	Tow
Cotapaxi 8 gr.g	c90	2	4,942	NAb Lin
Edge of The Glen 5 b.g	h76	1	1,587	Plu
Fred Splendid 10 b.g	c94	3	7,829	NAb Plu NAb
General Merchant 13 br.g	c89	4	10,726	Fnt Tow Lin Tow
Indian Run (IRE) 4 b.g	h123	1	2,793	San
Jurz (IRE) 5 b.h	h117	1	2,794	War
Lapiaffe 9 b.g	c94	1	2,201	Exe
Lavalight 6 b.g	h76	2	3,507	Tau Wnc
Miss Marigold 4 b.f	h81	1	1,793	Wol
Northern Saddler 6 ch.g	c90:h99	3	8,874	Tau Don Asc
Rare Bid (NZ) 10 br.g	c102	2	4,803	Exe Her
Setter Country 9 b.m	c123	2	12,762	NAb Asc
Shelly's Folly 8 b.h	h83	1	1,595	Tow
Smartie Express 11 b.g	c118	4	15,692	War Wnc Nwb Lud
Smiling Chief (IRE) 5 ch.g	h92	1	1,618	Wnc
Starlap 9 b.g	c94	1	2,385	Tow

Jy 0-0 Au 3-11 Se 0-14 Oc 0-19 No 4-33 De 1-25 Ja 1-34 Fe 6-27 Mr 10-43 Ap 2-25 My 5-28 Jn 0-0

J. M. JEFFERSON   **14**   **36,580**

Ardlussa Bay 5 b.m	h112	3	6,533	Crl Ayr Wth
Dolikos 6 b.g	c100	2	4,872	Hun Crl
Persian House 6 ch.g	c114	2	7,950	MRa Crl
Tindari (FR) 5 ch.g	h117	3	6,089	Edi Edi Crl
West Ender 10 gr.g	c113	4	11,136	MRa Hun MRa Hun

Jy 0-0 Au 0-1 Se 0-2 Oc 3-6 No 2-8 De 3-12 Ja 1-5 Fe 2-7 Mr 2-8 Ap 1-11 My 0-5 Jn 0-0

J. R. JENKINS   **15**   **38,052**

Andrews Minstrel 6 br.g	h93	1	1,256	Plu
Atlaal 8 b.g	c137	1	9,990	Asc
Fierce 5 ch.g	h108	2	5,405	Hun Nwb
Greenhills Pride 9 b.g	h84	1	1,705	Sou
Ilewin 6 br.g	h96	1	1,298	Tow
Kaytak (FR) 6 b.g	h110	1	1,953	Not
Midday Show (USA) 6 b.h	h92	1	1,305	Wor
Shanaghey West 9 b.g	c81	1	2,287	Lin
Striding Edge 8 ch.g	c87:h101	2	3,972	Plu Fak
Weekday Cross (IRE) 5 b.g	h90	1	2,390	Fak
Wings of Freedom (IRE) 5 b.g	h104	3	6,491	Ban Tow Wor

Jy 0-1 Au 1-15 Se 2-15 Oc 1-23 No 1-30 De 0-18 Ja 2-31 Fe 3-26 Mr 3-22 Ap 0-20 My 2-12 Jn 0-0

J. H. JOHNSON   **19**   **60,700**

Abnegation 8 b.g	h126	1	5,117	Chl
Buck Owens 8 ch.g	c95	1	1,828	Sed
Cool Dude 7 b.g	h97	2	2,953	Cat Cat
Edberg 9 b.g	c132	1	3,488	San
Frozen Minstrel 9 b.g	c96	1	2,660	Cat
Glemot (IRE) 5 br.g	h77	1	1,996	Kel
Howe Street 10 gr.g	c129	1	5,918	Nwb
Mister Moody (FR) 8 ch.h	c90	1	2,259	Sed
Old Applejack 13 ch.g	c129	1	1,883	Nwc
Regan (USA) 6 b.m	c92	2	5,187	Sed Wth
Temple Garth 4 b.g	h97	2	2,942	Sed Crl
Tres Amigos 6 b.g	c103	3	6,457	Sed Cat Sed
Ushers Island 7 br.g	c113	2	18,012	Chl Wth

Jy 0-0 Au 0-2 Se 1-4 Oc 2-14 No 4-26 De 3-16 Ja 1-22 Fe 1-33 Mr 4-32 Ap 1-16 My 2-11 Jn 0-0

S. E. KETTLEWELL   **7**   **38,437**

Easby Hopes 7 b.g	h85	1	1,305	Hun
Easby Joker 5 b.g		1	1,304	Hex
Mr News (IRE) 4 b.c	h86	2	3,368	MRa Lud
Valiant Boy 7 b.g	c135	3	32,460	Asc Liv Ban

Jy 0-0 Au 0-0 Se 0-1 Oc 0-3 No 3-8 De 1-8 Ja 1-10 Fe 0-4 Mr 0-5 Ap 2-8 My 0-4 Jn 0-0

P. KIELY, IRELAND   **1**   **43,435**

Shuil Ar Aghaidh 7 b.m	h157	1	43,435	Chl

Jy 0-0 Au 0-0 Se 0-0 Oc 0-0 No 0-0 De 0-1 Ja 0-0 Fe 0-0 Mr 1-1 Ap 0-0 My 0-0 Jn 0-0

MISS H. C. KNIGHT   **37**   **79,635**

Assaglawi 11 b.g	c117	5	8,646	Wor Wor Wnc Exe Wor
Camelot Knight 7 br.g	c112	2	4,690	NAb Kem
Croft Mill 7 b.g	h90	1	1,305	Wnd
Delgany Run 9 ch.g	c100	1	2,574	Not
Easthorpe 5 b.g	h98	1	1,484	Wol
Factor Ten (IRE) 5 b.g	h104	2	3,638	Kem Lud
Glen Lochan (NZ) 8 gr.g	h137	4	13,442	Exe Kem Asc San
Grouseman 7 gr.g	h107	2	5,079	Tau Lud
Hymne d'Amour (USA) 5 b.m	h104	4	5,797	Wol Wol Wol Not
Lackendara 6 ch.g	h100	1	2,026	Wnd
Mickeen 6 b.g	h107	1	1,952	Str
Moving Out 5 b.g	h96	2	3,536	Wol War
Oatis Regrets 5 b.g	h110	4	9,460	War Lud Wnc Nwb
Pontoon Bridge 6 ch.g		1	1,476	San
Royal Saxon 7 b.g	c92	1	2,349	Wnd
Toureen Prince 10 b.g	c107	2	6,064	Asc Ban
Well Wrapped 9 b.g	c127	3	6,117	Sou Wol Wol

Jy 0-1 Au 1-1 Se 1-5 Oc 6-23 No 9-21 De 2-12 Ja 2-29 Fe 6-23 Mr 3-17 Ap 4-15 My 3-5 Jn 0-0

R. LEE   **29**   **94,528**

Always Ready 7 b.g	h95	2	3,277	Utt Lin
Annicombe Run 9 b.m	h121	1	2,803	Kem
Arrastra 5 b.m	h85	1	1,807	Flk
Bobby Socks 7 b.g	c106	3	7,723	Wol Hun Hun
Brompton Road 10 b.g	c112	1	3,193	Ban
Comedy Road 9 br.g	c95	1	3,453	Utt
Damers Cavalry 10 b.g	c115	1	3,707	Don
Donosti 9 b.g	h103	2	3,301	Lin Lin
Enchanted Man 9 b.g	c88	1	2,618	Str
Good For A Loan 6 b.g	h108	2	4,664	Lin Don
Leeswood 5 b.g	h91	2	4,541	Ban Ban
Major Kinsman 8 b.g	c111	4	10,585	Sed Lin Wol Hun
Market Leader 13 b.g	c84	2	5,345	MRa MRa
My New Best Friend 9 b.g	h108	1	1,392	Utt
Risk Factor 7 b.g	h82	1	2,242	Wor
Rochester 7 gr.g	c92:h99	2	4,048	Wol Tau
Space Fair 10 b.g	c143	2	29,829	Chl Chl

Jy 0-0 Au 2-6 Se 1-5 Oc 2-16 No 0-28 De 2-14 Ja 4-27 Fe 6-32 Mr 5-30 Ap 6-26 My 0-13 Jn 1-1

L. LUNGO   **22**   **44,188**

Attadale 5 b.g	h120	6	14,030	Nwc Wth Crl Sed Hex Nwc
Casual Pass 10 ch.g	h103	4	7,624	Kel Crl Hex Hex
Hthaal (USA) 5 b.g	h89	1	2,248	Kel
It's The Pits 6 b.g	h102	2	3,101	Per Hex
Justaserff 11 b.g	c91	1	2,916	Per
Kirstenbosch 6 b.g	h94	2	4,118	Crl Crt
Linngate 4 b.f		1	1,712	Ayr
Serphil 5 ch.g	h80	1	937	Hex

23

Valseur (USA) 4 ch.c   h95   4   7,502   Sed Sed Per Per
Jy 0-0 Au 0-2 Se 0-2 Oc 0-9 No 2-9 De 0-9 Ja 1-10 Fe 1-4 Mr 5-18 Ap 7-14 My 6-15 Jn 0-0

J. MACKIE   10   25,455

Andermatt 6 b.h	h121	2	5,776	Wth Utt
Lock Keeper (USA) 7 b.g	h77	1	1,214	Sou
Mr Setaside 8 br.g	c107	2	5,378	Utt Lei
Red Jam Jar 8 ch.g	h95	1	1,305	Wor
Sacre d'Or (USA) 8 b.g	c134	3	8,199	Utt Ban Lei
Wigtown Bay 10 br.g	c94	1	3,583	Utt

Jy 0-0 Au 1-3 Se 1-7 Oc 2-14 No 1-12 De 2-18 Ja 1-8 Fe 1-14 Mr 0-13 Ap 1-10 My 0-8 Jn 0-2

P. MONTEITH   14   34,683

Aragon Ayr 5 b.g	h97	1	2,304	Per
Beldine 8 gr.g	c106	1	2,201	Per
Dizzy (USA) 5 gr.m	h126	3	7,386	Edi Kel Kel
John Naman (IRE) 4 b.g	h82	1	1,914	Edi
Miliyel 4 ch.f	h97	1	1,725	Edi
Moment of Truth 9 b.g	c141:h122	2	5,975	Per Chl
Night Guest 11 br.g	c104	3	7,670	Kel Kel Crl
Run Pet Run 8 ch.m	c105	2	5,508	Kel Hex

Jy 0-0 Au 2-3 Se 0-7 Oc 1-18 No 1-18 De 1-15 Ja 2-24 Fe 1-14 Mr 4-16 Ap 1-8 My 1-9 Jn 0-0

A. MOORE   13   29,300

Bellezza 6 b.m	h113	3	11,730	Tau Tau Lin
Fighting Days (USA) 7 ch.g	c91	1	1,067	Plu
Masroug 6 b.g	h89	1	1,382	Plu
Roger's Pal 6 ch.h	h87	1	1,734	Plu
Sharpgun (FR) 7 ch.g	h95	1	2,303	Fak
Silverino 7 gr.g	c92	1	2,883	Lin
Solid Steel (IRE) 5 b.h	h101	3	3,551	Exe Plu Plu
Sure Pride (USA) 5 b.g	h105	2	4,650	Fnt Asc

Jy 0-0 Au 0-4 Se 2-10 Oc 1-24 No 3-32 De 1-8 Ja 1-22 Fe 1-32 Mr 2-26 Ap 2-13 My 0-15 Jn 0-0

G. M. MOORE   29   69,838

Awkas 8 b.g	c87	1	2,290	Cat
Bold Boss 4 b.g	h140	6	22,870	Edi Nwc Asc Hay Ayr Ayr
High Alltitude (IRE) 5 b.g	h136	4	13,735	Crl Hay Nwc Chp
Magic At Dawn (USA) 8 ch.g	c85	1	2,340	Per
No Sid No Stars (USA) 5 ch.g	h103	3	2,551	Sed Sed Sed
Nouvelle Cuisine 5 b.m	h87	2	3,012	Nwc Hex
Raiseamillion 5 b.g	h94	2	4,123	Sed Ban
Space Captain 6 b.g	h100	1	1,604	Crt
Ste-Jen (IRE) 4 b.g	h106	3	5,057	Crt Lei Lei
Tallywagger 6 b.g	h127	3	6,798	Hex Sed Nwc
Tapatch (IRE) 5 b.h	h111	3	5,458	Edi Hun Nwc

Jy 0-0 Au 3-7 Se 2-19 Oc 2-19 No 3-32 De 4-13 Ja 1-17 Fe 6-32 Mr 3-26 Ap 1-16 My 4-19 Jn 0-0

A. L. T. MOORE, IRELAND   1   26,040

Second Schedual 8 b.g	c149	1	26,040	Chl

Jy 0-0 Au 0-0 Se 0-0 Oc 0-0 No 0-2 De 0-1 Ja 0-0 Fe 0-4 Mr 1-4 Ap 0-0 My 0-1 Jn 0-0

K. A. MORGAN   13   29,257

Bill And Coup 8 br.m	c86	1	3,074	MRa
Exploration (USA) 6 b.g	h92	1	1,996	Crt
Favoured Victor (USA) 6 ch.g	h95	2	3,969	Cat Fak
Irish Ditty (USA) 6 ch.g	h96	2	3,907	Cat Cat
Isabeau 6 b.m	h108	1	1,172	Sou
Kind'a Smart 8 ch.g	c101	2	5,118	Wnd Cat
Nessfield 7 b.m	c86	2	5,556	MRa Cat
Nowhiski 5 b.h	h81	1	1,730	MRa

Ratify 6 br.g   h101   1   2,735 Fak
Jy 0-0 Au 1-2 Se 0-3 Oc 0-6 No 3-17 De 0-12 Ja 1-21 Fe 5-26 Mr 2-20 Ap 0-7 My 1-8 Jn 0-4

F. MURPHY   **23 105,279**
Brandeston 8 b.g   c128   2   9,618 Str Nwb
Dennington (IRE) 5 ch.g   h81   1   1,958 Hun
Emsee-H 8 br.g   c123   4   14,180 Hun Hun San Kem
Kev's Lass (IRE) 5 ch.m   h94   1   1,480 Wor
Man O Mine (IRE) 4 b.g   1   1,602 War
Mr-Paw 10 b.g   c87   1   3,020 MRa
Mrs Mayhew (IRE) 5 ch.m   h83   1   1,480 Wor
Notary-Nowell 7 b.g   h107   2   3,693 Fak Hun
Private Audition 11 b.g   c118   2   5,211 Hun Wor
Pry's-Joy 9 b.g   c96   3   7,127 Hun Str Wor
Scole 8 b.g   c114   1   2,271 Wor
Sibton Abbey 8 b.g   c161   4   53,639 Wor Chl Nwb Chl
Jy 0-0 Au 0-0 Se 3-10 Oc 6-22 No 3-22 De 0-10 Ja 3-22 Fe 2-15 Mr 0-11 Ap 4-18 My 1-9 Jn 1-2

P. G. MURPHY   **11 39,151**
Belafonte 6 br.g   h124   1   2,794 Asc
Beresfords Girl 8 b.m   c103   2   6,528 Exe Lei
Casienne (IRE) 5 ch.m   h84   1   1,876 Chp
Charmed I'm Sure 6 ch.m   h87   1   1,670 Exe
Elsa 4 gr.f   h80   1   1,670 Exe
Nan's Boy 5 b.h   h104   1   1,305 Wor
Sailors Luck 8 b.g   c94   1   2,345 Wnd
Sylvia Beach 7 b.m   h89   1   2,565 Her
Tomahawk 6 ch.g   h133   1   15,500 Kem
Viceroy Jester 8 br.g   h123   1   2,898 Asc
Jy 0-0 Au 0-0 Se 0-0 Oc 1-5 No 1-22 De 3-20 Ja 3-21 Fe 0-16 Mr 2-13 Ap 0-5 My 1-4 Jn 0-0

P. F. NICHOLLS   **20 54,727**
Its Nearly Time 10 br.g   c118   1   3,525 War
James The First 5 ch.g   h108   4   10,413 Str Her Wol Hay
Key Dear (FR) 6 ch.g   h87   1   1,452 Tau
Muddy Lane 5 b.g   h79   1   1,621 NAb
Olveston (NZ) 9 b.g   h114   2   3,759 Wor Lud
River Orchid 4 b.f   h80   1   1,721 Tau
Sunley Bay 7 gr.g   h112   1   2,129 Her
Thatcher Rock (NZ) 8 b.g   c105   4   10,504 Fnt Fak Wor NAb
Va Lute (FR) 9 b.g   h101   1   1,675 Lin
Vomero (NZ) 8 gr.m   h88   1   1,675 Lin
Welknown Character 11 b.g   c119   2   12,653 Wnc Asc
Western Legend 9 ch.g   c115   1   3,600 Wnc
Jy 0-0 Au 0-1 Se 0-4 Oc 3-12 No 2-13 De 0-10 Ja 3-20 Fe 5-26 Mr 4-20 Ap 2-22 My 1-4 Jn 0-0

D. NICHOLSON   **100 492,437**
Another Coral 10 br.g   c160   2   35,471 Chl Nwb
Banbridge 10 ch.g   c124   1   2,192 Lud
Barrica 6 b.m   c92   1   2,502 Her
Barton Bank 7 br.g   c142   4   30,368 Wor Wor Chl War
Baydon Star 6 br.g   h156   5   40,972 Asc Nwb Liv Asc Kem
Beauchamp Grace 4 b.f   h131   4   12,511 Chl Tow War Nwb
Belstone Fox 8 br.g   c115   2   6,584 Don Nwb
Bishops Island 7 b.g   c124   1   2,601 Utt
Canon Class 12 b.g   c90   1   1,534 Tow
Carrick Lanes 6 b.g   h103   2   3,560 Ban Hun
Clurican (IRE) 4 ch.g   h126   2   3,540 San Her
Dilleachta 6 b.m   1   1,969 War
Dreamers Delight 7 b.g   h126   3   8,315 Utt Liv Nwb

25

Duntree 8 ch.g	c131	1	10,699	Chl
Emperor Buck (IRE) 5 b.g		1	1,996	San
Fast Study 8 b.g	c102	2	4,925	Lei NAb
Formal Invitation (IRE) 4 ch.g	h124	2	2,959	Lud Wol
For The Grain 9 b.g	c135	1	10,820	Kem
Gambling Royal 10 ch.g	c138	1	7,293	Kem
Hebridean 6 b.g	h138	3	11,915	NAb Hun Asc
Kadi (GER) 4 b.g	h125	2	6,066	San Hun
King of The Lot 10 br.g	c141	2	9,121	Wth Chl
Little-Nipper 8 ch.g	c102	1	4,175	Chl
Master Jolson 5 b.g	h106	1	1,903	Not
Meleagris 9 b.g	h114	2	3,816	Lud Wol
Mighty Mogul 6 ch.g	h170	5	67,385	Nwb Chp Nwb Hay Kem
Moorcroft Boy 8 ch.g	c117	2	4,721	Asc Hun
Musthaveaswig 7 gr.g	c117	3	11,539	Don Not San
Now Your Talkin 7 b.g	h129	4	9,278	Lud War Wol Liv
Peajade 9 b.g	c108	2	6,520	Str Utt
Persian Sword 7 b.g	h92	2	3,672	War War
Sandybraes 8 ch.g	c107	3	8,296	Ban Plu Per
Scrutineer (USA) 4 b.g	h112	2	4,460	Nwb Wol
Setai's Palace 6 b.m	h94	1	1,480	Hun
Shamana 7 b.m	c132	3	11,968	Chl Wol San
Springholm 11 br.g	c98	1	3,659	San
Strong Beau 8 br.g	c123	2	20,031	Str Chl
Stylus 4 ch.g	h117	2	3,653	Lei Per
The Flying Footman 7 b.g	h84	1	2,484	Ban
Travelling Wrong 7 b.g	c115	4	15,045	Chp Nwb Chl Nwb
Tug of Gold 8 gr.g	c132	1	2,749	Utt
Uncle Mogy 7 ch.g	c93	1	2,840	Ban
Viking Flagship 6 b.g	c144	4	9,852	Wol Lei Wnc Chp
Waterloo Boy 10 ch.g	c159	3	39,080	Exe San Nwb
Winter Squall (IRE) 5 gr.g	h136	3	16,966	Lud San Chp
Wonder Man (FR) 8 ch.g	c151	3	18,952	Wol San Kem

Jy 0-0 Au 0-2 Se 0-7 Oc 11-34 No 19-47 De 15-42 Ja 16-64 Fe 18-64 Mr 12-51 Ap 7-43 My 2-10 Jn 0-2

M. J. P. O'BRIEN, IRELAND   1   34,275

| Shawiya (IRE) 4 b.f | h141 | 1 | 34,275 | Chl |

Jy 0-0 Au 0-0 Se 0-0 Oc 0-0 No 0-0 De 0-0 Ja 0-0 Fe 0-0 Mr 1-1 Ap 0-0 My 0-0 Jn 0-0

J. J. O'NEILL   21   43,663

Ambleside Harvest 6 b.g	h116	1	2,113	Ayr
Arrow Dancer 7 b.g	h83	1	816	Crl
Ballylord 9 ch.g	h99	2	4,626	Hay Utt
Beachy Head 5 gr.g	h135	1	2,500	Per
Boreen Owen 9 b.g	c113	3	7,209	Sed Sed Sed
Chic And Elite 6 b.m	h94	2	2,595	Crl Crl
Danny Connors 9 b.g	c129	1	2,916	Ban
Fantastical 5 br.g	h87	1	1,987	Edi
Impany 14 br.g	c82	1	2,192	Lud
Konvekta Control 6 ch.g		1	1,455	Ayr
Konvekta King (IRE) 5 br.g		1	1,277	Lud
Rifle Range 10 b.g	c124	2	6,835	Ayr Hay
Rose Tableau 10 ch.m	h100	1	1,079	Cat
Scottish Reform 6 b.g	c92	1	1,974	Crl
Tronchetto (IRE) 4 b.g	h103	2	4,089	Sed MRa

Jy 0-0 Au 0-11 Se 2-11 Oc 4-22 No 5-22 De 4-18 Ja 1-17 Fe 0-11 Mr 1-8 Ap 3-18 My 0-11 Jn 1-2

R. J. O'SULLIVAN   13   26,899

| Belmoredean 8 ch.g | c100 | 2 | 4,564 | NAb Tau |

Dwadme 8 b.g	c96	1	2,052	NAb
El Volador 6 br.h	h99	2	4,255	Tau Fnt
Mad Casanova 8 b.g	c105	2	4,850	Fnt Lin
Munday Dean 5 ch.g	h79	1	1,734	Lin
Scotoni 7 ch.g	c105	3	6,426	Fnt Lin Flk
Sparkler Gebe 7 b.g	h91	2	3,018	Str Lin

Jy 0-0 Au 0-0 Se 1-7 Oc 5-14 No 1-13 De 2-10 Ja 1-11 Fe 2-11 Mr 1-13 Ap 0-6 My 0-2 Jn 0-0

J. A. B. OLD		**19**	**56,430**	
Buddy Holly (NZ) 8 b.g	c95	1	3,231	NAb
Buonarroti 6 b.g	h125	2	6,868	Lin Asc
Corrarder 9 ch.g	c100	1	2,738	NAb
Mole Board 11 br.g	h157	1	10,114	San
Plastic Spaceage 10 b.g	c127	3	10,474	Chp Chp NAb
Quadrireme 4 b.g	h123	3	5,355	Wnc NAb Utt
Ramble (USA) 6 ch.m	h87	1	1,484	Sou
River Island (USA) 5 b.g	h116	2	2,975	Tau Hun
Sand-Dollar 10 ch.g	h122	1	2,327	Tau
Simpson 8 ch.g	h136	1	3,753	Nwb
Soothfast (USA) 4 b.g	h95	1	1,480	Tow
Wick Pound 7 b.g	c108	2	5,631	Kem Wnc

Jy 0-0 Au 0-0 Se 0-0 Oc 2-9 No 0-3 De 2-8 Ja 2-12 Fe 3-16 Mr 1-12 Ap 6-21 My 3-11 Jn 0-1

C. PARKER		**14**	**36,071**	
Boarding School 6 b.g	c98	3	8,802	Wol Ayr MRa
Caithness Prince 7 b.g	h88	1	2,010	Crl
Kushbaloo 8 b.g	c120	5	14,951	Crl Hex Kel Ayr Don
Lupy Minstrel 8 br.g	c97	1	1,581	Crl
Portavogie 9 b.g	c86	1	2,511	Nwc
Trump 4 b.g	h101	3	6,216	Edi Edi Crl

Jy 0-0 Au 0-1 Se 1-5 Oc 2-12 No 1-17 De 0-3 Ja 1-7 Fe 4-13 Mr 1-6 Ap 2-11 My 1-8 Jn 1-2

MISS L. A. PERRATT		**12**	**31,280**	
Family Line 5 b.g	h108	5	11,691	Per Not Don Ayr Ayr
Jimmy Mac Jimmy 6 b.g	c89	1	2,209	Hex
Kirsty's Boy 10 b.g	c123	2	7,079	Nwc Wth
Persuasive 6 b.m	h127	3	7,411	Hay Cat Per
Silver Hello 7 gr.g	c98	1	2,890	MRa

Jy 0-0 Au 0-0 Se 2-11 Oc 0-12 No 2-15 De 1-8 Ja 0-17 Fe 2-8 Mr 1-9 Ap 2-10 My 2-10 Jn 0-0

M. C. PIPE		**194**	**808,027**	
A Fortiori (IRE) 5 b.g		1	1,702	Nwb
Angels Kiss (SWE) 8 b.g	h97	1	1,530	NAb
Ankud (IRE) 4 b.f	h80	1	1,635	NAb
As du Trefle (FR) 5 ch.g	h124	3	7,077	Lei NAb Hay
Bighayir 6 gr.g	h103	1	1,548	Hay
Boogie Bopper (IRE) 4 b.g	h97	2	2,741	Not Flk
Cache Fleur (FR) 7 ch.g	c129	1	2,469	Kem
Capability Brown 6 b.g	c137	4	24,797	Wor Hay Chp Asc
Catch The Cross 7 gr.g	c124	2	6,666	War NAb
Celcius 9 b.g	h107	2	4,098	Lei Hay
Claxton Greene 9 b.g	c116	3	7,988	Chp Tau Tau
Cool Clown 6 b.g	h115	2	2,955	Flk Tow
Cyphrate (USA) 7 b.g	c147	1	10,143	Asc
Dagobertin (FR) 7 ch.g	c119	1	2,112	Fnt
Damier Blanc (FR) 4 b.g		1	1,675	Lin
Elite Reg 4 b.g	h122	6	16,097	Liv War Don Hay Chp Wor
Errant Knight 9 ch.g	c113	1	3,591	Str
Ess El Ar 5 b.m		1	828	Sou
Faithful Star 8 b.g	c126:h97	3	6,230	Her Exe Lei

Flying Speed (USA) 5 b.g	h125	3	5,948	Utt Wnc Wor
Galway Star 6 b.h	c89:h129	2	4,077	NAb NAb
Gay Ruffian 7 b.g	c132	4	11,127	Wor Lud Utt Her
Gold Medal (FR) 5 gr.g	h113	3	4,633	Exe Chp War
Grand Frere 7 br.g	h114	3	7,123	NAb Tau Wnc
Grand Hawk (USA) 5 b.g	h133	5	11,200	Exe Lei Asc Kem Kem
Granville Again 7 ch.g	h167	1	84,734	Chl
Grove Serendipity (IRE) 5 b.g	h101	2	2,519	Wol Wol
Hawthorn Blaze 7 br.g	c126:h145	4	13,792	Chl Nwb Lin Lei
Heathfield Gale 6 b.m	h106	2	10,355	Don Nwb
Her Honour 4 b.f	h127	3	6,694	Hay Tau Chl
Highland Spirit 5 ch.m	h119	10	16,681	Her Her Exe Tau Lud Exe
				Tau Tau MRa Chp
Just (FR) 7 b.g	h90	1	2,944	Tau
Land of The Free 4 b.f	h107	3	4,927	Tau Wnc Tau
Lemon's Mill (USA) 4 b.f	h132	3	15,107	Lud War Liv
Lord Relic (NZ) 7 b.g	h140	3	20,265	Utt Chp Nwb
Marshall Sparks 6 ch.g		1	1,529	Lud
Mick's Tycoon (IRE) 5 b.g	h93	2	3,034	Flk Flk
Milford Quay 10 ch.h	c134	2	10,967	Chp Chp
Millrous 5 b.m	h86	3	4,469	Tow Exe War
Miss Equilia (USA) 7 ch.m	h98	2	3,406	Her NAb
Mister Half-Chance 7 b.g	h109	1	2,295	Not
Mohana 4 br.f	h126	6	11,379	NAb NAb NAb Ban Chl Chl
Myverygoodfriend 6 b.g	h87	1	1,404	NAb
Noble Insight 6 ch.g	h116	1	4,403	Kem
Obie's Train 7 ch.g	c105	1	2,851	Exe
Old Brig 7 br.g	h99	1	1,772	Wnc
Olympian 6 ch.g	h135	3	59,890	Str San Chl
On The Sauce 6 b.g	h102	5	7,705	Fnt Her Exe Exe Utt
Passed Pawn 6 b.g	h117	3	6,005	NAb Her Fnt
Pharaoh Blue 9 ch.g	h110	1	1,772	Her
Pharly Story 5 b.h	h117	3	5,332	Wor Chp Wnc
Poacher's Delight 7 ch.g	c101	2	5,204	Tau Chp
Pragada 10 b.g	h160	1	9,380	Hay
Re-Release 8 ch.m	c106	1	2,204	Wnd
Riverside Boy 10 ch.g	c140	1	5,576	Tau
Robingo (IRE) 4 b.c	h125	3	7,182	Exe Chp Lei
Rovulenka 5 b.g	h107	1	2,490	Lei
Run For Free 9 b.g	c163	4	80,510	Hay Chp Chp Ayr
Rushing Wild 8 b.g	c172	2	17,410	Wnc San
Sabin du Loir (FR) 14 ch.g	c151	1	5,585	Wnc
Saraville 6 ch.m	c118	3	7,613	Wnc Wor Fnt
Sea Patrol 6 b.g	h88	1	1,480	Wor
Side of Hill 8 b.g	c112	3	7,905	Chp Wor NAb
Skipping Tim 14 b.g	c114	8	22,954	NAb NAb Chl Fnt Fnt Her
				Ban Exe
Slavi (FR) 5 ch.m	h110	2	3,580	NAb NAb
Snowy Lane (IRE) 5 ch.g	h123	1	1,744	Chp
Swahili Run 5 ch.g	h103	2	3,670	Exe Wnc
Sweet Glow (FR) 6 b.g	h156	2	23,831	Asc Asc
Sweet N' Twenty 7 b.m	h121	1	3,623	Asc
Takemethere 9 b.g	c104	1	3,319	Don
The Black Monk (IRE) 5 ch.g	h125	9	15,882	Exe Exe Lud Lei Chp
				Exe Chp NAb Her
The Leggett 10 b.g	c112	1	4,317	Exe
Tom Clapton 6 b.g	h108	1	1,313	NAb
Tri Folene (FR) 7 b.m	c118	2	4,990	Chl Fnt

Tudor Da Samba 4 b.g	h113	5	8,205	Tau Lei Exe Tau Chp
Tyrone Bridge 7 b.g	h153	1	9,500	Nwb
Vagog 8 b.g	h156	2	30,096	Chl Asc
Valfinet (FR) 6 b.g	h156	5	55,556	Chl San Hay Tau Wnc
Viardot (IRE) 4 b.c	h123	2	4,938	Wol San
Wingspan (USA) 9 b.g	c147	1	1,749	Plu

Jy 0-0 Au 16-34 Se 10-39 Oc 5-39 No 17-67 De 27-90 Ja 32-116 Fe 26-121 Mr 26-119 Ap 14-66 My 21-71 Jn 0-8

MRS J. PITMAN

			36	117,200
Almanzora 9 ch.g	h93	1	1,480	Str
Balzac Boy (IRE) 5 ch.g	h97	1	1,940	Wnc
Cavvies Clown 13 b.g	c144	1	9,870	Wnc
Do Be Brief 8 ch.g	c118	1	3,124	Hun
Ebony Gale 7 br.g	h115	1	2,784	Fnt
Egypt Mill Prince 7 b.g	c120	2	7,561	Chl Tow
Esha Ness 10 b.g	c137	1	4,305	Wnc
Heyfleet 10 b.g	c100	1	2,259	Plu
Hidden Oats 6 ch.g	h102	1	2,234	Str
Jakarrdi 7 ch.g	h131	1	3,787	Don
Lusty Light 7 b.g	h104	2	3,275	Tow Hun
Mailcom 7 b.g	h119	2	5,559	Hun Tow
Major Bush 6 b.g	h94	1	1,768	NAb
Precious Juno (IRE) 4 b.f		1	1,795	Lud
Royal Athlete 10 ch.g	h129	1	3,940	Wnd
Run To Form 8 br.g	c111	1	2,175	Plu
Ryde Again 10 ch.g	c147	1	5,865	Chl
Shannon Glen 7 b.g	c97	1	2,447	Lei
Smith Too (IRE) 5 br.g	h102	1	1,480	Tow
Spirit of Kibris 8 ch.g	h104	1	2,190	War
Star of The Glen 7 b.g	h121	4	9,061	Wnc Lud Lud Wnc
Superior Finish 7 br.g	c133	3	7,965	Kem Lei Ayr
Tammy's Friend 6 b.g	c102	3	6,209	Plu Utt Hun
The Illywhacker 8 b.g	c150	2	20,501	Wnc Wor
Willsford 10 b.g	h134	1	3,626	War

Jy 0-0 Au 0-0 Se 0-1 Oc 3-17 No 4-26 De 2-25 Ja 8-46 Fe 4-36 Mr 5-38 Ap 5-31 My 5-21 Jn 0-1

R. J. PRICE

			10	35,134
Al Skeet (USA) 7 b.g	h78	1	1,940	Wor
Flakey Dove 7 b.m	h153	2	19,834	War Utt
Handy Dove 6 b.m	h89	3	4,099	Wor Lud Her
Love On The Rocks 8 b.m	c88	1	2,413	NAb
Pithy 11 ch.g	c99	2	4,907	Wor Lud
Zealous Kitten (USA) 5 ch.m	h104	1	1,941	Wol

Jy 0-0 Au 0-4 Se 1-2 Oc 4-10 No 1-14 De 0-5 Ja 2-8 Fe 1-15 Mr 0-10 Ap 0-9 My 1-7 Jn 0-1

MRS J. G. RETTER

			24	74,135
Boscean Chieftain 9 b.g	h140	4	25,164	Tau Wnc Chp Hay
Broughton Manor 8 b.m	c114	3	10,416	Wnc Kem Wnc
Celtic Diamond 8 b.m	c110	2	4,232	NAb Fnt
Chip And Run 7 b.g	c110	1	1,724	Wol
Derechef 6 ch.m	h88	1	1,954	Str
Far Too Loud 6 b.g	h105	1	3,630	Nwb
Faux Pavillon 9 ch.g	h90	2	2,934	Exe Exe
Fearless Fred 6 ch.g	h95	1	1,996	Her
Forest Flame (USA) 8 ch.g	h108	1	2,259	Wnc
Meldon 6 b.g	h81	1	1,480	Tau
Rafiki 8 br.g	c98	3	8,493	War Exe Utt
Ricmar (USA) 10 ch.g	h96	1	2,064	NAb

Sabaki River 9 br.g   h128   3   7,789   Chp Chl Exe
Jy 0-0 Au 1-3 Se 2-11 Oc 3-14 No 0-5 De 3-15 Ja 3-23 Fe 4-19 Mr 2-17 Ap 1-19 My 5-21 Jn 0-5

MRS M. REVELEY		**90**	**250,587**	
Ambuscade (USA) 7 ch.g	h149	1	3,436	Ayr
Azureus (IRE) 5 ch.g	h101	1	1,188	Sou
Babcock Boy 8 b.g	h100	2	4,524	Kel Kel
Batabanoo 4 ch.g	h124	4	13,045	Wth Edi Edi Nwc
Bertie Boy 8 ch.g	c106	1	3,002	Wth
Bonanza 6 ch.g	c114	3	7,204	Sed Sed MRa
Brackenfield 7 ch.g	h137	6	20,865	Crl MRa MRa Ayr Chp Ayr
Broctune Bay 4 b.g		2	3,840	Edi MRa
Cab On Target 7 br.g	c154	5	47,555	Ayr Not Don Liv Ayr
Candy Tuff 7 b.g	c110	2	5,870	Ayr Wth
Firm Price 12 b.g	h121	3	5,714	Sed Hun Don
Flight Hill 9 br.g	c127	1	2,820	Sed
Friskney Dale Lad 8 b.g	c101	1	2,039	Sed
Grace Card 7 b.g	h141	1	2,560	Wth
Grey Power 6 gr.m	h113	2	3,980	Sed Wth
Hey Rawley 8 b.g	c96	1	2,924	Sed
Holdenby 8 b.g	c102	1	2,206	Cat
Imhotep 6 gr.g	h102	2	4,209	Cat Kel
Just Frankie 9 ch.g	c106	2	3,660	Hex Cat
Kayartis 4 b.f	h94	1	825	Sed
Majed (IRE) 5 b.h	h135	4	14,898	Ayr Hay Ayr Kel
Manettia (IRE) 4 b.f		1	1,497	Crl
Marra's Roscoe 7 b.g	h101	2	3,446	Ayr Sed
Maudlins Cross 8 ch.g	c115	4	9,569	Sou Sed Sed Kel
Monaru 7 b.g	h121	1	2,126	Cat
Mr Boston 8 b.g	c123	1	2,931	Utt
My Desire 5 ch.m	h97	1	1,305	Sed
Mystic Memory 4 b.f	h101	2	4,027	Per Wth
Mythical Storm 6 b.m	h96	1	1,484	Sed
Notable Exception 4 b.g	h96	2	3,251	Cat Nwc
Padaventure 8 b.g	c115	1	3,655	Wth
Pandessa 6 b.m	h106	3	5,625	Sou Edi Wth
Portonia 9 b.m	c115	4	10,026	Sed Cat Cat Cat
Programmed To Win 6 b.g	h110	2	4,315	Ayr Wth
Rare Fire 9 ro.g	c90	1	2,138	Hex
Shean Alainn (IRE) 5 b.m	h87	1	2,167	Tow
Snuffle Babe (IRE) 5 br.g		1	1,581	Crl
Srivijaya 6 b.h	c104	1	2,186	Cat
Starstreak 6 b.h	h95	1	1,872	Per
Stay Awake 7 ch.g	h115	2	5,711	Wth Wth
Terrible Gel (FR) 8 b.g	c102	3	6,594	Sou Kel Sed
Watertight (USA) 8 b.g	c90	2	3,409	Sed Hex
Wellwotdouthink 7 b.m	h92	1	2,654	Ayr
Whitwood 8 b.g	c102	1	2,330	MRa
Wild Bramble (IRE) 5 ch.m	h101	3	4,834	Her Utt Utt
Young Ty 9 br.g	c98	2	5,490	Don Ayr

Jy 0-0 Au 1-1 Se 5-11 Oc 8-32 No 21-69 De 6-33 Ja 18-53 Fe 9-39 Mr 7-41 Ap 9-34 My 6-27 Jn 0-1

G. RICHARDS		**104**	**327,790**	
Abbot of Furness 9 b.g	h134	4	11,493	Ayr Hay Nwc Wth
Algari 6 b.g	c98	3	7,269	Kel Nwc Crt
Arctic Skylight 9 ch.g	c113	3	6,602	Per Crl Ban
Barkin 10 b.g	c99	1	2,905	Crt
Bavard Bay 9 b.g	c98:h86	2	4,157	Cat Hex
Bee Dee Boy 5 b.g	h86	1	825	Hex

30

Better Times Ahead 7 ro.g	c117	3	7,649	Ban Ban Crt
Beyond Reason 7 b.g	h86	1	1,674	Crl
Big Mac 6 gr.g	h85	1	830	Crl
Byzantine 5 b.g	h88	2	3,024	Sed Utt
Clever Folly 13 b.g	c139	2	5,632	NAb Ban
Damanour (USA) 7 gr.g	h94	1	1,618	Ban
Folk Dance 11 b.g	c93	1	2,640	Ayr
Four Trix 12 gr.g	c121	1	2,762	Ban
Frickley 7 b.g	h134	5	17,234	Ayr Hex Don Ayr Don
Gallateen 5 gr.g	h135	4	18,478	Kel Ayr Liv Per
General Pershing 7 br.g	c144	6	29,260	Ayr Ayr Ayr Utt Wth Per
Jinxy Jack 9 b.g	h155	5	22,973	Ban Kem War Hay Kel
Jock's Burn 7 ch.g	h91	2	3,341	Hex Ayr
Kilhallon Castle 10 b.g	c100	1	2,884	Ayr
Last 'o' The Bunch 9 ch.g	c141	4	15,036	Hay Hay Wth Ayr
Mackinnon 8 b.g	c95	1	3,730	Hay
Mister Tuftie 8 b.g	c95	1	2,023	Ayr
Montpelier Lad 6 br.g	c112:h134	5	13,737	Ayr Ayr Don Ban Crt
Mutual Trust 9 ch.g	c110	5	14,735	Hex Ban Per Per Crt
On The Other Hand 10 b.g	c125	1	4,873	San
Osgathorpe 6 ch.g	h91	1	1,903	Per
Palm House 8 ch.g	h104	4	7,541	Ban Sed Ban Kel
Precipice Run 8 ch.g	h111	3	6,515	Hex Ban Crt
Preoblakensky 6 b.g	h120	1	2,325	Crl
Real Class 10 b.g	h84	1	1,033	Hex
River Pearl 8 b.m	h108	1	2,222	Ayr
Sweet City 8 ch.g	h116	1	2,038	Kel
Tartan Tailor 12 b.g	c116	1	2,948	Per
Tartan Tradewinds 6 b.g	h98	1	2,262	Crl
Tartan Tyrant 7 b.g	c103	2	5,439	Wth Ayr
The Demon Barber 11 b.g	c131	1	3,415	Ban
Thistle Monarch 8 b.g	h118	3	5,958	Crl Wth Ayr
Twin Oaks 13 br.g	c157	2	14,647	Hay Hay
Whaat Fettle 8 br.g	c123	4	11,089	Kel Kel Kel Kel
Whispering Steel 7 b.g	c120	5	24,851	Hay Hay Hay Hay Ayr
Wind Force 8 br.g	c137	7	26,220	Ban Crl Crl Wth Ayr Liv Utt

Jy 2-2 Au 4-21 Se 11-31 Oc 15-54 No 11-69 De 9-42 Ja 12-32 Fe 5-49 Mr 11-54 Ap 10-65 My 14-39 Jn 0-1

R. ROWE		**23**	**51,947**	
Baby Wizzard 4 b.f	h82	1	1,475	Plu
Charlton Yeoman 8 b.g	c90	1	1,714	Hun
Devil's Valley 10 ch.g	c115	1	2,108	Flk
Fotoexpress 5 ch.g	h117	4	7,696	Lin Plu Flk Plu
Glebelands Girl 6 b.m	h99	1	1,497	Fnt
Glebe Prince 13 b.g	c84	1	2,109	Fnt
Howaryadoon 7 b.g	h104	1	2,355	Nwb
Just Moss 7 b.g	c114	2	6,164	Lin Lei
Lake Teereen 8 ch.g	c116	2	7,639	Wor Flk
Little General 10 ch.g	c92	1	2,912	Not
Rampallion 10 b.g	c94	1	2,559	Tow
Rockmount Rose 8 b.m	c82	1	2,023	Hun
Stupid Cupid 9 b.m	c87	1	2,427	Not
Suffolk Road 6 br.g	h108	1	2,532	Wor
Thuhool 5 b.g	h99	2	3,797	Flk Flk
Trojan Call 6 b.g	c84	1	1,590	Plu
Whistling Buck (IRE) 5 br.g		1	1,350	Lud

Jy 0-0 Au 0-3 Se 0-7 Oc 4-15 No 1-18 De 4-11 Ja 1-31 Fe 6-33 Mr 4-25 Ap 1-13 My 2-12 Jn 0-0

MISS B. SANDERS   9   32,032

Absent Relative 5 ch.m	h120	4	8,787	Fnt Lin Wnd Fnt
Calapaez 9 gr.g	c131	3	15,149	Plu Kem Asc
Marlin Dancer 8 b.g	h136	2	8,096	Kem San

Jy 0-0 Au 0-1 Se 0-1 Oc 1-9 No 2-7 De 1-5 Ja 0-10 Fe 1-12 Mr 4-11 Ap 0-4 My 0-1 Jn 0-0

O. SHERWOOD   37   92,847

Bardesan 7 b.g	h107	3	4,764	Exe Sou Sou
Beauchamp Express 6 b.g	h105	2	3,875	NAb Wor
Boll Weevil 7 b.g	h99	1	1,924	Utt
Change The Act 8 b.g	c111	1	3,054	Wor
Copper Mine 7 b.g	c115	5	15,744	Str Don Nwb Wor Wor
Dissimulateur (FR) 4 b.c	h116	1	4,663	Don
Early Drinker 5 gr.g		1	1,534	Lin
Extra Grand 7 b.g	c93	2	4,526	Wor Utt
La Princesse 6 b.m	h111	2	3,659	War NAb
Large Action (IRE) 5 b.g		2	5,693	Don San
Leotard 6 b.g	h121	2	3,023	Utt Wor
Love Anew (USA) 8 b.g	c97	1	2,710	Fak
Mandraki Shuffle 11 b.g	c110	1	2,211	Fak
Mossy Fern 7 b.m	c123	3	9,442	Her Wor Utt
Royle Speedmaster 9 ch.g	c114	5	12,590	Wor Str Exe Chl Lud
Stormhead 5 ch.g	h108	2	5,517	NAb Asc
Woodland Flower 8 b.m	c95	1	1,553	Wol
Woody Will 7 b.g	c95	1	2,271	Wor
Young Pokey 8 b.g	c140	1	4,094	San

Jy 0-0 Au 1-3 Se 4-6 Oc 2-16 No 1-19 De 2-13 Ja 5-39 Fe 6-34 Mr 7-29 Ap 6-30 My 3-12 Jn 0-1

S. E. SHERWOOD   30   92,851

Archie Brown 6 b.g	h122	1	2,243	Ayr
Artful Abbot 9 ch.g	c100:h113	2	4,263	Sou Chl
Boycott 6 b.g	h129	1	1,480	Wnd
Derab (USA) 7 b.g	c100	2	5,669	Lud Lud
Dis Train 9 ch.g	c120	2	6,038	War NAb
Dragons Den 7 b.g	c104:h104	3	7,380	Utt Sou Wor
Duke of Monmouth (USA) 5 b.g	c112	2	4,479	Tau Hun
Dusty Miller 7 b.g	c124	2	11,734	Nwb Kem
Front Street 6 b.g	h89	1	1,912	Wnc
Gentleman Angler 10 ch.g	c99	1	2,213	Sou
Kino 6 b.g	c96	1	2,218	Str
Lake Mission 8 b.g	c113	1	4,115	San
Latent Talent 9 b.g	c133	1	8,538	Asc
Midnight Caller 7 br.g	c112	3	16,193	Wnd Lin NAb
Nocatchim 4 b.g	h118	3	4,918	Wnc Str Lud
Red Amber 7 ch.g	c91	2	4,746	Fnt Wor
Russell Dalus 6 b.g	h100	1	1,632	Hay
Tipp Mariner 8 ch.g	c95	1	3,080	Wnc

Jy 0-0 Au 0-0 Se 1-8 Oc 3-21 No 5-21 De 5-19 Ja 0-26 Fe 5-23 Mr 4-21 Ap 5-26 My 2-8 Jn 0-2

DENYS SMITH   14   35,240

Bow Handy Man 11 ch.g	c103	1	2,406	Cat
Cheeky Pot 5 b.g	h90	2	3,377	Sed Edi
Cornet 7 b.g	c129	3	10,927	Ayr Ayr Edi
Desert Mist 4 gr.f	h110	5	13,999	Per Kel Wth MRa Crt
Direct Interest 10 ch.g	c83	1	2,238	Hex
Thunderbird One (USA) 4 b.g	h88	1	1,484	Sou
Valkyrie Reef 4 ch.f	h82	1	809	Sed

Jy 0-0 Au 2-13 Se 1-18 Oc 3-17 No 1-17 De 2-5 Ja 0-17 Fe 4-16 Mr 0-9 Ap 0-2 My 1-6 Jn 0-0

MRS S. J. SMITH   6   29,483

Brambleberry 4 gr.c	h100	1	2,040	Wth
Island Jetsetter 7 ch.g	c101	1	2,522	Sou
Kildimo 13 b.g	c128	1	20,541	Liv
Regal Romper (IRE) 5 b.h	h96	2	3,075	Hex Hex
South Stack 7 b.g	h83	1	1,305	Sed

Jy 0-0 Au 0-0 Se 0-10 Oc 1-29 No 2-32 De 1-25 Ja 0-31 Fe 0-23 Mr 1-26 Ap 0-15 My 1-9 Jn 0-0

J. L. SPEARING   12   25,570

Casino Magic 9 b.g	c88	3	8,203	Hun Flk Her
Chelworth Raider 7 ch.g	h102	1	2,022	Hun
Eau d'Espoir 4 b.f	h87	1	1,830	Not
Jarrwah 5 ch.m	h95	2	4,283	Lin Lin
King William 8 b.g	h109	1	2,023	Hun
Raba Riba 8 gr.g	h117	4	7,209	Lin Lin Lin Lin

Jy 0-0 Au 0-5 Se 1-2 Oc 0-7 No 2-8 De 0-3 Ja 2-8 Fe 3-10 Mr 4-14 Ap 0-8 My 0-10 Jn 0-0

W. A. STEPHENSON   35   77,774

Bad Trade 11 ch.g	c113	1	2,217	Hay
Break The Chain 8 b.g	c107	1	2,775	Kel
Buckra Mellisuga 9 b.g	h105	1	1,431	Wor
Captain Mor 11 b.g	c117	1	1,918	Sed
Chief Raider (IRE) 5 br.g	h95	1	1,311	Hex
Dancing River 7 b.g	c116	3	8,086	Crt Utt Ban
Fettuccine 9 ch.g	h126	4	8,459	MRa Per Crt Chl
Gale Again 6 br.g	c137	2	6,832	Wth Nwc
He Who Dares Wins 10 b.g	c114	1	2,322	Hex
If You Say So 7 ch.g	h85	1	1,660	Kel
Kidlaw 5 b.g	h94	1	1,305	Nwc
Killula King 6 br.g	c101	1	1,813	Kel
Military Secret 7 ch.g	c94	1	2,247	Hex
One Man (IRE) 5 gr.g	h126	1	1,096	Nwc
Over The Deel 7 ch.g	c110	2	4,747	Sed Nwc
Palm Reader 9 b.g	c127	2	4,950	Per Sed
River House 11 ch.g	c105	1	2,920	Kel
Silver Haze 9 gr.g	c89	3	5,876	Ban Hex Crt
Spanish Fair (IRE) 5 b.g	h93	1	1,702	Nwc
Spree Cross 7 b.g	c110	2	5,929	Hex Wth
Strong Sound 6 b.g	c95	1	1,714	Sed
Strong Views 6 b.g	h109	2	4,860	Kel Kel
The Laughing Lord 7 b.g	h107	1	1,604	Kel

Jy 1-1 Au 8-35 Se 4-35 Oc 10-65 No 11-57 De 1-11 Ja 0-0 Fe 0-0 Mr 0-0 Ap 0-0 My 0-0 Jn 0-0

T. P. TATE   12   37,071

Ardbrin 10 ch.g	c125	2	11,031	Kem Wnc
Badastan (IRE) 4 b.c	h101	1	1,484	Sed
Captain Tancred (IRE) 5 b.g	h92	1	1,564	Sou
Lo Stregone 7 b.g	h132	3	6,353	Hay Hay Hay
Man's Best Friend 6 b.g	c101	2	4,457	Hex Hex
No More Trix 7 b.g	c102	2	4,932	Sed Sed
Peanuts Pet 8 b.h	h135	1	7,250	Nwc

Jy 0-0 Au 0-1 Se 1-1 Oc 0-5 No 2-12 De 1-11 Ja 3-12 Fe 3-14 Mr 2-7 Ap 0-3 My 0-3 Jn 0-0

T. THOMSON JONES   14   36,938

Alreef 7 b.g	h110	1	1,732	Lin
Express Reale 8 b.g	h102	1	2,008	Utt
Norman Conqueror 8 br.g	c117	1	3,395	Asc
Pamber Priory 10 b.g	c114	2	6,538	Flk Tow
Rathvinden House (USA) 6 b.g	c107:h110	2	7,058	Kem War
Sartorius 7 b.g	c99	1	1,817	Not

Sayyure (USA) 7 b.g	h134	1	4,370	Kem
Skinnhill 9 b.g	c101	1	2,364	Wol
Sleepline Royale 7 ch.g	h118	2	5,028	Flk Lin
Take The Buckskin 6 b.g		1	828	Sou
West Bay 7 b.g	h78	1	1,800	Wor

Jy 0-0 Au 0-0 Se 0-0 Oc 1-8 No 2-9 De 2-17 Ja 5-35 Fe 1-25 Mr 1-20 Ap 1-13 My 1-10 Jn 0-0

N. TINKLER — 25 81,989

Alum Bay 4 b.g	h91	1	1,924	Edi
Comstock 6 ch.g	h88	1	1,882	Edi
Dawadar (USA) 6 b.h	h120	2	3,767	Don Edi
Kanndabil 6 gr.h	c105	1	2,604	Nwc
Lara's Baby (IRE) 5 ch.m	h80	1	1,387	Crt
Le Temeraire 7 b.h	c102	1	1,165	Cat
Master Shikari 4 b.g	h89	2	1,843	Sou Crl
Operation Wolf 7 ch.g	h101	2	3,896	Wor Per
Pass The Key (IRE) 4 b.g	h83	1	1,719	Cat
Richmond (IRE) 5 ch.g	h83	1	1,670	MRa
Sacre d'Or (USA) 8 b.g	c134	1	25,499	Chl
Satin Lover 5 ch.g	h137	6	23,906	Chl Asc Asc Chl Kem San
Society Ball 6 b.m	h83	1	1,352	Fnt
Vain Prince 6 b.h	c113	4	9,375	Hun Nwc MRa Wth

Jy 0-0 Au 2-13 Se 3-6 Oc 2-19 No 5-23 De 3-12 Ja 3-14 Fe 2-23 Mr 3-14 Ap 2-9 My 0-6 Jn 0-0

M. H. TOMPKINS — 22 94,116

Arany 6 b.g	h93	1	2,323	Utt
Banana Cufflinks (USA) 7 b.g	h84	1	1,749	MRa
Brownside Brig 8 b.g	h88	1	1,607	Wor
Cadency 5 b.g	h121	1	3,392	Hun
Eden's Close 4 ch.g	h119	1	3,028	Nwb
Elegant Friend 5 ch.g	h96	2	4,438	MRa Fak
Glaisdale (IRE) 4 b.g	h121	1	1,480	Tow
Halkopous 7 b.g	h164	2	30,975	Nwc Chl
Highbrook (USA) 5 b.m	h111	1	1,925	Cat
Jungle Knife 7 b.g	h144	1	4,161	War
Millador 4 b.f	h107	2	4,101	MRa Wth
Moor Lodge (USA) 4 b.g	h110	3	4,267	Exe Str Exe
Rosgill 7 ch.g	h117	1	5,920	Nwb
Staunch Friend (USA) 5 b.g	h164	4	24,750	Nwb Chl Chp Ayr

Jy 0-0 Au 3-10 Se 2-2 Oc 4-14 No 3-17 De 2-16 Ja 1-16 Fe 2-8 Mr 2-9 Ap 2-11 My 1-7 Jn 0-0

ANDREW TURNELL — 37 161,491

Around The Horn 6 b.g	c99	2	4,802	Her Wth
Biloxi Blues 11 gr.g	c96	3	4,226	Her Flk Fnt
Bowl of Oats 7 ch.g	c104	3	9,979	MRa Lin Tow
Cogent 9 b.g	c136	3	13,459	Nwb Wnc Kem
Country Member 8 ch.g	c143	4	32,556	Wnc Nwb San San
Fenton Bridge 9 b.g	c95	2	5,363	Ban Chp
Giventime 5 ch.g	h134	3	5,516	Utt Lin Lin
Just Rosie 4 b.f	h95	2	3,220	Her Exe
Katabatic 10 br.g	c161	2	43,701	Asc Wth
Night Wind 6 b.g	h94	1	1,480	Hun
Sailor Blue 6 b.g	h102	1	2,532	Tow
Star of Italy 6 b.g	c85	2	4,433	Her Her
Storm Alert 7 b.g	c143	6	21,287	Str War Lud Not Nwb San
Washingtoncrossing 7 ch.g	c117	3	8,937	Lin Lin Nwb

Jy 0-0 Au 0-1 Se 0-3 Oc 6-26 No 5-20 De 7-19 Ja 6-24 Fe 4-21 Mr 2-18 Ap 2-16 My 5-9 Jn 0-0

N. A. TWISTON-DAVIES — 76 451,859

Arctic Kinsman 5 gr.g		1	2,400	Asc

34

Captain Dibble 8 b.g	c148	2	34,598	Wnc Asc
Celtic Prince 7 ch.g	c104	2	4,479	Per Utt
Classics Pearl (IRE) 5 gr.m	h84	2	3,216	NAb Ban
Dagaz 7 b.g	h115	1	2,783	Chl
Dakyns Boy 8 ch.g	c136	4	39,597	War Tow Kem Asc
Dandy Minstrel 9 br.g	c107	3	10,414	Wnd Hun Flk
Desperate 5 ch.g	h116	3	7,133	Chp Ban Str
Earth Summit 5 b.g	h101	1	1,954	Chp
Emily's Star 6 b.m	c101:h104	4	7,833	Per NAb Wth Not
Gaelstrom 6 b.m	h135	5	41,036	Str Chp Utt Chl Chl
Ghia Gneuiagh 7 b.g	h98	2	3,857	NAb Ban
Grange Brake 7 b.g	c110	3	23,705	Per Nwb Asc
Indian Tonic 7 br.g	c110	1	11,308	Asc
Kano Warrior 6 b.g	h92	1	1,898	Str
Knave of Clubs 6 ch.g	h121	3	10,006	Lud Chl Tow
Man of Mystery 7 b.g	c99	1	2,489	Her
Master Muck 10 b.g	c96	1	1,150	Tow
Miss Simone 7 b.m	h92	3	4,740	NAb NAb Her
Nougat Russe 12 b.g	c102	3	9,257	Lud Wor Lud
Paris of Troy 5 b.h	h132	3	5,413	Her Wor Wor
Petosku 5 b.g	h129	1	1,830	Per
Sausalito Boy 5 b.g	h106	2	5,785	San Lud
Sohrab (IRE) 5 ch.g	h107	1	2,166	Utt
Sweet Duke (FR) 6 b.g	h161	5	29,196	Per Chp Chl Asc Asc
Texan Baby (BEL) 4 b.g		1	1,625	War
Tipping Tim 8 b.g	c153	3	48,980	Chl Wth Chl
Tochenka 9 ch.m	c100	2	5,522	Her Fnt
Tompet 7 b.g	c92	2	5,574	Str Tau
Young Hustler 6 ch.g	c149	8	116,202	Ban Chl Nwb Wnc Don San Nwb Chl
Zamirah (IRE) 4 b.f	h121	2	5,713	Wnc Nwb

Jy 0-0 Au 2-6 Se 12-22 Oc 9-39 No 6-30 De 6-33 Ja 5-27 Fe 7-45 Mr 8-36 Ap 17-54 My 4-26 Jn 0-0

JOHN R. UPSON			**31 132,398**	
Askinfarney 6 ch.g	c106	1	2,505	Tow
Bakhtaran 6 b.g	h122	2	3,480	MRa Sou
Bentley Manor 4 ch.g	h80	1	943	Lud
Big Ben Dun 7 b.g	c104	3	9,520	Lin Wor Str
Clares Horse 6 b.g	c89	1	1,769	Wor
Duck Or Grouse 8 b.g	c78	1	2,018	MRa
Letterfore 6 br.m	c103	2	4,697	Flk Wnd
May-Day-Baby 7 ch.g	h89	1	1,302	Flk
No Grandad 9 br.m	c103	3	10,151	Utt Hun NAb
Overhereoverthere 10 ch.g	c100	2	4,606	Utt Tow
Some Obligation 8 b.g	c106	2	3,751	Her Fak
Southend United 7 b.g	c96	1	2,541	Lud
Sultan's Son 7 b.g	h97	2	4,424	Lud Fak
The Green Stuff 8 ch.g	c110	2	5,760	Lin Tow
Very Very Ordinary 7 b.g	c137	3	28,904	Tow Asc Asc
Zeta's Lad 10 b.g	c149	4	46,027	Utt Kem Wnd Kem

Jy 0-1 Au 3-12 Se 1-15 Oc 1-17 No 5-25 De 5-23 Ja 2-19 Fe 6-26 Mr 1-12 Ap 6-24 My 1-12 Jn 0-0

MRS F. WALWYN			**11 25,761**	
Bayphia 5 ch.g	h93	2	2,976	NAb Exe
Brora Rose (IRE) 5 b.m	h85	1	1,858	Exe
Cardinal Red 6 b.g	h136	2	8,955	Wor Liv
Fifth Amendment 8 b.g	c110	2	2,925	Wnd Str
Rope 7 b.g	h98	2	3,442	Sou Sou

35

Sheer Ability 7 b.g   c101   2   5,605 Tow Tow
Jy 0-0 Au 2-4 Se 0-7 Oc 1-8 No 0-8 De 0-3 Ja 2-8 Fe 2-9 Mr 1-11 Ap 2-9 My 1-6 Jn 0-0

J. WHITE		**38**	**88,935**	
Aahsaylad 7 b.h	h124	4	11,237	Wor Nwc Hex Ayr
Al Sahil (USA) 8 b.g	h92	1	1,810	NAb
Blushing Belle 5 b.m	h84	2	3,291	Lin Plu
Brave Defender 9 ch.g	c104	2	4,942	Sed Wnd
Cultured 4 b.g	h116	2	3,924	Wnd Per
Days of Thunder 5 ch.g	h94	1	1,631	Plu
Fogar (USA) 11 ch.g	c88	1	2,103	Plu
Into The Red 9 ch.g	c124	2	14,162	Nwc Nwc
Kingfisher Bay 8 b.g	c93	2	2,943	Plu Plu
Majority Holding 8 b.g	h90	1	1,778	Tow
Norstock 6 b.m	h102	3	5,309	Chp Utt Tow
Ok Corral (USA) 6 gr.g	c108	3	6,740	Flk Plu Plu
River Fly 8 ch.g	c90	1	2,120	Plu
River House 11 ch.g	c105	1	2,938	Str
Safety (USA) 6 b.g	c87:h105	3	5,809	NAb Plu Lin
Sand King (NZ) 7 gr.g	h88	1	2,334	Ban
Sayh 4 b.g	h108	1	3,818	Kem
So Discreet (USA) 5 b.g	h93	3	4,673	Exe Ban Crt
Take Two 5 b.g	h102	2	3,894	Crt Str
Well Done Rory 4 b.g	h89	2	3,479	Crt MRa

Jy 0-2 Au 6-23 Se 1-13 Oc 1-16 No 0-22 De 1-13 Ja 6-36 Fe 7-41 Mr 7-29 Ap 4-22 My 2-27 Jn 3-8

R. C. WILKINS		**5**	**35,371**	
Double Silk 9 b.g	c122	5	35,371	War Chl Liv Chl Chl

Jy 0-0 Au 0-0 Se 0-0 Oc 0-0 No 0-0 De 0-0 Ja 0-0 Fe 0-1 Mr 2-2 Ap 2-2 My 1-1 Jn 0-0

B. E. WILKINSON		**5**	**25,747**	
Armagret 8 b.g	c143	3	21,128	Nwc Wth Nwc
Ityful 7 gr.g	c94	2	4,619	Edi Edi

Jy 0-0 Au 0-1 Se 0-6 Oc 0-5 No 0-3 De 1-3 Ja 2-4 Fe 2-5 Mr 0-4 Ap 0-2 My 0-1 Jn 0-0

M. J. WILKINSON		**10**	**46,608**	
Andrew's First 6 br.g	h127	4	25,189	Not Nwb Hay Liv
Catchapenny 8 br.g	c96	3	16,090	Wol Utt MRa
Ronans Glen 6 b.g	h111	2	2,960	Tow Wor
Wicket 8 b.m	c90	1	2,369	Wor

Jy 0-0 Au 0-1 Se 0-2 Oc 0-6 No 0-7 De 1-8 Ja 0-7 Fe 4-14 Mr 3-18 Ap 2-8 My 0-12 Jn 0-0

MRS S. D. WILLIAMS		**7**	**27,837**	
Blasket Hero 5 gr.g	h92	1	2,260	Ban
Country Lad (IRE) 5 b.g	h110	2	17,850	Chl Chl
Grey Tornado 12 gr.g	c89	1	2,892	Tau
Morgans Man 4 b.c	h91	1	1,788	Her
Othet 9 b.g	h87	1	1,606	Her
Touch Tricky 5 b.m	h69	1	1,441	Tau

Jy 0-0 Au 0-4 Se 1-7 Oc 1-9 No 0-5 De 0-2 Ja 1-4 Fe 0-5 Mr 1-13 Ap 1-7 My 2-8 Jn 0-0

S. WOODMAN		**1**	**33,800**	
King Credo 8 b.g	h161	1	33,800	Nwb

Jy 0-0 Au 0-0 Se 0-0 Oc 0-0 No 0-1 De 0-2 Ja 0-0 Fe 1-1 Mr 0-1 Ap 0-0 My 0-1 Jn 0-0

If myths are promulgated about trainers they are even more commonplace about the racing characteristics passed down from a sire to his progeny. This record of winners by sire should be an invaluable source of reference for backers. Again the Timeform Rating, and the distance and going for each race, are listed for a complete picture. This section should also become a standard reference for anyone with an interest in the breeding of jumpers. Over the course of time it will become possible to build a definitive picture of the domestic career of any stallion's progeny.

Stallion & Progeny	Timeform Rating	Races Won	Value £	Distance & Going of races won
ABEDNEGO		**3**	**16,043**	
Abnegation 8 b.g	h126	1	5,117	22v
Chergo 8 b.g	c97	1	2,232	c25m
Repeat The Dose 8 b.g	c134	1	8,694	c20s
ABSALOM		**12**	**24,942**	
Absent Relative 5 ch.m	h120	4	8,787	18d a20g 16f 18g
Briggs Builders 9 b.g	c103	2	4,954	c16d c17g
Sheep Stealer 5 gr.g	h88	1	1,764	16g
Silver Haze 9 gr.g	c89	3	5,876	c18m c17f c18s
Silver Stick 6 gr.g	h106	2	3,561	22d 21m
ADONIJAH		**6**	**12,809**	
Front Page 6 ch.g	h105	3	7,741	16s 17d 18v
Operation Wolf 7 ch.g	h101	2	3,896	16m 17s
Peace King 7 ch.g	h126	1	1,172	18g
AFFIRMED (USA)		**2**	**3,409**	
Watertight (USA) 8 b.g	c90	2	3,409	c21d c21v
AHONOORA		**1**	**1,705**	
Comaneci (IRE) 5 b.m	h82	1	1,705	a16g
AKARAD (FR)		**1**	**1,988**	
Badrakhani (FR) 7 b.g	h126	1	1,988	17s
ALIAS SMITH (USA)		**9**	**20,473**	
Acre Hill 9 gr.g	c124	1	3,454	c16g
Catch The Cross 7 gr.g	c124	2	6,666	c21v c21m
Faux Pavillon 9 ch.g	h90	2	2,934	18m 18g
Folk Dance 11 b.g	c93	1	2,640	c25s
My Lindianne 6 gr.m	h71	1	1,811	16v
Ragtime Cowboy Joe 8 gr.g	h84	2	2,968	a20g a22g
ALLEGED (USA)		**5**	**14,357**	
Derab (USA) 7 b.g	c100	2	5,669	c20d c16d
Ruling (USA) 7 b.h	h165	1	3,460	16d
Straight Laced (USA) 6 b.g	h103	1	2,898	21d
Yaheeb (USA) 9 b.h	c98	1	2,330	c20s
ALLEGING (USA)		**1**	**1,587**	
Edge of The Glen 5 b.g	h76	1	1,587	17v
AL NASR (FR)		**5**	**13,247**	
Albemine (USA) 4 b.g	h113	3	9,000	16f 17f 17g
Gaveko (USA) 4 b.g	h97	2	4,247	17g 16m
ALPHABATIM (USA)		**2**	**3,360**	
Dublin Indemnity (USA) 4 b.g	h81	1	1,435	17g
Highbrook (USA) 5 b.m	h111	1	1,925	16g
AL SIRAT (USA)		**7**	**21,721**	
Clares Own 9 b.g	c94	3	6,887	c18s c16g c16s
Direct Interest 10 ch.g	c83	1	2,238	c21f
Express Reale 8 b.g	h102	1	2,008	25v
Far Senior 7 ch.g	c132	2	10,588	c24g c25d
ALZAO (USA)		**16**	**43,260**	
Beaucadeau 7 b.g	h107	2	4,250	16f 18m
Hawthorn Blaze 7 br.g	c126:h145	4	13,792	17v 21s c21v c21s
Here He Comes 7 b.g	h129	2	4,895	17v 17v

La Raptotte 6 b.m	h99	1	1,604	16d
Master of The Rock 4 b.c	h85	2	3,511	17s 18d
Polar Region 7 br.g	c112	5	15,208	c24d c27g c28g c24s c27g
ANAX		**2**	**3,837**	
Eastern Oasis 10 b.g	c110	1	2,294	c24g
Master Eryl 10 gr.g	c90	1	1,543	c24f
ANFIELD		**4**	**9,023**	
Mel's Rose 8 ch.g	h97	1	1,475	17g
Stay Awake 7 ch.g	h115	2	5,711	16f 16g
Wessex Warrior 7 b.g	h98	1	1,837	17f
ARAGON		**5**	**8,530**	
Aragon Ayr 5 b.g	h97	1	2,304	17s
Arran View 7 br.g	h92	1	2,064	21d
Obeliski 7 b.g	c110	1	1,161	c16g
Spanish Whisper 6 b.g	h85	1	988	16g
Tip Top Lad 6 b.g	h97	1	2,013	17f
ARAPAHO		**5**	**8,480**	
Well Wrapped 9 b.g	c127	3	6,117	c21d c21g c21d
West Street 9 br.g	c95	2	2,363	c21m c21g
ARAPAHOS (FR)		**3**	**11,408**	
Hurdy 6 ch.g	h111	3	11,408	16g 20g 17f
ARCTIC TERN (USA)		**4**	**7,659**	
Bay Tern (USA) 7 b.h	h119	3	6,367	23g 17d 17m
Legal Win (USA) 5 ch.h	h67	1	1,292	19h
ARDOON		**1**	**1,734**	
Lough Brown 10 ch.g	h83	1	1,734	18v
ARDROSS		**37**	**102,528**	
Aahsaylad 7 b.h	h124	4	11,237	22v 20d 24d 22g
Ard T'Match 8 b.g	c95	1	2,247	c25d
Attadale 5 b.g	h120	6	14,030	20g 25s 21g 22g 21s 20f
Avro Anson 5 b.g	h136	2	7,814	17m 17g
Beauchamp Grace 4 b.f	h131	4	12,511	17v 16v 16v 17g
Bellezza 6 b.m	h113	3	11,730	20g 20d 20f
Burgoyne 7 b.g	h158	1	7,845	25g
Cairncastle 8 b.g	h114	3	7,526	24g 27d 23d
Kovalevskia 8 ch.m	h94	2	3,556	17v a20g
Lasting Memory 7 b.m	h104	1	2,075	22s
Macarthur 8 b.g	c121	1	2,301	c16s
Murphys Way 4 br.f		1	1,679	F16s
My Rossini 4 b.g		1	1,602	F16d
Piper O'Drummond 6 ch.g	c100	2	5,654	c23d c23g
Sweet George 6 b.g	h79	1	3,302	21f
Vado Via 5 b.m	h119	4	7,419	24d 22d 22v 22v
ARISTOCRACY		**1**	**2,147**	
Noble Eyre 12 br.g	c89	1	2,147	c16g
ASCERTAIN (USA)		**6**	**12,833**	
John Corbet 10 b.g	c83	1	1,203	c21g
Portonia 9 b.m	c115	4	10,026	c27d c26d c26s c29s
Straight Pilot 11 br.g	c95	1	1,604	c27g
ASHFORD (USA)		**1**	**1,305**	
Real Progress (IRE) 5 ch.g	h102	1	1,305	16s

ATLANTIC BOY		1	1,530	
Angels Kiss (SWE) 8 b.g	h97	1	1,530 17v
AUCTION RING (USA)		3	5,815	
Bold Choice 7 b.g	c87	1	2,120 c23g
Emerald Moon 6 b.g	h72	1	1,453 17g
Risk Factor 7 b.g	h82	1	2,242 22v
AUK (USA)		1	2,247	
Auk Eye (NZ) 9 b.g	c89	1	2,247 c21d
AVOCAT		3	13,721	
Rowlandsons Jewels 12 br.g	c131	2	12,246 c26d c25f
The Holy Golfer 6 br.g	h72	1	1,475 17f
AYYABAAN		2	3,670	
Swahili Run 5 ch.g	h103	2	3,670 18g 16f
BABY TURK		1	1,625	
Texan Baby (BEL) 4 b.g		1	1,625 F16s
BAILLAMONT (USA)		3	23,477	
Dare To Dream (IRE) 4 b.g	h132	3	23,477 17v 17v 17s
BAIRN (USA)		6	16,050	
Batabanoo 4 ch.g	h124	4	13,045 16d 16g 16m 17m
Kinoko 5 ch.g	h101	1	1,700 16v
Saskia's Hero 6 ch.g	h93	1	1,305 16s
BALAK		2	4,803	
Rare Bid (NZ) 10 br.g	c102	2	4,803 c23h c19g
BALINGER		4	12,386	
Bertie Boy 8 ch.g	c106	1	3,002 c21s
Bollinger 7 ch.g	h131	1	2,846 25d
Pamber Priory 10 b.g	c114	2	6,538 c26s c25v
BALLACASHTAL (CAN)		12	25,145	
Ballystate 5 ch.m	h105	2	4,966 19g 18d
Carabali Dancer 5 ch.g	h97	1	1,772 21s
Gymcrak Sovereign 5 b.g	h103	2	4,287 16s a16g
Irish Velvet 7 b.g	c88	1	2,443 c21f
Mecado 6 b.g	h79	2	3,617 18v 21d
Middlewick 8 b.g	h99	1	2,355 17f
Pontynyswen 5 b.g	h127	2	3,556 17d a16g
Secret Liason 7 b.g	h99	1	2,149 17d
BALLIOL		1	2,231	
Va Utu 5 b.g	h93	1	2,231 17f
BALLYMORE		1	1,079	
Rose Tableau 10 ch.m	h100	1	1,079 26m
BAPTISM		2	3,724	
Baptismal Fire 9 ch.g	c126	1	1,520 c18g
Re-Release 8 ch.m	c106	1	2,204 c21v
BARON BLAKENEY		5	10,555	
High Baron 6 gr.g	h136	3	7,613 18s 16v 16v
Temple Garth 4 b.g	h97	2	2,942 22g 21d
BATES MOTEL (USA)		2	4,650	
Sure Pride (USA) 5 b.g	h105	2	4,650 18m 20g

40

BAY EXPRESS		2	2,976	
Bayphia 5 ch.g	h93	2	2,976	17d 18f
BEAU CHARMEUR (FR)		5	14,029	
Not So Soon 8 b.g	c95	1	2,348	c22s
Sandy Beau 7 ch.g	c87	1	2,232	c24m
Smooth Escort 9 b.g	c109	1	3,522	c26s
Vicompt de Valmont 8 b.g	c90	1	2,301	c26d
Willsford 10 b.g	h134	1	3,626	21v
BEECHCRAFT (NZ)		2	4,610	
Riva (NZ) 6 ch.g	h116	1	2,276	17v
Sand King (NZ) 7 gr.g	h88	1	2,334	24g
BELDALE FLUTTER (USA)		12	51,507	
El Volador 6 br.h	h99	2	4,255	17d 18m
Greek Flutter 8 b.g	c116	1	3,056	c16s
Halkopous 7 b.g	h164	2	30,975	17g 17v
Peak District 7 b.g	h92	1	1,492	20g
Show The Flag 5 b.g	h85	1	1,822	17f
Stated Case 8 b.g	h113	5	9,907	21v 28g 24g 25d 28m
BELFALAS		4	7,619	
Alpha One 8 ch.g	c98	2	2,848	c25v c25g
Padaventure 8 b.g	c115	1	3,655	c25s
York Imperial 12 br.g	c93	1	1,116	c26d
BELFORT (FR)		5	8,553	
Beldine 8 gr.g	c106	1	2,201	c16m
Casa Bella 6 b.m	h73	2	2,848	16v 22f
Kamart 5 gr.m	c84	1	1,394	c17g
On The Line 5 b.g	h95	1	2,110	18g
BELLYPHA		4	8,747	
Bellton 5 gr.g	h118	2	4,128	16g 16s
Ityful 7 gr.g	c94	2	4,619	c20g c20g
BE MY GUEST (USA)		11	36,914	
Belmoredean 8 ch.g	c100	2	4,564	c17d c17f
Be My Habitat 4 ch.g	h107	3	8,521	17d 20s 21f
Burnet 8 b.g	c95	2	3,590	c21m c20m
Formal Invitation (IRE) 4 ch.g	h124	2	2,959	16m 17m
Quai d'Orsay 8 b.g	h102	1	1,780	20f
Tomahawk 6 ch.g	h133	1	15,500	16v
BE MY NATIVE (USA)		15	37,900	
Briggs Lad (IRE) 4 ch.g	h98	2	3,669	16f 20m
Driving Force 7 ch.g	c109	1	3,518	c17s
Make Me Proud (IRE) 4 b.f	h94	1	2,010	17g
Native Crown (IRE) 5 b.g	h104	1	1,796	24m
Native Field (IRE) 4 b.g		3	10,746	F17m F17f F17f
Native Pride 6 ch.g	c120	2	6,305	c17d c24d
Native Scot 7 ch.m	c80	1	1,553	c21v
Reggae Beat 8 b.g	c108	2	5,285	c16g c17d
Sparkler Gebe 7 b.g	h91	2	3,018	23m a22g
BIG SPRUCE (USA)		2	6,287	
Lumberjack (USA) 9 b.g	c127	2	6,287	c18d c21d
BIKALA		1	1,940	
Big Diamond (FR) 9 b.g	h94	1	1,940	17m

BILLION (USA) 3 37,138
Gold Options 11 ch.g c154 1 30,987 c20s
High Finance 8 ch.g h91 1 2,756 17g
Sure Metal 10 b.g c138 1 3,395 c16d

BIVOUAC 1 2,174
Yorkshire Holly 10 br.g c87 1 2,174 c21g

BLACK MINSTREL 21 60,569
Amtrak Express 6 ch.g h115 4 16,419 F17g 17s 16d 16m
Andrews Minstrel 6 br.g h93 1 1,256 17v
City Kid 8 br.g c97 2 4,134 c21g c21d
Classic Minstrel 9 br.g c87 1 2,151 c24g
Dandy Minstrel 9 br.g c107 3 10,414 c24v c24s c26g
Frozen Minstrel 9 b.g c96 1 2,660 c16s
Kentish Piper 8 br.g c116 2 5,875 c22m c21s
Killula King 6 br.g c101 1 1,813 c17g
Lupy Minstrel 8 br.g c97 1 1,581 c24m
Mister Tuftie 8 b.g c95 1 2,023 c25g
Pats Minstrel 8 b.g c100 2 5,559 c16g c16f
Southend United 7 b.g c96 1 2,541 c16s
Southern Minstrel 10 ch.g c116 1 4,143 c21s

BLAKENEY 12 25,006
Barcham 6 b.g h90 2 3,128 17g 17g
Bluechipenterprise 7 br.m c75 1 2,042 c19h
Hurricane Blake 5 b.g h120 2 4,133 23g 22f
Lake Mission 8 b.g c113 1 4,115 c21d
Nan's Boy 5 b.h h104 1 1,305 22v
Newton Point 4 b.g h109 1 1,953 17g
Passed Pawn 6 b.g h117 3 6,005 27m 26g 22f
Preoblakensky 6 b.g h120 1 2,325 21m

BLAKENEY POINT 3 7,723
Bobby Socks 7 b.g c106 3 7,723 c16m c21g c21g

BLUEBIRD (USA) 1 3,818
Sayh 4 b.g h108 1 3,818 21d

BLUE CASHMERE 5 9,069
Pandessa 6 b.m h106 3 5,625 21s 20d 16g
Pharaoh Blue 9 ch.g h110 1 1,772 26g
Sing The Blues 9 b.g h97 1 1,672 a20g

BLUE REFRAIN 5 9,666
Biloxi Blues 11 gr.g c96 3 4,226 c26f c21m c27f
Rejoinus 8 ch.g c104 2 5,440 c17s c21s

BLUSHING SCRIBE (USA) 1 1,910
Mister Lawson 7 ch.g h91 1 1,910 17m

BOB BACK (USA) 4 8,866
Chapel of Barras (IRE) 4 b.g 1 1,684 F12d
Robingo (IRE) 4 b.c h125 3 7,182 18s 17v 21s

BOCO (USA) 1 1,050
Cawkwell Tom 9 b.g c92 1 1,050 c26g

BOLD FORBES (USA) 1 2,285
Windsor Park (USA) 7 br.g h97 1 2,285 20m

BON CHAT 3 7,988
Claxton Greene 9 b.g c116 3 7,988 c24s c27d c24g

42

BONNE NOEL		**1**	**2,310**
Fort Noel 10 br.g	c106	1	2,310 c20s
BOREEN (FR)		**6**	**12,898**
Boll Weevil 7 b.g	h99	1	1,924 21v
Boreen Jean 9 ch.m	h106	1	1,606 25f
Boreen Owen 9 b.g	c113	3	7,209 c27d c27d c27d
Stunning Stuff 8 b.g	c101	1	2,159 c19m
BRAVE INVADER (USA)		**1**	**2,109**
Glebe Prince 13 b.g	c84	1	2,109 c27f
BREZZO (FR)		**1**	**2,024**
Astings (FR) 5 b.g	h90	1	2,024 22v
BRILLIANT INVADER (AUS)		**1**	**1,287**
Super Sharp (NZ) 5 ch.g		1	1,287 F16g
BROADSWORD (USA)		**13**	**38,508**
Alan Ball 7 b.g	c99	2	6,606 c17m c18m
Ashfold Copse 7 ch.g	c124	3	7,798 c21m c21s c24g
Cappuccino Girl 6 ch.m	h90	1	1,475 20g
Clever Shepherd 8 b.g	c107	1	3,259 c24d
Mackinnon 8 b.g	c95	1	3,730 c16d
Persian Sword 7 b.g	h92	2	3,672 16s 16v
Shamana 7 b.m	c132	3	11,968 c17v c16d c16g
BUCKFINDER (USA)		**1**	**1,758**
Dollar Seeker (USA) 9 b.h	h89	1	1,758 20m
BUCKSKIN (FR)		**36**	**120,846**
Allo George 7 ch.g	h83	1	1,973 22d
Belstone Fox 8 br.g	c115	2	6,584 c17g c17g
Black Humour 9 b.g	c145	3	15,711 c23v c26s c25f
Boycott 6 b.g	h129	1	1,480 16v
Brave Buccaneer 6 ch.g	h112	1	2,763 25s
Buck Owens 8 ch.g	c95	1	1,828 c27m
Carrikins 6 b.m	h90	1	929 20d
Emperor Buck (IRE) 5 b.g		1	1,996 F17f
Givus A Buck 10 br.g	c147	3	35,292 c18v c24f c25m
Grouseman 7 gr.g	h107	2	5,079 20s 22d
K C'S Dancer 8 ch.g	c98	2	4,167 c26d c27f
Menebuck 7 b.g	c105:h128	5	12,121 c21d c21d 23g 20g 17g
Mount Eaton Fox 10 b.g	c90	1	1,514 c21g
Obie's Train 7 ch.g	c105	2	5,675 c18s c18s
Peajade 9 b.g	c108	2	6,520 c24d c26v
Saddler's Choice 8 b.g	c99	2	5,590 c24s c24d
Skircoat Green 8 ch.g	h101	2	3,647 22g 21s
Take The Buckskin 6 b.g		1	828 aF16g
Winabuck 10 ch.g	c114	2	4,722 c23m c21v
Yellow Spring 8 b.g	h131	1	2,427 21g
BULLDOZER		**4**	**18,631**
Ardbrin 10 ch.g	c125	2	11,031 c21v c21f
Lion of Vienna 6 b.g	h95	1	2,255 25v
San Fernando 7 b.g	h123	1	5,345 17s
BURSLEM		**2**	**6,705**
Bo Knows Best (IRE) 4 ch.g	h128	1	5,208 17m
Glebelands Girl 6 b.m	h99	1	1,497 18d

BUSTED		5	9,052	
Awkas 8 b.g	c87	1	2,290	c16s
Duncan Idaho 10 b.g	h109	1	2,624	25v
Material Girl 7 b.m	c109	3	4,138	c22g c21s c19s
BUSTINETO		2	4,222	
Mr Matt (IRE) 5 b.g	h111	2	4,222	20v 20v
BUSTINO		9	15,801	
Arrastra 5 b.m	h85	1	1,807	18g
Giventime 5 ch.g	h134	3	5,516	16s 17v 20v
Peacock Feather 5 b.m	h77	1	1,684	17v
Prince Tino 5 b.g	h101	1	1,858	17m
Romola Nijinsky 5 b.m	h71	1	1,481	18m
Surcoat 6 b.h	h91	2	3,455	18g 25m
BUSTOMI		2	3,167	
Creeshla 6 b.g	c95	1	1,865	c26d
Placid Lad 6 b.g	h104	1	1,302	20g
BUZZARDS BAY		6	12,789	
Baybeejay 6 b.m	h76	1	1,480	16d
Mariolino 6 b.g	h100	2	3,491	23d 20g
Pintail Bay 7 b.g	c88	1	2,790	c17s
Sleepline Royale 7 ch.g	h118	2	5,028	18v 17v
BYBICELLO		5	10,849	
Fettuccine 9 ch.g	h126	5	10,849	22m 25m 26s 24g 27f
CAERLEON (USA)		3	5,790	
Bahrain Queen (IRE) 5 ch.m	h82	1	1,672	22m
Kirstenbosch 6 b.g	h94	2	4,118	17m 22m
CALLERNISH		16	56,220	
Bit of A Clown 10 b.g	c113	3	11,386	c22s c25v c25v
Break The Chain 8 b.g	c107	3	8,245	c23s c27d c21g
Call Home (IRE) 5 b.g		2	3,880	F16f F17m
Doonloughan 8 b.g	c99	1	3,835	c26g
Lake Teereen 8 ch.g	c116	2	7,639	c21s c21s
Midnight Caller 7 br.g	c112	3	16,193	c21s c24v c27s
Mweenish 11 b.g	c108	1	3,035	c26d
The Widget Man 7 b.g	c119	1	2,007	c27g
CAMDEN TOWN		6	10,791	
Dolikos 6 b.g	c100	2	4,872	c17s c16d
Mr Felix 7 b.g	c92	2	3,522	c17f c16v
Towny Boy 7 b.g	h90	2	2,397	17f 17m
CANDY CANE		2	5,870	
Candy Tuff 7 b.g	c110	2	5,870	c25g c25s
CAP MARTIN (FR)		1	2,593	
Viva Bella (FR) 6 b.g	c94	1	2,593	c21s
CAPRICORN LINE		2	3,773	
Acrow Line 8 b.g	h122	1	2,332	26v
Touch Tricky 5 b.m	h69	1	1,441	20f
CARDINAL FLOWER		1	1,865	
Red Under The Bed 6 b.g	c103	1	1,865	c27g
CARLINGFORD CASTLE		12	26,576	
Anthony Bell 7 b.g	c96	2	3,902	c17m c17g

Pontoon Bridge 6 ch.g	h99	2	4,444	F17d 17f
Rathmore 7 b.g	c101	2	6,343	c24g c26g
Sheer Ability 7 b.g	c101	2	5,605	c22v c22v
Unholy Alliance 6 b.g	h119	4	6,282	22g 24f 22g 22g
CARO		**1**	**2,248**	
Hthaal (USA) 5 b.g	h89	1	2,248	17d
CARRIAGE WAY		**1**	**2,209**	
Jimmy Mac Jimmy 6 b.g	c89	1	2,209	c17v
CARWHITE		**5**	**9,559**	
Fierce 5 ch.g	h108	2	5,405	17s 17f
Luthior (FR) 7 gr.g	h70	1	1,364	20f
Whitewebb 6 br.g	h88	2	2,790	16s 16g
CASINO BOY		**3**	**8,203**	
Casino Magic 9 b.g	c88	3	8,203	c21d c21s c19m
CASTLE KEEP		**8**	**14,669**	
Beauchamp Express 6 b.g	h105	2	3,875	22v 22v
Castle Courageous 6 b.g	h130	3	5,953	18s 22d 17d
Five Castles 5 b.g	h69	1	774	18f
Jinga 8 b.g	h107	1	3,132	20g
Secret Castle 5 b.g	h95	1	935	16m
CELESTIAL STORM (USA)		**6**	**12,066**	
Hold Your Hat On 4 ch.g		1	2,088	F14m
Nirvana Prince 4 ch.g		1	1,030	F17f
Storm Drum 4 ch.g	h100	2	3,343	17s 16f
Storm Dust 4 b.g	h129	2	5,605	16g 16d
CELIO RUFO		**4**	**18,532**	
Roving Report 6 gr.g	c85	1	1,566	c21m
Winter Squall (IRE) 5 gr.g	h136	3	16,966	16s 17s 17m
CELTIC CONE		**30**	**77,181**	
Bossburg 6 b.m	c84	1	1,436	c17s
Buddington 8 b.g	c109	2	5,537	c27v c26s
Celtic Breeze 10 b.g	h105	1	2,295	25g
Celtic Diamond 8 b.m	c110	2	4,232	c27s c27g
Celtic Prince 7 ch.g	c104	2	4,479	c24d c23s
Celtic Song 6 ch.m	h96	1	1,954	21s
Chief Celt 7 ch.g	h110	2	2,785	21s 24g
Crystal Cone 7 b.g	h77	1	1,769	17v
Distillation 8 b.g		1	3,460	c26g
Earth Summit 5 b.g	h101	1	1,954	24s
Fairfields Cone 10 ch.m	h113	3	7,221	22g 22s 21v
I'm Toby 6 b.g	h104	2	4,150	25g 25d
Latent Talent 9 b.g	c133	1	8,538	c25g
Master Cornet 8 ch.g	c97	2	4,730	c26m c25d
M I Babe 8 ch.m	c106	1	2,837	c16s
Reltic 6 b.g	h78	1	1,847	25g
Ryde Again 10 ch.g	c147	1	5,865	c21s
Singlesole 8 ch.g	c109	3	7,280	c25m c25d c24s
Welsh Singer 7 ch.g	h95	1	1,758	18f
Woodlands Genhire 8 ch.g	c92	1	3,054	c25g
CHABRIAS (FR)		**1**	**1,594**	
Moulton Bull 7 ch.g	c86	1	1,594	c21g

45

CHEVAL 5 12,836
La Cienaga 9 ch.g c99 1 2,879 c21m
Rufus 7 ch.g c105 2 3,893 c27s c21s
Toureen Prince 10 b.g c107 2 6,064 c20s c25g

CHIEF'S CROWN (USA) 4 6,535
Crown Baladee (USA) 6 b.g h89 1 1,749 a20g
Master's Crown (USA) 5 ch.g h103 3 4,786 18d 16f 20g

CHIEF SINGER 6 13,993
Bankroll 6 b.g h111 1 2,448 22m
Clean Singer 4 b.f h69 1 1,617 16d
Khojohn 5 ch.g h98 4 9,928 a24g 21g 25s a24g

CHUKAROO 1 2,637
Chucklestone 10 b.g h109 1 2,637 24f

CHURCH PARADE 3 5,836
Full O'Praise (NZ) 6 br.g h99 2 4,161 18d 17m
Vomero (NZ) 8 gr.m h88 1 1,675 a20g

CIDRAX (FR) 1 3,294
Feile Na Hinse 10 b.g c100 1 3,294 c29d

CIMON 2 2,955
Roc Color (FR) 4 b.g h102 2 2,955 18v 17d

CLASS DISTINCTION 3 9,643
Daring Class 7 b.m h88 1 2,334 18f
Mere Class 7 b.g c110 2 7,309 c20d c24m

CLAUDE MONET (USA) 2 4,209
Imhotep 6 gr.g h102 2 4,209 16g 18m

COMEDY STAR (USA) 11 24,681
Cosmic Ray 8 b.g h95 1 1,764 16d
Emily's Star 6 b.m c101:h104 4 7,833 21g 22s 25g c22v
Gymcrak Stardom 7 gr.g h127 2 5,331 16s 17d
Master Comedy 9 b.g c80 1 2,196 c18s
Seven of Diamonds 8 b.g c107 1 1,900 c21d
Starstreak 6 b.h h95 1 1,872 21m
Thamesdown Tootsie 8 b.m c87 1 3,785 c26g

COMMANCHE RUN 7 12,010
Chiparopai (IRE) 5 b.m h76 1 1,730 17s
Indian Run (IRE) 4 b.g h123 1 2,793 17g
Miss Capulet 6 b.m h87 2 3,119 22d 25v
Snowy Lane (IRE) 5 ch.g h123 1 1,744 24s
Someone Brave 5 b.g h89 1 1,151 25g
Suez Canal (IRE) 4 b.g h95 1 1,473 16s

CONCORDE JR (USA) 1 2,036
Le Ginno (FR) 6 ch.g 1 2,036 F16v

CONNAUGHT 10 48,455
Ardcroney Chief 7 ch.g c96 2 3,568 c17d c21d
Gaelic Frolic 10 ch.g c104 3 6,888 c22m c23m c21f
Tresidder 11 b.g c108 2 5,539 c16f c17m
Valiant Boy 7 b.g c135 3 32,460 c16s c16f c18g

CONQUISTADOR CIELO (USA) 1 2,478
Hamanaka (USA) 4 b.f h97 1 2,478 16d

COOL GUY (USA) | | **2** | **4,078**
Davy Blake 6 b.g | c115 | 2 | 4,078 c25g c25m

COQUELIN (USA) | | **16** | **42,567**
Co-Chin (IRE) 4 gr.c | h112 | 2 | 3,754 17d 16s
Coe 7 b.g | c111 | 1 | 3,068 c24f
Comstock 6 ch.g | h88 | 1 | 1,882 16g
Cornet 7 b.g | c129 | 3 | 10,927 c20g c20g c24m
High Alltitude (IRE) 5 b.g | h136 | 4 | 13,735 21d 20s 20g 21d
Palm House 8 ch.g | h104 | 4 | 7,541 20m 22m 20m 18g
Sexy Mover 6 ch.g | h99 | 1 | 1,660 21d

CORVARO (USA) | | **3** | **5,798**
Coonawara 7 b.g | h130 | 3 | 5,798 17v 17v 16s

CRAFTY PROSPECTOR (USA) | | **2** | **3,582**
Lonesome Train (USA) 4 ch.g | h114 | 2 | 3,582 17m 17g

CRANLEY | | **1** | **3,236**
Harley 13 ch.g | c99 | 1 | 3,236 c33m

CRASH COURSE | | **16** | **192,551**
Barkin 10 b.g | c99 | 1 | 2,905 c22v
Bel Course 11 b.g | c102 | 1 | 2,427 c21s
Captain Dibble 8 b.g | c148 | 2 | 34,598 c26g c25s
Castle King 6 b.g | c116 | 3 | 10,614 c20g c20m c20m
Esha Ness 10 b.g | c137 | 1 | 4,305 c26d
Fast Study 8 b.g | c102 | 2 | 4,925 c24s c27v
Jodami 8 b.g | c174 | 3 | 122,322 c27s c24v c27m
Kittinger 12 b.g | c101 | 1 | 2,710 c19s
Romany King 9 br.g | c149 | 1 | 3,420 c25d
Rustic Air 6 ch.g | c90 | 1 | 4,325 c23d

CREETOWN | | **2** | **3,480**
Aldington Peach 4 ch.f | h87 | 1 | 1,866 16g
Cobb Gate 5 b.h | h75 | 1 | 1,614 17d

CREVER | | **1** | **1,996**
Fearless Fred 6 ch.g | h95 | 1 | 1,996 20d

CRIMSON BEAU | | **2** | **5,211**
Private Audition 11 b.g | c118 | 2 | 5,211 c17d c16v

CROFTHALL | | **1** | **1,484**
Chadwick's Ginger 5 ch.m | h77 | 1 | 1,484 a16g

CROGHAN HILL | | **5** | **15,726**
Musthaveaswig 7 gr.g | c117 | 3 | 11,539 c24g c25g c25g
Positive Action 7 b.g | c90 | 2 | 4,187 c17v c17s

CROONER | | **11** | **22,707**
Arr Eff Bee 6 b.g | h93 | 1 | 1,764 22g
Durrington 7 b.g | h85 | 1 | 1,138 17s
St Athans Lad 8 b.g | c121 | 9 | 19,805 c18f c18g c19f c18d c19m c18g c18g c19f c18f

CRUISE MISSILE | | **4** | **17,454**
May Run 7 b.m | h75 | 1 | 2,080 25g
Miss Fern 8 b.m | c96 | 1 | 2,192 c26g
Snitton Lane 7 b.m | c117 | 2 | 13,182 c20d c21g

CRYSTAL GLITTERS (USA) | | **6** | **31,064**
Cyprus (FR) 5 b.g | h96 | 2 | 3,827 16g 17f

Miss Equilia (USA) 7 ch.m	h98	2	3,406	20d 17d
Sweet Glow (FR) 6 b.g	h156	2	23,831	24s 24d
CURE THE BLUES (USA)		2	3,756	
Play The Blues 6 gr.m	c84	1	2,752	c18f
Reilton 6 b.g	h88	1	1,004	18g
CURRENT MAGIC		3	12,914	
Dusty Miller 7 b.g	c124	2	11,734	c20d c21s
Lingham Magic 8 b.m	c83	1	1,180	c21g
CUT ABOVE		4	10,479	
Duncan 8 b.g	c105	1	1,590	c20g
Nodform Wonder 6 b.g	h125	3	8,889	21g 23g 24d
CZARIST		1	2,916	
Justaserff 11 b.g	c91	1	2,916	c16s
DALSAAN		3	4,958	
Aldahe 8 ch.g	h69	1	1,734	a20g
Sciacca 6 ch.m	h91	2	3,224	17m 17m
DAMISTER (USA)		5	10,789	
Beachy Head 5 gr.g	h135	1	2,500	21s
Broom Isle 5 b.m	h96	1	3,590	20f
Byzantine 5 b.g	h88	2	3,024	18m 16f
Damier Blanc (FR) 4 b.g		1	1,675	17v
DANCING BRAVE (USA)		4	5,803	
Hunting Ground 5 b.h	h102	2	2,853	18f 24f
Kabayil 4 b.f	h92	2	2,950	17v 17d
DANZIG CONNECTION (USA)		2	4,460	
Scrutineer (USA) 4 b.g	h112	2	4,460	17s 17m
DARA MONARCH		5	8,977	
Caribbean Prince 5 ch.g	h104	1	1,474	17s
Clurican (IRE) 4 ch.g	h126	2	3,540	17d 17v
Dara Melody (IRE) 4 b.g	h84	1	1,940	a16g
King William 8 b.g	h109	1	2,023	17f
DARING MARCH		6	11,504	
Allimac Nomis 4 b.g	h101	2	4,222	18m 18g
Good For A Loan 6 b.g	h108	2	4,664	a20g 17m
South Stack 7 b.g	h83	1	1,305	22s
Tom Clapton 6 b.g	h108	1	1,313	17m
DARLY (FR)		1	1,452	
Key Dear (FR) 6 ch.g	h87	1	1,452	17f
DARSHAAN		1	2,349	
Baladiya 6 b.m	c91	1	2,349	c16m
DAWN REVIEW		2	20,501	
The Illywhacker 8 b.g	c150	2	20,501	c21g c21g
DAY IS DONE		1	10,699	
Duntree 8 ch.g	c131	1	10,699	c26v
DECENT FELLOW		4	8,730	
Ambleside Harvest 6 b.g	h116	1	2,113	20s
Foolish Affair 9 b.g	c94	1	1,358	c21g
Scobie Boy (IRE) 5 ch.g		1	1,940	F16s
Takemethere 9 b.g	c104	1	3,319	c20g

DECOY BOY   **1**   **2,085**

Wide Boy 11 b.g	c120	1	2,085	c21s

DEEP RIVER   **1**   **1,822**

Debt of Honor 5 ch.g	h79	1	1,822	a22g

DEEP RUN   **93 620,519**

Annincombe Run 9 b.m	h121	1	2,803	21g
Archie Brown 6 b.g	h122	1	2,243	16g
Armala 8 ch.g	c97	2	5,217	c21g c21f
Askinfarney 6 ch.g	c106	1	2,505	c25s
Bally Clover 6 ch.g	h124	2	4,174	18d 17d
Balzac Boy (IRE) 5 ch.g	h97	1	1,940	16v
Book of Runes 8 b.g	h96	2	4,187	16d 20v
Brightling Boy 8 ch.g	h94	2	3,905	23f 22g
Carrickmines 8 ch.g	c95	1	1,553	c24m
Chic And Elite 6 b.m	h94	2	2,595	17m 17m
Clares Horse 6 b.g	c89	1	1,769	c23g
Dakyns Boy 8 ch.g	c136	4	39,597	c26v c22v c24s c25s
Deep Sensation 8 ch.g	c148	3	135,054	c20d c16m c20f
Delgany Run 9 ch.g	c100	1	2,574	c22s
Dennington (IRE) 5 ch.g	h81	1	1,958	22g
Dis Train 9 ch.g	c120	2	6,038	c16g c21d
Duo Drom 8 ch.m	c95	1	2,561	c24g
Egypt Mill Prince 7 b.g	c120	2	7,561	c16d c17m
Elite Boy 11 ch.g	c90	1	2,640	c19g
Errant Knight 9 ch.g	c113	1	3,591	c22g
Funny Old Game 6 ch.g	c96	1	2,868	c20s
Granville Again 7 ch.g	h167	1	84,734	17m
Knockelly Castle 13 ch.g	c103	2	3,489	c21d c19v
Konvekta Control 6 ch.g		1	1,455	F16g
Laurie-O 9 b.g	c108	1	2,326	c21d
Mole Board 11 br.g	h157	1	10,114	17s
Morley Street 9 ch.g	h169	2	52,858	17v 20f
Mr-Paw 10 b.g	c87	1	3,020	c18m
Mrs Mayhew (IRE) 5 ch.m	h83	1	1,480	16v
Notary-Nowell 7 b.g	h107	2	3,693	21g 26g
Plenty Crack 10 b.g	c129	2	6,185	c24s c28d
Precipice Run 8 ch.g	h111	3	6,515	16d 20g 18d
Real Class 10 b.g	h84	1	1,033	21s
Redgrave Girl 11 b.m	h103	1	1,861	17g
Rochestown Lass 7 b.m	h106	3	5,658	23s 25d 24s
Royal Day 7 ch.g	c84	1	2,012	c22v
Royal Flamingo 7 gr.m	c94:h94	4	10,292	16v c22m c22d c22g
Run Fast For Gold 6 ch.m	h81	1	1,805	17g
Run For Free 9 b.g	c163	4	80,510	c24s c24v c30s c33g
Run Pet Run 8 ch.m	c105	2	5,508	c28g c25g
Run To Form 8 br.g	c111	1	2,175	c21f
Run Up The Flag 6 ch.g	h133	3	9,573	21d 21s 22v
Ru Valentino 9 ch.g	c106	1	2,957	c24d
Scole 8 b.g	c114	1	2,271	c23g
Skipping Tim 14 b.g	c114	8	22,954	c27s c21s c21v c19m c27m c26g c21g c24g
Sorbiere 6 b.g	h102	1	2,653	21f
Tammy's Friend 6 b.g	c102	3	6,209	c18s c21m c24f
Waterloo Boy 10 ch.g	c159	3	39,080	c18d c16s c17g
Whatever You Like 9 b.g	c124	1	3,563	c16s
Wicket 8 b.m	c90	1	2,369	c21s
Wild Bramble (IRE) 5 ch.m	h101	3	4,834	F17v 21v 21v

DENEL (FR)   2   3,595

A Fortiori (IRE) 5 b.g		1	1,702 F17s
Mr Five Wood (IRE) 5 ch.g	h95	1	1,893 22g

DEROULEDE   4   9,443

Carrickrovaddy 7 ch.g	c99	1	3,014 c24m
The Yank 7 b.g	c95	3	6,429 c24g c24d c24m

DERRING ROSE   9   28,248

Brompton Road 10 b.g	c112	1	3,193 c33s
Decent Man 10 b.g	c102	3	14,124 c27g c25d c26m
Dont Tell The Wife 7 br.g	h100	1	1,480 22d
The Red One 9 b.g	c110	4	9,451 c25d c24m c24f c25g

DERRYLIN   10   21,992

Belafonte 6 br.g	h124	1	2,794 20g
Derechef 6 ch.m	h88	1	1,954 17m
Derring Valley 8 b.g	c97	2	5,406 c25g c22m
Easter Baby 7 ch.m	h91	1	1,857 16v
Glossy 6 ch.g	h65	1	1,484 a16g
Irish Bay 7 b.g	h108	2	3,301 16v 22m
Little-Nipper 8 ch.g	c102	1	4,175 c21s
Saintly Lad 11 b.g	h79	1	1,021 16d

DIAGRAMATIC (USA)   1   1,744

Cosmic Force (NZ) 9 b.g	h83	1	1,744 20m

DIAMOND PROSPECT (USA)   1   2,340

Magic At Dawn (USA) 8 ch.g	c85	1	2,340 c16m

DIAMOND SHOAL   7   17,634

No Sid No Stars (USA) 5 ch.g	h103	3	2,551 22f 22d 18g
Secret Summit (USA) 7 b.g	c92:h90	4	15,083 18d c18d c16g c16g

DIESIS   5   12,501

Favoured Victor (USA) 6 ch.g	h95	2	3,969 16d 17g
Knight's Spur (USA) 6 b.g	c98	2	5,996 c17f c16d
Nathir (USA) 7 b.h	c93	1	2,536 c16v

DISC JOCKEY   2   3,219

Blue Disc 8 br.g	h97	2	3,219 a18g 17d

DIXIELAND BAND (USA)   9   15,418

Band of Hope (USA) 6 ch.m	h88	2	4,059 16d 17s
Hymne d'Amour (USA) 5 b.m	h104	4	5,797 17d 17s 17g 22m
Mrs Jawleyford (USA) 5 b.m	h110	3	5,562 18d a16g a16g

DOMINEAU (USA)   2   4,900

Frisco City (CHI) 7 b.g	c90	2	4,900 c20g c18g

DOMINION   18   82,785

Ankud (IRE) 4 b.f	h80	1	1,635 17s
Capability Brown 6 b.g	c137	4	24,797 c23v c20v c24vF c25d
Dominant Serenade 4 b.g	h130	4	20,903 16g 17g 17v 16d
Land Afar 6 b.g	h131	3	7,666 16d 17d 17g
Rich Pickings 4 b.f	h83	1	1,537 17d
Touch 'n' Pass 5 ch.g	h84	1	1,793 22g
Trainglot 6 ch.h	h129	4	24,454 20g 16s 22s 21m

DON   2   3,152

Mount Argus 11 ch.g	c116	1	1,089 c26g
Vodka Fizz 8 ch.g	c92	1	2,063 c18m

DON'T FORGET ME | | 2 | 2,976 |
And Me 4 ch.f | h71 | 1 | 1,674 17s
Qualitair Memory (IRE) 4 ch.g | h80 | 1 | 1,302 16v

DOUBLE SCHWARTZ | | 1 | 1,637 |
Milly Black (IRE) 5 b.m | h89 | 1 | 1,637 18s

DOULAB (USA) | | 1 | 1,876 |
Casienne (IRE) 5 ch.m | h84 | 1 | 1,876 21f

DOWN THE HATCH | | 1 | 2,788 |
Roy's Dream 10 b.g | c89 | 1 | 2,788 c23d

DR CARTER (USA) | | 2 | 3,327 |
Dr Maccarter (USA) 6 gr.g | h92 | 2 | 3,327 25s 25d

DREAMS TO REALITY (USA) | | 2 | 4,661 |
In Truth 5 ch.g | h101 | 1 | 2,696 18g
Rarfy's Dream 5 b.g | h101 | 1 | 1,965 a16g

DRUMALIS | | 1 | 1,858 |
Brora Rose (IRE) 5 b.m | h85 | 1 | 1,858 18s

DRUMS OF TIME (USA) | | 1 | 3,435 |
Casting Time (NZ) 9 br.g | c98 | 1 | 3,435 c21f

DUBASSOFF (USA) | | 17 | 100,521 |
Boutzdaroff 11 ch.g | c134 | 2 | 25,698 c17g c16f
Broughton Manor 8 b.m | c114 | 3 | 10,416 c16d c16v c16v
Double Silk 9 b.g | c122 | 5 | 35,371 c26g c27m c22f c27m c27m
Dubacilla 7 b.m | c124 | 5 | 20,577 c16v c19s c24d c21d c25g
Dubalea 10 b.g | c86 | 1 | 2,724 c16m
Dubious Jake 10 b.g | c104 | 1 | 5,735 c33v

DUKY | | 2 | 5,814 |
Duke of Aprolon 6 ch.g | h99 | 1 | 2,898 17g
Wrekin Hill 11 b.g | c109 | 1 | 2,916 c25g

DUNBEATH (USA) | | 6 | 13,289 |
Masroug 6 b.g | h89 | 1 | 1,382 20s
Osgathorpe 6 ch.g | h91 | 1 | 1,903 17m
Rexy Boy 6 b.g | h80 | 2 | 3,736 20s 20g
Silk Degrees 7 gr.g | c119 | 2 | 6,268 c17d c17d

EFISIO | | 1 | 2,005 |
Any Dream Would Do 4 b.f | h84 | 1 | 2,005 16f

ELA-MANA-MOU | | 18 | 45,828 |
Aslan (IRE) 5 gr.g | | 3 | 6,890 F18d F17s F17v
Buonarroti 6 b.g | h125 | 2 | 6,868 20v 24g
Grace Card 7 b.g | h141 | 1 | 2,560 25s
Home Counties (IRE) 4 ch.g | h117 | 1 | 1,730 17v
Mardood 8 b.g | h116 | 3 | 7,464 22d 18d 22d
Metal Oiseau (IRE) 5 ch.g | h123 | 3 | 12,300 22v 24v 25g
Mystic Memory 4 b.f | h101 | 2 | 4,027 17m 21g
Shafayif 4 ch.f | h78 | 1 | 1,582 18m
Tel E Thon 6 b.g | h108 | 2 | 2,407 17g 20m

EL BADR | | 2 | 4,190 |
Uranus Collonges (FR) 7 b.g | c103 | 2 | 4,190 F17d c26s

ELECTRIC | | 11 | 26,078 |
Alternation (FR) 4 ch.f | h106 | 1 | 1,940 23g
Elite Reg 4 b.g | h122 | 6 | 16,097 17s 16v 17g 20f 17f 22f

51

Marshall Sparks 6 ch.g		1	1,529 F16s
Nova Spirit 5 b.m	h98	1	2,373 18g
Switch 7 ch.g	h129	1	2,820 18v
Taurian Princess 4 b.f	h74	1	1,319 16v
ELEGANT AIR		**7**	**16,578**
Montpelier Lad 6 br.g	c112:h134	5	13,737 c16g c16s 17m c18g c18m
Vienna Woods 6 b.g		2	2,841 F16d F18v
EL GRAN SENOR (USA)		**4**	**8,388**
San Lorenzo (USA) 5 b.g	h121	4	8,388 18d 17d 17s 16f
ENCHANTMENT		**1**	**2,618**
Enchanted Man 9 b.g	c88	1	2,618 c20d
ENTRE NOUS		**2**	**4,048**
Rochester 7 gr.g	c92:h99	2	4,048 c16s 17g
ESPRIT DU NORD (USA)		**1**	**2,786**
Albertito (FR) 6 b.g	h117	1	2,786 17d
EXCELLER (USA)		**2**	**3,767**
Dawadar (USA) 6 b.h	h120	2	3,767 20g 24m
EXPLODENT (USA)		**1**	**1,996**
Exploration (USA) 6 b.g	h92	1	1,996 18m
FAIRY KING (USA)		**4**	**8,834**
Soleil Dancer (IRE) 5 b.g	h107	1	2,343 16d
Wings of Freedom (IRE) 5 b.g	h104	3	6,491 20m 16g 22f
FAPPIANO (USA)		**3**	**4,452**
Munir (USA) 4 b.c	h97	3	4,452 a18g a20g a20g
FARAWAY TIMES (USA)		**1**	**4,317**
The Leggett 10 b.g	c112	1	4,317 c26g
FAR NORTH (CAN)		**5**	**9,804**
Flying Speed (USA) 5 b.g	h125	3	5,948 16v 16d 16f
Himlaj (USA) 8 b.g	h90	1	1,471 17g
Ling (USA) 8 b.g	h98	1	2,385 18v
FAUSTUS (USA)		**1**	**1,940**
Overlord 4 b.g		1	1,940 F16s
FEELINGS (FR)		**1**	**3,678**
Fast Thoughts 6 b.g	h111	1	3,678 22g
FIDEL		**4**	**28,478**
Glenshane Lad 7 b.g	h108	1	1,954 17g
Thumbs Up 7 b.g	h128	3	26,524 17s 16s 17m
FINAL STRAW		**8**	**19,055**
Always Alex 6 b.m	h90	1	1,697 18g
Coulton 6 ch.g	h157	1	4,760 16g
Rapid Mover 6 ch.g	h84	1	2,008 16m
Scotoni 7 ch.g	c105	3	6,426 c19f c16v c16s
Shahmiraj 5 b.m	h73	1	1,800 17d
Skinnhill 9 b.g	c101	1	2,364 c25m
FINE BLADE (USA)		**3**	**9,366**
Tareesh 6 br.m	h94	1	2,738 25g
The Demon Barber 11 b.g	c131	1	3,415 c25m
The Nigelstan 12 b.g	c106	1	3,213 c24f

FINE BLUE		4	**9,303**
Channels Gate 9 b.g	c104	2	3,781 c26g c27s
Tochenka 9 ch.m	c100	2	5,522 c26d c27g
FIT TO FIGHT (USA)		9	**20,908**
Fighting Days (USA) 7 ch.g	c91	1	1,067 c21m
Fight To Win (USA) 5 b.g	c103	3	6,425 c21f c21g c24m
King's Shilling (USA) 6 b.g	h121	5	13,416 17m 17d 17m 16g 17g
FITZWILLIAM (USA)		1	**1,165**
I'm Fine 8 b.m	h74	1	1,165 16s
FLASH OF STEEL		4	**4,856**
Captain My Captain (IRE) 5 ch.g	h93	1	1,305 17d
Solid Steel (IRE) 5 b.h	h101	3	3,551 18d 17d 17v
FLYING TYKE		1	**1,969**
Hunmanby Gap 8 ch.g	h75	1	1,969 22g
FOGGY BELL		1	**1,488**
Sandy's Beacon 8 b.g	c92	1	1,488 c21g
FORMIDABLE (USA)		15	**30,538**
Arcot 5 b.g	h123	2	4,908 16d 17d
Casual Pass 10 ch.g	h103	4	7,624 18g 17d 16s 21g
Fearsome 7 gr.g	h101	2	4,257 17v 22v
Forge 5 ch.g	h96	2	3,247 a18g a18g
Fox Chapel 6 b.g	h114	1	3,002 21s
Marzocco 5 ch.g	h88	1	1,954 17v
Riyadh Lights 8 b.g	h87	1	1,749 a20g
Thuhool 5 b.g	h99	2	3,797 18s 18g
FORTIES FIELD (FR)		1	**1,614**
Glencommon 12 ch.g	h97	1	1,614 18f
FREE STATE		1	**1,484**
State of Affairs 6 b.g	h96	1	1,484 16s
FULL OF HOPE		5	**10,078**
Baby Ashley 7 b.m	h79	2	4,924 a16g a16g
Easby Hopes 7 b.g	h85	1	1,305 22d
Magic Bloom 7 br.m	h91	2	3,849 17m 16g
FULL ON ACES (AUS)		4	**7,066**
Innocent Princess (NZ) 6 ch.m	h103	2	3,817 22s 23g
Mine's An Ace (NZ) 6 br.g	h95	2	3,249 17d 17m
FUNNY MAN		3	**9,978**
Jimmy O'Dea 6 br.g	c93	2	4,402 c25m c22f
Riverside Boy 10 ch.g	c140	1	5,576 c35s
FURRY GLEN		57	**170,907**
Beresfords Girl 8 b.m	c103	2	6,528 c24s c24v
Bibendum 7 b.g	c118	2	7,267 c16s c20g
Change The Act 8 b.g	c111	1	3,054 c16m
Cool Dude 7 b.g	h97	2	2,953 16d 16s
Croft Mill 7 b.g	h90	1	1,305 23s
Danny Connors 9 b.g	c129	1	2,916 c21s
Dragons Den 7 b.g	c104:h104	3	7,380 21d c25g c21f
Freeline Finishing 9 b.g	c135	2	10,303 c18g c17d
Frickley 7 b.g	h134	5	17,234 16g 16g 17d 16g 17g
Furry Baby 6 b.m	h103	3	3,282 25d 28g 28v
Gandouge Glen 6 b.g	h116	3	4,425 18g 18g 18g

Glen Cherry 7 b.g	c104	1	1,956	c21d
Jim Valentine 7 b.g	c94	1	2,738	c20d
Kano Warrior 6 b.g	h92	1	1,898	23m
Now Your Talkin 7 b.g	h129	4	9,278	22m 21d 23d 20d
Raglan Road 9 b.g	c95	2	4,845	c23d c21g
Seon 7 b.g	h117	5	8,190	17m 17g 16g 16v 17s
Shannon Glen 7 b.g	c97	1	2,447	c21v
Side of Hill 8 b.g	c112	3	7,905	c20s c23g c27m
Strath Royal 7 b.g	h118	4	7,211	16s 16m 16m 16d
The Flying Footman 7 b.g	h84	1	2,484	17g
Very Very Ordinary 7 b.g	c137	3	28,904	c22s c25s c25d
Whispering Steel 7 b.g	c120	5	24,851	c24d c20s c24d c20s c25d
Woodland Flower 8 b.m	c95	1	1,553	c25g
GABITAT		**1**	**1,534**	
Early Drinker 5 gr.g		1	1,534	aF16g
GAITER (NZ)		**2**	**3,581**	
Happy Horse (NZ) 6 ch.g	h92	1	1,480	23d
Rutland Gate (NZ) 6 b.g		1	2,101	F16g
GALA PERFORMANCE (USA)		**3**	**8,703**	
Billy Bathgate 7 ch.g	c125	2	5,255	c16d c19f
Gala's Image 13 br.g	c107	1	3,448	c26d
GARDA'S REVENGE (USA)		**1**	**1,425**	
Clare Lad 10 ch.g	h80	1	1,425	22d
GARRYOWEN		**2**	**3,741**	
Joker Jack 8 ch.g	h91	2	3,741	20v 27m
GATE DANCER (USA)		**4**	**7,269**	
Ringland (USA) 5 b.h	h100	2	3,658	17g 16g
Wishing Gate (USA) 5 br.g	h104	2	3,611	24g 24m
GAY MECENE (USA)		**1**	**1,753**	
Van Dyke Brown 12 b.g	c82	1	1,753	c22g
GENERAL IRONSIDE		**6**	**20,743**	
Farm Week 11 gr.g	c113	2	5,589	c26g c29f
Generals Boy 11 b.g	c117	1	6,775	c28f
Little General 10 ch.g	c92	1	2,912	c28m
Off The Bru 8 b.g	c104	1	4,327	c25m
Pigeon Island 11 b.g	c80	1	1,140	c21g
GIACOMETTI		**1**	**2,128**	
Saskia's Reprieve 9 ch.g	h94	1	2,128	22f
GINGER BOY		**2**	**3,194**	
Ginger Tristan 7 ch.g	h100	1	1,475	22g
Red Bean 5 ch.g	h86	1	1,719	a16g
GIOLLA MEAR		**1**	**1,688**	
Bee Garden 12 b.g	c103	1	1,688	c21g
GLEASON (USA)		**6**	**14,562**	
Fenton Bridge 9 b.g	c95	2	5,363	c25d c24m
Gaelic Cherry 10 b.g	c103	2	5,448	c25f c25g
Some Obligation 8 b.g	c106	2	3,751	c19d c17d
GLEN QUAICH		**2**	**2,960**	
Ronans Glen 6 b.g	h111	2	2,960	21g 22m

GLENSTAL (USA)

		22	**44,931**	
Boarding School 6 b.g	c98	3	8,802	c16m c16g c20m
Bonanza 6 ch.g	c114	3	7,204	c21d c21d c23d
Dancing Days 7 ch.g	h86	2	2,995	22d a20g
Deb's Ball 7 b.m	h141	4	9,437	17m 18g 22d 23f
Gleneliane (IRE) 5 b.m	h81	1	1,235	16g
Grove Serendipity (IRE) 5 b.g	h101	2	2,519	17s 17g
Saint Bene't (IRE) 5 b.g	h85	1	988	17m
Sanawi 6 b.g	h83	1	1,350	17m
Star of The Glen 7 b.g	h121	4	9,061	16g 16m 16d 16m
Windsor Highness 6 ch.m	h81	1	1,340	17g

GLINT OF GOLD

		19	**115,742**	
Dawson City 6 ch.g	c123	4	25,572	c16d c20d c21s c20d
Millador 4 b.f	h107	2	4,101	18m 16m
Only A Rose 4 br.f	h110	3	5,047	18d 20s 16s
Punchbag (USA) 7 b.g	h98	3	6,381	17v 17v 17s
Shimmering Scarlet (IRE) 5 b.m	h99	3	5,340	a20g a22g 20m
Spinning 6 b.g	h151	2	39,205	17f 16f
Vagog 8 b.g	h156	2	30,096	26d 26s

GLOW (USA)

		10	**19,253**	
Alcoy (IRE) 4 b.g	h118	6	11,842	a18g a16g a18g a16g 20f a18g
Sea Breaker (IRE) 5 b.g	h97	3	4,324	22m 22m 22m
The Glow (IRE) 5 b.g	h112	1	3,087	20d

GODSWALK (USA)

		1	**1,710**	
Gaelgoir 9 gr.g	h76	1	1,710	16v

GOLD CLAIM

		1	**1,480**	
Singing Gold 7 b.g		1	1,480	16v

GOLDEN ACT (USA)

		4	**9,660**	
Dizzy (USA) 5 gr.m	h126	3	7,386	16g 18g 18m
Golden Reverie (USA) 5 b.g	h80	1	2,274	20g

GOLDEN FLEECE (USA)

		2	**4,750**	
Golden Isle 9 b.h	h113	2	4,750	16g 16f

GOLDEN LOVE

		1	**26,040**	
Second Schedual 8 b.g	c149	1	26,040	c21m

GOLDHILL

		1	**1,607**	
Brownside Brig 8 b.g	h88	1	1,607	16f

GO MARCHING (USA)

		1	**5,585**	
Sabin du Loir (FR) 14 ch.g	c151	1	5,585	c21v

GOOD THYNE (USA)

		9	**75,451**	
Fine Thyne (IRE) 4 ch.g		1	2,013	F17m
Howaryadoon 7 b.g	h104	1	2,355	25s
Linkside 8 b.g	h103	1	1,903	16g
Mighty Mogul 6 ch.g	h170	5	67,385	17g 21s 17s 20d 16d
Precious Juno (IRE) 4 b.f		1	1,795	F16s

GOOD TIMES (ITY)

		3	**5,247**	
Charlycia 5 b.m	h88	1	1,918	18m
Kidlaw 5 b.g	h94	2	3,329	17m 17d

GORYTUS (USA)

		8	**14,452**	
Amphigory 5 b.g	h88	1	1,481	18f
Arrow Dancer 7 b.g	h83	1	816	17m
Grand Frere 7 br.g	h114	3	7,123	17s 17g 16f

55

Myhamet 6 b.g	h98	3	5,032	22d 18s 20d
GREAT NEPHEW		1	**2,820**	
Choctaw 9 gr.g	c94	1	2,820	c27m
GREEN DANCER (USA)		2	**5,233**	
Eden's Close 4 ch.g	h119	1	3,028	17g
Greenwine (USA) 7 br.g	c90	1	2,205	c16g
GREEN FOREST (USA)		1	**2,259**	
Forest Flame (USA) 8 ch.g	h108	1	2,259	16d
GREEN RUBY (USA)		1	**1,670**	
Elsa 4 gr.f	h80	1	1,670	20m
GREEN SHOON		16	**74,029**	
Another Coral 10 br.g	c160	2	35,471	c21v c20s
Gladtogetit 7 br.m	c98	1	3,152	c24g
Overhereoverthere 10 ch.g	c100	2	4,606	c26d c25s
Rather Sharp 7 b.g	c82	1	2,469	c17v
Royle Speedmaster 9 ch.g	c114	5	12,590	c21g c24m c25f c26d c24d
Shoon Wind 10 b.g	c125	2	6,944	c24g c25g
The Green Stuff 8 ch.g	c110	2	5,760	c16v c17v
Viridian 8 b.g	c108	1	3,037	c23f
GREGORIAN (USA)		1	**2,056**	
Chuck Curley (USA) 5 b.g	h98	1	2,056	16s
GREY DESIRE		2	**3,121**	
My Desire 5 ch.m	h97	1	1,305	28d
Rich Desire 4 b.f		1	1,816	F16g
GUEST OF HONOUR (NZ)		1	**2,150**	
Invite d'Honneur (NZ) 11 ch.g	h87	1	2,150	26d
GUNNER B		1	**4,163**	
The Master Gunner 9 ch.g	c103	1	4,163	c20g
HADEER		1	**1,534**	
Harry The Cab 4 ch.c		1	1,534	aF13g
HALYUDH (USA)		1	**2,931**	
Mr Boston 8 b.g	c123	1	2,931	c26f
HARDBOY		2	**10,404**	
Solidasarock 11 ch.g	c118	2	10,404	c24f c26f
HARD FOUGHT		3	**10,478**	
Gold Shot 7 ch.g	c111	3	10,478	c24m c23v c26f
HARVEST SPIRIT		3	**14,161**	
Sikera Spy 11 b.m	c120	3	14,161	c30s c25m c25g
HASTY WORD		1	**2,330**	
Whitwood 8 b.g	c102	1	2,330	c20d
HATIM (USA)		7	**13,500**	
Loxley Range (IRE) 5 ch.g	h80	1	2,043	16s
Richmond (IRE) 5 ch.g	h83	1	1,670	18d
Simone's Son (IRE) 5 ch.g	h113	5	9,787	18m 16f 17g 17m 16d
HAWAIIAN RETURN (USA)		3	**9,030**	
Champagne Lad 7 ch.g	c116	3	9,030	c21d c21f c20s
HELLO GORGEOUS (USA)		2	**3,423**	
Mubaaris 10 ch.g	h93	2	3,423	26s 24s

HELLO HANDSOME | | **1** | **1,214**
Thistleholm 7 ro.g | h107 | 1 | 1,214 21m

HE LOVES ME | | **3** | **5,889**
Hard To Hold 10 b.g | h116 | 3 | 5,889 a20g a20g a20g

HENBIT (USA) | | **19** | **86,642**
Corrupt Committee 10 ch.g | c88 | 1 | 2,174 c20m
Crafty Copper 9 b.g | c90 | 2 | 3,606 c21s c23d
Drumstick 7 ch.g | c110 | 5 | 12,335 c18s c16m c16m c17f c18f
Hardihero 7 b.g | h92 | 1 | 1,918 26s
Holdenby 8 b.g | c102 | 1 | 2,206 c16d
Hutner 8 b.g | c104 | 3 | 7,470 c17g c17m c21s
Sartorius 7 b.g | c99 | 1 | 1,817 c16v
Sybillin 7 b.g | c156 | 5 | 55,116 c16d c16d c17s c16s c16g

HERO'S HONOR (USA) | | **3** | **4,267**
Moor Lodge (USA) 4 b.g | h110 | 3 | 4,267 18f 17m 18m

HIGHLAND PARK (USA) | | **1** | **1,484**
Ramble (USA) 6 ch.m | h87 | 1 | 1,484 a18g

HIGH LINE | | **15** | **129,896**
Family Line 5 b.g | h108 | 5 | 11,691 17d 16g 17m 16g 16g
Linebacker 9 b.g | c90 | 1 | 2,006 c26g
Muse 6 ch.g | h165 | 3 | 49,638 20d 16s 22s
Olympian 6 ch.g | h135 | 3 | 59,890 23g 17f 21m
Poacher's Delight 7 ch.g | c101 | 2 | 5,204 c24f c24f
Viaggio 5 b.g | h97 | 1 | 1,467 17v

HIGH TOP | | **3** | **7,673**
Aal El Aal 6 br.h | | 1 | 1,998 F14d
Dwadme 8 b.g | c96 | 1 | 2,052 c27s
Sweet N' Twenty 7 b.m | h121 | 1 | 3,623 20d

HOMEBOY | | **2** | **3,479**
Well Done Rory 4 b.g | h89 | 2 | 3,479 18v 18m

HOMING | | **1** | **2,924**
Jopanini 8 b.g | h139 | 1 | 2,924 17v

HORAGE | | **7** | **11,307**
Azureus (IRE) 5 ch.g | h101 | 1 | 1,188 21m
Cosmic Dancer 6 ch.g | h112 | 3 | 5,438 a22g a22g a22g
Houghton 7 b.g | c97 | 1 | 2,559 c20m
Temporale 7 ch.h | h83 | 2 | 2,122 21d 18g

HOSTAGE (USA) | | **2** | **7,058**
Rathvinden House (USA) 6 b.g | c107:h110 | 2 | 7,058 25d c21s

HOT BRANDY | | **3** | **6,589**
Bird of Spirit 13 b.g | c95 | 2 | 4,706 c26m c25m
Old Applejack 13 ch.g | c129 | 1 | 1,883 c20m

HOTFOOT | | **3** | **11,928**
Ben Adhem 11 b.g | h121 | 1 | 3,470 16g
Flown 6 b.g | h165 | 1 | 5,222 18m
Ketti 8 br.m | h128 | 1 | 3,236 21v

HUMDOLEILA | | **1** | **1,231**
Shermago 11 b.m | c77 | 1 | 1,231 c24m

IDIOT'S DELIGHT | | **33** | **92,635**
Cavvies Clown 13 b.g | c144 | 1 | 9,870 c26d

Chiaroscuro 7 b.g	h85	1	1,632	20v
Clever Folly 13 b.g	c139	2	5,632	c17m c21m
Cool Clown 6 b.g	h115	2	2,955	23v 21v
Dreamers Delight 7 b.g	h126	3	8,315	F12d 17s 17s
Easby Joker 5 b.g		1	1,304	F16v
Front Street 6 b.g	h89	1	1,912	16d
Ima Delight 6 b.m	h97	1	2,431	21v
Leading Prospect 6 b.g	h99	2	4,020	18g 18d
Lunabelle 5 b.m	h95	1	1,604	16d
Martha's Son 6 b.g	h128	3	13,799	18f 16d 17s
Mr Flanagan 7 b.g	h109	1	2,460	21d
Sabaki River 9 br.g	h128	3	7,789	17s 17g 20g
Sailors Luck 8 b.g	c94	1	2,345	c16d
Sausalito Boy 5 b.g	h106	2	5,785	22v 22m
Simple Pleasure 8 b.g	c104	3	9,076	c16g c17d c21g
Stupid Cupid 9 b.m	c87	1	2,427	c22g
Tangled String 9 b.g	c99	1	2,330	c20s
Vulrory's Clown 15 b.g	c90	3	6,949	c23s c19m c18g
ILE DE BOURBON (USA)		**9**	**17,203**	
Celcius 9 b.g	h107	2	4,098	16s 20s
Djebel Prince 6 b.g	h103	2	4,845	17v 17v
Ilewin 6 br.g	h96	1	1,298	16m
Lucky Again 6 br.h	c98	1	2,222	c17g
Miss Simone 7 b.m	h92	3	4,740	17s 22d 20d
ILIUM		**1**	**1,621**	
Muddy Lane 5 b.g	h79	1	1,621	17d
IMPECUNIOUS		**1**	**1,604**	
Jokester 6 b.g	h84	1	1,604	16v
IMPERIAL FLING (USA)		**1**	**3,522**	
Kitchi Koo 9 b.m	h100	1	3,522	21s
IMPORT		**8**	**116,202**	
Young Hustler 6 ch.g	c149	8	116,202	c21m c21g c24s c26v c24m
				c21d c20g c25m
INDIAN KING (USA)		**1**	**1,411**	
Little Big 6 b.g	h85	1	1,411	19g
IN FIJAR (USA)		**2**	**5,543**	
Fit For Firing (FR) 9 b.m	c114	2	5,543	c21d c21v
INSTANT FAME		**1**	**1,480**	
Power Happy 8 ch.m	h84	1	1,480	16f
IRISH RIVER (FR)		**3**	**6,617**	
Flowing River (USA) 7 b.h	h104	1	2,710	17g
Irish Ditty (USA) 6 ch.g	h96	2	3,907	16s 16d
IRON DUKE (FR)		**7**	**34,505**	
Gris Et Violet (FR) 6 ch.g	h110	2	5,309	18v 20d
Sweet Duke (FR) 6 b.g	h161	5	29,196	21g 24s 25v 24s 24d
ITALIC (FR)		**5**	**60,056**	
Antonin (FR) 5 ch.g	c135	4	15,556	c16g c17s c17f c20s
The Fellow (FR) 8 b.g	c171	1	44,500	c24s
JALMOOD (USA)		**5**	**11,032**	
Cabochon 6 b.g	h127	2	5,326	17s 16d
Diamond Prospector 4 b.g		1	2,136	F17g

My Senor 4 b.g	h101	2	3,570	17g 18v
JASMINE STAR		2	**4,706**	
Starmine 7 ch.g	c95	1	3,101	c21s
Welshman's Gully 9 ch.g	c80	1	1,605	c21m
JEFFERSON		1	**4,663**	
All Jeff (FR) 9 b.g	c127	1	4,663	c33d
JELLABY		2	**5,766**	
Tinas Lad 10 b.g	c105	2	5,766	c18d c16f
JESTER		2	**4,628**	
No More The Fool 7 ch.g	c90	1	1,730	c22g
Viceroy Jester 8 br.g	h123	1	2,898	20s
JIMMY REPPIN		2	**5,225**	
James My Boy 13 ch.g	c93	2	5,225	c21s c21s
JIMSUN		3	**6,745**	
Betty Hayes 9 b.m	c96	1	1,744	c26m
Jimstro 8 b.g	c99	2	5,001	c24g c24s
JOHN DE COOMBE		2	**4,942**	
Cotapaxi 8 gr.g	c90	2	4,942	c17m c16f
JOHN FRENCH		1	**1,898**	
Shrewd John 7 b.h	h82	1	1,898	17d
JOSHUA		2	**3,764**	
Final Chant 12 br.g	c104	1	1,968	c25d
Needwood Sprite 7 ch.m	h107	1	1,796	23m
JULIO MARINER		10	**19,102**	
Bee Dee Boy 5 b.g	h86	1	825	24g
Dextra Dove 6 gr.g	h119	2	5,947	16f 17s
Gentleman Angler 10 ch.g	c99	1	2,213	c25m
Major Bush 6 b.g	h94	1	1,768	17s
Nuns Jewel 7 ch.m	h89	1	895	21g
Sailor Blue 6 b.g	h102	1	2,532	21g
Sea Barn 10 ch.g	h91	2	3,276	17m 17g
Shannon Juliette 6 b.m	h79	1	1,646	22d
JUPITER ISLAND		5	**9,430**	
Curtain Factory 4 ch.g	h86	1	1,811	17g
Island Jewel 5 ch.g	h84	1	1,953	16v
Jupiter Moon 4 b.c	h85	1	1,772	17m
Take Two 5 b.g	h102	2	3,894	18v 17f
JUPITER PLUVIUS		1	**1,607**	
Gembridge Jupiter 15 b.g	c97	1	1,607	c24f
KABOUR		1	**2,657**	
Precious Memories 8 br.g	c89	1	2,657	c23m
KALAGLOW		5	**10,154**	
Beautiful Dream 5 b.m	h96	1	1,999	22v
Blasket Hero 5 gr.g	h92	1	2,260	20m
Kalamoss 4 ch.f	h86	1	1,763	20m
Kalko 4 b.c	h102	2	4,132	17d 17g
KALA SHIKARI		12	**21,211**	
Market Leader 13 b.g	c84	2	5,345	c18m c18m
Marsh's Law 6 br.g	h106	3	6,318	18m 18s 16d

Master Shikari 4 b.g	h89	2	1,843 18g 17m
On The Sauce 6 b.g	h102	5	7,705 22m 26v 18m 20g 21m
KAMBALDA		**34**	**101,903**
Ask The Governor 7 b.g	h110	3	7,143 22v 22d 21m
Bardesan 7 b.g	h107	3	4,764 22d a18g a16g
Barton Bank 7 br.g	c142	4	30,368 c21s c23v c21v c26m
Case Harden 6 ch.g	h104	1	2,367 21g
Copper Mine 7 b.g	c115	5	15,744 c18d c17m c20f c21f c21f
Earlham 7 ch.g	h85	1	1,675 a24g
Height of Fun 9 b.g	c93	2	4,536 c21s c26f
Knockumshin 10 ch.g	c103	4	5,536 c24f c27g c24d c26m
Kushbaloo 8 b.g	c120	5	14,951 c21m c25g c23g c25d c24m
Portavogie 9 b.g	c86	1	2,511 c20f
Sandybraes 8 ch.g	c107	3	8,296 c25g c26s c24m
This Nettle Danger 9 b.g	h96	2	4,012 24f 26f
KAMPALA		**4**	**8,028**
Braida Boy 7 b.g	h89	2	3,951 21s 21m
Galway Star 6 b.h	c89:h129	2	4,077 17m c17s
KASHNEB (FR)		**1**	**2,469**
Cache Fleur (FR) 7 ch.g	c129	1	2,469 c24v
KAYTU		**1**	**825**
Kayartis 4 b.f	h94	1	825 18d
KEMAL (FR)		**24**	**60,032**
Beyond Reason 7 b.g	h86	1	1,674 25s
Clyde Ranger 6 b.g	h104	2	2,951 24s 24v
Factor Ten (IRE) 5 b.g	h104	2	3,638 16g 22d
Fantasy World 7 ch.m	h97	2	5,441 18v 22d
Kev's Lass (IRE) 5 ch.m	h94	1	1,480 16v
King of Steel 7 b.g	h96	1	1,778 26s
Kissane 12 br.g	c110	1	1,996 c19g
Nevada Gold 7 ch.g	c117	3	11,645 c21s c21f c21g
No More Trix 7 b.g	c102	2	4,932 c21d c21g
Richville 7 b.g	c101	1	3,028 c19v
Saraville 6 ch.m	c118	3	7,613 c21m c23d c27g
Spree Cross 7 b.g	c110	3	10,072 c17d c16d c16s
Squires Tale (IRE) 5 b.g		1	1,984 F16m
West Bay 7 b.g	h78	1	1,800 22f
KENMARE (FR)		**1**	**1,688**
Un Souverain 5 b.g	h86	1	1,688 20m
KEY TO THE MINT (USA)		**4**	**11,652**
Green Island (USA) 7 b.g	c113	4	11,652 c16g c19m c18d c18g
KIND OF HUSH		**9**	**17,538**
Kind'a Smart 8 ch.g	c101	2	5,118 c16s c16g
Master of Hounds 7 b.g	c94	1	2,023 c21m
Munday Dean 5 b.g	h79	1	1,734 a16g
Quiet Miss 4 b.f	h86	2	2,789 16m 18f
Second Call 4 ch.f	h101	3	5,874 18s 17f 18f
KING AMONG KINGS		**1**	**1,646**
Palacegate King 4 ch.g	h110	1	1,646 17s
KINGLET		**2**	**35,280**
King Credo 8 b.g	h161	1	33,800 17g
Spinning Steel 6 b.g	h76	1	1,480 16f

KING OF CLUBS		5	13,142	
Jamestown Boy 5 b.g	h94	1	1,534	17s
King of Normandy (IRE) 4 ch.g	h74	1	1,602	18v
Knave of Clubs 6 ch.g	h121	3	10,006	22s 22m 21f
KING PERSIAN		2	3,055	
King Optimist 4 ch.g	h86	1	875	18f
Whippers Delight (IRE) 5 ch.g	h101	1	2,180	16d
KINGS LAKE (USA)		6	19,661	
Royal Print (IRE) 4 ch.g	h100	2	3,363	17f 16g
Sea Trout 9 b.g	h114	1	2,374	22m
Sultan's Son 7 b.g	h97	2	4,424	16m 17d
Tyrone Bridge 7 b.g	h153	1	9,500	25s
KING'S RIDE		6	57,155	
Camelot Knight 7 br.g	c112	2	4,690	c21s c24s
Cool And Easy 7 b.g	c99	1	3,485	c24d
Tipping Tim 8 b.g	c153	3	48,980	c21g c25g c21d
KIRRAMA (NZ)		1	2,616	
Colonel O'Kelly (NZ) 9 br.g	c89	1	2,616	c25d
KNOWN FACT (USA)		2	5,975	
Moment of Truth 9 b.g	c141:h122	2	5,975	17m c17g
KRIS		11	43,484	
Alosaili 6 ch.g	h98	2	3,467	16d 17d
Dare Say 10 b.g	c97	1	2,346	c19g
Jungle Knife 7 b.g	h144	1	4,161	16s
Kisu Kali 6 ch.g	c84	3	16,298	c18g c17v c21f
Qannaas 9 br.g	c97	1	1,871	c24f
Royal Circus 4 b.g	h91	1	1,705	a18g
Srivijaya 6 b.h	c104	1	2,186	c16g
Thinking Twice (USA) 4 ch.c	h123	1	11,450	16f
LASHKARI		4	39,373	
Seraphim (FR) 4 b.f	h97	3	5,098	18g 18g 17m
Shawiya (IRE) 4 b.f	h141	1	34,275	17m
LAST FANDANGO		2	3,873	
Mr Murdock 8 b.g	c96	2	3,873	c24f c21f
LAST TYCOON		9	16,981	
Jawani (IRE) 5 b.g	h92	2	4,013	20m 22f
Kiveton Tycoon (IRE) 4 b.c	h129	2	3,718	16d 16s
Mick's Tycoon (IRE) 5 b.g	h93	2	3,034	23s 23s
Trump 4 b.g	h101	3	6,216	16d 20g 21d
LATEST MODEL		1	3,480	
Upstanding 11 b.g	c86	1	3,480	c25m
LAW SOCIETY (USA)		6	8,701	
Isabeau 6 b.m	h108	1	1,172	21g
J P Morgan 5 b.g	h93	1	1,882	16g
Lynch Law (IRE) 5 b.h	h112	2	2,659	16g 17d
Major's Law (IRE) 4 b.c	h99	1	1,636	17g
Society Ball 6 b.m	h83	1	1,352	22s
LEADER OF THE BAND (USA)		3	8,654	
Buddy Holly (NZ) 8 b.g	c95	1	3,231	c27d
Musical Monarch (NZ) 7 ch.g	h112	2	5,423	21v 21g

LEADING MAN		3	8,300
Winnie The Witch 9 b.m	c109	3	8,300 c21d c16s c16s

LEAD ON TIME (USA)		1	1,570
Daphnis (USA) 4 b.c		1	1,570 F14s

LEANDER		1	1,368
Sweatshirt 8 ch.g	c90	1	1,368 c22d

LEAR FAN (USA)		2	5,187
Regan (USA) 6 b.m	c92	2	5,187 c21s c16d

LE BAVARD (FR)		21	75,652
Bavard Bay 9 b.g	c98:h86	2	4,157 c26s 21s
Belmount Captain 8 ch.g	c137	2	11,031 c24s c28d
Cogent 9 b.g	c136	3	13,459 c20s c21d c21v
Fair Brother 7 ch.g	h95	1	2,775 17d
Habton Whin 7 b.g	c100:h100	2	3,750 24g c21d
He Who Dares Wins 10 b.g	c114	1	2,322 c25g
Kildimo 13 b.g	c128	1	20,541 c27d
La Princesse 6 b.m	h111	2	3,659 21s 22v
Master Bavard (IRE) 5 ch.g		2	3,238 aF16g aF16g
Mickeen 6 b.g	h107	1	1,952 23m
Niyaka 6 b.g		1	828 aF16g
Tompet 7 b.g	c92	2	5,574 c24m c24g
What A To Do 9 b.g	c92	1	2,366 c27v

LE COQ D'OR		5	19,133
Ardesee 13 ch.g	c100	1	1,506 c24s
Glenbrook d'Or 9 b.g	c122	1	3,420 c26s
Merry Master 9 br.g	c128	3	14,207 c25m c25g c25s

LEGAL EAGLE		3	8,343
Aldington Bell 10 b.g	c91	3	8,343 c16m c17f c20f

LEGAL TENDER		4	10,726
General Merchant 13 br.g	c89	4	10,726 c18v c17v c16f c17m

LEGEND OF FRANCE (USA)		1	4,663
Dissimulateur (FR) 4 b.c	h116	1	4,663 17g

LE GRAND SEIGNEUR (CAN)		5	13,070
Thatcher Rock (NZ) 8 b.g	c105	4	10,504 c18v c24g c21s c21v
Village Reindeer (NZ) 6 b.g	h116	1	2,566 25g

LEMHI GOLD (USA)		4	33,698
Sacre d'Or (USA) 8 b.g	c134	4	33,698 c21s c21d c21s c21m

L'EMIGRANT (USA)		3	5,689
Al Skeet (USA) 7 b.g	h78	1	1,940 16g
John Shaw (USA) 5 b.h	h97	2	3,749 a16g 20m

LE MOSS		27	65,619
Ask Moss 8 ch.g	h125	1	2,290 23s
Balloo House 8 ch.g	h96	2	3,465 26g 26m
Brackenfield 7 ch.g	h137	6	20,865 21m 24s 24v 20s 24s 20g
Captain Dolford 6 ch.g	h108	1	1,475 18v
Do Be Brief 8 ch.g	c118	1	3,124 c24g
Flight of Steel 8 ch.g	c76	1	1,757 c18m
Garston La Gaffe 8 b.g	h97	1	1,826 23m
Hazel Leaf 7 b.m	h93	1	1,935 17d
Just Moss 7 b.g	c114	2	6,164 c24v c24s
May-Day-Baby 7 ch.g	h89	1	1,302 23s

Mossy Fern 7 b.m	c123	3	9,442	c26d c23s c26v
Murphaideez 6 b.g	h93	1	2,198	22d
Orchipedzo 8 ch.g	c80	1	1,580	c16m
Shean Alainn (IRE) 5 b.m	h87	1	2,167	21v
Special Account 7 b.g	h103	2	2,849	24v 25s
Taramoss 6 b.g	h102	1	1,660	24s
Tort 9 b.g	c103	1	1,520	c25d
LE NAIN JAUNE (FR)		**2**	**4,177**	
Le Metayer (FR) 5 b.g	h115	2	4,177	16s 16d
LEPANTO (GER)		**4**	**15,261**	
Ballyanto 8 b.g	h99	1	2,827	19m
Naval Battle 6 ch.g		1	1,842	F16d
Panto Prince 12 br.g	c123	2	10,592	c20f c20m
LE SOLARET (FR)		**4**	**7,937**	
Hilltown Blues 4 gr.g	h87	3	6,468	16d 16d 17v
Tip It In 4 gr.g	h86	1	1,469	18v
LE SOLEIL		**3**	**7,815**	
Cythere 9 gr.g	c111	3	7,815	c27s c25v c27d
LIBRATE		**4**	**7,696**	
Fotoexpress 5 ch.g	h117	4	7,696	20v 20d 18g 20s
LIDHAME		**4**	**4,888**	
Emsboy 5 b.g	h93	3	4,100	17s 20m 17d
Tapestry Dancer 5 b.g	h76	1	788	18g
LIGHTER		**14**	**30,582**	
Arctic Skylight 9 ch.g	c113	3	6,602	c21d c16m c18d
Don't Light Up 7 b.g	h100	1	2,273	21s
Elltee-Ess 8 ch.g	c86	1	1,684	c23f
Interim Lib 10 b.g	c115	1	1,848	c24m
Lavalight 6 b.g	h76	2	3,507	17f 22f
Quiet Dawn 7 b.m	h84	1	1,896	26m
Sonsie Mo 8 b.g	c101	2	5,342	c16g c16f
Warner Forpleasure 7 b.g	h81	1	1,940	22f
Young Ty 9 br.g	c98	2	5,490	c20m c20g
LINKAGE (USA)		**1**	**1,351**	
Burn Bridge (USA) 7 b.g	h98	1	1,351	18d
LIR		**2**	**4,474**	
Lirie Lad 7 ch.g	c83	1	2,740	c22g
Roger's Pal 6 ch.h	h87	1	1,734	17g
LITTLE WOLF		**2**	**4,541**	
Leeswood 5 b.g	h91	2	4,541	17s 17m
LOCAL SUITOR (USA)		**3**	**4,775**	
Blushing Belle 5 b.m	h84	2	3,291	a20g 17f
Local Flyer 4 b.g	h101	1	1,484	a16g
LOCHNAGER		**10**	**22,297**	
Ashdren 6 b.h	h94	1	2,233	17g
Delpiombo 7 br.g	h98	1	1,822	16m
Elgin 4 b.g	h98	1	1,924	16g
J J Jimmy 9 b.g	c97	1	2,950	c20f
Loch Garanne 5 br.m	h112	3	6,564	16d 17s 16d
Polder 7 b.g	c87:h80	2	4,653	16g c17m
Tough Cookie 8 gr.g	c87	1	2,151	c16m

LOMOND (USA)		4	8,367
Child of The Mist 7 b.g	h124	2	5,412 17g 17g
Desert Force (IRE) 4 b.c	h103	1	1,475 18s
Glaisdale (IRE) 4 b.g	h121	1	1,480 16v

LORD DURHAM (CAN)		1	2,365
Turn'em Back Jack (CAN) 10 ch.g	c85	1	2,365 c21m

LORD GAYLE (USA)		3	12,257
Logamillion 7 b.g	c123	3	12,257 c17d c16s c21s

LORD HA HA		5	11,548
Ballylord 9 ch.g	h99	2	4,626 16d 21v
The Hidden City 7 b.g	h82	1	1,630 16d* dis
The Laughing Lord 7 b.g	c94:h107	2	5,292 23g c20d

LUCIFER (USA)		2	3,564
Certain Light 15 br.g	c104	1	1,456 c21s
Devil's Valley 10 ch.g	c115	1	2,108 c16s

LYDIAN (FR)		3	7,971
Lady Ghislaine (FR) 6 b.m	h83	1	1,537 17s
Ricmar (USA) 10 ch.g	h96	1	2,064 22m
Sayyure (USA) 7 b.g	h134	1	4,370 25s

LYPHARD'S SPECIAL (USA)		4	7,102
Fettle Up 5 ch.g	h77	1	1,631 a20g
Green's Van Goyen (IRE) 5 b.g	h117	1	2,448 20d
Leotard 6 b.g	h121	2	3,023 16d 16g

LYPHARD'S WISH (FR)		1	9,440
Lift And Load (USA) 6 b.g	h153	1	9,440 21f

LYPHARD (USA)		7	14,154
Galagames (USA) 6 ch.g	c85	1	2,411 c16g
Valseur (USA) 4 ch.c	h95	4	7,502 28m 22d 25v 25m
Zamil (USA) 8 b.g	c101	2	4,241 c16v c21v

LYPHEOR (USA)		8	14,020
Damanour (USA) 7 gr.g	h94	1	1,618 17m
Lyph (USA) 7 b.g	h85	1	1,660 a20g
Suluk (USA) 8 b.h	h113	6	10,742 a18g a22g a16g a18g a16g a20g

MACMILLION		2	4,123
Raiseamillion 5 b.g	h94	2	4,123 18g 20g

MAGIC MIRROR		2	2,242
Alice's Mirror 4 gr.f	h86	2	2,242 18g 17g

MAIN REEF		1	2,502
Barrica 6 b.m	c92	1	2,502 c19d

MAIYMAD		5	55,556
Valfinet (FR) 6 b.g	h156	5	55,556 17d 17v 16s 17s 16g

MAJESTIC MAHARAJ		6	20,675
Stirrup Cup 9 b.g	c123	6	20,675 c26v c26v c28s c27v c25s c23d

MAJESTIC STREAK		2	7,079
Kirsty's Boy 10 b.g	c123	2	7,079 c24f c25g

MALINOWSKI (USA)		3	6,740
Ok Corral (USA) 6 gr.g	c108	3	6,740 c21v c26g c26g

MANDALUS		28	86,860
Baydon Star 6 br.g	h156	5	40,972 17g 21g 17d 17s 25g

Carrigeen Lad 6 b.g	h104	2	3,254 20v 23m
Dilleachta 6 b.m		1	1,969 F16v
Duck Or Grouse 8 b.g	c78	1	2,018 c23m
Early Man 6 b.g	h110	3	5,921 23s 25v 20v
Konvekta King (IRE) 5 br.g		1	1,277 F16m
Mandraki Shuffle 11 b.g	c110	1	2,211 c24d
Maneree 6 b.m	h90	1	1,480 20d
Manettia (IRE) 4 b.f		1	1,497 F17d
Man's Best Friend 6 b.g	c101	2	4,457 c25v c32d
Royal Saxon 7 b.g	c92	1	2,349 c21m
Russell Dalus 6 b.g	h100	1	1,632 16d
Springholm 11 br.g	c98	1	3,659 c21f
Tallywagger 6 b.g	h127	3	6,798 24d 28d 24m
The Link Man 6 b.g	h79	2	3,478 23f 22v
The Mrs 7 b.m	h79	1	1,617 22s
Woody Will 7 b.g	c95	1	2,271 c21m
MANDRAKE MAJOR		**6**	**26,031**
Armagret 8 b.g	c143	3	21,128 c20d c21d c20g
Herbalist 4 b.c		1	1,285 F16g
Majority Holding 8 b.g	h90	1	1,778 16g
Speedy Sioux 4 ch.f	h76	1	1,840 16g
MARSHALSEA		**1**	**2,287**
Shanaghey West 9 b.g	c81	1	2,287 c16v
MARTINMAS		**14**	**33,719**
In The Zone 8 b.g	c91	1	1,580 c19f
Love On The Rocks 8 b.m	c88	1	2,413 c17v
Martin's Lamp 6 b.g	h124	2	4,063 16s 16v
Mr Jamboree 7 b.g	c112	3	10,587 c16g c24f c21g
Mr Taylor 8 b.g	h108	2	5,334 21v 21s
Peaceman 7 b.g	h122	3	5,483 16s 17s 16v
Poors Wood 6 b.g	h109	2	4,259 16s 18g
MART LANE		**1**	**1,464**
Liams Pride 10 ch.g	c85	1	1,464 c16g
MASHHOR DANCER (USA)		**8**	**14,405**
Mohana 4 br.f	h126	6	11,379 17m 17s 17s 17m 17d 17d
Muizenberg 6 b.g	h95	1	1,305 17d
River Orchid 4 b.f	h80	1	1,721 17f
MASTER THATCH		**1**	**2,259**
Mister Moody (FR) 8 ch.h	c90	1	2,259 c27m
MASTER WILLIE		**1**	**2,190**
Willesdon (USA) 9 ch.h	h82	1	2,190 18h
MATCHING PAIR		**1**	**1,303**
Castlerichardking 8 b.g	h70	1	1,303 17g
MAZAAD		**6**	**12,852**
Golden Gunner (IRE) 5 ch.g	h102	1	2,952 16s
Qualitair Sound (IRE) 5 b.g	h128	1	3,407 17d
Set The Standards (IRE) 5 b.g	h109	1	2,092 20g
Trendy Auctioneer (IRE) 5 b.g	h75	3	4,401 17g 17g 17f
M DOUBLE M (USA)		**3**	**18,793**
Bentley Manor 4 ch.g	h80	1	943 22s
Country Lad (IRE) 5 b.g	h110	2	17,850 17s 17g

MEADOWBROOK		1	**1,763**
Beanley Brook 5 ch.m	h87	1	1,763 18d
MELDRUM		4	**15,036**
Last 'o' The Bunch 9 ch.g	c141	4	15,036 c16s c16d c21s c20g
MELYNO		1	**1,845**
Mizyan (IRE) 5 b.g	h120	1	1,845 a18g
MIAMI SPRINGS		3	**7,069**
Miami Splash 6 ch.g	h121	3	7,069 16g 18s 16d
MIDLAND GAYLE		3	**6,584**
Midland Glenn 9 ch.g	h126	1	2,616 24d
Midland Lad 8 br.g	h114	2	3,968 28f 28m
MIDYAN (USA)		2	**3,840**
Broctune Bay 4 b.g		2	3,840 F16g F14g
MILAN		1	**2,792**
Thats The Business 9 br.g	c89	1	2,792 c24f
MILFORD		3	**14,785**
Milford Quay 10 ch.h	c134	2	10,967 c20v c20d
Threeoutoffour 8 b.g	c104	1	3,818 c21g
MILK OF THE BARLEY		1	**2,999**
Super Malt (IRE) 5 ch.m	h106	1	2,999 21s
MILLER'S MATE		1	**1,480**
The Minder (FR) 6 b.g	h86	1	1,480 17s
MILL REEF (USA)		1	**5,920**
Rosgill 7 ch.g	h117	1	5,920 17f
MINER'S LAMP		1	**828**
Miner Jackson 6 b.g	h97	1	828 21v
MIRAMAR REEF		4	**7,342**
Ardlussa Bay 5 b.m	h112	3	6,533 20s 25g 21s
Valkyrie Reef 4 ch.f	h82	1	809 18d
MIRROR BOY		1	**3,048**
Diamond Fort 8 b.g	c107	1	3,048 c24v
MISTER MAJESTIC		2	**3,494**
Mistic Glen (IRE) 4 b.f	h95	2	3,494 20m 22g
MISWAKI (USA)		4	**6,494**
Court Circular 4 b.c	h107	4	6,494 a16g a20g a16g 17f
MONKSFIELD		6	**13,813**
Bishop's Tipple 7 b.g	h100	1	1,484 28d
Ghia Gneuiagh 7 b.g	h98	2	3,857 17d 24g
Lackendara 6 ch.g	h100	1	2,026 16d
Ross Venture 8 b.g	c129	1	3,340 c24m
Young Miner 7 ch.g	c89	1	3,106 c25m
MONSANTO (FR)		6	**11,386**
Calabrese 8 ch.g	c123	1	2,234 c19v
Eau d'Espoir 4 b.f	h87	1	1,830 16d
Just Cracker 8 ch.g	h91	3	4,482 17s 26d 17g
Uncle Mogy 7 ch.g	c93	1	2,840 c18g
MONSIEURE EDOUARDE		2	**27,152**
Mister Ed 10 ch.g	c127	2	27,152 c27m c34d

MONTEKIN		**1**	**2,126**	
Monaru 7 b.g	h121	1	2,126	26s
MONTELIMAR (USA)		**5**	**40,831**	
Martomick 6 br.m	h122	1	2,233	22f
Montelado 6 b.g	h150	1	30,014	17m
Pims Gunner (IRE) 5 b.g	c101	2	6,966	c20m c20m
Smiling Chief (IRE) 5 ch.g	h92	1	1,618	16d
MORGANS CHOICE		**1**	**1,788**	
Morgans Man 4 b.c	h91	1	1,788	17g
MOUKTAR		**3**	**5,433**	
Bakhtaran 6 b.g	h122	2	3,480	18m 16g
Kaytak (FR) 6 b.g	h110	1	1,953	16g
MOVE OFF		**2**	**5,517**	
Stormhead 5 ch.g	h108	2	5,517	17v 17s
MR FLUOROCARBON		**4**	**12,461**	
Carbonate 8 b.g	c111	3	9,383	c16g c16v c16s
Momser 7 ch.g	h111	1	3,078	20m
MUFRIJ		**1**	**1,688**	
Dancing Holly 6 br.g	h93	1	1,688	20d
MUMMY'S GAME		**6**	**12,074**	
Prime Mover 5 b.g	h74	1	1,900	16m
Sheer Jest 8 b.g	c117	5	10,174	c24g c24g c25m c22m c17m
MUSCATITE		**3**	**6,847**	
Rupples 6 b.g	c85	1	2,827	c18d
Who's Tef (IRE) 5 b.g	h106	2	4,020	18m 17f
MUSIC BOY		**4**	**7,508**	
Elegant Friend 5 ch.g	h96	2	4,438	18d 17g
Greenwich Bambi 5 b.m	h93	1	1,475	18s
Shelly's Folly 8 b.h	h83	1	1,595	16f
MY DAD TOM (USA)		**1**	**1,599**	
Head Turner 5 b.m	h74	1	1,599	17g
NAIN BLEU (FR)		**2**	**4,328**	
Salman (USA) 7 b.g	h105	2	4,328	17g 17g
NATIONAL TRUST		**7**	**18,961**	
Guiburn's Nephew 11 ch.g	c125	3	13,252	c21v c20f c16g
Teaplanter 10 b.g	c114	2	2,695	c24g c25d
Trust The Gypsy 11 br.g	c102	2	3,014	c17g c19g
NATROUN (FR)		**3**	**3,467**	
Natral Exchange (IRE) 4 b.c	h108	3	3,467	18g*dis 17m 18s
NEARLY A HAND		**11**	**41,375**	
Beech Road 11 ch.g	c143	3	22,546	c21s c21g c22m
Bow Handy Man 11 ch.g	c103	1	2,406	c26s
Came Down 10 gr.g	c96	1	2,989	c17f
Glove Puppet 8 ch.g	c97	1	2,726	c25d
Little Tom 8 b.g	c92	2	5,480	c21f c19d
Mister Half-Chance 7 b.g	h109	1	2,295	22s
Never A Penny 10 b.g	c90	1	1,182	c18f
Penultimate Hand 5 ch.m		1	1,751	F18g
NEBOS (GER)		**2**	**4,990**	
Tri Folene (FR) 7 b.m	c118	2	4,990	c21d c27f

67

NELTINO   **6**   **13,518**

Lumumba Days 7 gr.g	h96	2	3,153 17m 17m
Montalino 10 gr.g	c100	1	3,012 c16g
Mr Entertainer 10 gr.g	c129	1	3,908 c20g
Neltama 9 gr.g	c94	1	2,140 c22g
Neltegrity 4 b.g	h100	1	1,305 16s

NEPOTISM   **4**   **10,585**

Major Kinsman 8 b.g	c111	4	10,585 c21s c21v c21s c21g

NETHERKELLY   **5**   **9,359**

Handsome Ned 7 br.g	h95	2	3,982 17d 18s
Highland Poacher 6 ch.g	h90	1	1,632 16s
Nicklup 6 ch.m	h94	2	3,745 22s 20s

NEVER SO BOLD   **1**   **1,305**

Bold Melody 4 b.f		1	1,305 16f

NEW BRIG   **4**   **18,351**

Bluff Knoll 10 b.g	c121	2	12,179 c28s c23d
Forth And Tay 11 b.g	c94	2	6,172 c24d c24s

NEW MEMBER   **6**   **37,612**

Country Member 8 ch.g	c143	4	32,556 c26d c24d c25s c25d
Friendly Lady 9 b.m	c96	1	3,610 c28f
Judicious Captain 6 b.g	h107	1	1,446 21d

NEWSKI (USA)   **4**   **12,633**

Its Nearly Time 10 br.g	c118	2	7,176 c16v c16v
My Skiway 10 b.g	c106	2	5,457 c24d c21g

NICHOLAS BILL   **14**   **32,328**

Bill And Coup 8 br.m	c86	1	3,074 c18m
Bill Quill 9 ch.g	c94	2	3,832 c17s c16g
Bollin William 5 b.h	h140	3	8,445 17d 17s 20s
Charmed I'm Sure 6 ch.m	h87	1	1,670 18s
One For The Pot 8 ch.g	c103	3	7,101 c16s c17d c16f
Tax The Devil 5 b.g		1	1,697 F17s
The Titan Ghost 4 ch.c	h92	1	1,581 17d
What If 9 ch.m	h98	2	4,928 16s 16v

NIELS   **2**   **5,495**

Sandstone Arch 10 b.g	c88	2	5,495 c26m c23g

NIGHT SHIFT (USA)   **3**   **5,381**

Have A Nightcap 4 ch.g	h96	2	3,407 18g a16g
Scottish Reform 6 b.g	c92	1	1,974 c21d

NIKOS   **2**   **3,580**

Slavi (FR) 5 ch.m	h110	2	3,580 17s 17s

NINISKI (USA)   **23**   **57,738**

Brave Defender 9 ch.g	c104	2	4,942 c21g c29f
Dancing River 7 b.g	c116	3	8,086 c18d c21f c21m
Fishki 7 b.m	c96	1	2,424 c25g
Jarrwah 5 ch.m	h95	2	4,283 a20g a24g
Julietski 5 gr.m	h88	3	5,557 21m 25d 23d
Kino 6 b.g	c96	1	2,218 c18g
Macedonas 5 b.h	h112	2	6,508 16s 17f
Marlin Dancer 8 b.g	h136	2	8,096 21d 22f
Nijmegen 5 b.g	h122	3	7,773 16v 16s 16d
Sandro 4 b.g	h75	2	2,220 18g 18d
Wick Pound 7 b.g	c108	2	5,631 c21d c21d

NISHAPOUR (FR)   14   44,151

Calapaez 9 gr.g	c131	3	15,149 c21v c21s c20s
For The Grain 9 b.g	c135	1	10,820 c21d
Jackson Flint 5 b.g	h96	1	1,958 20m
Kanndabil 6 gr.h	c105	1	2,604 c17d
Mandalay Prince 9 b.g	h96	3	3,434 22m 22f 24f
Nishkina 5 b.g	h91	1	2,103 18s
Propaganda 5 b.g	h108	1	2,532 17g
Silver Hello 7 gr.g	c98	1	2,890 c25m
Sovereign Niche (IRE) 5 gr.g	h79	1	1,657 17d
Wingcommander Eats 8 b.g	h95	1	1,004 16m

NOALTO   1   1,702

Golden Spinner 6 ch.g		1	1,702 F17s

NODOUBLE (USA)   1   2,042

Perfay (USA) 5 ch.h	h101	1	2,042 16s

NOIR ET OR   1   2,334

Gold Cap (FR) 8 ch.g	c111	1	2,334 c27v

NO LUTE (FR)   1   1,675

Va Lute (FR) 9 b.g	h101	1	1,675 a18g

NOMINATION   12   32,799

Bold Boss 4 b.g	h140	6	22,870 16g 17s 17d 16d 16g 16g
Dibloom 5 b.g	h91	1	1,302 16s
Nomadic Rose 4 b.f	h103	2	2,819 18g 16s
Northern Nation 5 b.g	h102	3	5,808 a16g a16g a16g

NORDANCE (USA)   5   16,099

Dancing Paddy 5 b.h	h132	3	12,973 18v*dis 17s 17d
Nordansk 4 ch.g	h87	2	3,126 16f 18f

NORDICO (USA)   5   9,291

Lyn's Return (IRE) 4 b.c	h117	5	9,291 a16g a16g a16g a16g a16g

NORTHERN BABY (CAN)   15   23,810

Al Haal (USA) 4 b.c	h86	1	1,793 a16g
Arctic Circle (IRE) 4 ch.g	h105	3	4,783 16m 17m 17g
Aremef (USA) 4 b.g	h118	2	3,350 17d 17g
Cheveley Dancer (USA) 5 b.g	h82	1	2,334 16s
Edward Seymour (USA) 6 b.g	h93	1	1,814 16s
Mabthul (USA) 5 b.g	h81	1	1,595 17f
Nornax Lad (USA) 5 b.h	h109	4	6,250 17m 20g 22f 22f
Northern Rarity (USA) 4 gr.g		2	1,891 aF16g F16g

NORTHERN GUEST (USA)   3   7,670

Night Guest 11 br.g	c104	3	7,670 c23s c23d c16g

NORTHERN TEMPEST (USA)   1   1,606

Northern Optimist 5 b.m	h86	1	1,606 20m

NORTHERN TREAT (USA)   2   9,618

Brandeston 8 b.g	c128	2	9,618 c22g c20g

NORTHERN VALUE (USA)   2   3,819

Fedneyhill 9 b.g	c85	1	1,253 c24m
Northern Meadow 12 b.g	c102	1	2,566 c26g

NORTHFIELDS (USA)   1   1,703

Solar Cloud 11 ch.g	c83	1	1,703 c21m

NORWICK (USA)   21   47,570

Hebridean 6 b.g	h138	3	11,915 17v 22s 20d
Liability Order 4 b.g	h104	2	3,469 16s 18d
Miss Marigold 4 b.f	h81	1	1,793 17m
Norstock 6 b.m	h102	3	5,309 17v 21v 16v
Northern Saddler 6 ch.g	c90:h99	3	8,874 c19g 17f 17s
Northern Village 6 ch.g	h108	1	1,811 a20g
Nortino 5 ch.g	h83	2	3,329 17s 16m
Texas Scramble 4 b.g	h99	3	4,613 17f 18d 16s
Tres Amigos 6 b.g	c103	3	6,457 c17f c26d c21m

OATS   38   97,094

Avena 6 b.m		1	1,350 F17m
Bartondale 8 br.m	c80	1	2,164 c20m
Bowl of Oats 7 ch.g	c104	3	9,979 c20v c21v c22v
Carrick Lanes 6 b.g	h103	2	3,560 20s 26g
Ceilidh Boy 7 b.g	h114	3	5,932 23g 23s 23d
Charlotte's Emma 6 b.m	h105	1	1,872 26d
Chelworth Raider 7 ch.g	h102	1	2,022 17d
Chichell's Hurst 7 ch.m	h107	1	2,075 21v
Coraco 6 br.g	h99	1	2,093 16v
Couldnt Be Better 6 br.g	h106	1	1,870 17v
Extra Grand 7 b.g	c93	2	4,526 c21g c23m
Flakey Dove 7 b.m	h153	2	19,834 21m 21f
Hidden Oats 6 ch.g	h102	1	2,234 17m
How Doudo 6 b.m	h81	1	1,814 21s
Manhattan Boy 11 b.g	h95	2	2,345 20g 17v
Mighty Frolic 6 b.m	c91	1	2,773 c24f
Oatis Regrets 5 b.g	h110	4	9,460 F16d 16d 16v 21g
Oriel Dream 6 br.m	h113	1	2,128 21s
Percy Smollett 5 br.g	h88	1	1,667 20g
Raba Riba 8 gr.g	h117	4	7,209 a22g a20g a22g a20g
River Pearl 8 b.m	h108	1	2,222 22g
Superior Finish 7 br.g	c133	3	7,965 c24v c24s c25g

OLD JOCUS   1   3,453

Comedy Road 9 br.g	c95	1	3,453 c21m

OLMETO   1   1,480

Veleda II (FR) 6 ch.g	h90	1	1,480 22f

ORANGE BAY   3   6,810

Pithy 11 ch.g	c99	2	4,907 c16s c20s
Swinhoe Croft 11 b.g	c105	1	1,903 c25s

ORCHESTRA   6   13,619

Dante's Inferno 7 ch.g	c116	4	10,054 c16d c16d c16g c21d
Philharmonic (IRE) 5 b.g		1	1,984 F16f
Snuffle Babe (IRE) 5 br.g		1	1,581 F17g

OUR MIRAGE   3   5,714

Firm Price 12 b.g	h121	3	5,714 22d 22s 20f

OUR NATIVE (USA)   1   3,200

Yorkshireman (USA) 8 ch.g	c103	1	3,200 c20d

OVAC (ITY)   5   23,613

Boston Rover 8 b.g	c109	4	12,305 c18d c17s c20m c17d
Indian Tonic 7 br.g	c110	1	11,308 c25s

OVER THE RIVER (FR)   34   146,490

Bad Trade 11 ch.g	c113	1	2,217 c20s

Ballyroe Lady 7 ch.m	c103	2	4,691	c21g c21g
Grange Brake 7 b.g	c110	3	23,705	c24g c20f c20s
In Deep Water 6 ch.m	h78	1	1,734	a22g
Into The Red 9 ch.g	c124	2	14,162	c30d c33g
Into The Trees 9 b.g	c90	2	3,584	c20s c24m
Mr Dynamic 11 b.g	c81	1	2,624	c27v
No Rebasse 11 b.g	c85	1	1,592	c26m
On The Hooch 8 ch.m	c106	1	2,918	c21m
Overheard 6 ch.g	c109	2	3,414	c24s c25g
Over The Deel 7 ch.g	c110	2	4,747	c27d c30m
Over The Stream 7 b.g	c92	1	2,862	c24f
Postman's Path 7 ch.g	c99	1	1,873	c21v
Poulstone 6 ch.g		1	1,732	F18s
River Fly 8 ch.g	c90	1	2,120	c21f
River House 11 ch.g	c105	3	12,796	c23d c24m c22f
Spy Hill 7 b.g	c90	1	2,801	c26m
Teenage Scribbler 8 br.g	h99	1	1,954	16d
Washingtoncrossing 7 ch.g	c117	3	8,937	c21v c21v c20g
Zeta's Lad 10 ch.g	c149	4	46,027	c23v c24d c24d c24g

PADDY'S STREAM
		13	32,059	
Banbridge 10 ch.g	c124	1	2,192	c16g
Emsee-H 8 br.g	c123	4	14,180	c17g c21d c16s c16g
Jock's Burn 7 ch.g	h91	2	3,341	21d 20g
L'Uomo Piu 9 b.g	c92	1	2,063	c16m
Meldon 6 b.g	h81	1	1,480	25d
Paddysway 6 b.g	h96	3	7,799	22v 24f 22m
Padrigal 10 ch.m	c94	1	1,004	c25d

PAICO
| | | 1 | 2,196 | |
| Le Chat Noir 10 br.g | c118 | 1 | 2,196 | c21s |

PALM TRACK
		5	9,049	
Handy Dove 6 b.m	h89	3	4,099	22f 16g 17g
Palm Reader 9 b.g	c127	2	4,950	c21m c21m

PAMPABIRD
| | | 1 | 2,658 | |
| Imperial Flight 8 b.g | h95 | 1 | 2,658 | 16g |

PARASANG
| | | 1 | 2,192 | |
| Impany 14 br.g | c82 | 1 | 2,192 | c16m |

PAS DE SEUL
| | | 2 | 5,795 | |
| Chain Shot 8 b.g | c107 | 2 | 5,795 | c18m c16d |

PATCH
		2	5,574	
Mountain Cabin 11 ch.g	c81	1	2,626	c25g
Tartan Tailor 12 b.g	c116	1	2,948	c21g

PAUPER
| | | 2 | 5,609 | |
| Clonroche Driller 8 b.g | c97 | 2 | 5,609 | c21g c21s |

PEACOCK (FR)
| | | 1 | 2,762 | |
| Four Trix 12 gr.g | c121 | 1 | 2,762 | c25m |

PENNINE WALK
		4	8,170	
Ambassador Royale (IRE) 5 gr.g	h88	2	2,823	16d 18m
Cooley's Valve (IRE) 5 b.g	h116	1	2,553	17g
Jurz (IRE) 5 b.h	h117	1	2,794	16m

PERSIAN BOLD
		12	45,484	
Arabian Bold (IRE) 5 br.g	h131	2	4,277	16f 16m
General Pershing 7 br.g	c144	6	29,260	c20g c25d c20d c21d c25s c24v

Persian House 6 ch.g	c114	2	7,950	c18g c21g
Sand-Dollar 10 ch.g	h122	1	2,327	20f
Schweppes Tonic 7 br.g	h97	1	1,670	20v

PETERHOF (USA)   1   **1,749**
| Banana Cufflinks (USA) 7 b.g | h84 | 1 | 1,749 | 18m |

PETITIONER   3   **7,269**
| Algari 6 b.g | c98 | 3 | 7,269 | c17m c20f c18v |

PETIT MONTMORENCY (USA)   3   **7,077**
| As du Trefle (FR) 5 ch.g | h124 | 3 | 7,077 | 16v 22s 20d |

PETONG   1   **1,548**
| Bighayir 6 gr.g | h103 | 1 | 1,548 | 20d |

PETORIUS   5   **10,816**
| Admiralty Way 7 b.g | h118 | 3 | 6,310 | a16g 17d 17g |
| Corrin Hill 6 b.g | h128 | 2 | 4,506 | 17s 18s |

PETOSKI   4   **6,937**
Cheeky Pot 5 b.g	h90	2	3,377	18s 20m
Nowhiski 5 b.h	h81	1	1,730	18s
Petosku 5 b.g	h129	1	1,830	25g

PHARDANTE (FR)   4   **6,705**
Bell Staffboy (IRE) 4 b.g		1	1,795	F17g
Capiche (IRE) 4 b.g		1	1,182	F16g
John Naman (IRE) 4 b.g	h82	1	1,914	16d
Phargold (IRE) 4 ch.g	h74	1	1,814	17m

PHARLY (FR)   5   **8,571**
| Charly Pharly (FR) 6 b.g | h97 | 2 | 3,239 | 17m 18f |
| Pharly Story 5 b.h | h117 | 3 | 5,332 | 18g 17f 16d |

PIAFFER (USA)   8   **21,315**
Fred Splendid 10 b.g	c94	3	7,829	c17v c16v c17s
Lapiaffe 9 b.g	c94	2	4,192	c23f c20g
Northern Jinks 10 b.m	c115	3	9,294	c16v c18d c16s

PIPERHILL   1   **2,411**
| Royal Piper (NZ) 6 br.g | h111 | 1 | 2,411 | 16v |

PITPAN   7   **10,963**
Heathview 6 b.g	h87	1	1,822	18g
No Escort 9 b.g	c111	2	3,583	c22g c26m
Pantechnicon 13 b.g	c88	1	1,684	c18g
Precis 5 b.m	h90	1	1,776	17s
Tartan Trix 10 b.g	c111	2	2,098	c24v c26d

PITSKELLY   1   **1,305**
| Le Pelley's Isle 6 b.g | h79 | 1 | 1,305 | 16v |

POLITICO (USA)   8   **47,297**
Benghazi 9 b.g	h108	1	2,416	27d
Captain Frisk 10 bl.g	c114	2	9,896	c25d c26d
Gala Water 7 ch.m	c83	1	2,326	c25v
Party Politics 9 br.g	c156	1	27,018	c29d
Pollibrig 9 br.m	c82	2	2,847	c25g c22g
Traprain Law 10 b.g	c101	1	2,794	c24g

POLLERTON   15   **32,244**
| Dark Dawn 9 b.g | c116 | 3 | 5,314 | c21g c21v c23g |
| Master William 9 b.g | h87 | 1 | 1,024 | 24g |

Mutual Trust 9 ch.g	c110	5	14,735 c25d c21g c21v c21m c22m
Owen 9 b.g	c92	2	3,975 c21g c21g
Pollerton's Pride 6 b.m	h95	2	2,881 16d 23d
Programmed To Win 6 b.g	h110	2	4,315 20g 21s
PONGEE		4	**11,136**
West Ender 10 gr.g	c113	4	11,136 c25g c24g c25s c21s
PONY EXPRESS		5	**18,690**
News Review 10 b.g	c98	1	2,998 c24d
Smartie Express 11 b.g	c118	4	15,692 c21m c21m c20f c20s
PORTO BELLO		1	**2,265**
Ringmore 11 ch.g	c88	1	2,265 c16s
POSSE (USA)		1	**2,327**
Sheriff's Band 6 ch.g	c84	1	2,327 c25g
POTENT COUNCILLOR		3	**3,924**
Ellerton Hill 10 br.g	c102	3	3,924 c21g c24m c25m
PRAGMATIC		4	**16,547**
Dagaz 7 b.g	h115	1	2,783 24d
Pragada 10 b.g	h160	1	9,380 24v
Renagown 10 b.g	c104	1	1,590 c21m
Super Sense 8 b.g	h145	1	2,794 21s
PRECOCIOUS		3	**5,601**
Arany 6 b.g	h93	1	2,323 16d
Careless Lad 7 ch.g	h102	1	809 18f
Scarlet Express 6 b.g	h99	1	2,469 17s
PRIMO DOMINIE		3	**4,823**
Lake Dominion 4 b.g	h89	1	1,690 a16g
Prima Aurora 5 br.m	h79	1	1,506 a21g
Smiles Ahead 5 ch.g	h97	1	1,627 16d
PRINCE BEE		6	**16,122**
Babcock Boy 8 b.g	h100	2	4,524 23d 23m
Fighting Words 7 ch.g	c122	3	10,206 c16m c16g c21g
My New Best Friend 9 b.g	h108	1	1,392 21f
PRINCE OF PEACE		2	**5,650**
Jailbreaker 6 ch.g	c107	2	5,650 c17s c27v
PRINCE REGENT (FR)		6	**39,214**
Barkisland 9 b.g	c91	2	3,962 c16d c20g
Regent Lad 9 b.g	h100	1	1,305 17d
Remittance Man 9 b.g	c163	2	26,767 c21d c21s
Tinryland 9 b.g	c141	1	7,180 c17m
PRINCES GATE		1	**1,480**
Martell Boy (NZ) 6 b.g	h104	1	1,480 24s
PRINCE TENDERFOOT (USA)		5	**9,452**
Caithness Prince 7 b.g	h88	1	2,010 17d
Colway Prince (IRE) 5 b.g	h80	2	3,725 16d 16s
Lady Llanfair 7 b.m	c93	1	2,153 c21m
Shoehorn 6 br.g	h98	1	1,564 16f
PRINCE VANDEZEE		1	**937**
Serphil 5 ch.g	h80	1	937 21v
PROCIDA (USA)		1	**1,305**
Miss Hyde (USA) 4 br.f	h94	1	1,305 16g

73

PROVERB		**13**	**94,054**	
Almanzora 9 ch.g	h93	1	1,480	17g
Ask For More 8 b.g	h98	1	1,484	23s
On The Other Hand 10 b.g	c125	1	4,873	c25f
Otterburn House 9 b.g	c123	2	7,309	c26d c24s
Proplus 11 ch.g	c107	3	7,352	c25g c25s c24f
Rockmount Rose 8 b.m	c82	1	2,023	c21f
Topsham Bay 10 b.g	c148	2	62,416	c27f c30d
Truth Be Told 9 ch.g	h125	1	3,517	22s
Western Legend 9 ch.g	c115	1	3,600	c21g
PRY		**4**	**9,512**	
Pry's-Joy 9 b.g	c96	3	7,127	c24f c24g c21v
Starlap 9 b.g	c94	1	2,385	c17m
QUAYSIDE		**2**	**4,559**	
Regardless 11 b.g	c100	1	2,369	c24g
Spirit of Kibris 8 ch.g	h104	1	2,190	16s
RABDAN		**1**	**2,355**	
It's Varadan 9 ch.h	h100	1	2,355	17d
RADICAL		**2**	**3,672**	
Radical Views 8 b.g	c120	2	3,672	c21s c24d
RAGAPAN		**4**	**9,186**	
Dr Rocket 8 b.g	c113	3	8,080	c16v c17g c17v
Hiram B Birdbath 7 b.g	c95	1	1,106	c21g
RAINBOW QUEST (USA)		**3**	**6,621**	
Indian Quest 4 b.g	h130	2	4,276	16s 16v
Tactical Mission (IRE) 5 b.g	h103	1	2,345	20g
RAISE A CUP (USA)		**1**	**1,861**	
Druso (USA) 9 b.g	h83	1	1,861	a24g
RAISE YOU TEN		**2**	**14,647**	
Twin Oaks 13 br.g	c157	2	14,647	c29s c24d
RAISINGELLE (USA)		**3**	**6,594**	
Terrible Gel (FR) 8 b.g	c102	3	6,594	c16s c17d c17s
RANDOM SHOT		**7**	**26,497**	
Beech Grove 12 b.g	c90	1	2,268	c26m
Jinxy Jack 9 b.g	h155	5	22,973	17m 16g 16d 16v 17d
Random Place 11 ch.g	c85	1	1,256	c26m
RANKSBOROUGH		**1**	**1,480**	
Gabriella Mia 8 b.m	h102	1	1,480	24v
RAPID RIVER		**1**	**1,646**	
Riverboat Queen 10 br.m	c86	1	1,646	c25g
RARE ONE		**1**	**1,467**	
Jack The Hiker 10 b.g	c86	1	1,467	c17s
RARITY		**1**	**2,138**	
Rare Fire 9 ro.g	c90	1	2,138	c17d
R B CHESNE		**4**	**24,149**	
Sun Surfer (FR) 5 ch.g	h127	4	24,149	16d 17d 21s 17v
REACH		**1**	**1,954**	
Master Reach 4 br.g	h99	1	1,954	17f

REASONABLE (FR)		2	3,216	
Classics Pearl (IRE) 5 gr.m	h84	2	3,216	17d 20s
REBEL PRINCE		1	4,386	
Mighty Mark 14 b.g	c105	1	4,386	c25m
RECORD TOKEN		2	3,992	
Donna's Token 8 br.m	h94	2	3,992	16m 18f
RED JOHNNIE		4	9,870	
Johnsted 7 ch.g	h94	4	9,870	a16g 21g a18g 17d
RED SUNSET		6	11,455	
Corinthian God (IRE) 4 b.c	h84	1	1,705	18g
Dyflin 7 b.g	c100	1	2,176	c16f
Emerald Sunset 8 b.g	h115	1	3,704	25g
It's Not My Fault (IRE) 5 b.g	h79	1	943	22s
Red Jack (IRE) 4 b.g	h96	1	1,564	16s
Sunset Rock 6 b.g	h93	1	1,363	16d
REFERENCE POINT		1	1,924	
Alum Bay 4 b.g	h91	1	1,924	16d
REFORMED CHARACTER		2	12,653	
Welknown Character 11 b.g	c119	2	12,653	c21g c25d
REGAL AND ROYAL (USA)		1	2,047	
Old Road (USA) 7 b.g	c90	1	2,047	c16v
RELKINO		10	28,331	
Arctic Kinsman 5 gr.g		1	2,400	F17d
Cherrykino 8 b.g	c145	4	14,816	c21s c21d c20v c21d
Connaught Crusader 5 b.g		1	2,400	F17d
Flight Hill 9 br.g	c127	1	2,820	c21g
Herlin 5 b.g		1	1,206	F17g
Miramac 12 br.g	h93	1	1,806	27d
Silverino 7 gr.g	c92	1	2,883	c24v
REMAINDER MAN		5	9,877	
One Man (IRE) 5 gr.g	h126	3	5,017	20m 22s 20d
Strong Views 6 b.g	h109	2	4,860	17g 18d
RHODOMANTADE		1	3,028	
Under Offer 12 br.g	c90	1	3,028	c26v
RIBOBOY (USA)		2	4,269	
Rampallion 10 b.g	c94	1	2,559	c17g
Ribovino 10 b.g	h88	1	1,710	22d
RISK ME (FR)		4	7,388	
Aedean 4 ch.g	h94	1	1,302	17d
Daily Sport Girl 4 b.f	h81	1	1,480	17g
Personal Hazard 4 ch.g	h104	2	4,606	16s 16s
RIVERMAN (USA)		4	6,563	
Al Sahil (USA) 8 b.g	h92	1	1,810	22s
Cavo Greco (USA) 4 b.g	h85	1	2,059	17d
Lock Keeper (USA) 7 b.g	h77	1	1,214	16g
Soothfast (USA) 4 b.g	h95	1	1,480	16v
ROBELLINO (USA)		6	10,482	
Fluidity (USA) 5 b.g	h89	3	5,157	a16g 17f 16f
Maamur (USA) 5 gr.g	h128	1	1,302	20g
Prosequendo (USA) 6 b.g	h107	2	4,023	16s 17v

ROBERTO (USA)   7   24,206

Ambuscade (USA) 7 ch.g	h149	1	3,436 25g
Cambo (USA) 7 b.g	h95	2	4,358 16d 22d
Lemon's Mill (USA) 4 b.f	h132	3	15,107 16d 16g 20f
Midday Show (USA) 6 b.h	h92	1	1,305 18g

ROI DAGOBERT (FR)   1   2,112

Dagobertin (FR) 7 ch.g	c119	1	2,112 c19v

ROI GUILLAUME (FR)   3   6,581

Colour Cost (IRE) 5 b.g	h87	1	2,038 17s
Willie Sparkle 7 b.g	h115	2	4,543 16d 20g

ROLFE (USA)   8   17,590

Father Ralph 7 ch.g	h89	1	1,485 16s
Leading Role 9 ch.g	h95	1	1,866 22d
Peatswood 5 ch.h	h130	1	2,058 21s
Rope 7 b.g	h98	2	3,442 a16g a21g
Shaston 8 ch.g	c104	2	5,841 c26v c26g
Uncle Eli 10 br.g	c123	1	2,898 c21g

ROMAN WARRIOR   4   8,867

Jomana 7 ch.m	c90	2	4,120 c18m c16g
Warner For Winners 7 b.g	c91	2	4,747 c26g c21f

RONTINO   3   5,958

Thistle Monarch 8 b.g	h118	3	5,958 17s 25s 22g

ROSCOE BLAKE   10   57,859

Docklands Express 11 b.g	c165	3	40,547 c25f c26m c22g
Goodshot Rich 9 b.g	c115	2	6,733 c27s c24v
Lady Token 9 b.m	c94	1	2,761 c26g
Marra's Roscoe 7 b.g	h101	2	3,446 25d 28g
Old Brig 7 br.g	h99	1	1,772 22g
Roscoe Harvey 11 br.g	c108	1	2,600 c19d

ROSELIER (FR)   9   23,673

Inconclusive 6 b.g	c86	1	2,924 c21d
Lucky Villain 8 b.g	c87	1	2,179 c24s
Moorcroft Boy 8 ch.g	c117	2	4,721 c25d c24g
Mr Pickpocket (IRE) 5 b.g		1	2,219 F16v
Royal Athlete 10 ch.g	h129	1	3,940 23s
Smith Too (IRE) 5 br.g	h102	1	1,480 24g
Stay On Tracks 11 gr.g	c118	1	5,248 c24d
Tryumphant Lad 9 gr.g	c99	1	962 c26f

ROUSER   2   5,846

Grenagh 12 ch.g	h121	2	5,846 24v 24d

ROUSILLON (USA)   9   15,776

Miliyel 4 ch.f	h97	3	5,952 16g 18g 17g
Millrous 5 b.m	h86	3	4,469 16v 20d 16m
Quadrireme 4 b.g	h123	3	5,355 16f 17m 16m

ROYAL BOXER   1   1,576

Opal's Tenspot 6 b.g	h88	1	1,576 18m

ROYAL FOUNTAIN   7   19,221

Here Comes Tibby 6 b.m	h84	1	1,564 16v
Larksmore 8 br.m	c98	1	4,570 c22v
Mr Setaside 8 br.g	c107	2	5,378 c26v c24s
Norman Conqueror 8 br.g	c117	1	3,395 c25d
Royal Jester 9 b.g	c89	1	2,088 c25s

Truely Royal 9 b.g	c94	1	2,226 c26g
ROYAL MATCH		**3**	**12,492**
Gambling Royal 10 ch.g	c138	1	7,293 c24s
Prize Match 4 ch.f	h89	1	1,446 17v
Simpson 8 ch.g	h136	1	3,753 25g
ROYAL PALACE		**6**	**14,035**
Palanquin 11 ch.g	h102	2	5,153 24m 25m
Regal Estate 9 ch.g	c104	3	7,402 c27g c26s c27d
Setai's Palace 6 b.m	h94	1	1,480 22g
ROYAL VULCAN		**1**	**2,490**
Rovulenka 5 b.g	h107	1	2,490 16s
RUGANTINO		**1**	**2,892**
Grey Tornado 12 gr.g	c89	1	2,892 c24g
RUNNETT		**3**	**3,703**
Copy Lane (IRE) 4 b.g	h103	3	3,703 17g 17g 18g
RUSHMERE		**2**	**17,410**
Rushing Wild 8 b.g	c172	2	17,410 c26d c30s
RUSTICARO (FR)		**7**	**15,946**
Donosti 9 b.g	h103	2	3,301 a16g a16g
Station Express (IRE) 5 b.g	h78	3	6,541 18d 16g 22m
Tara Boy 8 b.g	c84	1	1,864 c21m
Up-A-Point 8 gr.g	c105	1	4,240 c17v
RUSTINGO		**3**	**5,780**
Goldingo 6 ch.g	h98	2	4,250 17s 17v
Rusty Roc 12 b.g	h104	1	1,530 17g
RYMER		**3**	**9,698**
Dublin Flyer 7 b.g	c118	2	7,044 c24g c26d
Wellwotdouthink 7 b.m	h92	1	2,654 16g
SADLER'S WELLS (USA)		**3**	**7,223**
Rainham 6 b.g	h89	1	2,285 17d
Viardot (IRE) 4 b.c	h123	2	4,938 17s 17s
SAGARO		**2**	**4,074**
Hey Rawley 8 b.g	c96	1	2,924 c21d
Master Muck 10 b.g	c96	1	1,150 c22m
SAINT CYRIEN (FR)		**6**	**18,700**
Cultured 4 b.g	h116	2	3,924 16v 17s
Cyphrate (USA) 7 b.g	c147	1	10,143 c16s
Gold Medal (FR) 5 gr.g	h113	3	4,633 18h 17s 21s
SALLUCEVA		**3**	**10,800**
Boraceva 10 b.g	c137	3	10,800 c29g c24d c25d
SALLUST		**2**	**4,006**
Lustreman 6 ch.g	h93	1	1,564 17g
Marquee Cafe 9 ch.g	h95	1	2,442 22m
SALMON LEAP (USA)		**3**	**12,023**
Kilcash (IRE) 5 b.g	h139	2	10,543 17s 17d
Salmonid 7 ch.g	h92	1	1,480 17g
SANDALAY		**7**	**31,306**
Once Stung 7 br.g	c116	4	10,214 c24f c25g c25d c26g
Tipp Mariner 8 ch.g	c95	1	3,080 c26d

Ushers Island 7 br.g	c113	2	18,012	c32m c25f
SANDHURST PRINCE		5	11,678	
Taylors Prince 6 ch.g	h91	1	2,303	16g
Vain Prince 6 b.h	c113	4	9,375	c17f c17m c18s c16s
SAXON FARM		3	7,133	
Desperate 5 ch.g	h116	3	7,133	21s 24g 27g
SAYF EL ARAB (USA)		1	1,302	
Come Home Alone 5 ch.g	h89	1	1,302	22d
SAY PRIMULA		4	6,272	
Chantry Bartle 7 ch.g	h108	2	3,784	17m 17s
Ess El Ar 5 b.m		1	828	aF16g
If You Say So 7 ch.g	h85	1	1,660	23g
SAYYAF		1	1,756	
Sayant 8 b.g	h91	1	1,756	17m
SCALLYWAG		13	31,641	
Better Times Ahead 7 ro.g	c117	3	7,649	c25s c21s c26d
Comedy Spy 9 gr.g	h99	1	1,805	25v
Coole Dodger 8 gr.g	c105	1	4,208	c26f
First Crack 8 b.m	h103	1	1,812	23d
Greenhill Raffles 7 ch.g	h109	2	3,660	18g 22m
Hearts Are Wild 6 ch.g	h97	1	1,737	17g
Mega Blue 8 gr.m	c106	3	9,877	c16d c17g c21g
Robins Choice 9 b.m	c88	1	893	c25m
SCORPIO (FR)		2	4,850	
Mad Casanova 8 b.g	c105	2	4,850	c18d c21v
SCOTTISH REEL		12	19,461	
Baby Wizzard 4 b.f	h82	1	1,475	17f
Charmonix 4 ch.f	h78	1	1,305	17d
Highland Spirit 5 ch.m	h119	10	16,681	20g 17g 19m 20g 16m 18d 20f 20m 20g 21f
SEA ANCHOR		2	3,759	
Olveston (NZ) 9 b.g	h114	2	3,759	16v F13m
SECRETO (USA)		10	36,171	
Duke of Monmouth (USA) 5 b.g	c112	2	4,479	c17g c17g
So Discreet (USA) 5 b.g	h93	3	4,673	19h 17m 22s
Staunch Friend (USA) 5 b.g	h164	4	24,750	17g 17d 17s 16g
Thunder Bug (USA) 5 ch.m	h90	1	2,269	17m
SENSITIVE PRINCE (USA)		2	5,784	
Love Anew (USA) 8 b.g	c97	2	5,784	c22g c22g
SEXTON BLAKE		13	24,027	
Fiery Sun 8 b.g	h111	2	3,726	a18g 18m
Nathan Blake 8 gr.g	c99	2	4,419	c26g c24f
The Black Monk (IRE) 5 ch.g	h125	9	15,882	18m 18f 22g 16s 21v 18s 21s 22m 20g
SEYMOUR HICKS (FR)		1	2,074	
Saymore 7 ch.g	h98	1	2,074	17g
SHAAB		6	28,442	
Boscean Chieftain 9 b.g	h140	4	25,164	25s 22d 21d 24f
The Mine Captain 6 b.g		2	3,278	aF16g aF16g

SHADEED (USA)		1	**1,484**
Trust Deed (USA) 5 ch.g	h77	1	1,484 a24g
SHARDARI		5	**9,013**
Badastan (IRE) 4 b.c	h101	1	1,484 22d
Dari Sound (IRE) 5 b.g	h113	1	2,611 22m
Nocatchim 4 b.g	h118	3	4,918 16d 17d 16f
SHAREEF DANCER (USA)		3	**16,056**
Atlaal 8 b.g	c137	1	9,990 c16d
Kadi (GER) 4 b.g	h125	2	6,066 17v 17g
SHARPO		7	**15,090**
Persuasive 6 b.m	h127	3	7,411 16s 16g 17s
Sharpgun (FR) 7 ch.g	h95	1	2,303 17s
Sharp Top 5 b.m	h84	1	1,723 17d
Stylus 4 ch.g	h117	2	3,653 16s 17d
SHARROOD (USA)		7	**17,519**
Brambleberry 4 gr.c	h100	1	2,040 16s
Desert Mist 4 gr.f	h110	5	13,999 17m 17g 16g 24d 26m
Sharriba 4 gr.f	h123	1	1,480 17d
SHEER GRIT		4	**11,558**
Charlton Yeoman 8 b.g	c90	1	1,714 c21f
Clay County 8 b.g	c138	3	9,844 c17g c17d c16g
SHERNAZAR		6	**12,394**
Enfant du Paradis (IRE) 5 b.m	h79	2	3,586 16g 17g
Officer Cadet 6 b.g	h100	1	2,553 26d
Sohrab (IRE) 5 ch.g	h107	1	2,166 16d
Tronchetto (IRE) 4 b.g	h103	2	4,089 22m 22m
SHIRLEY HEIGHTS		8	**13,157**
Antiguan Flyer 4 b.c	h89	1	1,484 a16g
Doradus 5 br.g	h98	2	3,569 18g 18g
Heliopsis 5 b.g	h113	2	2,734 24d 21s
Military Honour 8 b.g	c84	1	1,155 c17v
Ratify 6 br.g	h101	1	2,735 17g
Sea Patrol 6 b.g	h88	1	1,480 22f
SHOW-A-LEG		3	**8,493**
Rafiki 8 br.g	c98	3	8,493 c16v c18g c26m
SHRIVENHAM		1	**2,120**
Master South Lad 9 b.g	c94	1	2,120 c18f
SHY GROOM (USA)		1	**1,700**
Reluctant Suitor 4 ch.g		1	1,700 F16m
SHY RAMBLER (USA)		1	**4,163**
Rocktor (NZ) 8 b.g	c122	1	4,163 c24m
SIBERIAN EXPRESS (USA)		5	**16,430**
Amazon Express 4 b.c	h137	2	11,704 17g 16g
Chill Wind 4 gr.c	h86	2	2,896 17m 17m
Siberian Breeze 5 gr.g	h82	1	1,830 17g
SIDE TRACK		1	**2,039**
Friskney Dale Lad 8 b.g	c101	1	2,039 c21m
SILVER HAWK (USA)		6	**12,723**
Grand Hawk (USA) 5 b.g	h133	5	11,200 18d 16s 20s 21v 21g
Silver Age (USA) 7 b.h	h101	1	1,523 17d

79

SILVER SEASON		1	1,712
Linngate 4 b.f		1	1,712 F16d
SIMPLY GREAT (FR)		3	6,695
Caromandoo (IRE) 5 b.g	h92	1	2,208 18m
Fly For Gold (IRE) 4 b.f	h88	1	1,644 16s
Sea Buck 7 b.g	h112	1	2,843 22g
SIR IVOR		6	12,704
Hudson Bay Trader (USA) 6 b.g	h125	4	8,023 20g 20s 20s 22s
Staunch Rival (USA) 6 b.g	h114	2	4,681 22d 23s
SIR MAGO		1	1,672
Lord Purna 11 ch.g	c105	1	1,672 c25m
SIT IN THE CORNER (USA)		4	11,282
Amari King 9 b.g	c124	1	3,968 c21g
Mulbank 7 b.g	c105	1	2,445 c17s
Playpen 9 b.g	c101	2	4,869 c27d c21v
SIZZLING MELODY		5	8,205
Tudor Da Samba 4 b.g	h113	5	8,205 17s 16s 18g 17m 21s
SLEW O' GOLD (USA)		2	5,651
Cariboo Gold (USA) 4 b.c	h128	2	5,651 16d 17g
SLIP ANCHOR		2	3,536
Moving Out 5 b.g	h96	2	3,536 17d 16m
SLIPPERED		1	1,576
Many A Slip 8 ch.g	c106	1	1,576 c27d
SMOOTH STEPPER		1	2,374
Super Spell 7 ch.g	h108	1	2,374 17s
SOLFORD (USA)		4	8,600
Able Player (USA) 6 b.g	h123	4	8,600 16d 16m 16g 20g
SOLO DANCER (GER)		1	2,758
Sagaman (GER) 7 b.g	h126	1	2,758 17g
SONG		1	2,008
Recording Contract 5 b.g	h82	1	2,008 17g
SONNEN GOLD		4	6,384
Cheap Metal 8 br.g	h85	1	788 20m
Titus Gold 8 b.g	h107	1	1,574 16s
Toogood To Be True 5 br.g	h99	2	4,022 16s 18d
SOUGHAAN (USA)		1	2,026
Fired Earth (IRE) 5 b.g	h95	1	2,026 16s
SOUTHERN MUSIC		3	5,862
Simple Arithmetic 5 ch.g		1	1,679 F16v
The Green Fool 6 ch.g	h113	2	4,183 20m 18d
SPACE KING		4	38,950
King of The Lot 10 br.g	c141	2	9,121 c16g c16d
Space Fair 10 b.g	c143	2	29,829 c17m c17m
SPANISH PLACE (USA)		1	1,702
Spanish Fair (IRE) 5 b.g	h93	1	1,702 17m
SPARKLING BOY		1	1,705
Greenhills Pride 9 b.g	h84	1	1,705 a20g

SPARTAN JESTER		1	2,295	
Little Lemon 9 b.m	c78	1	2,295	c27d
SPECTACULAR BID (USA)		1	1,473	
Spectacular Dawn 4 gr.f	h109	1	1,473	16s
SPEND A BUCK (USA)		4	8,206	
Doolar (USA) 6 b.g	h118	2	5,231	16d 21f
River Island (USA) 5 b.g	h116	2	2,975	17s 17d
SPIN OF A COIN		3	19,908	
Roll A Dollar 7 b.g	h136	3	19,908	17g 16g 17f
SPUR ON		2	5,182	
Black Spur 11 br.g	c101	2	5,182	c21s c16s
STALKER		6	13,124	
Sillars Stalker (IRE) 5 b.g	h132	3	8,067	21d 22d 20d
Ste-Jen (IRE) 4 b.g	h106	3	5,057	18g 16s 16s
STANFORD		1	3,707	
Damers Cavalry 10 b.g	c115	1	3,707	c26m
STAR APPEAL		3	5,269	
Hand In Glove 7 b.g	h80	1	1,305	17d
Space Captain 6 b.g	h100	1	1,604	18g
Warleggan 12 br.g	c112	1	2,360	c26g
STARCH REDUCED		2	4,051	
Super Ritchart 5 b.g	h108	2	4,051	23s 16s
STAR DE NASKRA (USA)		1	1,484	
Thunderbird One (USA) 4 b.g	h88	1	1,484	a16g
ST COLUMBUS		5	9,301	
Rio Haina 8 ch.g	c109	1	3,716	c26d
Tenesaint 12 ch.g	c112	3	4,381	c25g c25g c25v
The Malakarma 7 b.g	c108	1	1,204	c24g
STEP TOGETHER (USA)		2	7,631	
Stepfaster 8 gr.m	c104	2	7,631	c20g c23m
STORM BIRD (CAN)		5	8,765	
Battle Standard (CAN) 6 b.g	h90	2	2,588	16m 17d
Cardinal Bird (USA) 6 b.g	h91	2	4,428	16v 16v
Wingspan (USA) 9 b.g	c147	1	1,749	c16s
STRONG GALE		96	479,455	
Air Commander 8 br.g	c96	4	9,544	c17m c18m c20f c20f
Around The Horn 6 b.g	c99	2	4,802	c16g c16s
Blustery Fellow 8 b.g	c104	1	2,636	c16g
Cab On Target 7 br.g	c154	5	47,555	c20g c22s c20d c25f c20g
Charming Gale 6 b.m	c93	3	7,768	c23g c23d c24m
Chief Raider (IRE) 5 br.g	h95	1	1,311	21d
Chip And Run 7 b.g	c110	1	1,724	c21g
Ebony Gale 7 br.g	h115	1	2,784	22v
Edberg 9 b.g	c132	1	3,488	c21d
Emerald Storm 6 br.g	h93	1	1,302	16s
Fragrant Dawn 9 br.g	c134	2	7,587	c17d c17f
Gaelstrom 6 b.m	h135	5	41,036	17g 21s 21d 26d 21m
Gale Again 6 br.g	c137	4	20,074	c21m c17s c20s c20d
Glemot (IRE) 5 br.g	h77	1	1,996	17s
Heathfield Gale 6 b.m	h106	2	10,355	F17g 21g
Katabatic 10 br.g	c161	2	43,701	c16g c16s

81

Killula Chief 6 b.g	h99	1	2,271	17g
Knayton Prospect 5 br.g	h97	1	1,746	20m
Letterfore 6 br.m	c103	2	4,697	c21s c24v
Lusty Light 7 b.g	h104	2	3,275	16d 22d
Mailcom 7 b.g	h119	2	5,559	22g 21f
Man O Mine (IRE) 4 b.g		1	1,602	F16m
Montagnard 9 b.g	h119	1	5,768	25d
Mythical Storm 6 b.m	h96	1	1,484	18d
Night Wind 6 b.g	h94	1	1,480	17d
No Grandad 9 br.m	c103	3	10,151	c26s c24s c27d
Peace Officer 7 br.g	c114	1	4,202	c19d
Rocket Launcher 7 b.g	c106	2	5,843	c16v c20f
Sibton Abbey 8 b.g	c161	4	53,639	c21g c25v c27s c26s
Storm Alert 7 b.g	c143	6	21,287	c18m c16d c16d c16s c17s c16d
Strong Approach 8 br.g	c113	1	2,762	c16d
Strong Beau 8 br.g	c123	2	20,031	c22d c25m
Strong Medicine 6 b.g	h109	3	5,041	16f 22f 23f
Strong Sound 6 b.g	c95	1	1,714	c21d
Tartan Tradewinds 6 b.g	h98	1	2,262	21m
Touch of Winter 7 b.g	h99	1	1,837	a20g
Travado 7 br.g	c152	4	50,918	c17g c17s c16v c16m
Travelling Wrong 7 b.g	c115	4	15,045	c24d c24s c26v c24g
Wadeley 6 br.g	h101	1	1,484	26d
Whaat Fettle 8 br.g	c123	4	11,089	c25g c25g c25g c28d
Wind Force 8 br.g	c137	7	26,220	c25m c21m c16m c21g c20g c20f c21f
Windy Ways 8 br.g	c124	1	4,143	c25g
Yorkshire Gale 7 br.g	h115	2	6,242	21s 22v
SULA BULA		**3**	**4,939**	
Just Rosie 4 b.f	h95	2	3,220	17f 18g
Philip's Woody 5 b.g	h107	1	1,719	a16g
SUNLEY BUILDS		**2**	**4,409**	
Jimmy The Gillie 7 b.g	h125	1	2,280	16d
Sunley Bay 7 gr.g	h112	1	2,129	26s
SUNOTRA		**2**	**4,614**	
Phils Pride 9 b.g	c115	2	4,614	c16s c18v
SUNYBOY		**5**	**10,796**	
Highland Son 12 b.g	c89	1	1,548	c24f
Master Jolson 5 b.g	h106	1	1,903	22g
Sonofagipsy 9 b.g	c80	1	1,448	c26g
Sunbeam Talbot 12 b.g	c113	2	5,897	c26g c28d
SUPER CONCORDE (USA)		**2**	**6,272**	
Big Beat (USA) 5 br.g	h128	2	6,272	18s 17v
SUPERLATIVE		**2**	**4,433**	
Star of Italy 6 b.g	c85	2	4,433	c16v c16v
SUPREME LEADER		**1**	**1,910**	
Capenwray (IRE) 4 br.g		1	1,910	F16d
SURE BLADE (USA)		**3**	**5,215**	
Rimouski 5 b.h	h98	1	1,784	25m
Wheeler's Wonder (IRE) 4 br.f	h109	2	3,431	16m 17s
SWEET MONDAY		**2**	**3,522**	
Easthorpe 5 b.g	h98	1	1,484	17d
Sweet City 8 ch.g	h116	1	2,038	17d

SWEET STORY		**3**	**9,257**
Nougat Russe 12 b.g	c102	3	9,257 c24d c23m c24d
SWING EASY (USA)		**3**	**14,957**
Easy Buck 6 b.g	h131	2	13,553 17d 16f
Myverygoodfriend 6 b.g	h87	1	1,404 22s
TACHYPOUS		**6**	**13,517**
Carfax 8 ch.g	h105	3	5,360 a24g a22g a24g
Heyfleet 10 b.g	c100	1	2,259 c21v
Munka 7 b.g	h96	1	3,179 17g
Sooner Still 9 b.g	c105	1	2,719 c26m
TAKACHIHO		**1**	**2,890**
Ben Tirran 9 b.g	c91	1	2,890 c21g
TAMPERO (FR)		**1**	**1,807**
Falcon Flight 7 ch.g	h101	1	1,807 a16g
TAP ON WOOD		**2**	**5,996**
Buckingham Gate 7 gr.g	c91	1	2,853 c20d
On Tap 9 ch.g	c106	1	3,143 c20d
TARRAGO (ITY)		**2**	**5,200**
Powder Boy 8 ch.g	c95	2	5,200 c24f c24g
TATE GALLERY (USA)		**1**	**1,627**
Classic Exhibit 4 b.g	h79	1	1,627 16d
TAUFAN (USA)		**8**	**17,944**
Boogie Bopper (IRE) 4 b.g	h97	2	2,741 16v 18v
Far Too Loud 6 b.g	h105	1	3,630 21f
Rabsha (IRE) 5 b.m	h77	1	1,604 16d
Seagull Hollow (IRE) 4 b.g	h103	3	7,579 16g 16s 18d
Weekday Cross (IRE) 5 b.g	h90	1	2,390 17g
TAWFIQ (USA)		**2**	**6,752**
Avonburn (NZ) 9 ch.g	c112	2	6,752 c24s c21d
TEENOSO (USA)		**9**	**20,225**
Bollin Magdalene 5 b.m	h90	1	2,233 21g
Cadency 5 b.g	h121	1	3,392 17g
Gort 5 b.g		1	1,502 F17v
Her Honour 4 b.f	h127	3	6,694 16d 17d 17m
Playing Truant 5 b.g	h95	1	1,744 16g
Sir Peter Lely 6 b.g	c100	1	2,065 c17d
Street Kid 5 b.g	h108	1	2,595 22m
TELSMOSS		**1**	**2,072**
Commanchero 6 gr.g	h75	1	2,072 21d
TEMPERENCE HILL (USA)		**1**	**1,604**
Auvillar (USA) 5 br.g	h84	1	1,604 17s
TENDER KING		**17**	**47,128**
Andrew's First 6 br.g	h127	4	25,189 22s 21g 20d 25f
Broughton's Tango (IRE) 4 b.g	h98	1	1,669 17g
Candle King (IRE) 5 b.g	h72	1	1,375 17g
Emerald Ruler 6 b.g	h104	1	1,305 16g
Hallo Mam (IRE) 4 br.f	h86	3	5,812 16f 16f 16m
It's The Pits 6 b.g	h102	2	3,101 21s 21g
Please Please Me (IRE) 5 b.m	h79	2	3,650 17m 16g
Regal Romper (IRE) 5 b.h	h96	2	3,075 16g 16d
Wee Wizard (IRE) 4 br.g	h91	1	1,952 16s

TEOFANE		1	**1,856**
Father Dowling 6 br.g	c93	1	1,856 c27d
TEPUKEI		7	**15,064**
Curaheen Boy 13 b.g	c97	2	2,932 c20f c26m
Just Frankie 9 ch.g	c106	2	3,660 c17g c16m
Palmrush 9 b.g	c103	3	8,472 c21g c21f c21f
THATCHING		6	**15,906**
Gallant Effort (IRE) 5 b.h	h107	1	1,562 20v
Major Bugler (IRE) 4 b.g	h135	2	8,886 17s 17s
Tapatch (IRE) 5 b.h	h111	3	5,458 16g 17f 17f
THATCH (USA)		1	**1,606**
Othet 9 b.g	h87	1	1,606 17g
THE MINSTREL (CAN)		6	**11,598**
Bravo Star (USA) 8 b.g	h108	2	4,102 18f 26g
Lark Rise (USA) 5 ch.g	h79	1	1,616 a20g
Mingus (USA) 6 b.g	h84	1	2,058 22m
Singing Reply (USA) 5 b.m	h78	1	1,881 18m
Zealous Kitten (USA) 5 ch.m	h104	1	1,941 17s
THE NOBLE PLAYER (USA)		2	**6,411**
Bridge Player 6 ch.m	h86	1	2,008 25d
Noble Insight 6 ch.g	h116	1	4,403 16s
THE PARSON		54	**185,285**
Abbot of Furness 9 b.g	h134	4	11,493 20g 22s 20s 21s
Artful Abbot 9 ch.g	c100:h113	2	4,263 c25g 21d
Big Ben Dun 7 b.g	c104	3	9,520 c24v c23g c24g
Bishops Island 7 b.g	c124	1	2,601 c23v
Canon Class 12 b.g	c90	1	1,534 c22d
Captain Tancred (IRE) 5 b.g	h92	2	3,762 16s 16s
Cardinal Red 6 b.g	h136	2	8,955 22s 25f
Direct 10 b.g	c116	2	8,529 c27v c29s
Fifth Amendment 8 b.g	c110	2	2,925 c21d c24g
High Padre 7 b.g	c109	3	8,875 c25d c25s c28g
Holy Foley 11 b.g	c99	2	2,534 c21s c24m
Large Action (IRE) 5 b.g		2	5,693 F17g F17d
Le Piccolage 9 b.g	c123	2	11,025 c22v c27g
Loch Scavaig (IRE) 4 b.f		1	1,786 F16s
Lo Stregone 7 b.g	h132	3	6,353 22d 22s 20v
Monsieur Le Cure 7 b.g	h123	1	1,663 17v
Mr Glen 8 ch.g	h92	1	2,850 23g
Never Forgotten 8 ch.g	h104	2	2,682 17m 18g
Pardon Me Mum 8 ch.g	h119	3	5,905 22s 22d 20d
Parsons Green 9 b.g	c133	1	3,600 c20s
Plastic Spaceage 10 b.g	c127	3	10,474 c20s c24s c27d
Queen's Chaplain 9 b.g	c92	2	2,514 c21g c25s
Red Amber 7 ch.g	c91	2	4,746 c27v c23g
Sacrosanct 9 b.g	h109	2	5,380 25s 25m
Shelton Abbey 7 br.g	h106	2	5,451 28g 25s
Shuil Ar Aghaidh 7 b.m	h157	1	43,435 25m
Sylvia Beach 7 b.m	h89	1	2,565 20m
Wont Be Gone Long 11 b.g	c128	1	4,172 c25g
THE WONDER (FR)		4	**21,896**
Just (FR) 7 b.g	h90	1	2,944 17d
Wonder Man (FR) 8 ch.g	c151	3	18,952 c16d c16s c16d

THREE LEGS		**4**	**13,442**	
Glen Lochan (NZ) 8 gr.g	h137	4	13,442	19m 21d 20d 22v
TICKLED PINK		**3**	**8,722**	
Pink Gin 6 ch.g	c98	3	8,722	c16d c20g c25g
TILDEN		**3**	**6,230**	
Faithful Star 8 b.g	c126:h97	3	6,230	c19g c18m 21s
TIMOLIN (FR)		**1**	**2,605**	
Tammy My Girl 10 ch.m	c87	1	2,605	c25d
TINA'S PET		**11**	**38,285**	
Brigtina 5 b.g	h74	1	1,601	20g
Peanuts Pet 8 b.h	h135	1	7,250	17m
Petmer 6 b.g	h82	1	1,495	17s
Satin Lover 5 ch.g	h137	6	23,906	17d 17g 17d 17v 16s 17d
Tigers Pet 9 b.g	c101	2	4,033	c21g c21f
TINOCO		**1**	**1,431**	
Oco Royal 4 b.c	h78	1	1,431	17f
TIP MOSS (FR)		**2**	**5,712**	
Merano (FR) 10 ch.g	c130	1	2,846	c24s
Tim Soldier (FR) 6 ch.g	c88	1	2,866	c21s
TOLOMEO		**1**	**2,522**	
Island Jetsetter 7 ch.g	c101	1	2,522	c16m
TOM NODDY		**1**	**1,631**	
Doubting Donna 7 gr.m	c82	1	1,631	c24s
TOM'S SHU (USA)		**5**	**10,629**	
Shu Fly (NZ) 9 ch.g	c128	2	6,372	c17g c18g
Sydney Barry (NZ) 8 b.g	h83	3	4,257	17g 20f 17m
TOPSIDER (USA)		**3**	**5,809**	
Safety (USA) 6 b.g	c87:h105	3	5,809	c17m c16f a16g
TOP VILLE		**12**	**25,434**	
Andermatt 6 b.h	h121	2	5,776	21s 23d
Le Temeraire 7 b.h	c102	1	1,165	c16m
Mountain Retreat 7 br.g	h107	1	2,285	18m
Notable Exception 4 b.g	h96	2	3,251	16d 17g
Our Slimbridge 5 b.g	h112	3	7,402	16s 18d 17g
St Ville 7 b.g	h102	3	5,555	28s a24g a20g
TORENAGA		**1**	**2,054**	
Master Salesman 10 b.g	c97	1	2,054	c16g
TORUS		**15**	**69,023**	
Bradbury Star 8 b.g	c151	1	13,420	c25d
Coombesbury Lane 7 b.m	h85	2	2,755	19f 22d
False Economy 8 ch.g	c111	1	3,493	c25v
Flashthecash 7 b.g	c134	6	30,326	c18v c24d c20f c20f c26m c21m
Howe Street 10 gr.g	c129	1	5,918	c17s
Jakarrdi 7 ch.g	h131	1	3,787	20g
Man of Mystery 7 b.g	c99	1	2,489	c19s
Rifle Range 10 b.g	c124	2	6,835	c25g c20d
TOUCHING WOOD (USA)		**25**	**78,363**	
Annio Chilone 7 b.h	c117	3	14,976	c25d c26v c25d
Fingers Crossed 9 b.m	h94	2	2,515	21f 25m
Gallateen 5 gr.g	h135	4	18,478	18s 20d 20f 21s

85

Jadidh 5 b.m	h95	2	3,131	22s 20g
Light Veneer 8 ch.g	c113	6	17,859	c25g c26v c25s c24s 25f c21s
Loving Omen 6 ch.g	h89	1	2,976	18d
Nikitas 8 b.g	h119	4	9,826	17m 17m 16d 17s
Polishing 6 ch.g	h119	2	7,178	16s 20m
White Diamond 5 b.g		1	1,424	F17m
TOWER WALK		**2**	**6,534**	
Doc's Coat 8 b.g	h117	1	4,902	17s
Top Scale 7 b.g	h81	1	1,632	18m
TOWN AND COUNTRY		**7**	**26,280**	
Circulation 7 b.g	c98	1	3,270	c18s
Kilhallon Castle 10 b.g	c100	1	2,884	c25g
Mister Feathers 12 b.g	c102	2	4,480	c20m c19m
Setter Country 9 b.m	c123	2	12,762	c17v c16d
The Slater 8 ch.g	c106	1	2,884	c16s
TRANSWORLD (USA)		**2**	**11,933**	
Fogar (USA) 11 ch.g	c88	1	2,103	c16f
Lonesome Glory (USA) 5 ch.g	h150	1	9,830	22v
TREASURE KAY		**1**	**1,719**	
Pass The Key (IRE) 4 b.g	h83	1	1,719	16g
TRIMMINGHAM		**10**	**32,626**	
Our Survivor 9 b.g	c87:h80	3	6,409	a20g a20g c18g
Retail Runner 8 b.g	c118	2	12,560	c20g c20s
Trimlough 8 b.g	c127	5	13,657	c18m c16d c16d c16d c16g
TROJAN FEN		**10**	**19,424**	
Mr News (IRE) 4 b.c	h86	2	3,368	18d 16d
Paris of Troy 5 b.h	h132	3	5,413	20g 22f 22g
Sport of Fools (IRE) 4 b.f	h99	2	3,340	17d 17d
Trojan Call 6 b.g	c84	1	1,590	c21d
Zamirah (IRE) 4 b.f	h121	2	5,713	16d 17f
TROY		**5**	**8,646**	
Assaglawi 11 b.g	c117	5	8,646	c21m c23f c26m c24m c23f
TRUE SONG		**9**	**28,542**	
Catchapenny 8 br.g	c96	3	16,090	c25d c26d c25s
Corrarder 9 ch.g	c100	1	2,738	c17d
Finally Fantazia 4 ch.f		1	1,245	F17d
Give Me An Answer 7 ch.m	h89	1	1,030	21f
Meleagris 9 b.g	h114	2	3,816	22s 26d
Wild Illusion 9 ch.g	c101	1	3,623	c26m
TRY MY BEST (USA)		**3**	**4,533**	
Gabish 8 b.g	c81	1	1,590	c16g
Kingfisher Bay 8 b.g	c93	2	2,943	c26m c26d
TUG OF WAR		**9**	**61,515**	
Bonsai Bud 10 b.g	c120	2	6,962	c24d c26s
Fissure Seal 7 ch.g	h137	1	20,858	26m
Military Secret 7 ch.g	c94	1	2,247	c25d
Sirrah Jay 13 b.g	c112	3	26,965	c21s c21s c22f
Tug of Gold 8 gr.g	c132	1	2,749	c26d
Victory Anthem 7 ch.g	h95	1	1,734	a16g
TUMBLE WIND (USA)		**5**	**9,995**	
Buckra Mellisuga 9 b.g	h105	1	1,431	16m
Faynaz 7 ch.h	h91	1	1,807	a16g

Nessfield 7 b.m	c86	2	5,556	c20s c26d
See Now 8 ch.g	h72	1	1,201	17m
TURN BACK THE TIME (USA)		2	**2,909**	
Cleeveland Lady 6 b.m	h83	2	2,909	F17m 17g
TURNPIKE		2	**15,714**	
Fiddlers Pike 12 b.g	c132	2	15,714	c29v c30s
TYCOON II		3	**7,838**	
Point Made 10 b.g	c92	1	2,399	c25d
Tartan Tyrant 7 b.g	c103	2	5,439	c25s c25g
TYRNAVOS		2	**3,277**	
Always Ready 7 b.g	h95	2	3,277	16d a16g
UNCLE POKEY		4	**8,697**	
Old Mortality 7 b.g	h87	1	1,996	18m
Related Sound 7 b.g	h72	1	1,119	21g
Uncle Ernie 8 b.g		1	1,488	F10d
Young Pokey 8 b.g	c140	1	4,094	c16g
UNCLE REMUS (NZ)		1	**2,398**	
Interpretation (NZ) 7 b.g	c102	1	2,398	c20m
VACARME (USA)		3	**6,089**	
Tindari (FR) 5 ch.g	h117	3	6,089	24g 24d 25d
VAGUELY NOBLE		2	**2,785**	
Holy Wanderer (USA) 4 b.g	h119	1	1,480	16g
Landed Gentry (USA) 4 b.c	h108	1	1,305	16s
VAGUELY TENDER (USA)		1	**2,252**	
Noble Ben (NZ) 9 b.g	c101	1	2,252	c16d
VAIGLY GREAT		9	**18,030**	
Days of Thunder 5 ch.g	h94	1	1,631	17d
Joli's Great 5 ch.m	h88	3	5,595	a18g a16g 17d
Maudlins Cross 8 ch.g	c115	4	9,569	c16m c17d c17d c17g
Pusey Street Boy 6 ch.g	h80	1	1,235	16m
VALIYAR		5	**8,267**	
Land of The Free 4 b.f	h107	3	4,927	20s 16v 17f
Lara's Baby (IRE) 5 ch.m	h80	1	1,387	18g
Valiant Warrior 5 br.g	h101	1	1,953	21m
VAN DER LINDEN (FR)		2	**2,807**	
Ercall Miller 6 b.g	h97	2	2,807	24s 26g
VAYRANN		2	**4,253**	
Shahdjat (IRE) 5 ch.m	h101	2	4,253	24s 25f
VELOSO (NZ)		5	**11,869**	
Crystal Bear (NZ) 8 b.g	h132	1	2,233	21m
Kiwi Velocity (NZ) 6 b.m	h112	2	5,129	24v 22d
Top Javalin (NZ) 6 ch.g	h129	2	4,507	24v 24s
VERBATIM (USA)		1	**1,649**	
Exact Analysis (USA) 7 b.g	h92	1	1,649	17s
VICE REGAL (NZ)		3	**6,306**	
Knights (NZ) 7 br.g	h107	3	6,306	18d 22g 25m
VIKING (USA)		7	**15,734**	
Eurotwist 4 b.g	h94	1	1,910	16d

Striding Edge 8 ch.g	c87:h101	2	3,972	17f c17g
Viking Flagship 6 b.g	c144	4	9,852	c16d c17s c16d c17s

VISION (USA) — 9 — 15,471

Aberfoyle (IRE) 5 b.g	h94	1	1,893	a22g
Fantastical 5 br.g	h87	1	1,987	16g
Keen Vision (IRE) 5 b.g	h111	2	3,556	a18g a18g
Mr Reiner (IRE) 5 br.g	h101	4	5,946	18m 22f 18d 18d
Vision of Freedom (IRE) 5 b.g	h92	1	2,089	17m

VITAL SEASON — 1 — 1,320

Dexterous Lady 7 b.m	h76	1	1,320	18m

VIVADARI — 2 — 5,068

Sam Shorrock 11 b.g	c98	2	5,068	c21d c26v

WAR HAWK — 1 — 1,822

Grey Hussar (NZ) 7 gr.g	h90	1	1,822	23v

WARPATH — 6 — 9,308

Apache Brave 8 gr.g	h88	1	1,305	16d
Big Mac 6 gr.g	h85	1	830	21m
Gunmetal Boy 9 b.g	c89	1	2,138	c25g
Jasmin Path 8 ro.m	h94	1	1,537	18s
Rain-N-Sun 7 gr.g	h80	1	872	16g
Washakie 8 gr.g	c93	1	2,626	c24m

WASSL — 4 — 6,727

Alreef 7 b.g	h110	1	1,732	a18g
Haitham 6 b.h	h107	1	2,093	18f
Kanooz (IRE) 5 br.g	h95	1	1,340	23m
Ullswater 7 b.g	h80	1	1,562	18m

WAVERING MONARCH (USA) — 1 — 1,484

Emperor Chang (USA) 6 b.g	h93	1	1,484	22g

WELSH CAPTAIN — 5 — 7,370

Black Jewel 10 b.g	h94	2	2,280	16m 17s
Brandon Grove 5 b.m	h86	1	1,484	a16g
Captain Mor 11 b.g	c117	1	1,918	c21f
Wordy's Wonder 5 b.m		1	1,688	F14s

WELSH PAGEANT — 4 — 10,871

Alkinor Rex 8 ch.g	c126	1	3,655	c17v
Emrys 10 ch.g	c97	3	7,216	c16f c16g c18m

WELSH SAINT — 1 — 2,107

Captain Barney 10 b.g	h77	1	2,107	21v

WELSH TERM — 4 — 11,127

Gay Ruffian 7 b.g	c132	4	11,127	c16v c20s c21v c19g

WHAT A GUEST — 3 — 4,798

As d'Eboli (FR) 6 b.g	h90	1	1,277	21g
Tharsis 8 ch.g	h97	1	2,265	20m
Wylam 6 b.g	c87	1	1,256	c21m

WHERE TO DANCE (USA) — 2 — 37,344

Rhythm Section (IRE) 4 ch.g		1	12,720	F17m
Titled Dancer (IRE) 4 ch.f	h132	1	24,624	17f

WHISTLEFIELD — 1 — 2,285

Steveyvul 9 ro.h	h98	1	2,285	17d

WHISTLING DEER   8   24,160
Carousel Calypso 7 ch.g   c100   2   5,115 c24s c26g
Carousel Rocket 10 ch.g   c103   3   8,662 c24d c26g c24d
Forest Sun 8 ch.g   c139   2   9,033 c21v c21s
Whistling Buck (IRE) 5 br.g   1   1,350 F16d

WHITE PRINCE (USA)   1   2,271
Romful Prince 10 b.g   c95   1   2,271 c21f

WIND AND WUTHERING (USA)   3   9,239
Icarus (USA) 7 b.g   c119   3   9,239 c20d c21g c22m

WINDJAMMER (USA)   3   4,095
Ardiles 9 b.g   h72   1   1,021 22d
Great Gusto 7 b.g   c88   1   1,769 c21m
Red Jam Jar 8 ch.g   h95   1   1,305 16f

WOLF POWER (SAF)   2   3,980
Grey Power 6 gr.m   h113   2   3,980 22m 21d

WOLVER HEIGHTS   5   11,718
James The First 5 ch.g   h108   4   10,413 17m 17d 17d 16d
War Beat 5 b.g   h88   1   1,305 22g

WOLVERLIFE   4   14,898
Majed (IRE) 5 b.h   h135   4   14,898 16g 16d 16g 18g

WORLINGWORTH   2   3,863
Troodos 7 b.g   h99   2   3,863 22g 28g

YASHGAN   2   4,400
Suffolk Road 6 br.g   h108   1   2,532 24s
Yaslou 6 ch.g   h79   1   1,868 18d

YAWA   2   3,012
Nouvelle Cuisine 5 b.m   h87   2   3,012 17f 16g

YOUNG GENERATION   1   4,143
Young Benz 9 ch.g   c141   1   4,143 c16v

YOUNG MAN (FR)   1   1,892
Jimmy River 10 br.g   c109   1   1,892 c24s

YOUNG NELSON   1   3,583
Wigtown Bay 10 br.g   c94   1   3,583 c21d

ZAMAZAAN (FR)   3   20,265
Lord Relic (NZ) 7 b.g   h140   3   20,265 21v 21s 21s

ZAMBRANO   5   16,650
Mazmoor 7 gr.m   h127   1   7,440 20g
Moss Bee 6 br.g   c88   1   2,130 c16m
Zam Bee 7 gr.g   c98   3   7,080 c20g c21s c21g

ZIAD (USA)   2   3,825
Flying Ziad (CAN) 10 ch.g   c95   2   3,825 c21m c21m

TRAINERS

The following is a list of licenced trainers. The figures in brackets are the number of winners each trainer has had over the past five seasons, from 1988/89 to 1992/93 inclusive. Quarters and telephone numbers are given.

Aconley, Mrs V. A. (3:7:10:12:8)
Westow (065381) 594 and (0653)
695042 (home)
Akehurst, J. (—:—:6:5:9)
Lambourn (0488) 72688
Akehurst, R. P. J. (43:30:35:17:13)
Epsom (0372) 748800 and fax (0372)
739410
Allan, A. R. (6:10:3:10:6)
Cornhill-on-Tweed (0890) 820581
Allen, C. N. (2:2:1:1:0)
Newmarket (0638) 667870 and
mobilephone (0831) 349629
Alston, E. J. (0:5:1:3:0)
Preston (0772) 612120
Arbuthnot, D. W. P. (0:0:1:2:4)
Newbury (0635) 578427
Armstrong, R. W. (0:0:0:0:0)
Newmarket (0638) 663333/4
Armytage, R. C. (1:2:2:3:3)
Middleham (0969) 23970
Austin, Mrs S. M. (1:0:0:3:2)
Malton (065385) 200
Avison, M. (3:4:1:0:3)
Nawton (0439) 71672
Ayliffe, N. G. (1:0:0:0:0)
Minehead (064385) 265

Bailey, A. (0:0:0:0:2)
Tarporley (0829) 760762
Bailey, K. C. (18:34:33:38:57)
Lambourn (0488) 71483
Balding, G. B. (59:42:48:53:38)
Weyhill
Balding, I. A. (1:5:4:12:6)
Kingsclere (0635) 298210
Balding, J. (0:0:0:0:0)
Doncaster (0302) 710096 and (0777)
818407 (stable)
Banks, J. E . (—:—:0:6:3)
Newmarket (0638) 667997 (office)
and 661472 (home)
Barker, Mrs P. A. (2:6:2:3:2)
Wetherby (0937) 582151
Barker, W. L. (—:—:0:0:2)
Scorton (0325) 378266 and
mobilephone (0836) 260149
Barnes, M. A. (0:0:0:2:7)
Penrith (0768) 881257
Barons, D. H. (36:40:34:25:16)
Kingsbridge (0548) 550326
and 550411
Barr, R. E. (1:2:4:0:2)
Stokesley (0642) 710687
Barraclough, M. F. (0:1:2:3:2)
Claverdon (092684) 3332
Barratt, L. J. (0:0:0:0:0)
Oswestry (069 188) 209
Barron, T. D. (6:4:1:1:5)
Thirsk (0845) 587 435

Barrow, A. K. (4:4:6:4:4)
Bridgwater (0278) 732522
Barwell, C. R. (—:—:2:2:6)
Tiverton (03985) 537
and 224
Bastiman, R. (0:0:1:0:0)
Wetherby (0937) 583050
Baugh, B. P. J. (—:—:—:—:2)
Stafford (0889) 882114
Beasley, B. J. (—:—:—:—:0)
Thirsk (0845) 597288
Beaumont, P. (8:4:12:5:19)
Brandsby (03475) 208
Beever, C. R. (10:17:8:4:0)
Grantham (0476) 870177
Bell, D. J. (0:1:0:0:0)
Chipping Norton (0608) 730070
Bell, M. L. W. (—:0:0:0:0)
Newmarket (0638) 666567
Bennett, J. A. (2:3:2:0:0)
Sparsholt (023559) 635
Bennett, R. A. (1:0:3:0:1)
Maidenhead (0628) 30290
Benstead, C. J. (0:5:2:0:1)
Epsom (037 22) 73152
Bentley, W. (1:5:5:11:7)
Middleham (0969) 22289
Berry, J. (3:1:4:2:1)
Lancaster (0524) 791179
Bevan, P. J. (3:3:3:9:2)
Kingstone (0889) 500647 (yard) or
500670 (home)
Bill, T. T. (6:8:3:9:2)
Ashby-de-la-Zouch (0530) 415881
Birkett, J. J. (1:2:0:0:1)
Workington (0900) 604189
Bishop, K. S. (5:1:2:5:1)
Bridgwater (0278) 671437
Blanshard, M. T. W. (0:1:3:3:0)
Lambourn (0488) 71091
Bolton, M. J. (1:1:1:0:1)
East Grinstead (0980) 621059
Booth, C. B. B. (0:0:0:0:0)
Flaxton (065 381) 586
Bosley, J. R. (2:5:6:4:3)
Bampton (0993) 850212
Boss, R. (0:0:0:0:0)
Newmarket (0638) 661335
Bostock, J. R. (0:2:2:4:2)
Swaffham (0366) 47870
Bottomley, J. F. (—:1:1:6:3)
Malton (0653) 694597 (stable)
Bower, Miss L. J. (4:2:2:0:1)
Alresford (0962) 771552
Bowring, S. R. (0:0:0:0:0)
Mansfield (0623) 822451
Bradburne, Mrs S. C. (1:6:9:9:18)
Cupar (033781) 325
Bradley, J. M. (12:4:15:2:7)
Chepstow (0291) 622486

Bradstock, M. F. (1:1:5:0:4)
East Garston (0488) 648801
Bramall, Mrs S. A. (11:6:11:0:16)
Hutton Sessay (0845) 401333
Bravery, G. C. (—:—:—:4:4)
Newmarket (0638) 668985
Brazington, R. G. (2:2:4:2:0)
Redmarley, Glos. (0452) 840384
Brennan, O. (14:16:15:13:25)
Newark (063 686) 332
Bridger, J. J. (1:0:1:0:0)
Chichester (0428) 722528
Bridgwater, K. S. (3:8:12:6:8)
Solihull (056478) 2895
Brisbourne, W. M. (—:—:—:0:0)
Shrewsbury (074381) 536 and 360
Brittain, C. E. (—:0:3:0:0)
Newmarket (0638) 663739 and 664347
Brittain, M. A. (0:0:0:0:0)
Warthill (0759) 71472
Broad, C. D. (—:1:5:4:17)
Westbury-upon-Severn (0452) 760835
(office) and 830015 (home)
Brooks, C. P. E. (41:56:27:29:16)
Lambourn (0488) 72077 (office) and
72909 (home)
Brotherton, R. (1:2:0:0:3)
Evesham (0386) 710772
Buckler, R. H. (—:—:—:2:12)
Bridport (0308) 88318
Buckley, E. T. (—:—:—:—:4)
Wythall (Birmingham) (0564) 824989
Burchell, W. D. (12:11:18:18:12)
Ebbw Vale (0495) 302551
Burgoyne, P. V. J. P. (4:1:0:1:0)
Upper Lambourn (0488) 71980
Burke, K. R. (—:—:4:4:10)
Wantage (0235) 821455
Butler, P. (2:1:3:1:1)
Lewes (0273) 890124
Bycroft, N. (2:0:2:3:3)
Brandsby (03475) 641

Caldwell, T. H. (4:2:2:1:3)
Warrington (0565) 777275
Callaghan, N. A. (8:4:6:9:2)
Newmarket (0638) 664040
Callow, R. (1:2:4:3:1)
Somerton (Somerset) (0458) 72194
Calver, P. (0:0:2:3:3)
Ripon (0765) 600313
Camacho, M. J. C. (0:1:0:2:5)
Malton (0653) 694901
Cambidge, B. R. (0:2:0:1:1)
Shifnal (095 276) 249
Campbell, I. (5:2:3:4:7)
Newmarket (0638) 660829
Campion, A. M. (—:—:—:—:0)
Worthing (0903) 873047
Candy, H. D. N. B. (0:1:1:0:0)
Wantage (0367) 820276
Caroe, Miss C. J. E. (0:1:1:0:0)
Tarporley (0829) 51920
Carr, J. M. (—:—:—:—:0)
Malton (0653) 694671
Carr, T. J. (—:—:—:0:5)
Great Ayton (0642) 722596 and (0287)
660506

Casey, W. T. (12:4:9:10:3)
Lambourn (0488) 73004
Cecil, Mrs J. (—:—:—:—:5)
Newmarket (0638) 560634 (office)
and 662420 (home) and
fax 560636
Chamberlain, A. J. (1:0:2:1:0)
Swindon (0285) 861347
Chamberlain, N. (0:0:1:0:0)
West Auckland (0388) 832465 and
834636 (office)
Champion, R. (6:2:2:1:5)
Newmarket (0638) 666546
Channon, M. R. (—:1:8:6:6)
Lambourn (0264) 810225 (home) and
(0488) 71149 (stable)
Chapman, D. W. (3:1:0:0:0)
Stillington (0347) 21683
Chapman, M. C. (10:4:8:9:4)
Market Rasen (0673) 843663
Chappell, D. N. (—:—:—:—:0)
Blewbury (0635) 28294
Chapple-Hyam, P. W. (—:—:0:—:0)
Manton (0672) 514901
Charles, M. J. (0:1:2:5:2)
Warwick (0926) 493878
Charles-Jones, G. F. H. (—:—:—:7:2)
Wantage (0235) 767713
Charlton, J. I. A. (5:8:6:9:9)
Stocksfield (0661) 843247
Cheesbrough, P. (—:—:—:—:30)
Bishop Auckland (0388) 720213 and
720432 (hostel)
Christian, S. P. L. (15:12:12:19:6)
Kinnersley (0905) 371233
Chugg, J. (1:7:6:2:1)
Oxford (0993) 830219
Clarke, P. C. (—:0:1:0:2)
Ashburnham (0323) 832098
Clay, W. (14:11:0:5:21)
Fulford (0782) 392131
Coatsworth, G. M. R. (—:—:0:1:0)
Hartburn (067072) 671
Codd, L. J. (1:4:7:0:0)
Tarporley (0829) 760402
Cole, P. F. I. (—:0:0:1:0)
Whatcombe (04882) 433 or 434
Cole, S. N. (0:0:0:1:0)
Rackenford (088488) 205
Collingridge, H. J. (1:0:2:1:3)
Newmarket (0638) 665454
Colston, J. (1:2:1:0:0)
Worcester (0905) 830 252
Cosgrove, D. J. S. (—:—:—:0:0)
Newmarket (0638) 661961 and mobile
(0831) 242596
Cottrell, L. G. (1:0:2:0:0)
Cullompton (088 46) 320
Cowley, C. (—:—:—:0:0)
Marchwiel (0978) 355945
Craig, T. (0:0:2:0:0)
Dunbar (0368) 62583
Cundell, P. D. (6:5:0:0:8)
Newbury (0635) 578267
Cunningham, W. S. (—:—:—:—:0)
Northallerton (060982) 695
Cunningham-Brown, K. O. (0:4:1:2:6)
Stockbridge (0264) 781611

91

Curley, B. J. (13:4:7:1:1)
Newmarket (0638) 508251
Curtis, R. (11:6:12:7:14)
Epsom (0372) 277645
Cuthbert, T. A. K. (1:3:0:2:0)
Carlisle (0228) 560822 and
561317 (stables)
Cyzer, C. A. (0:1:0:0:0)
Horsham (0403) 730255

Dalton, P. T. (—:—:5:3:11)
Burton-on-Trent (0283) 701318
Dawe, Mrs J. C. (1:2:1:1:4)
Bridgwater (027 874) 588
Dickin, R. (11:6:15:17:15)
Dymock (0531) 890644
Dixon, M. (—:—:—:1:3)
Epsom (0372) 279308
Dods, M. J. K. (—:—:3:0:3)
Darlington (0325) 374270
Donnelly, T. W. (0:0:2:1:4)
Hartshorne (0283) 226046
and 216965 (office)
Dooler, J. (1:3:0:0:1)
Goole (0405) 861903
Dow, S. L. (3:6:6:24:4)
Epsom (0372) 721490 (home)
Doyle, Miss J. S. (—:—:—:—:4)
Compton (0635) 578885
Dunn, A. J. K. (2:1:3:3:4)
Minehead (0643) 862573

Easterby, M. H. (45:29:33:42:39)
Malton (065 386) 566
Easterby, M. W. (22:10:18:22:0)
Sheriff Hutton (034 77) 368
Eckley, M. W. (1:1:3:2:11)
Ludlow (058 472) 372
Eckley, R. J. (1:0:0:0:0)
Kington (05448) 216
Eddy, D. (—:—:1:4:3)
Ponteland (0661) 886356
Eden, G. H. (—:0:1:0:1)
Newmarket (0638) 667938
Edwards, J. A. C. (78:47:54:39:29)
Ross-on-Wye (098 987) 259 and
639 (home)
Egerton, C. R. (—:—:—:4:15)
Wantage (0488) 2771
Ellerby, M. W. (0:0:0:0:0)
Pickering (0751) 74092
Ellison, B. (—:2:3:3:3)
Consett
Elsey, C. C. (0:1:1:1:1)
Lambourn (0488) 71242
Elsey, C. W. C. (4:1:1:3:0)
Malton (0653) 693149
Elsworth, D. R. C. (54:24:23:20:18)
Fordingbridge (07253) 220 (home) or
528 (office)
Enright, G. P. (6:6:5:1:1)
Haywards Heath (0273) 479183
Esden, D. (—:—:—:0:0)
East Langton (Leices) (0858) 84734
and 84736
Etherington, J. (3:0:0:0:0)
Malton (0653) 692842

Etherington, T. J. (3:4:6:10:2)
Beare Green (0306) 631529
Evans, P. D. (1:3:4:5:6)
Welshpool (0938) 570288 and (0831)
815603
Eyre, J. L. (—:8:4:2:4)
Mirfield (0924) 492058

Fairhurst, T. (5:3:0:2:0)
Middleham (0969) 23362
Fanshawe, J. R. (—:0:1:3:5)
Newmarket (0638) 660153 and 664525
Feilden, P. J. (0:2:0:0:0)
Newmarket (0638) 577637
Felgate, P. S. (2:4:0:0:0)
Melton Mowbray (0664) 812019
Fetherston-Godley, M. J. (0:0:0:0:1)
East Ilsley (063 528) 250
Ffitch-Heyes, J. R. (12:15:2:6:9)
Lewes (0273) 480804
Fierro, G. (—:—:—:—:0)
Hednesford (0543) 879611
Fisher, R. F. (6:8:1:3:3)
Ulverston (0229) 55664 and 55819
(office)
FitzGerald, J. G. (59:58:45:33:62)
Malton (0653) 692718
Flower, R. M. (—:—:—:—:0)
Jevington (0444) 440774
Forbes, A. L. (—:—:2:3:8)
Uttoxeter (0889) 568145
Forsey, B. (3:4:5:0:2)
Crowcombe (098 48) 270
Forster, T. A. (34:23:37:44:29)
Letcombe Bassett (023 57) 3092
Forte, A. M. (—:—:—:—:1)
Teignmouth (0626) 779006
Fowler, A. (2:4:0:1:0)
Melton Mowbray (0664) 840016
(home) and 840203
Frost, R. G. (20:15:11:14:12)
Buckfastleigh (03644) 2267

Gallie, Miss S. L. (—:—:—:—:0)
Woldingham (0860) 797848
Gandolfo, D. R. (8:14:6:14:12)
Wantage (023 57) 3242
Garraton, D. T. (0:0:—:1:1)
Rillington, N. Yorks. (09442) 506
Gaselee, N. A. D. C. (13:19:19:15:13)
Lambourn (0488) 71503
Gifford, J. T. (64:50:62:49:49)
Findon (0903) 872226
Gillen, J. C. (0:0:—:0:0)
Cambusnethan (0698) 386412
Glover, J. A. (3:13:7:9:8)
Worksop (0909) 475962 or 475425
(stable)
Goldie, R. H. (1:1:0:0:0)
Dundonald (0292) 314323 and 317222
Goulding, J. L. (1:1:2:0:1)
Brigham (0900) 825393
Graham, N. A. (—:0:0:0:0)
Newmarket (0638) 665202 (office) and
667851 (home)
Green, Miss Z. A. (0:0:0:1:1)
Carlisle (09657) 219

Grissell, D. M. (14:16:14:5:18)
Heathfield (042 482) 241
Gubby, B. (0:2:0:2:0)
Bagshot (0276) 63282 and 71030
(evenings)

Haggas, W. J. (0:0:1:0:0)
Newmarket (0638) 667013
Haigh, W. W. (1:4:4:3:1)
Malton (0653) 694428
Haine, Mrs D. E. S. (6:11:14:6:6)
Newmarket (0638) 561001
Haldane, J. S. (3:0:1:1:1)
Kelso (0573) 224956
Hall, Miss P. J. (1:0:0:0:0)
Grantham (0476) 84538 or
mobilephone (0831) 431308
Hall, Miss S. E. (0:2:1:6:0)
Middleham (0969) 40223
Hallett, T. B. (2:13:11:3:0)
Saltash (0752) 846829
Ham, G. A. (25:21:13:9:9)
Axbridge (0934) 750331
Hambly, A. A. (—:—:—:—:4)
Southwell (0602) 412139
Hammond, M. D. (—:—:31:35:51)
Middleham (0969) 40228
Hannon, R. M. (0:0:1:4:1)
Marlborough (0264) 850254
Hanson, J. (2:6:1:1:4)
Wetherby (0937) 582841 and 586776
(yard)
Harris, J. L. (2:3:6:6:7)
Melton Mowbray (0949) 60671
Harris, P. W. (6:4:3:0:1)
Berkhamsted (0442) 842 480
Harris, R. (—:—:—:—:0)
Exning (0638) 578140
Harrison, R. A. (—:0:1:2:4)
Middleham (0969) 23788
Harwood, G. (6:19:13:16:12)
Pulborough (0798) 873011 or 873012
Haslam, P. C. (2:—:0:10:3)
Middleham (0969) 24351
Haynes, M. J. (1:4:3:7:1)
Epsom (073 73) 51140
Hayward, P. A. (3:0:0:0:0)
Netheravon (0980) 70585
Heaton-Ellis, M. J. B. (—:—:—:—:1)
Wroughton (0793) 815009
Hedger, P. R. (14:13:12:8:8)
Arundel (0243) 543863
Henderson, N. J. (43:41:49:52:53)
Lambourn (0488) 72259
Hern, W. R. (—:—:—:—:0)
Lambourn (0488) 73300 (office) and
(063528) 251 (home) or fax (0488)
71728
Herries, Lady (2:1:0:2:9)
Arundel (090 674) 421
Hetherton, J. (0:1:0:0:0)
Malton (0653) 696778
Hewitt, Mrs S. A. (2:1:3:4:4)
Malpas (0829) 782314
Hickman, Mrs V. S. (—:—:—:—:0)
Much Wenlock (0746) 34256
Hide, A. G. (0:0:4:3:1)
Newmarket (0638) 662063

Hills, B. W. (3:2:0:1:0)
Lambourn (0488) 71548 and fax (0488)
72823
Hills, J. W. (0:0:0:0:2)
Lambourn (0488) 73144 and fax (0488)
73099
Hoad, R. P. C. (2:1:6:3:3)
Lewes (0273) 477124
Hobbs, P. J. (24:45:33:51:37)
Watchet (0984) 40366
Hodges, R. J. (18:19:19:21:32)
Somerton (045 822) 3922
Hollinshead, R. (4:15:8:13:10)
Upper Longdon (0543) 490298 and
490490
Honeyball, J. (3:1:0:0:0)
Taunton (0823) 451266
Horgan, C. A. (0:1:3:2:2)
Billingbear (0344) 425382
Houghton, R. F. J. (3:3:6:5:2)
Blewbury (0235) 850480
Howe, H. S. (—:—:—:—:0)
Tiverton (0398) 5224
Howling, P. (0:1:0:1:0)
Brook (0428) 684065
Humphrey, G. L. (—:—:—:—:2)
Vernham Street (0264) 87244

Ingram, R. (—:—:0:0:1)
Fiskerton (0636) 815742
Ivory, K. T. (0:0:0:0:0)
Radlett (0923) 855337

Jackson, C. F. C. (1:1:0:1:1)
Malvern (0886) 880463
James, A. P. (2:7:5:8:1)
Evesbatch (0885) 410240
James, C. J. (0:0:0:3:3)
Newbury (048 839) 280
Jarvis, A. P. (—:—:—:—:2:2)
Abingdon (0235) 851341
Jarvis, M. A. (0:1:0:2:0)
Newmarket (0638) 661702 and 662519
Jarvis, W. (—:—:—:—:0)
Newmarket (0638) 669873 (office) or
662677 (home)
Jefferson, J. M. (8:6:5:3:14)
Malton (0653) 697225
Jenkins, J. R. (29:31:30:20:15)
Royston (0763) 241141 (office) and
246611 (home)
Jermy, D. C. (1:0:0:0:0)
Warminster (0985) 213155
Jewell, Mrs L. C. (—:—:—:—:3)
Sutton Valence (0622) 842788
Johnson, J. H. (14:14:10:20:19)
Bishop Auckland (0388) 762113 and
730872
Johnston, M. S. (0:1:0:1:0)
Middleham (0969) 22237
Jones, A. P. (—:2:8:4:7)
Lambourn (0488) 72637
Jones, A. W. (1:1:0:0:0)
Oswestry (0691) 659720
Jones, C. H. (—:—:0:0:1)
Witney (0993) 702508
Jones, D. H. (1:3:0:2:0)
Pontypridd (0443) 202515

93

Jones, G. H. (1:2:2:0:0)
  Tenbury Wells (056887) 676 and 305
  (stable)
Jones, H. Thomson (0:0:0:0:1)
  Newmarket (0638) 664884
Jones, P. J. (6:4:3:4:5)
  Marlborough (067286) 427
Jones, R. W. (—:—:0:0:1)
  Wickhambrook (0440) 820342
Jones, T. M. (1:0:1:0:0)
  Guildford (048 641) 2604
Jones, T. Thomson (6:17:21:23:14)
  Lambourn (0488) 71596 and 72933
Jordan, F. T. J. (16:21:17:5:3)
  Leominster (056882) 281
Jordan, Mrs J. (—:—:3:1:0)
  Lambourn (0488) 73446
Joynes, Mrs P. M. (—:—:0:3:3)
  Shipston-on-Stour (0608) 61206
Juckes, R. T. (3:3:6:7:2)
  Abberley, Worcs. (0299) 896471

Kelleway, Miss G. M. (—:—:—:0:4)
  Newmarket (0638) 669511 and mobile
  (0860) 860198
Kelleway, P. A. (0:1:4:4:8)
  Newmarket (0638) 661461
Kelly, G. P. (0:0:0:1:0)
  Sheriff Hutton (03477) 518 and 770
Kemp, W. T. (6:2:1:1:0)
  Duns (03615) 242
Kersey, T. (1:1:0:1:0)
  West Melton (0709) 873166
Kettlewell, S. E. (2:11:5:9:7)
  Middleham (0969) 40411
King, Mrs A. L. M. (2:2:2:8:0)
  Stratford-on-Avon (0789) 205087
King, J. S. (16:16:16:5:11)
  Swindon (0793) 731481
Knight, Mrs A. J. (3:2:7:2:4)
  Cullompton (0823) 680959
Knight, Miss H. C. (—:15:24:14:37)
  Wantage (0235) 833535

Laing, D. R. (0:—:0:0:1)
  Lambourn (0488) 72381
Lamb, R. R. (—:3:2:0:1)
  Seahouses (0665) 720 260
Leach, P. S. (1:2:4:6:10)
  Taunton (0823) 433249
Leadbetter, S. J. (2:2:3:5:2)
  Ladykirk (0289) 382519
Lee, A. N. (1:0:0:0:0)
  Newmarket (0638) 662734 (home)
Lee, D. (4:3:0:1:0)
  Pickering (0751) 32425
Lee, F. H. (7:1:1:0:0)
  Wilmslow (0625) 529672 and 533250
  (stud)
Lee, R. A. (29:37:22:20:29)
  Presteigne (0544) 267672 and
  mobilephone (0836) 537145
Leigh, J. P. (1:4:5:3:2)
  Willoughton, Lincs. (0427) 668210
Lines, C. V. (—:—:—:—:0)
  Exning (0638) 577531
Long, J. E. (3:2:4:0:2)
  Plumpton (0273) 890244

Long, Mrs M. E. (—:—:—:—:0)
  Limpsfield (0883) 347313
Lungo, L. (—:—:6:8:22)
  Carrutherstown (0387) 84691

Macauley, Mrs N. J. (0:1:4:1:0)
  Sproxton (0476) 860578 and
  860090 (office)
Mackie, W. J. W. (11:18:6:11:10)
  Derby (0283) 585604
Mactaggart, B. (0:0:1:1:3)
  Hawick (0450) 72086
Madgwick, M. J. (4:2:5:2:4)
  Denmead (0705) 258313
Makin, P. J. (1:0:1:1:0)
  Ogbourne Maisey (0672) 512973
Mann, W. G. (0:0:0:0:0)
  Leamington Spa (0926) 612659
Manning, R. J. (1:3:2:0:0)
  Winterbourne, Avon (0454) 773274
Marks, D. (0:2:0:0:1)
  Lambourn (0488) 71767
Marvin, R. F. (—:1:0:0:1)
  Newark (0623) 822714
McCain, D. (13:13:8:9:6)
  Cholmondeley (0829) 720352
McConnochie, J. C. (—:7:10:7:3)
  Stratford-on-Avon (0789) 450607
McCormack, M. (3:4:5:1:1)
  Wantage (0235) 751433
McDonald, R. (0:0:0:3:1)
  Duns (089081) 218 and 446
McEntee, P. M. (—:—:—:0:0)
  Bracknell (0344) 891211
McGovern, T. P. (4:6:4:0:4)
  Haywards Heath (0444) 881594
McKie, Mrs V. J. (6:7:6:13:6)
  Buckingham (0296) 730707
McMahon, B. A. (8:11:5:5:1)
  Tamworth (0827) 62901
McMath, B. J. (1:3:2:0:0)
  Newmarket (0638) 665868
McNeill, M. P. (—:—:1:0:0)
  Salisbury (0725) 89375
Meade, C. M. (—:2:1:1:8)
  Malmesbury (0666) 840465
Meehan, B. J. (—:—:—:—:0)
  Lambourn (0488) 73125
Mellor, S. T. E. (11:21:34:8:4)
  Wanborough (0793) 790230
Miller, C. J. V. (2:2:0:2:0)
  Shipston-on-Stour (0608) 82357
Millman, B. R. (—:0:1:1:2)
  Cullompton (0884) 6620 and
  mobile (0860) 459170
Mills, T. G. (—:—:—:—:1)
  Leatherhead (0372) 377209
Mitchell, N. R. (17:12:5:1:3)
  Piddletrenthide (0300) 4739
Mitchell, P. (7:4:4:5:0)
  Epsom (037 22) 73729
Mitchell, Pat K. (0:0:0:0:0)
  Newmarket (0638) 660013
Moffatt, D. (5:3:3:7:11)
  Cartmel (05395) 36689
Monteith, P. (6:10:17:23:14)
  Rosewell (031) 440-2309

94

Moore, A. (5:11:9:11:13)
Woodingdean (0273) 681679
Moore, G. L. (—:—:—:—:0)
Epsom (0372) 271526
Moore, G. M. (37:53:46:38:29)
Middleham (0969) 23823
Moore, J. S. (—:—:2:14:3)
Thruxton (0264) 889538 (office) and
(0380) 728526 (home) and
mobilephone (0831) 256532
Morgan, B. C. (2:4:0:5:2)
Barton-under-Needwood (028 375)
304
Morgan, K. A. (20:12:15:8:13)
Waltham-on-the-Wolds (066478) 711
Morley M. F. D. (—:—:—:0:0)
Newmarket (0638) 667175
Morris, D. (—:0:0:1:2)
Newmarket (0638) 667959
Muggeridge, M. P. (—:0:2:5:3)
Fyfield (0264) 850872
Muir, W. R (—:—:0:3:5)
Chaddleworth (04882) 463
Mullins, J. W. (—:—:—:—:1)
Andover (0264) 75363
Murphy, F. (—:—:11:19:23)
Woodbridge (072876) 243 or 554
Murphy, P. G. (—:—:—:—:10)
Portbury (0275) 372192 and fax
374185
Murray, B. W. (—:0:0:3:2)
Malton (0653) 692879
Murray-Smith, D. J. G. (35:17:11:13:6)
Upper Lambourn (0488) 71041
Musson, W. J. (0:3:4:1:0)
Newmarket (0638) 663371

Nash, C. T. (—:1:0:9:1)
Wantage (0367) 820510
Naughton, M. P. (5:3:1:3:6)
Richmond, N. Yorks. (0748) 822803
and mobilephone (0831) 414217
Naughton, T. J. (—:—:0:1:2)
Epsom (0372) 745112
Nicholls, P. F. (—:—:—:10:20)
Ditcheat (074986) 656 and
mobilephone (0860) 225692
Nicholson, D. (39:42:55:63:100)
Temple Guiting (038673) 209/219 or
fax 218
Nolan, D. A. (—:—:—:—:1)
Wishaw (0698) 381106
Norton, J. (0:2:0:1:2)
Barnsley (0226) 387633
Norton, S. G. (0:2:1:1:0)
Barnsley (0924) 830450 and 830406
(office)

O'Donoghue, J. (0:0:0:0:1)
Reigate (073 72) 45241
Old, J. A. B. (9:2:10:21:19)
Barbury Castle (0793) 845200 or
845900
Oldroyd, G. R. (2:3:2:3:0)
O'Leary, R. M. (0:2:9:8:4)
Malton (065386) 684 and 404
Oliver, J. K. M. (7:4:4:3:1)
Hawick (045 087) 216

O'Mahony, F. J. (3:1:1:4:3)
Dormansland (0342) 833278
O'Neill, J. J. (29:34:27:26:21)
Penrith (07684) 84555
O'Neill, O. (10:4:5:4:1)
Cheltenham (024 267) 3275
O'Shea, J. G. M. (3:3:1:5:3)
Wythall (0564) 794631
O'Sullivan, R. J. (13:6:6:14:13)
Bognor (02432) 67563
Owen, E. H. (2:3:1:2:0)
Denbigh (0824) 790264 and 790356

Palling, B. (1:3:0:3:2)
Cowbridge (0446) 772089
Parker, C. (9:2:8:7:14)
Lockerbie (05765) 232
Parkes, J. E. (11:14:3:4:10)
Malton (0653) 697570
Parrott, Mrs H. K. (2:5:4:5:1)
Deerhurst (0684) 292214
Payne, J. W. (0:0:0:0:0)
Newmarket (0638) 668675
Payne, S. G. (0:3:1:1:0)
Carlisle (06973) 20010
Peacock, J. H. (—:—:—:0:0)
Longville (0952) 506150
Peacock, R. E. (2:0:0:0:0)
Tetbury (0666) 577238
Pearce, J. N. (4:2:3:4:2)
Newmarket (0638) 664669
Perratt, Miss L. A. (—:—:—:15:12)
Ayr (0292) 266232
Phillips, R. T. (—:—:—:—:0)
Sparsholt (0235) 59552
Pickering, J. A. (2:1:1:2:0)
Wigston (0455) 220535
Piggott, Mrs S. E. (0:0:0:0:0)
Newmarket (0638) 662584
Pipe, M. C. (208:224:230:224:194)
Wellington, Somerset (0884) 840715
Pitman, Mrs J. S. (62:93:43:50:36)
Lambourn (0488) 71714
Popham, C. L. (20:17:16:3:8)
Bishop's Lydeard (0823) 432769
Potts, A. W. (0:2:0:1:0)
Barton-on-Humber (065 261) 750
Poulton, J. C. (—:—:—:—:0)
Lewes (0273) 603824
Preece, W. G. (10:22:4:6:2)
Telford (095 286) 249
Prescott, Sir Mark (0:0:0:0:0)
Newmarket (0638) 662117
Price, R. J. (0:1:3:8:10)
Leominster (0568) 615638 and 612333
Price, W. J. (2:1:1:1:1)
Ebbw Vale (0495) 303655
Pritchard, P. A. (5:0:0:3:1)
Shipston-on-Stour (0295) 680689
Pritchard-Gordon, G. A. (5:5:6:4:3)
Newmarket (0638) 662824

Ramsden, Mrs L. E. (1:4:7:6:4)
Sandhutton (0845) 587226
Reed, W. G. (1:2:2:3:9)
Hexham (0434) 344201
Reid, A. S. (—:1:1:3:2)
Thurleigh (071-723 1824)

95

Renfree-Barons, Mrs J. R.
(—:—:—:—:2)
Stockbridge
Retter, Mrs J. G. (11:3:11:24:24)
Whitestone (0392) 81410
Reveley, Mrs M. (23:41:58:99:90)
Saltburn (0287) 650456 and 652000
(hostel)
Richards, G. W. (69:78:118:67:104)
Greystoke (07684) 83392
Richards, Mrs L. (2:2:2:3:3)
Arundel (0243) 551440
Richmond, B. A. (2:3:3:2:4)
Wellingore (0522) 810578
Rodford, P. R. (0:0:1:3:3)
Martock (0935) 823459
Roe, C. G. A. M. (4:1:0:3:0)
Chalford (0453) 885487
Rothwell, B. S. (—:—:—:7:4)
Catwick (0964) 542583
Rowe, R. (—:—:—:7:23)
Storrington (0903) 742871
Ryan, M. J. (8:11:9:7:5)
Newmarket (0638) 664172

Sanders, Miss B. V. J. (8:14:9:18:9)
Epsom (03722) 78453
Saunders M. S. (—:—:—:1:3)
Bath (0749) 841011
Scargill, Dr J. D. (2:1:0:0:4)
Newmarket (0638) 663254
Scott, A. A. (—:—:0:—:0)
Newmarket (0638) 661998
Scudamore, M. J. (2:2:7:3:2)
Hoarwithy (0432) 840253
Sharpe, Mrs N. S. A. (0:0:1:0:0)
Clifford (097) 3465
Shaw, D. (—:—:—:0:0)
Ashington (0903) 893031
Sherwood, O. M. C. (53:58:56:48:37)
Upper Lambourn (0488) 71411
Sherwood, S. E. H. (—:—:12:17:30)
East Ilsley (063528) 678
Siddall, Miss L. C. (3:3:6:0:5)
York (090484) 291
Simpson, B. (3:3:3:9:6)
Lambourn (0488) 71622
Sly, Mrs P. M. (0:1:3:5:7)
Peterborough (0733) 270212
Smart, B. (6:2:1:3:3)
Lambourn (0488) 71632
Smith A. (3:0:1:0:2)
Beverley (0482) 882520
Smith, Charles (—:0:0:0:0)
Wellingore (0526) 833245
Smith, C. A. (—:—:0:2:4)
Malvern (06845) 5900
Smith, D. (20:13:21:19:14)
Bishop Auckland (0388) 603317 and
606180
Smith, J. P. (1:1:1:2:1)
Rugeley (054 36) 6587
Smith, N. A. (1:3:1:2:1)
Evesham (0386) 793263
Smith, Mrs S. J. (—:0:2:12:6)
Bingley (0274) 564930
Spearing, J. L. (6:4:9:7:12)
Alcester (0789) 772639

Spicer, R. C. (0:0:0:0:0)
Spalding (077587) 444
Stevens, B. (5:5:7:0:3)
Winchester (0962) 883030
Storey, W. L. (4:9:6:6:3)
Consett (0207) 55259
Stoute, M. R. (3:4:0:0:0)
Newmarket (0638) 663801
Stringer, A. P. (1:2:2:3:4)
Carlton Husthwaite (0845) 401329
Sutcliffe, J. R. E. (3:2:0:4:1)
Epsom (037 22) 72825
Swinbank, Mrs A. (—:—:—:—:5)
Darlington (0325) 377318

Tate, F. M. (3:2:1:1:0)
Kidderminster (0562) 777243
Tate, R. (0:3:1:0:3)
Thirsk (0845) 537375
Tate, T. P. (5:9:9:8:12)
Tadcaster (0937) 836036
Taylor, Mrs S. (—:—:—:0:2:0)
Alnwick (0665) 570553
Thom, D. T. (1:5:0:0:1)
Newmarket (0638) 577288
Thompson, R. (3:0:2:4:0)
Grantham (0780) 410812
Thompson, Ronald (1:3:2:0:0)
Doncaster (0302) 842857, 845904 and
840174
Thompson, V. (2:0:0:2:2)
Alnwick (0665) 576272
Thomson, N. B. (1:0:1:0:0)
Shaftesbury (074785) 262
Thorner, G. E. (0:0:2:5:4)
Letcombe Regis (023 57) 3003
Thornton, C. W. (6:4:15:10:11)
Middleham (0969) 23350
Tinkler, C. H. (5:5:2:2:0)
Malton (0653) 695981
Tinkler, N. D. (54:49:29:38:25)
Malton (065385) 245 and 512
Tompkins, M. H. (7:17:25:15:22)
Newmarket (0638) 661434
Trietline, C. C. (8:4:10:13:7)
Welford-on-Avon (0789) 750294
Tucker, D. R. (3:0:0:1:1)
Cullompton (0823) 680159
Turnell, A. (11:16:7:18:37)
East Hendred (0235 833) 297
Turner, W. G. (3:6:1:0:1)
Tavistock (0822) 810237
Turner, W. (Bill) G. M. (10:11:9:8:5)
Corton Denham (096322) 523
Twiston-Davies, N. A. (2:8:19:31:76)
Cheltenham (0451) 850278

Upson, J. R. (—:22:27:24:31)
Towcester (0327) 860043
Usher, M. D. I. (2:01:5:4)
East Garston (0488) 398953/4 (office)
and 71307 (home)

Voorspuy, R. (5:4:2:2:1)
Polegate (0323) 485006

Wainwright, J. S. (0:2:0:2:0)
Malton (065385) 537

Wall, C. F. (0:1:0:0:0)
Newmarket (0638) 661999 (office) and
668896 (home)
Walwyn, Mrs C. (—:—:15:2:11)
Lambourn (0488) 71555
Walwyn, P. T. (0:0:4:0:0)
Lambourn (0488) 71347
Wane, M. (—:—:—:—:0)
Richmond (0325) 718046
Waring, Mrs B. H. (0:0:0:0:0)
Malmesbury (0225) 742044
Watson, F. (0:1:2:0:0)
Sedgefield (0740) 20582
Weaver, R. J. (2:6:3:3:2)
Leicester (0533) 414112
Webber, J. H. (15:9:9:16:10)
Banbury (0295) 750226 and 750466
(stable) and mobilephone (0836)
580129
Weedon, C. V. (1:11:5:7:5)
Chiddingfold (0428) 683344
Weymes, E. (1:3:1:0:0)
Leyburn (0969) 40229
Wharton, J. (4:6:10:7:1)
Melton Mowbray (0664) 78334
(stable) and 65225 (home)
Whitaker, R. M. (5:3:0:1:0)
Wetherby (0532) 892265 and (0937)
582122 (office)
White, J. R. (14:16:20:39:38)
Wendover (0296) 623387
White, K. B. (6:8:3:6:3)
Craven Arms (058 476) 200
Whitfield, Miss A. J. (0:0:0:1:7)
Lambourn (0488) 72342
Wightman, W. G. R. (3:1:1:0:1)
Upham (0489) 892565
Wildman, C. P. (2:7:3:0:2)
Salisbury (0980) 52226
Wilkinson, B. E. (5:8:5:6:5)
Middleham (0969) 23385
Wilkinson, M. J. (4:2:3:4:10)
Chipping Warden (029586) 713
Williams, C. N. (0:0:0:1:3)
Newmarket (0638) 665116
Williams, D. L. (1:5:2:2:3)
Lambourn (0488) 2636 and 38530 and
(0836) 547894
Williams, M. (—:—:—:—:4)
Wellington (0823) 665156
Williams, R. J. R. (0:0:0:0:0)
Newmarket (0638) 663218
Williams, Mrs S. D. (0:0:2:2:7)
South Molton (07697) 291
Willis, H. (1:0:1:1:0)
Twyford, Hants. (0962) 712159
Wilson, A. J. (3:8:6:6:2)
Cheltenham (0242) 244713
Wilson, D. A. (2:2:1:2:4)
Headley (03722) 78327 (office) and
73839 (home)
Wilson, Capt. J. H. (0:0:0:2:1)
Preston (0772) 812780
Wilton, Miss S. J. (22:17:4:8:2)
Stoke-on-Trent (0782) 550861
Wingrove, K. G. (4:3:5:0:1)
Norwich (0263) 735299 and 733685

Wintle, D. J. (10:5:4:5:10)
Westbury-on-Severn (0452) 760459
and 760825
Wonnacott, Mrs J. (0:16:6:5:1)
Tavistock (082287) 215
Woodhouse, R. D. E. (4:4:4:6:2)
York (065 381) 637
Woodman, S. (1:2:3:4:1)
Chichester (0243) 527136
Woods, S. P. C. (—:—:—:—:3)
Newmarket (0638) 711067

Yardley, F. J. (0:0:0:0:6)
Ombersley (0905) 620477
Yardley, G. H. (1:0:0:0:0)
Malvern (0905) 830245

The following relinquished their licence
during the season:

Baker, R. J. (—:—:—:1:6)
Barclay, Miss J. E. (—:—:0:1:0)
Blum, G. (0:0:2:—:0)
Brown, M. L. (1:1:3:0:0)
Castell, M. (0:0:1:0:0)
Cosgrave, J. (0:—:—:—:0)
Cox, C. G. (—:—:—:0:0)
Davison, A. R. (7:5:4:9:1)
Denson, A. W. (1:5:0:2:1)
Earnshaw, R. (0:1:1:0:4)
Elliott, J. P. D. (0:1:5:1:1)
Eustace, J. M. P. (—:—:0:0:0)
Fleming, G. (—:—:—:0:0)
Guest, R. (1:0:0:0:0)
Hanbury B. (—:—:—:0:0)
Harris, S. T. (0:0:0:0:0)
Holden, W. (4:1:0:3:0)
Holder, R. J. (25:33:29:31:1)
James, M. B. C. (0:0:0:0:0)
Keddy, T. (—:—:—:—:1)
Lewis, G. (—:0:—:0:0)
Lunness, B. W. (—:—:—:0:0)
McCourt, M. The late (2:0:9:6:3)
Miller, N. (1:2:4:2:0)
Minns, Mrs S. A. (0:0:0:1:0)
O'Connor, Miss P. (1:1:2:0:0)
Oliver, Mrs S. (12:10:14:10:0)
O'Neill, M. J. (0:2:8:2:0)
Richards, G. (—:0:0:1:0)
Ringer D. J. (5:1:0:0:0)
Ripley, G. (0:0:0:0:0)
Roberts, J. D. (3:7:4:3:0)
Sneyd, Miss E. (1:0:0:0:0)
Stephenson, W. A. The late
(89:116:83:101:35)
Thomas, J. D. (—:0:2:2:1)
Tucker, D. C. (0:0:0:0:0)
Wheeler, E. A. (2:6:2:2:0)
Wigham, P. (—:0:0:0:0)

97

PERMIT HOLDERS

The following is a list of permit holders. The figures in brackets are the number of winners each permit holder has had over the past five seasons, from 1988/89 to 1992/93 inclusive. Quarters and telephone numbers are given.

Adam, J. R. (—:—:—:—:1)
Gordon (0578) 4229
Alexander, N. W. (—:—:—:—:0:0)
Kinross (059284) 223
Allen, J. S. (0:0:0:0:2)
Warwick (092684) 2026
Allison, Miss K. S. (—:—:—:0:2:4)
Lambourn (0488) 73125
Alner, R. H. (—:2:1:4:3)
Blandford (0258) 817271
Anderson, I. F. F. (0:0:0:0:0)
Welshpool (093875) 509
Andrews, Mrs E. M. (2:0:0:0:0)
Luton (046276) 263
Andrews, J. (4:0:2:0:1)
Ladybank (0337) 30335
Avery, S. B. (0:1:1:0:0)
Ulceby (0469) 72078 and (0652) 680744
Aylett, A. R. (—:—:—:—:0)
Isle of Wight (0983) 882909
Aynsley, J. W. F. (0:0:0:0:0)
Rothbury (0669) 20271

Babbage, N. M. (—:—:—:—:0:0)
Cheltenham (0242) 233090
Baker, Miss D. J. (0:0:0:1:1)
Cranleigh (0483) 277306
Banks, M. C. (0:1:2:1:2)
Sandy (0767) 50563
Barber, G. H. (0:0:0:0:0)
Chelmsford (0621) 828213
Barclay, Mrs A. (1:1:1:2:0)
Moreton-in-Marsh (0451) 30680
Barlow, G. B. (0:0:2:0:0)
Sandbach (0270) 762036
Barnett, G. W. (0:0:0:0:6)
Stoke-on-Trent (0782) 316777
Barton, R. B. (1:0:0:—:0)
Wadswick (0225) 810700
Batey, A. C. (0:1:3:1:0)
Prudhoe (0661) 842284
Bell, C. H. P. (0:0:—:0:0)
Morpeth (0670) 760560
Bell, Mrs H. L. (—:—:—:1:0)
Northallerton (0609) 776015 and (0845) 587207
Birchall, E. F. (—:—:—:0:0)
Kidderminster (0299) 250320
Bishop, V. R. (1:0:0:1:2)
Hereford (04973) 221
Bissill, W. H. (0:2:1:4:2)
Newark (0949) 50226
Black, Mrs C. J. (—:—:—:0:0)
Wigan (02575) 2844
Bloomfield, D. E. F. (1:3:0:2:0)
Launceston (056682) 232
Bloor, D. R. (0:2:0:2:0)
Nuneaton (0455) 291739

Bousfield, B. (4:0:0:2:0)
Brough (07683) 41391
Bowen, S. A. (0:0:0:2:0)
Canterbury (0304) 841876
Bowlby, Lady A. L. M. (0:0:0:0:0)
Thirsk (0845) 597331
Brackenbury, Mrs R. (—:—:2:2:1)
Totnes (054882) 326
Bradley, P. (—:—:—:—:1)
Breese, Mrs J. C. (—:—:0:—:0)
Ledbury (053183) 642
Brewis, R. (3:1:3:1:2)
Belford (0668) 213239
Bridgett, C. J. (0:—:0:0:0)
Market Drayton (063087) 2329 and 2501
Broad, Mrs B. K. (0:0:0:0:0)
Bedale (0677) 22267
Brockbank, J. E. (3:0:2:0:0)
Wigton (06973) 42391
Brooks, Mrs E. M. (0:1:0:0:0)
Bideford (0805) 23156
Brown, D. H. (—:—:—:0:1)
Rotherham (0709) 812854 (home) and 546671 (office)
Brown, R. L. (3:1:0:1:2)
Abergavenny (087386) 278
Browning, D. W. (2:0:1:0:0)
Heathfield (04352) 2425
Brunt, Mrs B. (0:0:0:0:0)
Newark (0623) 860109
Bulwer-Long, W. H. (—:—:—:—:0)
Butterworth, Mrs B. (0:0:—:0:0)
Appleby (0930) 61117
Byford, B. (0:1:0:0:0)
Colchester (0206) 240235

Campion, S. W. (—:—:—:1:2:0)
Wragby (0673) 858919
Cantillon, D. E. (—:—:—:0:1:3)
Newmarket (0638) 668507
Carden, J. (0:0:0:0:0)
Macclesfield (0625) 829748
Carey, D. N. (1:—:0:1:0)
Brynmawr (0495) 310794
Carr Evans, Mrs J. A. (—:—:—:—:0)
Ampleforth (04393) 243
Carter, O. J. (0:1:1:4:1)
Ottery St Mary (0404) 812436
Casey, R. F. (3:0:2:1:0)
Lambourn (0488) 648363 and mobilephone (0831) 104775
Chadwick, S. G. (—:—:—:5:2)
Aspatria (06973) 21226
Chesney, Dr D. (0:0:1:0:0)
Dorchester (0305) 65450
Churches, M. R. (0:2:1:1:0)
Wells (0458) 31141
Clutterbuck, K. F. (—:—:—:—:0:0)
Royston (0763) 263143

Coathup, S. (—:—:—:—:1)
Neston (Wirral) 051-336 8911
Cole, H. T. (—:—:—:—:5)
Taunton (0823) 480430
Collinson, J. E. (—:—:0:1:0)
Exeter (0395) 32038
Corbett, L. C. (1:4:—:—:0)
Marlborough (0672) 86491
Corner, A. S. (—:0:—:1:0)
Richmond (032577) 308
Coton, F. (—:0:—:0:0)
Nottingham (0602) 663048
Cottrell, A. J. (—:—:—:—:1)
Cullompton (0823) 680904
Cresswell, J. K. S. (—:—:—:0:0)
Stoke-on-Trent (0538) 702362
Criddle, J. V. (0:0:0:0:0)
Newport, Gwent (0633) 400401
and 400491
Csaky, A. (0:1:0:0:0)
Wolland, Dorset (02586) 543
Culham, Mrs G. P. (2:0:0:0:0)
Dumfries (038778) 225
Curson, I. L. (—:—:—:—:0)
Downham Market (0336) 386052
Curtis, J. W. P. (—:—:—:—:3)
Duffield (0262) 488225

Dalgetty, T. N. (1:0:0:0:2)
Jedburgh (08354) 324
Dalton, J. N. (1:0:0:0:0)
Shifnal (095271) 656
Davies, M. W. (2:2:1:1:1)
Abergavenny (0873) 2292
Davis, N. H. (0:1:0:0:1)
Bridgwater (0278) 732722
Deacon, D. J. (—:—:—:1:1)
Cheltenham (0242) 680298
Dean, R. (0:—:—:0:2)
Maidstone (0622) 850230
Dennis, P. J. (—:—:—:—:0)
Thirsk (0609) 83616
Dennis, W. W. (—:—:—:—:0)
Bude (0288) 352849
Dixon, J. E. (0:0:0:0:0)
Carlisle (0228) 710318
Dowson, Mrs P. A. (0:0:1:0:0)
Pershore (0386) 552029
Drewe, C. J. (—:—:0:2:0)
Didcot (0235) 813124
Dun, T. D. C. (0:0:0:0:1)
Heriot (087535) 225
Dutfield, Mrs P. N. (—:—:2:0:2)
Seaton (0297) 53560
Dyer, T. H. (—:—:—:—:6)
Dundee (082622) 622

Eaton, Miss J. M. (1:0:0:2:1)
Lancaster (05242) 21374
Edmunds, D. J. W. (—:—:0:0:0)
Retford (0427) 880375
Edwards, G. F. (—:0:1:2:2)
Minehead (064383) 549
Emery, R. W. (—:—:—:—:0)
Rugby (0788) 547584
England, Miss E. M. V. (—:—:—:—:0)
Rugby (0327) 60437

Eubank, A. (1:0:0:3:1)
Cockermouth (0900) 823027
Evans, R. R. (—:—:—:—:0:0)
Stratford-on-Avon (0789) 205277

Farr, Mrs S. M. (—:—:—:0:0)
Tonypandy (0443) 435060
Fort, J. R. (0:1:2:1:0)
Willington 091-378 2319
Francis, M. E. D. (7:5:1:1:0)
Lambourn (0488) 71700
Frank, Mrs S. (—:1:0:0:0)
Stockton (0642) 760538
Fullerton, Mrs H. J. (0:0:0:0:0)
Dorchester (0305) 65323

George, Miss K. M. (—:1:0:0:0)
Princes Risborough (08444) 2284
Gibbon, D. H. (—:—:—:—:0)
Colchester (0206) 250832
Gibson, F. (0:0:0:0:0)
Sheffield (0909) 771591
Gibson, T. M. (—:—:0:0:0)
Newcastle-upon-Tyne (0207) 544013
Giddings, G. W. (—:—:0:—:0)
Warminster (0831) 245344
Gill, H. J. (—:0:1:1:1)
Aberford (0532) 813273
Gledson, J. L. (0:0:1:0:0)
Hexham (0434) 220218
Goldie, J. S. (—:—:—:—:0)
Newcastle-upon-Tyne 091-487 7222
Gollings, S. (—:—:—:—:0)
Louth (0507) 343204
Goodfellow, Mrs A. C. D. (2:1:2:5:7)
Earlston (089684) 541
Graham, G. M. (—:—:—:—:0)
Rothwell, Leeds (0532) 826306
Graham, G. R. (0:0:0:0:0)
Wadhurst (089288) 2034
Gray, F. (2:1:2:0:1)
Warninglid (044485) 235
Gray, R. (0:—:—:—:0)
Gateshead 091-487-7222
Greathead, T. R. (2:1:1:0:0)
Chipping Norton (0608) 642954
Greig, D. R. (0:0:0:0:0)
Cranleigh (0483) 272737
Griffiths, S. G. (3:1:2:1:0)
Carmarthen (0267) 290321

Hackett, A. W. (0:0:0:0:0)
Leicester (066474) 535
Haley, P. R. (0:—:—:0:4)
Tadcaster (0937) 834816
Hamilton, Mrs A. (0:0:0:—:0)
Newcastle (0830) 30219
Hamilton, W. (0:—:—:0:2)
Hawick (045086) 229
Harper, H. C. (0:0:0:0:0)
Banbury (0295) 811223
Harper, R. C. (—:—:—:—:—)
Banbury (0295) 810997
Harriman, J. (0:1:0:0:0)
Tredegar (049525) 3724
Harry, Mrs R. L. M. (0:0:—:0:0)
Dinas Powys (0222) 512308

99

Hawker, R. L. (0:—:0:0:0)
Chippenham (06663) 269
Haynes, H. E. (0:0:0:1:0)
Swindon (0793) 762437
Haynes, J. C. (0:0:0:0:0)
Levens (044852) 280
Heffernan, B. J. (—:—:—:—:0)
Shaugh Prior (0755) 39645
Hellens, J. A. (0:1:7:6:3)
Durham (091) 388-5403
Henderson, Mrs R. G. (—:—:—:—:2)
Okehampton (0837) 52914
Hiatt, P. W. (—:—:—:0:1)
Hook Norton (0608) 737255
Hodge, H. B. (0:1:0:0:0)
Ware (0920) 3624
Holcombe, J. (—:—:—:0:0:0)
Rugeley (05436) 74958
Hollis, F. G. (0:1:0:—:0)
Cullompton (08847) 342 and (08846)
398
Horler, Miss C. J. (0:0:0:0:0)
Bath (037387) 216
Houlbrooke, T. J. (2:1:0:0:0)
Ledbury (053184) 368
Hubbuck, J. S. (0:1:0:0:0)
Hexham (0434) 602913
Hugill, J. D. (—:—:—:0:0)
Northallerton (0642) 701102
Humby, M. C. (—:—:—:—:0)
Andover (0264) 772990

Jenks, W. P. (—:—:—:0:1)
Bridgnorth (0746) 35288
Jestin, F. (2:0:2:0:0)
Wigton (06998) 439
Johnson, R. W. (0:0:1:0:0)
Newcastle (091) 267-4464
Johnson, Mrs S. M. (1:2:1:0:0)
Madley, Hereford (0981) 250214
Jones, D. G. (—:—:—:—:0)
Jones, G. E. (0:2:0:0:0)
Lampeter (057045) 261
Jones, I. R. (0:0:0:0:0)
Cwmbran (06333) 2399
Jones, Mrs M. A. (0:1:0:3:6)
Lambourn (0488) 72409
Joseph, J. (3:6:0:0:4)
Coleshill, Bucks (0494) 722239

Kavanagh, H. M (—:—:—:1:0)
Bodenham (0568) 847048
Kendall, Mrs M. A. (0:0:0:1:0)
Penrith (09312) 318
Kirby, J. (0:—:—:—:1)
Crowthorpe (0734) 732008

Lamyman, Mrs S. (0:1:0:1:1)
Louth (0507) 533260
Laxton, T. (3:0:0:0:0)
Clitheroe (0200) 23719
Le Blond, A. J. (0:0:0:0:0)
Houghton-le-Spring (091) 526-3442
Linton, K. A. (0:0:0:0:0)
Ladybank, Fife (0337) 30764
Llewellyn, B. J. (1:1:1:0:6)
Bargoed (0685) 841259

Love, J. (0:0:0:0:0)
Johnstone (0505) 612135

Mactaggart, A. H. (0:0:0:1:0)
Hawick (045086) 314
Madgwick, P. S. (—:—:0:0:0)
Petersfield (0730) 68949
Manners, H. J. (—:—:—:—:0)
Swindon (0793) 762232
Mason, A. J. (1:0:—:0:0)
Bibury (028574) 266
Mason, N. B. (—:—:—:0:1)
Crook, Co. Durham 091-373 6277
Mathew, R. K. (—:—:1:0:0)
Burford (04514) 311
Mays-Smith, Lady E. M.
(—:—:—:—:0)
Newbury (0488) 2209
McCune, D. (—:—:0:0:2)
Bishopton (0740) 30722
McInnes Skinner, Mrs C. (0:0:0:0:1)
Melton Mowbray (066477) 327
McKenzie-Coles, W. G. (1:2:0:1:0)
Taunton (09847) 334
McMillan, M. D. (—:—:0:3:0)
Bibury (028574) 341
Miller, N. (1:2:4:2:0)
Ferryhill 091-410 9696 (office) and
(0388) 721565
Mitchell, C. W. (1:0:0:0:1)
Dorchester (03005) 276
Morton, T. (1:0:0:0:0)
Leominster (056881) 488
Moscrop, Mrs E. (—:—:—:—:0)
Newcastle-upon-Tyne 091-236 2145
Mulhall, J. L. (0:0:0:0:0)
York (0904) 706321

Neaves, A. S. (0:0:0:0:0)
Faversham (079 589) 274
Needham, J. L. (0:0:0:1:0)
Ludlow (0584) 2112 and 4826
Nelson, W. M. (0:0:0:2:1)
Dumfries (038775) 237

O'Brien, D. C. (—:—:0:0:0)
Pembury, Kent (089282) 4072 and
4123
O'Neill, J. G. (—:—:—:—:0)
Bicester (0869) 277202

Paisley, R. (2:0:0:0:0)
Langholm (03873) 80698 and 80308
(office)
Panvert, J. F. (—:0:0:0:0)
Hildenborough (0732) 838443
Park, I. (0:0:1:2:0)
Eaglescliffe (0642) 580263
Patman, Miss R. J. (—:—:—:—:0)
Moreton-in-Marsh (0608) 74492
Payne, J. R. (1:1:0:0:0)
Dulverton (03987) 244
Peachey, H. E. (0:0:0:0:0)
Stratford (0789) 294520
Perrett, A. C. J. (0:1:0:0:0)
Cheltenham (0242) 820244 and
820841

Peter-Hoblyn, G. H. (—:0:0:—:0)
  Bodmin (0208) 84227
Phillips, Miss C. E. (0:0:—:0:0)
  Hereford (04973) 286 and 204
Pike, S. L. (1:0:0:0:1)
  Sidmouth (03957) 485
Pilkington, J. (0:1:1:0:0)
  Birtsmorton (068481) 580
Pilkington, Mrs J. St C. (0:0:0:0:1)
  Stow-on-the-Wold (0451) 30641
Pinney, C. W. (—:—:—:—:0)
  Louth (0507) 313234
Pittendrigh, S. I. (—:—:—:—:0)
  Wylam (0661) 852676
Plater, Miss L. C. (—:—:—:—:0)
  Bishop Auckland (0388) 832963
Plowright, Mrs G. S. (2:1:2:1:0)
  Sheffield (0226) 790472
Price, Mrs A. (1:0:1:—:0)
  Presteigne (0544) 267221
Price, G. M. (1:0:0:1:2)
  Brecon (087484) 212
Price, T. J. (0:0:0:—:0)
  Chepstow (0291) 421596
Price, W. (2:0:—:0:0)
  Leominster (056881) 439
Prince, O. R. (0:0:0:0:0)
  Barton-under-Needwood (028375) 229
Pritchard, P. L. J. (—:1:0:3:0)
  Purton, Glos. (0453) 811881
Pugh, R. C. (0:0:0:0:0)
  Worcester (0905) 640547 and 640211

Rae, Miss J. L. (—:—:—:—:0)
  Dunbar (03684) 217
Raw, W. (—:—:—:0:0)
  Richmond (0748) 818371
Reed, W. J. (0:0:0:0:3)
  Barnstaple (07694) 292
Rich, P. M. (—:—:—:0:0)
  Raglan (0291) 690864
Richards, Graham (—:—:—:—:0)
  Pontypridd (0443) 450029
Rimell, Mrs M. R. T. (—:—:—:0:1)
  Pershore (038682) 209
Robson, T. L. A. (1:0:0:1:0)
  Alnwick (066574) 307
Roe, G. L. (—:1:0:1:0)
  Yelverton (0822) 852850
Russell, Mrs P. A. (—:—:—:—:0)
  Flaxton (090486) 425
Ryall, B. J. M. (0:0:1:2:0)
  Yeovil (0935) 850222

Salmon P. (—:—:0:—:0)
  Wetherby (0937) 588525
Sample, W. N. (0:2:4:1:0)
  Morpeth (067074) 627
Sandys-Clarke, R. P. (3:3:1:0:0)
  Darlington (0833) 60215
Saul, Mrs M. M. (0:0:—:0:0)
  Spilsby, Lincs. (0790) 52034
Sawyer, H. (—:—:—:—:1)
  Newmarket (0638) 780749
Scott, D. D. (0:1:1:0:0)
  Minehead (0643) 2430
Scott, D. W. (0:0:0:0:0)
  Hexham (0434) 673313

Scott, Mrs E. B. (0:0:0:0:0)
  Keyworth (0509) 880489
Scriven, B. A. (0:0:3:0:0)
  Taunton (0823) 490208
Scrivens, Mrs J. (—:—:0:0:0)
  Bampton, Devon (0398) 331232
Sheridan, F. (—:0:0:0:0)
  Rowington (05643) 2011
Shiels, R. (—:—:0:0:0)
  Jedburgh (0835) 62743 and 64060
Simmons, J. C. (1:0:0:0:0)
  Abridge, Essex (037881) 2440
Skelton, J. (0:0:0:0:0)
  Skipton (0282) 842503
Slack, Mrs D. E. (0:0:0:0:0)
  Appleby (07683) 51354
Smith, F. G. (—:—:0:0:0)
  Gloucester (0452) 730265
Smith, M. J. (0:0:0:0:0)
  Thornaby (0642) 593198
Smith, S. G. (1:0:0:0:0)
  Grimsby (0472) 840276 or (0274)
    564930
Smith, W. J. (0:0:0:0:1)
  Islip (086733) 224
Smith, W. J. F. (0:0:0:0:1)
  Richmond (0748) 822629
Southall, Miss E. J. (—:—:—:0:0)
  Wincanton (0963) 32179
Sporborg, C. H. (3:1:0:0:0)
  Bishops Stortford (027974) 444
Spottiswood, P. (—:—:0:0:0)
  Hexham (0434) 240472
Stapleton, Mrs Y. E. (—:—:0:0:0)
  Bishop Auckland (0388) 710014
Stevens, S. R. (1:0:0:0:0)
  Exeter (0404) 822205
Stickland, G. W. (0:0:0:0:0)
  Stalbridge (0963) 62492
Stirk, Mrs M. K. (0:0:4:5:3)
  Ripon (0765) 658447
Stone, R. F. (—:—:—:—:0)
  Fareham (0329) 833573
Storey, F. S. (2:0:1:1:0)
  Carlisle (022875) 331
Stronge, R. M. (—:—:—:—:0)
  Newbury (0635) 248710
Supple, K. R. (0:0:—:0:0)
  Maidstone (0622) 6516
Swiers, J. E. (6:8:3:0:2)
  Helperby (0423) 322153
Swindlehurst, D. G. (0:0:2:2:0)
  Carlisle (022874) 289

Taplin, J. P. (0:—:0:0:0)
  Minehead (064384) 258
Teal, Mrs V. J. (0:0:0:—:0)
  St Clears (083483) 694
Temple, B. M. (0:0:0:0:0)
  Driffield (0377) 42321 and 241923
Tetley, Mrs P. A. (—:0:0:1:0)
  Cranleigh (0483) 274013
Thick, N. K. (0:0:0:0:0)
  Dymock (053185) 453
Thomson, A. M. (—:0:0:0:1)
  Greenlaw (03616) 514
Thomson, Mrs D. (1:1:0:—:0)
  Kinross (0577) 63418

101

Thornley, B. (—:—:—:0:0)
Standish (0257) 422932
Thorpe, J. G. (0:0:0:0:0)
Brigg (0652) 652135
Todd, D. T. (0:1:2:0:0)
Lincoln (0673) 858242
Tomkinson, Mrs A. (—:—:—:—:0:0)
Pocklington (0759) 302268
Townsend, R. D. (1:0:3:1:0)
Charing (023371) 2586
Tuck, J. C. (—:—:—:2:0)
Badminton (0454) 23236
Tucker, F. G. (—:—:—:0:0)
Wedmore, Somerset (0934) 712684
Turner, D. T. (—:—:0:0:1)
Spalding (0775) 87544
Turner, J. R. (1:0:0:1:0)
Helperby (0423) 322239
Turner, Miss S. J. (—:0:0:0:0)
Ripon (0423) 324096
Turton, S. F. (1:0:0:0:0)
Yealmpton (0752) 880105
Tutty, Mrs K. J. (—:0:0:0:0)
Northallerton (060983) 624 and (0748)
834184 (office)
Twibell, J. (0:1:0:0:0)
Dinnington (0909) 562338

Upson, P. N. (0:0:0:0:0)
Ashford, Kent (030381) 2320

Wade, J. (—:1:0:0:7)
Ferryhill (0740) 30310
Waggott, N. (0:0:0:0:0)
Spennymoor (0388) 819012
Wakely, P. (0:0:0:—:0)
Cullompton (08846) 357
Wales, W. A. (0:0:0:0:1)
Fakenham (032875) 580
Waley-Cohen, R. B. (3:1:0:1:2)
Banbury (029587) 632
Walton, F. T. (4:8:5:3:2)
Morpeth (0669) 40253
Ward, Mrs S. A. (0:1:0:0:0)
Northallerton (060982) 293
Ward, Mrs V. C. (0:0:0:0:2)
Grantham (05295) 260
Waring, L. E. (0:0:0:0:0)
Wellington, Somerset (082347) 2660
Waterman, Miss S. E. (0:0:1:0:0)
Dorchester (093583) 394

Wates, C. S. (0:1:1:0:0)
Rye (07974) 2125
Watson, A. (—:0:—:0:0)
Skipton (028284) 2228
Webb, H. J. M. (0:0:0:0:0)
Faringdon (0367) 20173
Wellicome, D. R. (4:2:0:0:0)
Northampton (0604) 740587
Welsh, D. D. G. (0:1:0:0:0)
Sevenoaks (0474) 813132
Whillans, A. C. (—:—:0:2:2)
Hawick (0450) 76642 and 73311
White, Mrs F. E. (0:0:0:1:0)
Chelmsford (0621) 742161
White, G. F. (—:—:—:—:1)
Alnwick (0665) 577430
White, Miss T. A. (0:0:0:0:0)
Newbury (063528) 608
Whyte, J. W. (—:—:—:0:2)
Beccles (0986) 81221
Wight, A. J. (0:0:0:—:0)
Cockburnspath (03683) 219
Wike, D. R. (—:—:1:1:0)
Taunton (0823) 400440
Williams, Mrs A. D. (—:—:—:—:0)
Kinver (0384) 873965
Williams, A. J. (0:0:—:0:0)
Newport (0633) 880255
Williams, D. G. (—:—:—:—:1)
Porth, Glamorgan (0443) 670269
Williams, Mrs F. A. W. (0:0:0:0:0)
Hitchin (0462) 34762
Williams, L. J. (—:—:—:—:0)
Williams, M. G. (0:0:1:0:0)
Newport, Gwent (0633) 880282
Williams, W. R. (0:0:2:1:1)
Idestone (0392) 81558
Wood, R. S. (—:—:—:0:2)
Nawton (0439) 71247
Woodrow, Mrs A. M. (0:0:0:0:0)
High Wycombe (024026) 2557
Wordingham, L. W. (—:0:1:0:1)
Fakenham (032875) 343

Young, B. R. J. (0:0:0:0:0)
Liskeard (0579) 20087
Young, Mrs J. A. F. (—:—:—:—:0)
Chippenham (0249) 720340
Young, W. G. (0:0:0:0:0)
Carluke (055586) 226

JOCKEYS

The following is a list of senior jockeys who held a licence for the season 1992/93. The figures in brackets show the number of winners each jockey has ridden in this country during the past five seasons, from 1988/89 to 1992/93 inclusive. Also included are their telephone numbers and riding weights.

Adams, A. J. (3:8:11:1:0)................. 9 7
(0488) 72238 and (0564) 794026
(agent)

Ahern, M. J. (3:10:10:10:3) 10 0
(0763) 41141

102

Akehurst, J. C. (3:2:1:0:0) 10   3
(0488) 72688

Armytage, Miss G. (4:6:2:11:4) ... 10   0
c/o (063528) 273 and (0831) 878662

Arnott, T. R. (2:3:0:0:0) 10   0
(07253) 504/520 and mobile (0860)
718654

Beggan, R. J. (24:22:13:22:6) 10   2
(0628) 667017 and fax 668178 and
mobilephone (0836)
507 343

Bellamy, R. J. (4:16:13:12:15) 10   0
(0451) 32477 and carphone (0836)
241458 and (agent) (0451) 850069 or
(0836) 774329

Bosley, M. R. (4:5:8:5:3) 10   2
(0367) 242224 and mobilephone (0831)
362262

Bradley, G. J. (34:30:26:29:30) 10   3
(0759) 371586 and mobilephone (0836)
753052 and fax (0759) 371028 (agent)
and (023559) 533 (home) and
mobilephone (0860) 722722

Brennan, Miss H. F. (0:0:0:2:2) .. 10   4
(063686) 322

Brennan, M. J. (17:22:17:10:23) .. 10   0
(0636) 703125 and (agent) (0636)
86654 and (0860) 707563

Bridgwater, D. G. (0:3:20:22:39)... 9   7
(0608) 50939 and (0831) 635817 and
(0451) 850069 and (0836) 774329
(agent)

Brownless, C. G. (—:—:—:1:1) ... 10   0
(06685) 317

Burchell, D. J. (13:12:13:15:13) ... 10   2
c/o (0495) 302551 and (0836) 329290

Burrough, S. C. (4:5:16:6:5) 10   0
(0860) 869374 and (agent) (0884)
820871

Byrne, D. C. (29:44:21:14:18) 10   0
(0235) 821250 or (0831) 547233 and
(0653) 600461 (home), mobilephone
(0836) 278374

Byrne, E. M. (—:0:2:3:2) 10   0
(0275) 374102 and c/o (0275) 372192
and 374185

Caldwell, P. (Pat) A.
(0:1:0:—:2) 10   2
(0831) 575879

Caldwell, P. H. (6:1:1:2:1) 10   2
(0925) 602679

Callaghan, J. G. (11:24:15:28:10). 10   0
(0347) 810825 (agent) and (0969)
22504 (home)

Campbell, R. (5:2:3:8:11) 10   1
(0638) 665357 and (0850) 712505

Carroll, A. W. (7:10:9:7:14) 10   0
(0836) 323090

Casey, D. (—:—:—:—:0) 9   10
(0274) 564930

Charlton, A. (9:9:0:9:3) 10   0
(026477) 2583

Clay, Miss D. L. (12:3:—:1:19) 10   0
(0782) 392131

Corkell, J. D. (0:3:12:1:0) 10   0
(0742) 586273

Cowley, S. (1:5:0:2:0) 10   0
(0242) 528634

Crosse, M. J. (3:0:1:0:1) 10   0
(0444) 85586

Davies, H. J. (50:60:51:44:33) 10   3
(079 371) 395 and (agent) (0423)
871624 and mobilephone (0860)
401683

Dawe, N. J. (1:2:2:2:2) 10   0
(0903) 884749 and (0295) 68619
(agent)

De Haan, B. (15:29:10:4:13) 10   0
(0488) 72163

Dennis, D. J. (—:1:1:2:0) 9   10
(0827) 716445

Doolan, K. J. (1:6:7:6:3) 9   13
(0207) 55259 and
502341 (home)

Doughty, D. N. (33:46:96:44:69) .. 10   6
(0768) 67800 and (0831) 204849
(mobile)

Duggan, D. J. (4:3:4:1:0) 10   4
(0235) 833767

Dunwoody, T. R.
(91:102:127:137:173) 10   2
(023559) 287 or carphone (0836)
502290 and (agent) (0451) 850069 or
(0836) 774329

Dwyer, M. P. (93:75:81:73:61) 10   3
(0944) 758841, (0860) 502233 and
(agent) (0759) 371586 and
mobilephone (0836) 753052 and fax
(0759) 371028

Earle, S. A. (13:22:16:8:4)............. 10   0
(0793) 782286 and mobilephone
(0860) 350116

Eccles, S. Smith
(45:56:56:21:30)............................ 10   5
(0638) 577238 and carphone (0836)
241780 and (agent) (0831) 865974

Elderfield, W. G. (—:—:0:0:0) 10   0
(0932) 563227

Farrell, P. A. (6:3:7:5:0) 9   10
(03475) 273 and 208

Fitzgerald, M. A. (2:1:11:38:54) .. 10   0
(0626) 854358 and (agent) (0932)
243913 or mobile (0860) 234342

Foster, M. R. (2:9:35:21:21) 9   11

Frost, J. D. (41:46:39:41:28) 10   4
(03644) 2267 and 2332 (home) and
mobile (0836) 723468 and (agent)
(0222) 615594

Gallagher, D. T. (3:23:12:16:17) .. 10   0
(0672) 40809, carphone (0836) 776937
and (agent) (0932) 243913 and
carphone (0860) 234342

Garritty, R. J. (21:22:14:17:21) 10   2
(0653) 600221 and (agent) (0347)
22410 or carphone (0836) 326084

Grant, C. (38:94:57:78:58)............. 10   0
(0388) 710425 and mobilephone (0860)
577998 and (agent) (0759) 371586 or
(0836) 753052

Grantham, T. O. (4:6:8:17:13) 10   0
(090671) 2432

103

Guest, R. C. (19:13:33:43:13) 10   1
(0264) 772907 (home), (0860) 883303
and (026477) 2278 and (agent) (0932)
243913 or (0860) 234342

Harker, G. A. (5:7:4:1:3) 10   0
(0642) 780995 and (0325) 378634
Harley, P. M (3:5:0:3:7) 10   0
(0932) 243913 and carphone (0860)
234342 (agent)
Harris, J. A. (3:2:10:4:8) 10   0
(0949) 60671
Harvey, L. J. (11:25:42:25:19)...... 10   0
(02357) 70551 and mobile (0850)
700287 and agent (0235) 821250 or
(0831) 547233
Hawke, N. J. (18:17:15:12:11)...... 10   0
(0803) 732891 or (0831)415473 and
(agent) mobile (0831) 865974
Hawkins, C. (12:11:7:4:13) 10   0
(0609) 748734 and (0374) 117997
Hazell, M. G. (0:1:0:—:0) 10   4
(0488) 71576
Hoad, M. R. (2:1:10:3:4)................ 10   1
(0932) 243913 and mobilephone (0860)
234342 (agent)
Hobbs, P. D. (47:43:9:31:51)......... 10   1
(0903) 877211 and mobilephone (0860)
608225
Hodge, R. J. (0:11:19:24:17) 10   0
(0751) 77142 (agent)
Hodgson, S. P. (9:6:8:9:2).............. 10   0
(0264) 772990 and (0831) 865974
(agent)
Holley, P. S. (22:11:19:11:21)......... 9 12
(07253) 504/520 and mobile (0860)
718654
Humphreys, W. G. (4:6:0:3:5) 10   0
(0451) 31515 mobilephone (0836)
777100 and (agent) (0451) 850069 or
(0836) 774329

Irvine, W. S. (23:14:12:10:13) 10   0
(0793) 870606 (agent)

Jarvis, T. O. (—:2:0:2:1) 10   0
(0235) 851361
Johnson, K. (14:14:24:12:6) 10   0
c/o (0388) 720213 or 091-267 4464 and
(0374) 131121
Jones, A. E. (7:2:1:3:1) 10   0
(0488) 648349 and (agent) (0235)
821250 or (0831) 547233
Jones, K. (1:0:2:2:2) 10   0
(0388) 663810
Jones, M. P. (12:9:11:8:0) 10   0
(0531) 822413

Kavanagh, J. R. (—:—:11:23:23)... 9   7
(0488) 72561 and mobile (0831)
376837 and (agent) (0932) 243913 or
mobile (0860) 234342
Keightley, S. L. (5:5:8:9:7)........... 10   0
(0638) 666070 and (agent)
(0964) 551135 or mobilephone (0860)
233041
Kent, T. J. (0:1:3:0:6)..................... 10   0
(0638) 668582

Kersey, Miss S. (1:1:0:1:0)............. 9 10
(0709) 873166

Lawrence, I. R. (15:21:16:15:6)..... 9   7
(02357) 69671 and mobile (0836)
211479
Leech, P. J. (—:3:1:2:0) 10   0
(0488) 71105
Llewellyn, C. (20:19:32:53:68) 10   0
(02357) 3410 and carphone (0836)
783223
Lodder, J. D. (10:25:18:6:5).......... 10   0
(0568) 611068 and carphone (0831)
486302 and (agent) (0235) 821250 or
(0831) 547233
Lower, J. A. (27:49:29:6:23) 10   0
(082347) 3580
Lynch, M. M. (12:17:16:23:7) 10   0
(029586) 713 or 767 (agent)
Lyons, Gary (8:31:10:7:3) 10   2
(0543) 876740 (home) and carphone
(0831) 330265 and (0543) 490298

Mackey, S. C. (6:8:2:0:1) 10   2
(0850) 434105
Maguire, A. (—:—:—:71:124) 10   0
(0932) 243913 or (0860) 234342
(agent)
Mann, N. J. W. (3:24:27:16:21) 10   0
mobilephone (0831) 236034 and agent
mobile (0831) 865974
Marley, R. J. (21:11:16:12:1) 10   0
mobile (0831) 890339
Martin, G. J. (0:2:0:0:0)................ 10   0
(0206) 240235
Maude, C. G. (3:12:28:20:11)........ 10   0
(0823) 278466 (home) and mobile
(0831) 094601 and (0793) 870606
(agent)
McCabe, A. J. (2:1:1:1:0).................. 9 10
(07253) 504/520 and mobile (0860)
718654
McCourt, G. M.
(86:100:83:102:70)....................... 10   4
(023559) 501, mobilephone (0836)
749191 and (agent) (0759) 371586 or
(0836) 753052
McDermott, P. S. (5:7:1:1:1)........ 10   0
(0452) 76459
McFarland, W. J.
(23:26:24:15:6)............................. 10   0
(0488) 73374 and mobilephone (0831)
317039 and (agent) (0225) 873882 or
(0831) 244659
McKeown, D. W. E.
(31:30:17:16:0)............................. 10   0
081-948 2764 or 879 3377 (agent)
McKinley, E. M. (3:0:7:1:1)............ 9   7
c/o (090671) 2226 and (0903) 872071
McNeill, S. R. O.
(22:15:20:31:51)........................... 10   0
(048839) 8861
Merrigan, A. T. A. (28:10:9:7:7).. 10   0
(0833) 690265
Moloney, M. J. (—:8:9:12:17)....... 10   0
(0768) 891325
Moore, G. L. (2:9:17:11:12) 10   4
(0273) 681679 and mobilephone (0860)

893042 and (agent) (0932) 243913 and mobilephone (0860) 234342

Morris, D. (4:6:15:9:15) 10   0
(0883) 344893 and mobilephone (0860) 758412

Morris, W. A. F. F. (0:2:4:1:0) 10   0
(0299) 250686 and (0562) 755625

Mulholland, A. B. (9:7:5:3:3) 10   0
(0924) 499857 and mobilephone (0836) 784439

Murphy, D. J. (19:15:29:48:45) 10   0
(0638) 577702 (home) and (0344) 872781 and 27178 (agent)

Murphy, E. R. (10:9:10:8:16) 10   0
(0903) 873957

Niven, P. D. (49:48:86:105:108) ... 10   2
(0751) 77142 and fax 77124 (agent) and mobilephone (0860) 260999 and (0642) 712974

Nolan, D. A. (0:6:2:0:1) 10   10
(0698) 381106

O'Hagan, A. T. (4:0:3:0:2) 10   0
(0584) 811214

O'Hara, L. S. (21:10:24:20:7) 10   0
mobilephone (0860) 596031 and (agent) (0759) 371586 or carphone (0836) 753052 or fax (0759) 371028

Oliver, Mrs J. (4:5:7:6:11) 10   0
(0989) 65219 and (agent) (0235) 821250 or (0831) 547233

O'Neill, S. J. (18:19:13:14:7) 10   2
(0829) 260660 and mobilephone (0831) 278860 and (agent) (029586) 713 or 767

Orkney, R. A. (4:11:20:28:21) 10   0
(0347) 810825 (agent) and (0969) 22845 and (0831) 112571

Osborne, J. A. (22:53:62:76:102).. 10   0
(0488) 73139 (home) and carphone (0860) 533422 and (agent) (0451) 850069 or (0836) 774329

Perrett, M. E. (27:52:58:22:27)...... 9   7
079-887 4894 (home), (agent) (0367) 820214 and (0793) 522359

Pitman, M. A. (40:57:27:35:22)... 10   5
c/o (0488) 71714

Potts, T. M. (0:2:0:1:0) 10   0
(065261) 750

Powell, B. G. (64:48:38:35:12) 9   7
(0793) 782286 (home) and Radiophone (0860) 314745 and (agent) (0451) 850069 or (0836) 774329

Quinn, J. J. (9:10:5:6:2) 10   0
(09446) 370

Railton, J. A. (18:21:27:11:33)...... 10   3
(0367) 820794 and mobilephone (0374) 149336

Ranger, M. (—:0:0:5:2) 10   0
(0526) 833245

Reed, W. T. (11:14:14:19:33) 10   3
(0434) 344016 or mobile (0850)

376088 and 081-879 3377 or 948 2764 (home)

Richards, M. R. (30:25:28:37:19). 10   0
(0243) 553821 and mobilephone (0831) 155266

Robinson, M. I. (—:0:0:0:0).......... 10   0

Rowe, G. T. (—:2:5:3:6) 10   0
(0903) 209908 and (agent) (0638) 577238 or (0831) 865974

Rowell, R. (1:1:2:0:0)..................... 10   4
(03212) 3331

Ryan, C. J. M. (7:1:2:1:0).............. 10   0
(03477) 794

Scudamore, P. M.
(221:170:141:175:129) 10   0
(0451) 850741 and carphone (0836) 514820

Sharratt, M. R. (0:0:—:1:0).......... 10   0
(0488) 73446

Shoemark, I. W. (4:11:3:7:4)......... 10   0
(0798) 873382 and (agent) (0793) 522359 and (0367) 820214

Skyrme, D. V. (9:15:18:6:8).......... 10   0
(044282) 7830 (home) and carphone (0836) 381957 and (agent) (0793) 870606

Smith, A. S. (4:8:24:14:11)............ 10   0
(0831) 272910

Smith, C. N. (3:14:10:8:5) 10   0
(0347) 22410 and carphone (0836) 326084 (agent)

Smith, V. (0:5:2:2:4)....................... 10   0
(0638) 668972 and (agent) 668974 or (0831) 865974

Stokell, Miss A. (0:1:0:3:1)............. 9   7
c/o (092684) 3332

Storey, B. (30:32:20:40:44) 10   0
(0347) 810825 (agent), (022875) 376 (home) and mobilephone (0860) 432881

Stronge, R. M. (9:2:3:10:5)........... 10   0
(063524) 8710 and (0884) 820871 (agent)

Supple, R. J. (8:34:29:31:27)......... 10   0
(0788) 890909 and (0860) 548901

Tegg, D. R. (21:12:21:19:18)......... 10   0
(0432) 352674 and mobilephone (0831) 117575 and (agent) (0793) 870606

Telfer, D. M. (1:1:0:1:1)................ 10   4
(0507) 533764

Turner, S. (29:25:5:6:4) 10   0
(0937) 582690 and (0831) 502899

Turner, Miss T. J.
(—:—:—:—:0) 10   0
(0822) 82458

Upton, G. (7:13:10:5:22) 10   1
(0488) 28883 and mobilephone (0831) 169766 and (agent) (0981) 22673 or (0831) 68075

Velfre, C. J. (—:—:—:0:0) 9   7
(0568) 2333

Vincent, Miss L. J. (5:5:11:10:8) ... 9   0
(0488) 73385 and mobilephone (0831) 532068

Wall, T. R. (15:15:10:12:8) 10   0
(074636) 569 and carphone (0860)
256211
Webb, A. (15:10:13:14:11) 10   0
(0295) 87756 and (agent) (0386)
858279
White, J. A. (27:31:14:11:7) 10   0
(0488) 72831
Wilkinson, D. (5:2:6:9:7) 9   7
(0969) 22060
Williamson, N. (—:20:33:33:41)... 10   0
(0981) 540411 and (0860) 902466 and
(agent) (0932) 243913 and mobile
(0860) 234342
Woods, W. (—:—:—:—:0) 8   1
(0638) 711260 and (agent) 081-471
5477 or (0836) 230335
Worthington, W. M. (1:7:5:3:2) ... 10   0
(0455) 619206

Wright, B. J. (3:5:—:—:0) 10   7
(023559) 533
Wyer, L. A. (36:33:44:35:48) 10   0
(0653) 628877 and mobilephone (0831)
218288 and (agent) (0751) 77142 and
fax 77124

The following relinquished their licence
during the season:

Brown J. L. (5:2:3:1:0)
Dowling, B. (17:23:14:7:2)
Fahey, R. A. (29:18:9:9:0)
McLaughlin, J. F. S. (7:4:8:2:2)
McWilliams, P. (—:—:—:—:4)
Tory, A. S. (15:15:32:26:14)

CONDITIONAL JOCKEYS

The following list shows the employer and riding weights of every conditional
jockey who held a licence for the 1992/93 season. The figures in brackets show
firstly the allowance claimed by each rider and secondly the number of winners
each jockey has ridden in this country during the past five seasons, from 1988/89
to 1992/93 inclusive.

Conditional jockeys are entitled to the following allowances in steeplechases
and hurdle races which are open to professional jockeys: 7 lb until they have won
15 races; thereafter 5 lb until they have won 30 races; thereafter 3 lb until they
have won 55 races (any win in any kind of race in any country included). The
allowances can be claimed in the following races, with the exception of conditional
races: (a) all handicaps except the Grand National (b) all selling races (c) all other
races with guaranteed prize money of not more than £5,000.

Allen, M. (7) (—:0:0:0:0) 9 12
(J. Edwards)
Appleby, M. (7) (—:—:—:—:0) 9   7
(B. Richmond)
Attwater, M. J. (7) (–:–:–:–:0) 10   0
(J. Sutcliffe)
Ayles, W. J. (7) (—:0:0:1:0) 9   7
(J. Gifford)

Barry, D. J. P. (0:1:0:1:1) 9   8
(G. Richards)
Bastiman, H. J. (7) (—:—:—:0:0) . 9   0
(R. Bastiman)
Bates, A. (7) (—:—:—:4:8) 9   7
(P. Kelleway)
Bazin, G. N. (7) (—:—:—:0:1) 9   7
(K. Bailey)
Bentley, D. B. (5) (—:0:2:12:9)...... 9   7
(M. Hammond) (0969) 23054
Bentley, N. A. (3) (—:—:3:16:25).. 9   7
(G. Moore) (0969) 23054
Berry, M. (7) (—:—:—:—:1) 10   0
(C. Brooks)
Billany, Miss A. L. (7)
(—:0:0:0:0) 8   6
(J. Thorpe)

Blythe, W. S. (7) (—:—:—:—:0).... 9   7
(R. Weaver)
Bohan, D. J. (7) (—:—:—:—:2) 9   7
(P. Murphy)
Bond, J. M. (7) (—:—:—:—:0) 9   0
(J. Peacock)
Braybrook, Miss T. J. (7)
(—:—:—:0:0) 9   7
(A. Forte)
Bridger, Miss R. J. (7) (0:0:0:0:0) . 9   0
(J. Bridger)
Brown, J. J. (7) (—:—:—:0:0) 9   7
(J. Gifford)
Brown, K. (7) (—:—:—:—:1) 9   7
(A. Wilson)
Burke, J. H. (7) (0:0:0:0:0) 10   0
(Mrs S. Bramall)

Caddell, J. J. (7) (—:—:—:—:1) 8 11
(W. Muir)
Cahill, G. P. (7) (—:0:—:0:1)........ 9   7
(B. Rothwell)
Carey, P. D. (7) (—:—:—:2:1) 9   7
(Bill Turner)
Carr, P. A. (7) (—:0:0:1:0) 9   7
(J. Johnson)

Clarke, J. (7) (3:1:0:1:3) 9 10
(A. Moore)
Clifford, B. M. (—:4:9:27:16).......... 9   7
(P. Hobbs) (0984) 40239 or (agent)
(0932) 243913 and mobilephone (0860)
234342
Codd, J. (7) (—:—:—:—:5).............. 9 10
(Mrs M. Reveley)
Collers, R. A. (7) (—:—:—:—:0) ... 9   7
(Mrs M. Reveley)
Comerford, K. C. (7)
(—:—:—:0:4) 9 12
(J. White)
Cooke, J. L. (7) (—:—:0:0:0) 9   7
(A. Jones)
Cooney, D. (7) (—:0:1:0:0) 10   9
(Mrs J. Pitman)
Crone, G. S. (7) (—:1:1:0:0) 9   7
(R. Curtis) (07982) 2423
Curran, J. M. (7) (—:0:0:0:0).......... 9   7
(Miss J. Doyle)
Cuthbert, Miss C. (7) (0:3:0:0:0) ... 9   0
(T. Cuthbert)

Dace, L. A. (7) (—:0:2:2:2) 9   7
(R. Rowe)
Dalton, B. P. (7) (—:1:5:3:1) 9   7
(J. Wharton) (0664) 78364
Darke, E. R. (7) (—:—:0:6:2) 10   0
(R. Frost)
Dascombe, T. G. (7)
(—:—:—:1:1) 9   7
(M. Pipe)
David, A. N. (7) (0:1:2:0:0) 9   7
(R. Ingram)
Davies, Miss J. A. (7)
(—:—:0:6:3) 9   7
(M. Charles) (0926) 493878 and
(agent) (0850) 205872
Davies, J. J. (7) (—:—:—:—:0) 9   7
(T. Tate)
Davies, K. (7) (—:—:—:—:0) 9   7
(R. O'Leary)
Davies, P. W. (7) (0:0:1:1:0)........... 9   7
(N. Henderson) (02357) 67547
Davis, R. J. (5) (0:0:3:0:14)............. 9 10
(D. Wintle) or (0989) 768974 (home)
and (0831) 592575 and agent (0932)
243913 or mobile (0860) 234342
Dennis, C. P. (3) (11:4:1:1:3).......... 9 11
(M. Naughton) (0325) 383295
Dicken, A. R. (5) (0:0:2:14:3) 9 12
(S. Dow)
Dimond, S. W. D. (7)
(—:—:—:—:0) 9   7
(M. Muggeridge)
Dobbin, A. G. (3) (—:—:—:14:23) . 9   0
(M. Barnes) (0768) 881257
Donohoe, S. S. (5) (0:—:8:1:1)....... 9 12
(P. Nicholls)
Downs, N. H. (7) (—:—:—:—:0) ... 9   7
(T. Hallett)
Doyle, M. A. (7) (0:0:2:0:0)............. 9   7
(F. Jordan)
Driscoll, J. P. (7) (—:1:0:4:1) 9 11
(M. W. Easterby)
Dwan, W. J. (5) (1:1:6:7:10) 9   7
(J. FitzGerald) (0751) 77142 (agent)

Eccles Smith, P. (7) (—:—:0:0:2).. 9   4
(M. Tompkins) (0638) 668974 and
(0831) 865974 (agent)
Edwards, R. (7) (—:—:0:0:0) 9   0
(D. McCain)
Eldredge, Miss L. C. (7)
(—:0:—:—:1) 9   7
(R. Lee)
Eley, T. J. (7) (—:—:—:4:14) 9   7
(T. Forbes) (0283) 585035 and (agent)
(0709) 866276 or (0831) 300935

Farrant, R. A. (5) (—:1:3:7:11)...... 9   7
(T. Forster) (02357) 70551 and mobile
(0850) 730733 and agent (0235)
821250 and (0831) 547233
FitzGerald, M. P. (7) (—:0:0:0:2).. 9   0
(M. Bradstock)
Flannigan, A. M. (7) (—:—:0:1:3) . 9   7
(C. Broad)
Fogarty, J. M. (7) (—:—:—:—:0) .. 9   7
(T. Casey)
Fortt, D. L. (7) (—:—:0:3:4).......... 9   7
(A. Turnell)
Fox, S. (7) (1:0:0:2:0) 9   8
(M. Muggeridge)
Fry, W. S. (7) (—:0:4:3:2) 9   7
(T. Tate)

Greene, R. J. (3) (2:12:8:14:17)...... 9 11
(P. Nicholls) (0749) 86656 and (0831)
272679 and (agent) (0793) 870606

Harding, B. P. (7) (—:—:—:—:2).. 9   7
(G. Richards)
Harmer, G. (7) (—:—:—:0:0) 10   0
(Mrs J. Pitman)
Heffernan, N. J. (7)
(—:—:—:—:0) 9 12
(F. Murphy)
Herrington, M. (7)
(—:—:—:—:2) 9   7
(Mrs M. Reveley)
Hide, P. E. (5) (—:—:—:8:18)........ 9   9
(J. Gifford)
Hobbs, D. M. (7) (—:—:—:—:1).... 9   4
(K. Bishop)
Hogg, S. R. (7) (—:—:—:—:0) 9 10
(M. Hammond)
Hope, G. (7) (—:—:—:—:0).......... 10   0
(D. Laing)
Hourigan, M. P. (3)
(—:—:—:24:21) 9   7
(P. Hobbs) (0932) 243913 and (0860)
234342 (agent)
Huggan, C. H. (7) (1:0:1:0:0).......... 9 10
(Mrs D. Haine)

James, J. L. D. (7)
(—:—:—:—:2) 9   0
(J. Upson)
Johnson, P. A. (7) (—:—:—:—:0).. 9   7
(M. W. Easterby)
Juckes, N. R. (7) (—:—:—:0:0)...... 9 12
(R. Juckes)

Keighley, M. H. (7)
(—:—:—:—:0) 9   7
(D. Nicholson)

Larnach, A. A. (3) (—:3:6:11:13)... 9 10
  (P. Cheesbrough)
Leach, N. R. (7) (1:1:2:5:5)............. 9 7
  (G. Richards)
Leahy, D. (5) (0:—:2:6:11)............. 9 7
  (Mrs H. Parrott) (0684) 297119 and
  (0831) 323736 and
  (agent) (0367) 820214/711 and
  (0793) 622359
Leahy, F. T. (7) (—:—:—:0:3) 9 7
  (J. FitzGerald)
Leigh, E. J. (7) (—:—:—:0:0) 9 7
  (J. Leigh)
Le Jeune, A. J. (7) (—:—:0:0:0)... 10 0
  (G. Balding)
Lillis, P. J. (7) (—:—:—:—:0) 9 7
  (Mrs J. Pitman)
Linton, A. (7) (—:0:0:0:1)................ 9 7
  (T. Dyer)
Long, Miss L. G. (7) (0:1:2:0:3) 9 7
  (J. Long)
Lycett, S. (7) (—:—:—:—:0) 9 7
  (G. Fierro)
Lynch, Miss A. J. (7)
  (—:—:—:—:0) 9 7
  (B. Palling)
Lyons, S. C. (5) (—:—:—:—:6) 9 10
  (M. Hammond) (0969) 23240

Madgwick A. P. (7)
  (—:—:—:0:0)................................. 9 9
  (P. Madgwick)
Marston, W. J. (3) (—:1:4:16:26)... 9 9
  (D. Nicholson) (0386) 73209 or
  071-409 1608 (agent)
Mason, S. T. (7) (1:0:1:1:7).............. 9 7
  (Mrs M. Reveley)
Massey, R. I. (7) (—:—:—:0:1)...... 9 7
  (D. Nicholson)
Matthews, D. D. (7) (—:0:1:7:2) ... 9 10
  (R. Holder)
  (0235) 821250 and (0831) 547233
  (agent)
McCabe, J. J. P. (7)
  (—:—:—:—:0)................................. 9 0
  (Bill Turner)
McCarthy, J. A. (5) (—:0:2:1:2:18) 9 10
  (O. Sherwood)
McDougall, S. J. (7) (0:0:—:—:0)... 9 7
  (W. Kemp)
McEntee, P. L. P. (7)
  (—:—:—:0:0)................................ 10 0
  (P. McEntee)
McEntee, P. (Paul) S. (7)
  (1:0:3:0:0).................................... 9 10
  (P. McEntee)
  (0273) 23889 or (0850) 725039 (agent)
McGonagle, M. (5) (—:1:3:9:2)... 10 0
  (S. Christian)
McGrath, G. J. (7) (—:—:—:0:0)... 9 7
  (A. Jarvis)
McKenna, R. P. (7)
  (—:—:—:—:0) 9 7
  (T. Forster)
McLoughlin, P. J. (7)
  (—:—:—:—:2)................................. 9 7
  (J. White) (0932) 243913 (agent) or
  (0860) 234342 (mobile)

Meredith, D. (3) (—:2:2:13:11) 9 2
  (R. Dickin) (0451) 850069 and
  (0836) 774329 (agent)
Middleton, A. (7) (—:—:—:—:0) . 10 5
  (J. White)
Midgley, P. T. (5) (2:5:6:10:1)...... 10 7
  (J. Dooler)
Moffatt, D. J. (5) (—:1:3:15:13) 9 7
  (D. Moffatt) (0327) 349700 (agent)
Moore, P. A. (7) (—:—:—:1:1)....... 9 10
  (J. Moore)
Moore, R. W. (7) (0:2:1:0:0) 9 10
  (G. Enright)
Munday, M. D. (7) (—:—:0:0:0) 9 7
  (N. Henderson) (0488) 72259 or 71099
Murphy, B. J. (7) (2:2:—:0:2)....... 10 0
  (F. Murphy)

Neaves, J. P. (7) (—:3:2:1:0) 9 7
  (N. Thomson) (0747) 52857

O'Brien, F. M. (7) (—:—:—:—:0) . 9 7
  (C. Cowley)
O'Hare, L. N. P. (7) (—:0:2:2:4).... 9 7
  (Mrs J. Pitman)
O'Sullivan, D. K. (3)
  (10:4:6:16:14)................................. 10 4
  (R. O'Sullivan) (0222) 615594 (agent)

Parker, N. (7) (—:—:—:0:0)........... 9 7
  (P. Hobbs)
Perratt, W. F. (7) (0:1:1:0:9).......... 9 7
  (L. Lungo)
Pratt, J. D. (7) (—:—:—:—:0)......... 9 0
  (C. Treitline)
Procter, A. R. (5) (—:—:1:4:4) 9 7
  (D. Elsworth) (07253) 504/520 and
  mobile (0860) 718654
Protheroe, T. S. (7) (—:0:1:1:0) 9 7
  (F. Jordan)
Pullin, J. R. (7) (0:0:1:5:0) 9 12
  (K. Bailey)

Rees, D. C. (7) (0:0:0:0:0) 9 10
  (B. Palling)
Reynolds L. R. (7) (—:—:—:1:2)... 9 7
  (M. Pipe)
Richmond, D. S. (5) (1:2:7:7:10).... 9 7
  (M. Pipe)
Roberts, M. A. (7) (—:—:0:—:1)... 9 7
  (Mrs A. Swinbank)
Robertson G. N. (7) (—:0:1:0)... 9 7
  (B. McMahon)
Robinson, S. (7) (—:—:0:0:0) 9 7
  (T. Forster) (02357) 3092 or 3295
Rooney, D. C. (7) (—:—:—:—:0) .. 9 7
  (N. Gaselee)
Ryan, D. A. (7) (—:—:—:0:4)......... 9 7
  (Mrs M. Reveley)
Ryan, J. B. (3) (1:11:1:9:8)............... 9 11
  (Mrs J. Renfree-Barons) (0932)
  243913) and (0860) 234342 (agent)
Ryan, S. (7) (—:—:1:0:0)................. 9 7
  (R. Akehurst)

Salter, D. G. (7) (0:0:0:0:11)............ 9 7
  (Mrs J. Retter)
Scholes, A. P. (7) (—:—:—:0:0).... 9 7

Sellars, Miss K. (7)
(—:—:—:—:1) 9 7
(M. Hammond)
Shakespeare, A. L. (7)
(—:—:—:—:0) 9 0
(N. Twiston-Davies)
Slattery, J. V. (3) (6:3:7:5:10) 9 0
(O. O'Neill) (0242) 603594 and (0831)
545789 or agent (0850) 205872
Spence, S. D. (7) (—:—:—:—:0:0) 9 7
(B. McMahon)
Stenning, J. (7) (—:0:0:0:0) 9 7
(J. Ffitch-Heyes)
Sterry, W. A. (7) (—:0:0:0:0) 9 7
(Mrs A. Knight)
Stevens, M. (7) (0:0:2:0:1) 9 13
(B. Stevens)
Stocks, N. A. (7) (—:—:—:0:2) 9 10
(G. Moore)
Supple, J. A. (7) (—:0:3:5:1) 9 7
(N. Mason)

Taylor, S. D. (7) (—:—:0:3:7) 9 0
(W. Bentley)
Thompson, P. A. (7) (—:—:1:0:1) . 9 7
(N. Henderson)
Thompson, T. P. (7) (—:—:0:0:3).. 9 7
(R. Hodges)
Tierney, E. (5) (0:6:6:7:0) 9 7
(Mrs J. Retter) c/o (0392) 81410
Twomey, G. E. (7)
(—:—:—:—:0) 9 7
(J. FitzGerald)
Towler, D. L. (7) (—:—:—:—:2) ... 9 0
(Mrs S. Smith)
Trott, M. A. (7) (—:—:—:0:0) 9 7
(T. McGovern)

Waggott, P. (5) (—:—:3:4:12) 9 7
(D. Smith) (0759) 71586 and mobile
(0836) 753052 or fax (0759) 71028
(agent)
Walsh, D. J. (5) (—:—:—:1:0) 9 7
(D. McCain)
Ward, P. D. (7) (—:—:0:1:0) 9 7
(M. Wilkinson)
Whelan, M. P. (7) (—:—:—:—:1) .. 9 5
(J. Eyre)
White, P. A. (7) (—:—:—:0:0) 9 7
(A. Bailey)
Whitham, A. D. (7) (—:1:—:—:0) . 9 7
(D. McCain)
Willer, Miss I. P. A. (7)
(—:—:—:—:0) 9 10
(K. Wingrove)

Williams, I. A. (7) (—:—:0:0:0) ... 10 0
(C. James)
Williams, P. D. (5) (0:0:1:6:11) 9 12
(Mrs S. Bradburne) (0636) 86654 and
(0860) 707563 (agent) and (0334)
828966
Williams, S. D. (3) (—:5:3:9:7) 9 7
(J. Glover) (0709) 866276 and (0831)
300935 (agent)
Wingate, A. (7) (—:—:0:3:0) 9 9
(J. Jenkins)
Winter, D. (7) (—:—:—:0:0) 9 7
(P. Dalton)
Woodall, C. (7) (0:0:—:0:6) 9 9
(Mrs V. Aconley)
Wright, C. D. (7) (—:—:—:—:0)... 9 7
(M. Channon)
Wynne, S. (3) (—:—:6:12:12) 8 11
(R. Hollinshead) (0543) 490298

The following relinquished their
licence during the season:

Brown, M. P. (1:1:—:1:0)
Donoghue, V. P. (—:—:—:1:0)
Geoghegan, D. P. (—:—:—:—:2)
Harris, M. P. (—:—:—:—:0)
Hartnett, K. C. (—:—:0:3:0)
Heaver, G. R. D. (0:1:1:2:3)
Hughes, P. (—:0:0:4:0)
Jones, J. J. (—:—:—:—:2)
Leech, J. P. (10:16:2:2:0)
Lees, D. W. (—:0:2:0:0)
Maddock, P. J. (—:—:—:2:0)
McCabe, J. B. (—:0:0:1:0)
McGrath, G. J. (—:—:—:0:0)
Meade, D. N. (—:0:0:2:4)
Mullaney, L. A. (0:0:3:7:1)
Murphy, J. J. (—:—:—:2:1)
Murtagh, F. P. (2:0:20:15:1)
Newsome, A. (—:—:—:0:0)
O'Connor, N. J. (—:—:—:—:0)
O'Donovan, E. F. (0:0:1:0:0)
O'Hanlon, J. (0:0:1:1:0)
O'Hare, J. P. (—:—:—:—:0)
O'Reilly, M. G. (—:—:—:—:0)
Roberts, R. W. (—:—:—:—:0)
Saunders, J. (—:—:0:—:0)
Skelton, J. A. (—:0:0:0:0)
Squire, L. A. (—:—:—:—:0)
Thomson, G. J. (0:0:1:2:1)
Twomey, J. G. (—:—:7:11:0)

AMATEUR RIDERS

The following is a list of 'Category B' amateur riders who hold a permit to ride in flat races, steeplechases, hurdle races and National Hunt Flat races. The figures in brackets show the number of winners each jockey has ridden in this country during the past five seasons, from 1988/89 to 1992/93 inclusive. Also included are their telephone numbers.

H. R. H. Princess Royal (0:0:0:0:0)
c/o (0451) 30417
Adkin, Mrs G. (—:—:—:—:0)
Alner, R. H. (1:2:5:8:1)
(02586) 271
Anderson, K. (6:4:4:2:0)
(04615) 482
Andrews, S. R. (4:0:2:0:2)
(046276) 263
Arbuthnot, Mrs D. (—:0:0:0:0)
Armson, R. J.(—:—:—:—:0)
Armytage, M. D. (7:6:6:20:4)
(036787) 637 and mobilephone (0860) 507447
Astaire, S. (—:—:0:1:0)
Atkinson, P. G. (1:0:0:—:0)

Bailey, E. D. (4:1:2:2:2)
(02357) 67547
Bailey, Mrs T. L. (0:1:1:1:1)
(063528) 253
Baker, D. K. D. (—:—:—:—:0)
Barfoot-Saunt, G. C. (—:—:—:—:0)
Barlow, C. J. B. (0:1:1:0:0)
Barlow, T. D. B. (1:0:0:0:0)
Barnett, Miss K. A. (—:—:—:0:0)
Barons, R. D. R. (0:0:—:—:0)
Batters, M. J. (1:0:0:2:0)
(07254) 609
Baxter, Miss S. E. (1:0:0:1:0)
c/o (0827) 62901
Bealby, C. C. (0:0:2:2:0)
(0476) 72749
Beardsall, J. H. (2:0:0:0:1)
(0748) 84551
Belcher, Miss S. J. (0:0:0:0:0)
(0580) 200039
Bell, S. B. (0:3:0:0:0)
Bethell, Mrs E. A. (0:0:0:0:0)
Billot, Miss S. A. (—:0:9:3:0)
(0488) 84285
Blackford, Miss L. A. (—:0:0:0:1)
(0964) 562996
Blackwell, S. C. (—:—:1:0:0)
Bloom, Miss C. A. (—:—:—:0:0)
(0953) 603137
Bloom, N. M. (1:1:0:1:0)
(0953) 603137
Bloor, D. R. (1:0:0:0:0)
(0455) 291739
Bonner, C. C. M. (—:—:—:0:3)
Bracegirdle, Miss T. (0:0:1:0:0)
Bradburne, J. G. (0:5:8:3:2)
(033 781) 325
Bradley, N. A. (—:—:1:0:2)
Brisby, S. W. (—:—:0:1:3)
(03477) 357

Bronson, Miss E. T. (0:0:0:0:0)
(0689) 54749
Brookshaw, S. A. (0:0:4:3:1)
Brown, H. S. L. (—:—:2:3:0)
Brown, R. H. (0:1:2:3:4)
(0439) 70026
Brunt, R. C. (0:0:0:0:0)
Buckley, M. A. (—:0:4:4:9)
(0653) 600295
Bulgin, T. S. M. (—:—:—:—:0)
Bull, P. A. (—:—:—:0:0)
Burgess, Miss C. A. (—:—:—:—:0)
Burnell, W. M. (0:0:0:2:0)
Burnett-Wells, C. P. (2:2:2:1:9)
(090671) 2226
Bush, S. (1:0:1:1:1)
(0249) 782317
Butler, Miss J. (—:0:0:2:2)
Byrne, T. (—:—:—:2:9)

Cambidge, J. R. (0:1:0:1:1)
(095 276) 249
Campbell, C. W. (0:0:0:0:0)
Chapman, M. (—:—:—:—:0)
Charlton, S. D. (0:0:0:0:0)
Cornelius, Miss M. (0:0:0:—:0)
Cosgrove, G. D. (1:0:0:0:0)
(0235) 833535
Cousins, K. G. (—:—:—:—:0)
Cowdrey, Mrs M. (0:0:0:0:0)
(0638) 662915
Cowell, S. A. (0:0:0:0:0)
Craggs, P. F. (1:6:0:0:1)
(067072) 260
Crawford, B. T. (0:0:0:0:0)
Cregan, M. J. (0:—:—:—:0)
Crow, A. H. (—:—:0:0:0)
Cumings, Miss J. M. (0:0:1:1:0)
Curling, Miss P. (1:0:1:2:2)
(027874) 405

Dalton, A. N. (0:0:0:0:0)
(095271) 656 and (0989) 62250
Dare, Miss A. (0:0:—:—:3)
Deasley, S. M. (—:—:—:1:1)
Deeprose, A. E. (0:1:0:0:0)
(0424) 712241 and (0831) 109947
Dickin, S. (0:0:0:1:0)
(095286) 439
Dowrick, I. S. (0:0:0:0:0)
Duggan, D. G. (0:2:1:2:1)
c/o (056) 882281
Dun, Mrs E. J. (—:—:0:0:0)
Dun, J. M. (1:0:1:1:3)
(087535) 307
Durkan, J. P. P. (1:7:6:4:9)
(0488) 71411 or 73241

Eaton, Miss L. V. (0:0:0:0:0)
(0468) 21374
Edwards, G. F. (0:0:1:1:0)
(064383) 549
Ellis, Miss K. J. (0:0:0:0:0)
(03643) 457
Ellwood, O. C. B. (0:0:1:1:0)
Embiricos, Miss A. E. (2:1:0:0:0)
Evatt, D. B. (0:0:0:0:0)
(0342) 810482
Ewart, C. J. (—:0:1:2:0)
Ewing, W. (—:—:—:—:0)

Farrant, A. J. (—:4:13:3:0)
(027581) 2192
Farrell, Mrs A. L. (6:3:7:4:7)
(03475) 273
Fellows, Miss L. K. (0:0:0:0:0)
(0684) 310275
Felton, M. J. (0:0:1:4:4)
(07255) 267
Ford, R. (0:3:1:2:1)
(0524) 733058 and mobilephone
(0860) 877883
Forster, Miss S. E. (—:—:1:1:0)
(0450) 87281
French, Miss S. (1:2:0:0:0)
(0474) 814397

Garton, T. A. (0:0:0:0:0)
(0625) 827892
Gault, Mrs J. E. (0:0:0:0:0)
Gee, M. P. (0:0:0:0:1)
(0909) 566666
George, T. R. (—:0:0:0:0)
Gibbon, Mrs L. J. (0:0:0:0:0)
(0206) 250832
Gingell, M. J. (—:0:0:0:1)
Gladders, Miss S. G. (0:0:0:0:0)
Gordon, C. E. (0:0:0:—:0)
Gray, Miss T. M. (—:—:—:0:0)
Greed, T. R. (1:0:0:0:0)
Green, K. A. (0:0:1:0:0)
Greenall, J. E. (7:6:3:11:12)
082 786 238
Greenway, C. E. R. (0:0:0:0:0)
(0606) 882387
Griffith, A. D. W. (2:1:1:2:0)
071-402 2572
Griffiths, G. R. T. (—:—:—:—:0)
Grossick, J. (0:1:1:0:0)
(0875) 52115

Hacking, W. P. (5:2:1:1:3)
(090671) 3984
Haine, G. W. V. (—:—:—:—:0)
Hale, R. A. (0:0:4:5:3)
(0845) 525595 (home) or 587226
(office)
Hambly, I. (—:—:—:0:0)
Hamer, M. P. (1:0:0:0:0)
(0656) 860275
Hammond, M. P. (—:—:0:1:0)
Hancock, C. T. C. (—:0:0:1:3)
Hanmer, G. D. (2:0:2:1:0)
(0283) 550035
Harding-Jones, P. (6:0:2:2:0)
(037882) 2183

Hargreave, N. E. H. (1:2:1:0:0)
Harper, R. C. (—:—:—:—:0)
Harris, M. C. M. (—:1:0:0:0)
052 784 428 and 0831 578566
Harris, N. J. (—:—:0:0:3)
Harvey, A. H. (0:0:0:1:1)
Harwood, Miss A. J. (3:6:5:2:1)
(079 82) 2195
Hawkins, Mrs J. E. (—:—:—:—:0)
Heathfield, R. R. (—:—:0:—:0)
Heffernan, B. J. (—:—:—:—:0)
Hembrow, Mrs S. J. R. (—:—:—:—:0)
(0823) 442546
Henderson, Mrs R. G. (0:—:—:2:2)
Henderson, W. J. (0:0:—:—:0)
Hewitt, R. J. (0:0:0:0:0)
Hickman, A. D. (0:0:2:1:0)
Higgins, Miss S. A. (—:—:—:—:0)
Hill, A. (3:3:1:1:5)
(0844) 51268
Hill, Mrs T. J. (—:—:0:0:0)
Hills, Mrs K. M. (0:0:0:0:0)
Hills, T. J. (0:0:0:0:0)
(023371) 2224
Hobbs, Mrs S. L. (0:2:0:0:0)
(0984) 40366
Hollowell, K. B. (0:—:—:1:0)
Holmes, Miss K. B. (0:0:—:—:1)
Honeyball, Miss T. E. (—:—:—:—:0)
Hurst, W. O. (—:—:—:2:0)

Jackson, M. J. (—:—:1:0:0)
Jackson, T. H. (0:3:0:0:0)
Jackson, Mrs V. S. (1:—:—:—:0)
Jefford, L. D. B. (—:0:0:0:0)
Jenks, T. P. (—:—:0:1:20)
c/o (0451) 30417
Johnson, P. (2:0:0:2:2)
(091) 2674464
Johnson Houghton, G. F. (5:3:0:4:2)
(0235) 850480
Jones, D. S. (0:0:0:0:0)
(026723) 6661
Jones, Miss I. D. W. (1:1:0:0:0)
(0691) 659720
Jones, R. G. (—:—:—:0:0)
Jones, T. L. (2:2:2:3:3)
(0222) 882217
Joynes, S. (—:—:—:0:0)
Judge, Miss R. M. (0:0:0:0:0)
Jukes, J. (—:—:0:—:0)

Kendall, Mrs M. A. (0:0:0:1:0)
(093 12) 318
Kille, G. G. (0:—:—:0:0)

Laidlaw, Miss S. D. (—:—:—:—:0)
Lamb, Miss S. K. (—:0:1:0:0)
Lawther, J. R. (—:—:1:1:0)
Lay, A. L. (0:0:0:2:0)
(060883) 608
Leavy, B. D. (0:—:—:—:1)
Ledger, Mrs C. (1:0:2:0:0)
(0795) 423360
Lewis, G. M. (—:—:—:1:8)
(0633) 413382 or (0984) 40366 (yard)
Litston, Mrs J. A. (0:0:1:2:0)
Llewellyn, J. A. (0:0:2:0:1)

111

Llewellyn, J. L. (—:0:2:0:6)
Long, S. P. (—:—:—:—:0)
Love, S. (0:0:0:0:0)
  (041330) 5700 and (041956) 5306

MacEwan, A. G. P. B. (1:3:0:0:0)
Mactaggart, D. C. (1:2:2:1:0)
  (045 086) 314
Marks, Miss A. K. (0:0:0:0:0)
  (0488) 71767
Maundrell, G. C. (1:0:0:0:1)
  (067284) 202
Maxse, J. J. I. (0:0:—:—:0)
McCain, D. R. (4:6:5:3:4)
  c/o (0638) 665432
McCarthy, T. D. (—:—:4:0:1)
McCaull, Miss H. (0:0:1:0:0)
  (0885) 482516 and mobile (0831)
  502720
McKie, I. R. (1:0:2:1:2)
  (029673) 707
McPherson, A. S. (—:—:—:0:0)
  (0506) 842815
Mellor, Mrs M. E. (—:—:—:—:0)
Miles, N. (—:—:—:1:0)
  (0495) 773847 or 302551
Millington, C. R. (—:—:0:0:0)
Mills, Mrs J. M. (0:0:0:0:0)
  (0364) 53223
Mills, R. C. (—:—:0:0:0)
Mitchell, R. N. (0:0:1:1:0)
  (0305) 251429
Mitchell, Miss S. L. (0:0:0:0:1)
Mitchell, T. L. J. (4:5:2:0:1)
  (0305) 251429 and 68069
Mobley, Miss C. J. (0:0:0:0:0)
Moore, N. P. (—:—:—:—:5)
Moore, T. W. (3:1:0:0:0)
  (0371) 821013
Morgan, W. G. N. (0:2:0:0:0)
Morris, Mrs M. A. (—:—:—:0:0)
Morrison, T. (1:0:0:1:0)
Mulcaire, S. P. (—:—:—:—:0)
Mulhall C. A. (—:—:—:0:0)
Mulligan, M. (—:—:—:0:0)
Murphy, P. T. J. (—:—:—:1:3)

Nash, Mrs P. L. (—:0:2:8:2)
  (036782) 510
Needham, Mrs F. E. (—:—:—:0:3)
Newport, C. J. (0:1:0:1:1)
Nichol, Miss S. A. (—:0:0:0:1)
  c/o (08534) 555
Nuttall, R. E. (0:0:1:0:0)

O'Brien, J. L. C. (0:0:0:0:0)

Parker, A. (0:0:—:1:1)
Parker, D. (—:—:1:0:4)
Parris, Mrs J. C. (1:0:0:0:0)
Payne, R. J. (—:—:—:0:0)
Percy, Miss J. D. (—:0:—:—:0)
Pewter, G. R. (—:0:1:—:1)
Pickering, A. W. (—:—:—:—:0)
Pipe, D. E. (—:—:—:—:1)
Pittendrigh, S. I. (—:—:—:0:0)
Pollock, B. N. (—:—:—:—:2)
Portman, M. H. B. (0:0:0:0:0)

Poulton, J. C. (0:0:0:0:0)
  (0273) 890244
Price, A. R. (—:—:0:0:0)
Pritchard, J. M. (0:0:0:1:3)
  (0684) 297119
Pritchard, P. L. J. (1:2:0:3:0)
  (0453) 811881

Rebori, A. D. (0:0:0:0:0)
Rees, Mrs G. S. (0:0:0:0:0)
  (077 473) 4409
Rees, J. (—:—:3:0:3)
  (0280) 701991
Ridout, N. T. (0:1:1:0:0)
Rimell, M. G. (—:—:1:1:3)
  (0451) 30417
Robertson, D. (0:0:0:0:0)
  (056 386) 201
Robinson, G. (2:0:1:0:0)
  (04612) 2852 and 2792
Robinson, R. (0:0:0:0:0)
  (04612) 2852
Robson, A. W. (0:1:1:0:0)
  (066 589) 276
Robson, Miss P. (0:—:1:5:1)
  (0830) 30241
Rowsell, H. G. M. (—:3:0:0:0)
  (0672) 86500
Russell, R. G. (1:3:6:0:6)
  (032736) 208

Sadler, Miss S. (—:—:—:0:0)
Sample, C. J. (2:1:2:1:0)
  (067074) 245
Sandys-Clarke, R. P. (3:3:1:0:0)
Sansome, A. D. (—:2:1:5:5)
  (0908) 542564 or 542139
Saunders, Mrs J. A. (6:1:0:0:0)
  (060124) 739
Sayer, Mrs H. D. (—:—:—:—:0)
Scott, D. W. (0:1:0:0:0)
  (043473) 313
Scott, J. A. (—:—:—:—:0)
Scott, Miss J. M. (0:0:0:0:0)
  (0509) 880489
Sharp, J. C. (3:1:1:0:0)
  (08012) 4578
Sharratt, Miss S. (—:—:—:—:0)
Sheppard, M. I. (0:—:—:—:1)
Shiels, R. (0:1:3:4:0)
  (0835) 62743
Shinton, S. N. (0:0:0:0:0)
  (0633) 50489
Smith, K. H. (0:0:0:0:0)
  (023371) 2768
Smith, M. V. (0:0:0:0:0)
Smith, N. F. (—:1:1:1:1)
Smith, T. E. G. (0:0:0:0:0)
  (0734) 761116
Smyth-Osbourne, J. G. (0:1:0:0:1)
Southcombe, Miss J. A. (3:0:0:1:0)
  (0488) 71041 (work) or (0672) 511425
  (home)
Sowersby, M. E. (0:0:1:0:1)
  (026288) 212
Spearing, Miss C. M. (—:0:0:0:0)
Spearing, Miss T. S. (0:0:0:0:0)
  (0789) 772639

Sporborg, W. H. (2:2:0:0:0)
  (027974) 444
Stephenson, T. M. (1:0:0:0:0)
  (068481) 312
Stickland, S. G. (0:0:0:0:0)
  (0963) 62492
Stockton, C. J. (0:2:2:0:1)
Storey, C. (—:—:—:1:1)
Swiers, S. J. (12:10:12:3:12)
  (0423) 324155
Swindlehurst, D. J. (0:0:1:1:0)
  (022 874) 289

Taiano, P. G. (0:0:0:0:0)
  (043871) 8506
Teal, R. A. (0:0:3:3:0)
  (099421) 396
Thomas, Miss C. J. (1:3:2:0:1)
  (05447) 530
Thornton, A. R. (—:—:—:10:26)
  (0388) 720213, (0740) 22322, (0325)
  730513 and (0751) 77142 (agent)
Thurlow, Miss J. (0:3:2:4:1)
  (06973) 20576 and (agent) 20723
Townsend, D. J. (0:0:2:1:0)
  (023371) 2586
Townsley, P. F. R. (0:0:0:—:0)
  (030677) 492
Treloggen, R. M. (0:0:0:2:5)
Trice-Rolph, J. C. (3:1:1:0:2)
  (0451) 32039
Tudor, J. W. (1:0:0:0:0)
  (0656) 50001
Turner, Miss A. J. (0:0:0:0:0)
  (075539) 231
Tutton, A. G. (0:0:0:0:0)
  (0327) 61083
Tutty, N. D. (0:4:1:1:0)
  (060983) 624 and (0642) 781894

Verco, D. I. (1:—:0:0:0)
Vickery, Mrs R. A. (1:0:2:1:0)
  (0963) 40421
Vigors, C. S. C. (—:—:—:1:5)

Waggott, Miss T. (0:0:0:0:0)
  (0388) 819012
Wales, W. A. (0:2:0:2:1)
  (032875) 580
Walker, S. A. (—:0:—:—:0)
Wallace, Miss L. (0:0:0:0:0)
  (0743) 860387
Walton, A. E. (0:0:0:2:0)
  (0400) 50531
Ward, C. E. (0:1:0:—:0)
Ward Thomas, C. R. F. (—:—:2:3:2)
Waring, Mrs J. (—:—:—:0:0)
Waterman, Miss S. E. (0:1:0:0:0)
  (093 583) 394
Watson, M. R. M. (0:1:0:0:0)
Weatherby, J. R. (—:3:1:0:0)
Welsh, A. (0:1:0:0:0)
  (0474) 813132
Weymes, J. R. (—:—:0:0:1)
Whitaker, S. R. (1:2:0:0:0)
  (0532) 892265
White, G. F. (—:—:0:0:0)
White, R. (2:0:2:0:0)
  (0488) 72831
White, R. H. (—:—:—:—:0)
Whiting, K. P. (—:—:—:0:0)
Wight, A. J. (0:—:—:—:0)
Wilding, M. W. (—:—:—:—:0)
Williams, R. E. R. (—:—:—:—:1)
Williamson, Miss S. L. (0:0:0:—:0)
Wilson, C. R. (0:0:0:1:2)
  (032574) 595
Wilson, N. (0:4:4:3:4)
Wingfield Digby, J. H. (0:1:0:0:1)
Winter, Miss J. D. (0:0:0:0:0)
Wintle, J. D. (—:—:0:1:1)
Wonnacott, A. J. (—:0:1:0:0)
  (082287) 215
Wonnacott, Mrs C. L. (1:5:4:1:0)
  (0822) 616416
Wragg, G. J. D. (0:0:0:0:0)
  071-370 0980

Yardley, Miss A. L. (0:—:—:0:0)
Young, Miss S. E. M. (0:0:0:0:0)

BIG RACE RESULTS

GRAND NATIONAL (Liverpool, 4m 856yds)

1946   £8,805
1. **Lovely Cottage** 9-10-8
   (Capt R. Petre)
2. Jack Finlay 7-10-2 *(W. Kidney)*
3. Prince Regent 11-12-5 *(T. Hyde)*
SP: 25/1; 100/1; 3/1   43 ran
   T. Rayson   4:3

1947   £10,007
1. **Caughoo** 8-10-0 *(E. Dempsey)*
2. Lough Conn 11-10-1 *(D. McCann)*
3. Kami 10-10-13 *(Mr J. Hislop)*
SP: 100/1; 33/1; 33/1   57 ran
   H. McDowell, in Ireland   20:4

1948   £9,103
1. **Sheila's Cottage** 9-10-7
   (A. Thompson)
2. First of the Dandies 11-10-4
   (J. Brogan)
3. Cromwell 7-10-11 *(Lord Mildmay)*
SP: 50/1; 25/1; 33/1   43 ran
   N. Crump   1:6

1949   £9,528
1. **Russian Hero** 9-10-8
   (L. McMorrow)
2. Roimond 8-11-12 *(R. Francis)*
3. Royal Mount 10-10-12 *(P. Doyle)*
SP: 66/1; 22/1; 18/1   43 ran
   G. Owen   8:1

1950   £9,314
1. **Freebooter** 9-11-11 *(J. Power)*
2. Wot No Sun 8-11-8 *(A. Thompson)*
3. Acthon Major 10-11-2
   (R. J. O'Ryan)
SP: 10/1; 100/7; 33/1   49 ran
   R. Renton   15:10

1951   £8,815
1. **Nickel Coin** 9-10-1 *(J. Bullock)*
2. Royal Tan 7-10-13 *(Mr A. O'Brien)*
3. Derrinstown 11-10-0 *(A. Power)*
SP: 40/1; 22/1; 66/1   36 ran
   J. O'Donoghue   6:bad

1952   £9,268
1. **Teal** 10-10-12 *(A. Thompson)*
2. Legal Joy 9-10-4 *(M. Scudamore)*
3. Wot No Sun 10-11-7 *(D. Dick)*
SP: 100/7; 100/6; 33/1   47 ran
   N. Crump   5:bad

1953   £9,330
1. **Early Mist** 8-11-2 *(B. Marshall)*
2. Mont Tremblant 7-12-5 *(D. Dick)*
3. Irish Lizard 10-10-6 *(R. Turnell)*
SP: 20/1; 18/1; 33/1   31 ran
   M. V. O'Brien, in Ireland   20:4

1954   £8,571
1. **Royal Tan** 10-11-7 *(B. Marshall)*
2. Tudor Line 9-10-7 *(G. Slack)*
3. Irish Lizard 11-10-5
   (M. Scudamore)
SP: 8/1; 10/1; 15/2   29 ran
   M. V. O'Brien, in Ireland   nk:10

1955   £8,934
1. **Quare Times** 9-11-0 *(P. Taaffe)*
2. Tudor Line 10-11-3 *(G. Slack)*
3. Carey's Cottage 8-10-11 *(T. Taaffe)*
SP: 100/9; 10/1; 20/1   30 ran
   M. V. O'Brien, in Ireland   12:4

1956   £8,695
1. **E.S.B.** 10-11-3 *(D. Dick)*
2. Gentle Moya 10-10-2 *(G. Milburn)*
3. Royal Tan 12-12-1 *(T. Taaffe)*
SP: 100/7; 22/1; 28/1   29 ran
   F. Rimell   10:10

1957   £8,868
1. **Sundew** 11-11-7 *(F. Winter)*
2. Wyndburgh 7-10-7 *(M. Batchelor)*
3. Tiberetta 9-10-0 *(A. Oughton)*
SP: 20/1; 25/1; 66/1   35 ran
   F. Hudson   8:6

1958   £13,719
1. **Mr What** 8-10-6 *(A. Freeman)*
2. Tiberetta 10-10-6 *(G. Slack)*
3. Green Drill 8-10-10 *(G. Milburn)*
SP: 18/1; 28/1; 28/1   31 ran
   T. Taaffe, in Ireland   30:15

1959   £13,646
1. **Oxo** 8-10-13 *(M. Scudamore)*
2. Wyndburgh 9-10-12 *(T. Brookshaw)*
3. Mr What 9-11-9 *(T. Taaffe)*
SP: 8/1; 10/1; 6/1   34 ran
   W. Stephenson   1½:8

1960   £13,134
1. **Merryman II** 9-10-12 *(G. Scott)*
2. Badanloch 9-10-9 *(S. Mellor)*
3. Clear Profit 10-10-1 *(B. Wilkinson)*
SP: 13/2 100/7; 20/1   26 ran
   N. Crump 15:12

1961   £20,020
1. **Nicolaus Silver** 9-10-1 *(H. Beasley)*
2. Merryman II 10-11-12 *(D. Ancil)*
3. O'Malley Point 10-11-4 *(P. Farrell)*
SP: 28/1; 8/1; 100/6   35 ran
   F. Rimell   5:nk

114

1962   £20,238
1. **Kilmore** 12-10-4 *(F. Winter)*
2. Wyndburgh 12-10-9 *(T. Barnes)*
3. Mr What 12-10-9 *(J. Lehane)*
SP: 28/1; 45/1; 22/1   32 ran
   R. Price   10:10

1963   £21,315
1. **Ayala** 9-10-0 *(P. Buckley)*
2. Carrickbeg 7-10-3 *(Mr J. Lawrence)*
3. Hawa's Song 10-10-0 *(P. Broderick)*
SP: 66/1; 20/1; 28/1   47 ran
   K. Piggott   ¾:5

1964   £20,280
1. **Team Spirit** 12-10-3
      (G. W. Robinson)
2. Purple Silk 9-10-4 *(J. Kenneally)*
3. Peacetown 10-10-1 *(R. Edwards)*
SP: 18/1; 100/6; 40/1   33 ran
   F. Walwyn   ½:6

1965   £22,041
1. **Jay Trump** 8-11-5 *(Mr C. Smith)*
2. Freddie 8-11-10 *(P. McCarron)*
3. Mr Jones 10-11-5 *(Mr C. Collins)*
SP: 100/6; 7/2; 50/1   47 ran
   F. Winter   ¾:20

1966   £22,334
1. **Anglo** 8-10-0 *(T. Norman)*
2. Freddie 9-11-7 *(P. McCarron)*
3. Forest Prince 8-10-8 *(G. Scott)*
SP: 50/1; 11/4; 100/7   47 ran
   F. Winter   20:5

1967   £17,630
1. **Foinavon** 9-10-0 *(J. Buckingham)*
2. Honey End 10-10-4 *(J. Gifford)*
3. Red Alligator 8-10-0 *(B. Fletcher)*
SP: 100/1; 15/2; 30/1   44 ran
   J. Kempton   15:3

1968   £17,848
1. **Red Alligator** 9-10-0 *(B. Fletcher)*
2. Moidore's Token 11-10-8
      (B. Brogan)
3. Different Class 8-11-5 *(D. Mould)*
SP: 100/7; 100/6; 17/2   45 ran
Denys Smith   20:nk

1969   £17,849
1. **Highland Wedding** 12-10-4
      (E. P. Harty)
2. Steel Bridge 11-10-0 *(R. Pitman)*
3. Rondetto 13-10-6 *(J. King)*
SP: 100/9; 50/1; 25/1   30 ran
   G. Balding   12:1

1970   £14,804
1. **Gay Trip** 8-11-5 *(P. Taaffe)*
2. Vulture 8-10-0 *(S. Barker)*
3. Miss Hunter 9-10-0 *(F. Shortt)*
SP: 15/1; 15/1; 33/1   28 ran
   F. Rimell   20:½

1971   £15,500
1. **Specify** 9-10-13 *(J. Cook)*
2. Black Secret 7-11-5 *(Mr J. Dreaper)*
3. Astbury 8-10-0 *(J. Bourke)*
SP: 28/1; 20/1; 33/1   38 ran
   J. E. Sutcliffe   nk:2½

1972   £25,765
1. **Well To Do** 9-10-1 *(G. Thorner)*
2. Gay Trip 10-11-9 *(T. Biddlecombe)*
3. Black Secret 8-11-2 *(S. Barker)*
3. General Symons 9-10-0 *(P. Kiely)*
SP: 14/1; 12/1; 40/1   42 ran
   T. Forster   2:3:d.h

1973   £25,486
1. **Red Rum** 8-10-5 *(B. Fletcher)*
2. Crisp 10-12-0 *(R. Pitman)*
3. L'Escargot 10-12-0 *(T. Carberry)*
SP: 9/1; 9/1; 11/1   38 ran
   D. McCain   ¾:25

1974   £25,102
1. **Red Rum** 9-12-0 *(B. Fletcher)*
2. L'Escargot 11-11-13 *(T. Carberry)*
3. Charles Dickens 10-10-0
      (A. Turnell)
SP: 11/1; 17/2; 50/1   42 ran
   D. McCain   7:sh

1975   £38,005
1. **L'Escargot** 12-11-3 *(T. Carberry)*
2. Red Rum 10-12-0 *(B. Fletcher)*
3. Spanish Steps 12-10-3 *(W. Smith)*
SP: 13/2; 7/2; 20/1   31 ran
   D. L. Moore, in Ireland   15:8

1976   £37,420
1. **Rag Trade** 10-10-12 *(J. Burke)*
2. Red Rum 11-11-10 *(T. Stack)*
3. Eyecatcher 10-10-7 *(B. Fletcher)*
SP: 14/1; 10/1; 28/1   32 ran
   F. Rimell   2:8

1977   £41,140
1. **Red Rum** 12-11-8 *(T. Stack)*
2. Churchtown Boy 10-10-0
      (M. Blackshaw)
3. Eyecatcher 11-10-1 *(C. Read)*
SP: 9/1; 20/1; 18/1   42 ran
   D. McCain   25:6

1978   £39,092
1. **Lucius** 9-10-9 *(R. Davies)*
2. Sebastian V 10-10-1 *(R. Lamb)*
3. Drumroan 10-10-0 *(G. Newman)*
SP: 14/1; 25/1; 50/1   37 ran
   G. Richards   ½:nk

1979   £40,506
1. **Rubstic** 10-10-0 *(M. Barnes)*
2. Zongalero 9-10-5 *(B. R. Davies)*
3. Rough And Tumble 9-10-7
      (J. Francome)
SP: 25/1; 20/1; 14/1   34 ran
   S. Leadbetter   1½:5

115

1980   £45,595

1. **Ben Nevis** 12-10-12
   (Mr C. Fenwick)
2. Rough And Tumble 10-10-11
   (J. Francome)
3. The Pilgarlic 12-10-4 *(R. Hyett)*

SP: 40/1; 11/1; 33/1   30 ran
   T. Forster   20:10

1981   £51,324

1. **Aldaniti** 11-10-13 *(R. Champion)*
2. Spartan Missile 9-11-5
   (Mr J. Thorne)
3. Royal Mail 11-11-7 *(P. Blacker)*

SP: 10/1; 8/1; 16/1   39 ran
   J. Gifford   4:2

1982   £52,507

1. **Grittar** 9-11-5 *(Mr R. Saunders)*
2. Hard Outlook 11-10-1 *(A. Webber)*
3. Loving Words 9-10-11 *(R. Hoare)*

SP: 7/1; 50/1; 16/1   39 ran
   F. Gilman   15:dist

1983   52,949

1. **Corbiere** 8-11-4 *(B. de Haan)*
2. Greasepaint 8-10-7
   (Mr C. Magnier)
3. Yer Man 8-10-0 *(T. O'Connell)*

SP: 13/1; 14/1; 80/1   41 ran
   Mrs J. Pitman   ¾:20

1984   £54,769

1. **Hallo Dandy** 10-10-2 *(N. Doughty)*
2. Greasepaint 9-11-2 *(T. Carmody)*
3. Corbiere 9-12-0 *(B. de Haan)*

SP: 13/1; 9/1; 16/1   40 ran
   G. Richards   4:1½

1985   £54,314

1. **Last Suspect** 11-10-5 *(H. Davies)*
2. Mr Snugfit 8-10-0 *(P. Tuck)*
3. Corbiere 10-11-10 *(P. Scudamore)*

SP: 50/1; 12/1; 9/1   40 ran
   T. Forster   1½:3

1986   £60,647

1. **West Tip** 9-10-11 *(R. Dunwoody)*
2. Young Driver 9-10-0 *(C. Grant)*
3. Classified 10-10-3 *(S. Smith Eccles)*

SP: 15/2; 66/1; 22/1   40 ran
   M. Oliver   2:20

1987   £64,710

1 **Maori Venture** 11-10-13
   (S. C. Knight)
2. The Tsarevich 11-10-5 *(J. White)*
3. Lean Ar Aghaidh 10-10-0
   (G. Landau)

SP: 28/1; 20/1; 14/1   40 ran
   A. Turnell   5:4

1988   £68,740

1. **Rhyme 'N' Reason** 9-11-0
   (B. Powell)
2. Durham Edition 10-10-9 *(C. Grant)*
3. Monanore 11-10-4 *(T. Taaffe)*

SP: 10/1; 20/1; 33/1   40 ran
   D. Elsworth   4:15

1989   £66,840

1. **Little Polveir** 12-10-3 *(J. Frost)*
2. West Tip 12-10-11 *(R. Dunwoody)*
3. The Thinker 11-11-10
   (S. Sherwood)

SP: 28/1; 12/1; 10/1   40 ran
   G. Balding   7:½

1990   £70,871

1. **Mr Frisk** 11-10-6 *(Mr M. Armytage)*
2. Durham Edition 12-10-9 *(C. Grant)*
3. Rinus 9-10-4 *(N. Doughty)*

SP: 16/1; 9/1; 13/1   38 ran
   K. Bailey   ¾:20

1991   £90,970

1. **Seagram** 11-10-6 *(N. Hawke)*
2. Garrison Savannah 8-11-1
   (M. Pitman)
3. Auntie Dot 10-10-4 *(M. Dwyer)*

SP: 12/1; 7/1; 50/1   40 ran
   D. Barons   5:8

1992   £112,091

1. **Party Politics** 8-10-7 *(C. Llewellyn)*
2. Romany King 8-10-3
   (R. Guest)
3. Laura's Beau 8-10-0 *(C. O'Dwyer)*

SP: 14/1; 16/1; 12/1   40 ran
   N. Gaselee   2½:15

1993   Void (false start)

GOLD CUP (Cheltenham, 3¼m 110yds)

1946   £1,130
1. **Prince Regent** 11-12-0 *(T. Hyde)*
2. Poor Flame 8-12-0 *(F. Rimell)*
3. Red April 9-12-0 *(G. Kelly)*
SP: 4/7; 5/1; 9/2   6 ran
  T. Dreaper, in Ireland   5:4

1947   £1,140
1. **Fortina** 6-12-0 *(Mr R. Black)*
2. Happy Home 8-12-0 *(D. L. Moore)*
3. Prince Blackthorn 9-12-0
  (R. Turnell)
SP: 8/1; 3/1; 8/1   12 ran
  H. Christie   10:6

1948   £1,911
1. **Cottage Rake** 9-12-0
  (A. Brabazon)
2. Happy Home 9-12-0 *(M. Molony)*
3. Coloured School Boy 8-12-0
  (E. Vinall)
SP: 10/1; 6/1; 10/1   12 ran
  M. V. O'Brien, in Ireland   1½:10

1949   £2,817
1. **Cottage Rake** 10-12-0
  (A. Brabazon)
2. Cool Customer 10-12-0
  (P. Murphy)
3. Coloured School Boy 9-12-0
  (E. Vinall)
SP: 4/6; 13/2; 8/1   6 ran
  M. V. O'Brien, in Ireland   2:6

1950   £2,936
1. **Cottage Rake** 11-12-0
  (A. Brabazon)
2. Finnure 9-12-0 *(M. Molony)*
3. Garde Toi 9-12-0
  (Marquis de Portago)
SP: 5/6; 5/4; 100/1   6 ran
  M. V. O'Brien, in Ireland   10:8

1951   £2,783
1. **Silver Fame** 12-12-0 *(M. Molony)*
2. Greenogue 9-12-0 *(G. Kelly)*
3. Mighty Fine 9-12-0 *(J. Bullock)*
SP: 6/4; 100/8; 10/1   6 ran
  G. Beeby   sh:2

1952   £3,232
1. **Mont Tremblant** 6-12-0 *(D. Dick)*
2. Shaef 8-12-0 *(F. Winter)*
3. Galloway Braes 7-12-0 *(R. Morrow)*
SP: 8/1; 7/1; 66/1   13 ran
  F. Walwyn   10:4

1953   £3,258
1. **Knock Hard** 9-12-0 *(T. Molony)*
2. Halloween 8-12-0 *(F. Winter)*
3. Galloway Braes 8-12-0 *(R. Morrow)*
SP: 11/2; 5/2; 33/1   12 ran
  M. V. O'Brien, in Ireland   5:2

1954   £3,576
1. **Four Ten** 8-12-0 *(T. Cusack)*
2. Mariner's Log 7-12-0 *(P. Taaffe)*
3. Halloween 9-12-0 *(G. Slack)*
SP: 100/6; 20/1; 100/6   6 ran
  J. Roberts   4:4

1955   £3,775
1. **Gay Donald** 9-12-0 *(A. Grantham)*
2. Halloween 10-12-0 *(F. Winter)*
3. Four Ten 9-12-0 *(T. Cusack)*
SP: 33/1; 7/2; 3/1   9 ran
  J. Ford   10:8

1956   £3,750
1. **Limber Hill** 9-12-0 *(J. Power)*
2. Vigor 8-12-0 *(R. Emery)*
3. Halloween 11-12-0 *(F. Winter)*
SP: 11/8; 50/1; 100/8   11 ran
  W. Dutton   4:1½

1957   £3,996
1. **Linwell** 9-12-0 *(M. Scudamore)*
2. Kerstin 7-12-0 *(G. Milburn)*
3. Rose Park 11-12-0 *(G. Nicholls)*
SP: 100/9; 6/1; 100/8   13 ran
  C. Mallon   1:5

1958   £5,788
1. **Kerstin** 8-12-0 *(S. Hayhurst)*
2. Polar Flight 8-12-0 *(G. Slack)*
3. Gay Donald 12-12-0 *(F. Winter)*
SP: 7/1; 11/2; 13/2   9 ran
  C. Bewicke   ½:bad

1959   £5,363
1. **Roddy Owen** 10-12-0 *(H. Beasley)*
2. Linwell 11-12-0 *(F. Winter)*
3. Lochroe 11-12-0 *(A. Freeman)*
SP: 5/1; 11/2; 100/9   11 ran
  D. Morgan, in Ireland   3:10

1960   £5,414
1. **Pas Seul** 7-12-0 *(W. Rees)*
2. Lochroe 12-12-0 *(D. Mould)*
3. Zonda 9-12-0 *(G. W. Robinson)*
SP: 6/1; 25/1; 8/1   12 ran
  R. Turnell   1:5

1961   £6,043
1. **Saffron Tartan** 10-12-0 *(F. Winter)*
2. Pas Seul 8-12-0 *(D. Dick)*
3. Mandarin 10-12-0 *(P. Madden)*
SP: 2/1; 100/30; 100/7   11 ran
  D. Butchers   1½:3

1962   £5,720
1. **Mandarin** 11-12-0 *(F. Winter)*
2. Fortria 10-12-0 *(P. Taaffe)*
3. Cocky Consort 9-12-0 *(C. Stobbs)*
SP: 7/2; 3/1; 50/1   9 ran
  F. Walwyn   1:10

1963 £5,958
1. **Mill House** 6-12-0
   (G. W. Robinson)
2. Fortria 11-12-0 *(P. Taaffe)*
3. Duke of York 8-12-0 *(F. Winter)*
SP: 7/2; 4/1; 7/1   12 ran
   F. Walwyn   12:4

1964 £8,004
1. **Arkle** 7-12-0 *(P. Taaffe)*
2. Mill House 7-12-0
   (G. W. Robinson)
3. Pas Seul 11-12-0 *(D. Dick)*
SP: 7/4; 8/13; 50/1   4 ran
   T. Dreaper, in Ireland   5:25

1965 £7,986
1. **Arkle** 8-12-0 *(P. Taaffe)*
2. Mill House 8-12-0
   (G. W. Robinson)
3. Stoney Crossing 7-12-0
   (Mr W. Roycroft)
SP: 30/100; 100/30; 100/1   4 ran
   T. Dreaper, in Ireland   20:30

1966 £7,674
1. **Arkle** 9-12-0 *(P. Taaffe)*
2. Dormant 9-12-0 *(M. Scudamore)*
3. Snaigow 7-12-0 *(D. Nicholson)*
SP: 1/10; 20/1; 100/7   5 ran
   T. Dreaper, in Ireland   30:10

1967 £7,999
1. **Woodland Venture** 7-12-0
   (T. Biddlecombe)
2. Stalbridge Colonist 8-12-0
   (S. Mellor)
3. What A Myth 10-12-0 *(P. Kelleway)*
SP: 100/8; 11/2; 3/1   8 ran
   F. Rimell   ¾:2

1968 £7,713
1. **Fort Leney** 10-12-0 *(P. Taaffe)*
2. The Laird 7-12-0 *(J. King)*
3. Stalbridge Colonist 9-12-0
   (T. Biddlecombe)
SP: 11/2; 3/1; 7/2   5 ran
   T. Dreaper, in Ireland   nk:1

1969 £8,129
1. **What A Myth** 12-12-0
   (P. Kelleway)
2. Domacorn 7-12-0
   (T. Biddlecombe)
3. Playlord 8-12-0 *(R. Barry)*
SP: 8/1; 7/2; 4/1   11 ran
   R. Price   1½:20

1970 £8,103
1. **L'Escargot** 7-12-0 *(T. Carberry)*
2. French Tan 8-12-0 *(P. Taaffe)*
3. Spanish Steps 7-12-0 *(J. Cook)*
SP: 33/1; 81; 9/4   12 ran
   D. L. Moore, in Ireland   1½:10

1971 £7,995
1. **L'Escargot** 8-12-0 *(T. Carberry)*
2. Leap Frog 7-12-0 *(V. O'Brien)*
3. The Dikler 8-12-0 *(B. Brogan)*
SP: 7/2; 7/2; 15/2   8 ran
   D. L. Moore, in Ireland   10:15

1972 £15,255
1. **Glencaraig Lady** 8-12-0 *(F. Berry)*
2. Royal Toss 10-12-0 *(N. Wakley)*
3. The Dikler 9-12-0 *(B. Brogan)*
SP: 6/1; 22/1; 11/1   12 ran
   F. Flood, in Ireland   ¾:hd

1973 £15,125
1. **The Dikler** 10-12-0 *(R. Barry)*
2. Pendil 8-12-0 *(R. Pitman)*
3. Charlie Potheen 8-12-0
   (T. Biddlecombe)
SP: 9/1; 4/6; 9/2   8 ran
   F. Walwyn   sh:6

1974 £14,572
1. **Captain Christy** 7-12-0
   (H. Beasley)
2. The Dikler 11-12-0 *(R. Barry)*
3. Game Spirit 8-12-0
   (T. Biddlecombe)
SP: 7/1; 5/1; 20/1   7 ran
   P. Taaffe, in Ireland   5:20

1975 £17,757
1. **Ten Up** 8-12-0 *(T. Carberry)*
2. Soothsayer 8-12-0 *(R. Pitman)*
3. Bula 10-12-0 *(J. Francome)*
SP: 2/1; 28/1; 5/1   8 ran
   J. Dreaper, in Ireland   6:½

1976 £18,134
1. **Royal Frolic** 7-12-0 *(J. Burke)*
2. Brown Lad 10-12-0 *(T. Carberry)*
3. Colebridge 12-12-0 *(F. Berry)*
SP: 14/1; 13/8; 12/1   11 ran
   F. Rimell   5:5

1977 £21,990
1. **Davy Lad** 7-12-0 *(D. T. Hughes)*
2. Tied Cottage 9-12-0 *(T. Carberry)*
3. Summerville 11-12-0 *(J. King)*
SP: 14/1; 20/1; 15/1   13 ran
   M. O'Toole, in Ireland   6:20

1978 £23,827
1. **Midnight Court** 7-12-0
   (J. Francome)
2. Brown Lad 12-12-0 *(T. Carberry)*
3. Master H 9-12-0 *(R. Crank)*
SP: 5/2; 8/1; 18/1   10 ran
   F. Winter   7:1

1979 £30,293
1. **Alverton** 9-12-0 *(J. J. O'Neill)*
2. Royal Mail 9-12-0 *(P. Blacker)*
3. Aldaniti 9-12-0 *(R. Champion)*
SP: 5/1; 7/1; 40/1   14 ran
   M. H. Easterby   25:20

118

1980 £35,997

1. **Master Smudge** 8-12-0 *(R. Hoare)*
2. Mac Vidi 15-12-0 *(P. Leach)*
3. Approaching 9-12-0
   (B. R. Davies)

SP: 14/1; 66/1; 11/1   15 ran
A. Barrow   5:2½

1981 £44,259

1. **Little Owl** 7-12-0
   (Mr A. J. Wilson)
2. Night Nurse 10-12-0 *(A. Brown)*
3. Silver Buck 9-12-0 *(T. Carmody)*

SP: 6/1; 6/1; 7/2   15 ran
M. H. Easterby   1½:10

1982 £48,386

1. **Silver Buck** 10-12-0
   (R. Earnshaw)
2. Bregawn 8-12-0 *(G. Bradley)*
3. Sunset Cristo 8-12-0 *(C. Grant)*

SP: 8/1; 18/1; 100/1   22 ran
M. Dickinson   2:12

1983 £45,260

1. **Bregawn** 9-12-0 *(G. Bradley)*
2. Captain John 9-12-0 *(D. Goulding)*
3. Wayward Lad 8-12-0
   (J. J. O'Neill)

SP: 100/30; 11/1; 6/1   11 ran
M. Dickinson   5:1½

1984 £47,375

1. **Burrough Hill Lad** 8-12-0
   (P. Tuck)
2. Brown Chamberlin 9-12-0
   (J. Francome)
3. Drumlargan 10-12-0 *(Mr F. Codd)*

SP: 7/2; 5/1; 16/1   12 ran
Mrs J. Pitman   3:8

1985 £52,560

1. **Forgive'N Forget** 8-12-0
   (M. Dwyer)
2. Righthand Man 8-12-0 *(G. Bradley)*
3. Earls Brig 10-12-0 *(P. Tuck)*

SP: 7/1; 15/2; 13/2   15 ran
J. FitzGerald   1½:2½

1986 £54,900

1. **Dawn Run** 8-11-9 *(J. J. O'Neill)*
2. Wayward Lad 11-12-0 *(G. Bradley)*
3. Forgive'N Forget 9-12-0
   (M. Dwyer)

SP: 15/8; 8/1; 7/2   11 ran
P. Mullins, in Ireland   1:2½

1987 £55,500

1. **The Thinker** 9-12-0 *(R. Lamb)*
2. Cybrandian 9-12-0 *(C. Grant)*
3. Door Latch 9-12-0 *(R. Rowe)*

SP: 13/2; 25/1; 9/1   12 ran
W. A. Stephenson   1½:2½

1988 £61,960

1. **Charter Party** 10-12-0
   (R. Dunwoody)
2. Cavvies Clown 8-12-0
   (S. Sherwood)
3. Beau Ranger 10-12-0
   (P. Scudamore)

SP: 10/1; 6/1; 33/1   15 ran
D. Nicholson   6:10

1989 £66,635

1. **Desert Orchid** 10-12-0
   (S. Sherwood)
2. Yahoo 8-12-0 *(T. Morgan)*
3. Charter Party 11-12-0
   (R. Dunwoody)

SP: 5/2; 25/1; 14/1   13 ran
D. Elsworth   1½:8

1990 £67,003

1. **Norton's Coin** 9-12-0 *(G. McCourt)*
2. Toby Tobias 8-12-0 *(M. Pitman)*
3. Desert Orchid 11-12-0
   (R. Dunwoody)

SP: 100/1; 8/1; 10/11   12 ran
S. Griffiths   ¾:4

1991 £98,578

1. **Garrison Savannah** 8-12-0
   (M. Pitman)
2. The Fellow 6-12-0 *(A. Kondrat)*
3. Desert Orchid 12-12-0
   (R. Dunwoody)

SP: 16/1; 28/1; 4/1   14 ran
Mrs J. Pitman   sh:15

1992 £98,028

1. **Cool Ground** 10-12-0 *(A. Maguire)*
2. The Fellow 7-12-0 *(A. Kondrat)*
3. Docklands Express 10-12-0
   (M. Perrett)

SP: 25/1; 7/2; 16/1   8 ran
G. Balding   sh:1

1993 £99,448

1. **Jodami** 8-12-0 *(M. Dwyer)*
2. Rushing Wild 8-12-0 *(R. Dunwoody)*
3. Royal Athlete 10-12-0 *(B. de Haan)*

SP: 8/1; 11/1; 66/1   16 ran
P. Beaumont   2:7

CHAMPION HURDLE (Cheltenham, 2m 110yds)

1946   £980

1. **Distel** 5-11-10 *(R. J. O'Ryan)*
2. Carnival Boy 5-11-10 *(F. Rimell)*
3. Robin O'Chantry 6-12-0
   (J. Goodgame)
SP: 4/5; 7/2; 100/6   8 ran
   C. Rogers, in Ireland   4:½

1947   £1,035

1. **National Spirit** 6-12-0
   (D. Morgan)
2. Le Paillon 5-11-10 *(A. Head)*
3. Freddy Fox 8-12-0 *(R. Smyth)*
SP: 7/1; 2/1; 8/1   13 ran
   V. Smyth   1:2

1948   £2,068

1. **National Spirit** 7-12-0 *(R. Smyth)*
2. D.U.K.W. 5-11-10 *(J. Maguire)*
3. Encoroli 5-11-10 *(M. Connors)*
SP: 6/4; 5/1; 20/1   12 ran
   V. Smyth   2:¾

1949   £2,299

1. **Hatton's Grace** 9-12-0
   (A. Brabazon)
2. Vatelys 9-12-0 *(R. Bates)*
3. Captain Fox 4-11-0 *(K. Mullins)*
SP: 1007; 10/1; 100/9   14 ran
   M. V. O'Brien, in Ireland   6:1

1950   £2,427

1. **Hatton's Grace** 10-12-0
   (A. Brabazon)
2. Harlech 5-11-12 *(M. Molony)*
3. Speciality 5-11-12 *(K. Mullins)*
SP: 5/2; 9/2; 100/6   12 ran
   M. V. O'Brien, in Ireland   1½:2

1951   £3,615

1. **Hatton's Grace** 11-12-0
   (T. Molony)
2. Pyrrhus III 8-12-0 *(A. Gill)*
3. Prince Hindou 5-11-12
   (M. Larraun)
SP: 4/1; 11/2; 9/2   8 ran
   M. V. O'Brien, in Ireland   5:½

1952   £3,632

1. **Sir Ken** 5-11-12 *(T. Molony)*
2. Noholme 5-11-12 *(B. Marshall)*
3. Approval 6-12-0 *(D. Dillon)*
SP: 3/1; 100/7; 9/1   16 ran
   W. Stephenson   2:4

1953   £3,479

1. **Sir Ken** 6-12-0 *(T. Molony)*
2. Galatian 6-12-0 *(B. Marshall)*
3. Teapot II 8-12-0 *(P. Taaffe)*
SP: 2/5; 4/1; 100/9   7 ran
   W. Stephenson   2:1½

1954   £3,657

1. **Sir Ken** 7-12-0 *(T. Molony)*
2. Impney 5-11-12 *(M. Pumfrey)*
3. Galatian 7-12-0 *(P. Taaffe)*
SP: 4/9; 9/1; 10/1   13 ran
   W. Stephenson   1:3

1955   £3,717

1. **Clair Soleil** 6-12-0 *(F. Winter)*
2. Stroller 7-12-0 *(T. P. Burns)*
3. Cruachan 7-12-0 *(G. Slack)*
SP: 5/2; 7/2; 50/1   21 ran
   R. Price   hd:4

1956   £3,300

1. **Doorknocker** 8-12-0
   (H. Sprague)
2. Quita Que 7-12-0 *(Mr J. Cox)*
3. Baby Don 6-12-0 *(T. Molony)*
SP: 100/9; 33/1; 100/8   14 ran
   W. Hall   ¾:4

1957   £3,729

1. **Merry Deal** 7-12-0
   (G. Underwood)
2. Quita Que 8-12-0 *(Mr J. Cox)*
3. Tout ou Rien 5-11-12 *(R. Emery)*
SP: 28/1; 15/2; 100/8   16 ran
   A. Jones   5:5

1958   £4,812

1. **Bandalore** 7-12-0 *(G. Slack)*
2. Tokoroa 7-12-0 *(D. Dick)*
3. Retour de Flamme 5-11-12
   (J. Lindley)
SP: 20/1; 5/1; 11/2   18 ran
   J. Wright   2:3

1959   £4,587

1. **Fare Time** 6-12-0 *(F. Winter)*
2. Ivy Green 9-12-0 *(P. Taaffe)*
3. Prudent King 7-12-0 *(T. P. Burns)*
SP: 13/2; 40/1; 13/2   14 ran
   R. Price   4:1

1960   £4,290

1. **Another Flash** 6-12-0 *(H. Beasley)*
2. Albergo 6-12-0 *(D. Page)*
3. Saffron Tartan 9-12-0 *(T. P. Burns)*
SP: 11/4; 11/2; 3/1   12 ran
   P. Sleator, in Ireland   2:3

1961   £5,211

1. **Eborneezer** 6-12-0 *(F. Winter)*
2. Moss Bank 5-11-12 *(J. J. Rafferty)*
3. Farmer's Boy 8-12-0
   (D. Nicholson)
SP: 4/1; 7/4; 8/1   17 ran
   R. Price   3:1½

1962   £5,143

1. **Anzio** 5-11-12 *(G. W. Robinson)*
2. Quelle Chance 7-12-0 *(D. Dick)*
3. Another Flash 8-12-0 *(H. Beasley)*

SP: 11/2; 11/2; 11/10   14 ran
  F. Walwyn   3:1½

1963   £5,585

1. **Winning Fair** 8-12-0
   (Mr A. Lillingston)
2. Farney Fox 8-12-0 *(P. Powell)*
3. Quelle Chance 8-12-0
   (B. Wilkinson)

SP: 100/9; 10/1; 100/7   21 ran
  G. Spencer, in Ireland   3:nk

1964   £8,161

1. **Magic Court** 6-12-0 *(P. McCarron)*
2. Another Flash 10-12-0 *(H. Beasley)*
3. Kirriemuir 4-11-4
   (G. W. Robinson)

SP: 100/6; 6/1; 100/6   24 ran
  T. Robson   4:¾

1965   £8,042

1. **Kirriemuir** 5-11-12
   (G. W. Robinson)
2. Spartan General 6-12-0
   (T. Biddlecombe)
3. Worcran 7-12-0 *(D. Nicholson)*

SP: 50/1; 8/1; 8/1   19 ran
  F. Walwyn   1:1½

1966   £7,921

1. **Salmon Spray** 8-12-0 *(J. Haine)*
2. Sempervivum 8-12-0 *(J. King)*
3. Flyingbolt 7-12-0 *(P. Taaffe)*

SP: 4/1; 20/1; 15/8   17 ran
  R. Turnell   3:¾

1967   £8,857

1. **Saucy Kit** 6-12-0 *(R. Edwards)*
2. Makaldar 7-12-0 *(D. Mould)*
3. Talgo Abbess 8-12-0 *(F. Carroll)*

SP: 100/6; 11/4; 100/8   23 ran
  M. H. Easterby   4:1

1968   £7,798

1. **Persian War** 5-11-12 *(J. Uttley)*
2. Chorus 7-12-0 *(A. Turnell)*
3. Black Justice 6-12-0 *(B. Scott)*

SP: 4/1; 7/2; 100/6   16 ran
  C. Davies   4:5

1969   £7,876

1. **Persian War** 6-12-0 *(J. Uttley)*
2. Drumikill 8-12-0 *(B. Brogan)*
3. Privy Seal 5-11-12 *(J. Cook)*

SP: 6/4; 100/7; 33/1   17 ran
  C. Davies   4:2½

1970   £7,739

1. **Persian War** 7-12-0 *(J. Uttley)*
2. Major Rose 8-12-0 *(J. Gifford)*
3. Escalus 5-11-12 *(D. Mould)*

SP: 5/4; 8/1; 25/1   14 ran
  C. Davies   1½:1½

1971   £7,466

1. **Bula** 6-12-0 *(P. Kelleway)*
2. Persian War 8-12-0 *(J. Uttley)*
3. Major Rose 9-12-0
   (T. Biddlecombe)

SP: 15/8; 9/2; 4/1   9 ran
  F. Winter   4:1

1972   £15,648

1. **Bula** 7-12-0 *(P. Kelleway)*
2. Boxer 5-11-12 *(J. Uttley)*
3. Lyford Cay 8-12-0 *(D. Cartwright)*

SP: 8/11; 25/1; 66/1   12 ran
  F. Winter   8:3

1973   £14,563

1. **Comedy of Errors** 6-12-0
   (W. Smith)
2. Easby Abbey 6-12-0 *(R. Barry)*
3. Captain Christy 6-12-0 *(H. Beasley)*

SP: 8/1; 20/1; 85/40   8 ran
  F. Rimell   1½:2

1974   £14,023

1. **Lanzarote** 6-12-0 *(R. Pitman)*
2. Comedy of Errors 7-12-0
   (W. Smith)
3. Yenisei 7-12-0 *(H. Beasley)*

SP: 7/4; 4/6; 100/1   7 ran
  F. Winter   3:8

1975   £14,459

1. **Comedy of Errors** 8-12-0
   (K. White)
2. Flash Imp 6-12-0 *(T. Stack)*
3. Tree Tangle 6-12-0 *(A. Turnell)*

SP: 11/8; 12/1; 10/1   13ran
  F. Rimell   8:hd

1976   £14,530

1. **Night Nurse** 5-12-0 *(P. Broderick)*
2. Bird's Nest 6-12-0 *(A. Turnell)*
3. Flash Imp 7-12-0 *(R. Mann)*

SP: 2/1; 100/30; 40/1   8 ran
  M. H. Easterby   2½:8

1977   £18,147

1. **Night Nurse** 6-12-0 *(P. Broderick)*
2. Monksfield 5-12-0 *(T. Kinane)*
3. Dramatist 6-12-0 *(W. Smith)*

SP: 15/2; 15/1; 6/1   10 ran
  M. H. Easterby   2:2

1978   £21,327

1. **Monksfield** 6-12-0 *(T. Kinane)*
2. Sea Pigeon 8-12-0 *(F. Berry)*
3. Night Nurse 7-12-0 *(C. Tinkler)*

SP: 11/2; 5/1; 3/1   13 ran
  D. McDonogh, in Ireland   2:6

1979 £22,730

1. **Monksfield** 7-12-0 *(D. T. Hughes)*
2. Sea Pigeon 9-12-0 *(J. J. O'Neill)*
3. Beacon Light 8-12-0 *(J. Francome)*

SP: 9/4; 6/1; 22/1   10 ran
  D. McDonogh, in Ireland   ¾:15

1980 £24,972

1. **Sea Pigeon** 10-12-0 *(J. J. O'Neill)*
2. Monksfield 8-12-0 *(D. T. Hughes)*
3. Bird's Nest 10-12-0 *(A. Turnell)*

SP: 13/2; 6/5; 11/1   9 ran
  M. H. Easterby   7:1½

1981 £32,260

1. **Sea Pigeon** 11-12-0 *(J. Francome)*
2. Pollardstown 6-12-0 *(P. Blacker)*
3. Daring Run 6-12-0 *(Mr T. Walsh)*

SP: 7/4; 9/1; 8/1   14 ran
  M. H. Easterby   1½:nk

1982 £37,043

1. **For Auction** 6-12-0
   (Mr C. Magnier)
2. Broadsword 5-12-0 *(P. Scudamore)*
3. Ekbalco 6-12-0 *(D. Goulding)*

SP: 40/1; 100/30; 7/2   14 ran
  M. Cunningham, in Ireland   7:1½

1983 £34,865

1. **Gaye Brief** 6-12-0 *(R. Linley)*
2. Boreen Prince 6-12-0 *(N. Madden)*
3. For Auction 7-12-0
   (Mr C. Magnier)

SP: 7/1; 50/1; 3/1   17 ran
  Mrs M. Rimell   3:7

1984 £36,680

1. **Dawn Run** 6-11-9 *(J. J. O'Neill)*
2. Cima 6-12-0 *(P. Scudamore)*
3. Very Promising 6-12-0
   (S. Morshead)

SP: 4/5; 66/1; 16/1   14 ran
  P. Mullins, in Ireland   ¾:4

1985 £38,030

1. **See You Then** 5-12-0
   (S. Smith Eccles)
2. Robin Wonder 7-12-0 *(J. J. O'Neill)*
3. Stans Pride 8-11-9 *(S. Morshead)*

SP: 16/1; 66/1; 100/1   14 ran
  N. Henderson   7:3

1986 £41,435

1. **See You Then** 6-12-0
   (S. Smith Eccles)
2. Gaye Brief 9-12-0 *(P. Scudamore)*
3. Nohalmdun 5-12-0 *(J. J. O'Neill)*

SP: 5/6; 14/1; 20/1   23 ran
  N. Henderson   7:1½

1987 £43,205

1. **See You Then** 7-12-0
   (S. Smith Eccles)
2. Flatterer 8-12-0 *(J. Fishback)*
3. Barnbrook Again 6-12-0
   (S. Sherwood)

SP: 11/10; 10/1; 14/1   18 ran
  N. Henderson   1½:1

1988 £52,225

1. **Celtic Shot** 6-12-0 *(P. Scudamore)*
2. Classical Charm 5-12-0
   (K. Morgan)
3. Celtic Chief 5-12-0 *(R. Dunwoody)*

SP: 7/1; 33/1; 5/2   21 ran
  F. Winter   4:3

1989 £50,207

1. **Beech Road** 7-12-0 *(R. Guest)*
2. Celtic Chief 8-12-0 *(G. McCourt)*
3. Celtic Shot 7-12-0 *(P. Scudamore)*

SP: 50/1; 6/1; 8/1   15 ran
  G. Balding   2:1

1990 £50,047

1. **Kribensis** 6-12-0 *(R. Dunwoody)*
2. Nomadic Way 5-12-0 *(P. Scudamore)*
3. Past Glories 7-12-0 *(J. Quinn)*

SP: 95/40; 8/1; 150/1   19 ran
  M. Stoute   3:¾

1991 £81,790

1. **Morley Street** 7-12-0 *(J. Frost)*
2. Nomadic Way 6-12-0 *(R. Dunwoody)*
3. Ruling 5-12-0 *(P. Niven)*

SP: 4/1; 9/1; 50/1   24 ran
  G. Balding   1½:hd

1992 £80,065

1. **Royal Gait** 9-12-0 *(G. McCourt)*
2. Oh So Risky 5-12-0 *(P. Holley)*
3. Ruling 6-12-0 *(P. Niven)*

SP: 6/1; 20/1; 20/1   16 ran
  J. Fanshawe   ½:sh

1993 £84,734

1. **Granville Again** 7-12-0
   (P. Scudamore)
2. Royal Derbi 8-12-0 *(M. Perrett)*
3. Halkopous 7-12-0 *(A. Maguire)*

SP: 13/2; 50/1; 9/1   18 ran
  M. Pipe   1:2½

FREE HANDICAP HURDLE (4-y-o) (Chepstow 2m)

1969	Country Retreat 11-3: 7/1	F. Walwyn	*M. Gifford*	9
1970	Harlech Lad 10-13: 5/1	J. Cann	*W. Smith*	16
1971	Boy Tudor 10-4: 25/1	R. Hezlet	*P. Kelleway*	14
1972	Freethinker 10-5: 7/1	F. Winter	*J. Francome*	9
1973	Bumble Boy 11-2: 6/1	W. Marshall	*W. Smith*	13
1974	Southern Darling 10-5: 8/1	J. Gifford	*R. Champion*	15
1975	Night Nurse 11-5: 11/10	M. H. Easterby	*P. Broderick*	16
1976	Romping To Work 10-7: 12/1	J. Edwards	*P. Blacker*	11
1977	Levaramoss 12-0: 15/2	A. Ingham	*B. R. Davies*	12
1978	Sean 11-0: 11/2	F. Rimell	*J. Burke*	8
1979	McAdam 10-5: 4/6	F. Rimell	*C. Tinkler*	4
1980	Gay George 11-10: 1/2	F. Walwyn	*W. Smith*	5
1981	York Cottage 10-3: 3/1	N. Gaselee	*R. Linley*	11
1982	Monza 10-5: 16/1	P. Cundell	*R. Rowe*	9
1983	Ra Nova 10-13: 4/1	Mrs N. Kennedy	*P. Farrell*	7
1984	Statesmanship 10-9: 14/1	R. Hannon	*P. Scudamore*	10
1985	Nebris 11-1: 15/8	R. Akehurst	*H. Davies*	10
1986	Tingle Bell 10-1: 10/1	G. Moore	*M. Hammond*	10
1987	Framlington Court 11-6: 7/2	P. Walwyn	*D. Browne*	7
1988	Rivers Secret 9-10: 8/1	Denys Smith	*A. Smith*	16
1989	Peer Prince 11-8: 11/4	G. Pritchard-Gordon	*S. Smith Eccles*	8
1990	Coe 10-0: 6/1	R. Akehurst	*L. Harvey*	16
1991	Bottles 11-9: 7/2	J. Banks	*S. Smith Eccles*	7
1992	Kilcash 10-10: 11/4	P. Hedger	*M. Richards*	8

DESERT ORCHID SOUTH WESTERN PATTERN CHASE
(Wincanton 2m 5f)

1990	Panto Prince 9-11-8: 4/6	C. Popham	*B. Powell*	3
1991	Sabin du Loir 12-11-8: 8/11	M. Pipe	*P. Scudamore*	7
1992	Remittance Man 8-11-8: 4/11	N. Henderson	*R. Dunwoody*	4

FLAVEL-LEISURE HURDLE (4-y-o) (Newbury 2m 110yds)

1980	Gay George 11-3: 8/13	F. Walwyn	*W. Smith*	8
1981	Ra Tapu 11-3: 6/1	P. Mitchell	*R. Hughes*	12
1982	Royal Vulcan 11-3: 9/4	N. Callaghan	*J. J. O'Neill*	9
1983	Connaught River 11-3: 12/1	D. Nicholson	*P. Scudamore*	12
1984	Statesmanship 11-3: 4/1	R. Hannon	*P. Scudamore*	9
1985	Ace of Spies 11-0: 100/30	L. Kennard	*B. Powell*	4
1986	Saffron Lord 11-3: 3/1	L. Kennard	*B. Powell*	8
1987	Celtic Chief 11-0: 7/2	Mrs M. Rimell	*P. Scudamore*	7
1988	Kribensis 11-7: 4/5	M. Stoute	*R. Dunwoody*	7
1989	Jopanini 11-0: 4/1	D. Thom	*D. Murphy*	9
1990	Spring Hay 11-0: 9/2	D. Nicholson	*R. Dunwoody*	8
1991	Bookcase 11-0: 5/4	D. Elsworth	*P. Holley*	3
1992	Staunch Friend 11-7: 8/11	M. Tompkins	*S. Smith Eccles*	4

GLYNWED INTERNATIONAL HANDICAP CHASE (Newbury 2½m)

1961	Frenchman's Cove 6-11-0: 100/30	H. T. Jones	*S. Mellor*	10
1962	Fortria 10-10-7: 4/11	T. Dreaper (Ir)	*P. Taaffe*	4
1963	King's Nephew 9-11-0: 5/2	F. Cundell	*D. Mould*	12
1964	No race			
1965	Abandoned because of fog			
1966	Kapeno 9-11-0: 100/7	P. Cazalet	*Mr N. Gaselee*	10
1967	Rondetto 11-10-7: 7/4	R. Turnell	*J. Haine*	5
1968	Chaou II 5-10-11: 3/1	P. Cazalet	*D. Mould*	5
1969	Moonduster 10-11-11: 5/2	F. Rimell	*T. Biddlecombe*	8
1970	Moonduster 11-10-12: —	F. Rimell	*C. G. Davies*	w.o.
1971	Into View 8-11-10: 8/13	F. Winter	*P. Kelleway*	3
1972	Spanish Steps 9-11-1: 11/10	E. Courage	*P. Blacker*	4
1973	Crisp 10-11-6: 4/5	F. Winter	*R. Pitman*	6
1974	Pendil 9-12-0: 1/3	F. Winter	*R. Pitman*	4
1975	Game Spirit 9-11-6: 2/7	F. Walwyn	*W. Smith*	2
1976	Game Spirit 10-11-6: 3/1	F. Walwyn	*W. Smith*	4
1977	Fort Devon 11-11-1: 10/11	F. Walwyn	*W. Smith*	4
1978	Party Line 9-11-10: 5/6	H. Poole	*R. R. Evans*	3
1979	Jack of Trumps 6-12-0: 1/1	E. O'Grady (Ir)	*Mr N. Madden*	3

123

1980 Stopped 8-11-1: 2/1	F. Winter	*B. de Haan*	9
1981 Fairy King 8-10-9: 1/1	J. FitzGerald	*S. Smith Eccles*	9
1982 Observe 6-10-7: 16/1	F. Winter	*B. de Haan*	9
1983 The Mighty Mac 8-10-13: 8/11	M. Dickinson	*Mr D. Browne*	6
1984 Observe 8-11-3: 4/1	F. Winter	*J. Francome*	7
1985 Tom's Little Al 9-11-7	W. Williams	*P. Scudamore*	2
1986 Voice of Progress 8-11-5: 3/1	D. Nicholson	*R. Dunwoody*	7
1987 Brave Hussar 9-10-0: 8/1	R. Curtis	*C. Llewellyn*	5
1988 Pegwell Bay 7-11-2: 2/1	T. Forster	*C. Llewellyn*	6
1989 Joint Sovereignty 9-10-11: 11/10	P. J. Hobbs	*P. Hobbs*	3
1990 Guiburn's Nephew 8-10-5: 3/1	P. Hobbs	*C. Maude*	5
1991 Espy 8-11-12: 4/1	C. Brooks	*G. Bradley*	6
1992 Brandeston 7-10-11: 9/2	F. Murphy	*D. Murphy*	9

UNITED HOUSE CONSTRUCTION HANDICAP CHASE (Ascot 2m)

1982 Artifice 11-10-7: 5/1	J. Thorne	*S. Smith Eccles*	7
1983 Western Rose 11-10-0: 11/10	Mrs M. Rimell	*S. Morshead*	2
1984 Little Bay 9-12-3: 2/1	G. Richards	*J. Francome*	7
1985 Admiral's Cup 7-10-7: 2/1	F. Winter	*B. de Haan*	4
1986 Far Bridge 10-10-7: 13/2	G. Balding	*S. Smith Eccles*	7
1987 Long Engagement 6-10-7: 12/1	D. Nicholson	*R. Dunwoody*	7
1988 Vodkatini 9-11-10: 6/1	J. Gifford	*P. Hobbs*	6
1989 Prize Asset 9-11-3: 100/30	P. Hobbs	*S. Earle*	9
1990 Fu's Lady 8-11-2: 6/1	M. Pipe	*P. Scudamore*	5
1991 Hogmanay 9-11-5: 11/2	R. Casey	*H. Davies*	7
1992 Katabatic 9-12-0: 2/1	A. Turnell	*S. McNeill*	6

TOTE SILVER TROPHY HANDICAP HURDLE (Chepstow 2½m 110yds)

1988 Buckskin's Best 6-10-3: 16/1	R. Dickin	*R. Dunwoody*	17
1989 Pipers Copse 7-10-4: 7/2	G. Harwood	*M. Perrett*	8
1990 Bradbury Star 5-10-11: 6/1	J. Gifford	*R. Rowe*	13
1991 Danny Harrold 7-11-10: 16/1	Mrs J. Pitman	*M. Pitman*	14
1992 Mighty Mogul 5-10-12: 11/8	D. Nicholson	*R. Dunwoody*	13

WENSLEYDALE JUVENILE HURDLE (3-y-o) (Wetherby 2m)

1990 Native Mission 10-12: 4/1	J. FitzGerald	*M. Dwyer*	10
1991 Swift Sword 10-12: 11/8	Mrs M. Reveley	*P. Niven*	9
1992 Desert Mist 10-7: 8/1	D. Smith	*C. Grant*	11

TOTE WEST YORKSHIRE HURDLE (Wetherby 3m 1f)

1990 Battalion 6-11-7: 11/8	C. Brooks	*P. Scudamore*	10
1991 Cab On Target 5-11-4: 5/2	Mrs M. Reveley	*P. Niven*	6
1992 Burgoyne 6-11-0: 4/1	M. H. Easterby	*L. Wyer*	9

TETLEY BITTER CHARLIE HALL CHASE (Wetherby 3m 110yds)

1969 Arcturus 8-11-10: 11/4	N. Crump	*P. Buckley*	3
1970 Kildrummy 5-11-7: 100/30	W. Crawford	*R. Barry*	8
1971 Abandoned because of snow and frost			
1972 Coxswain 7-11-10: 4/5	W. A. Stephenson	*Mr G. Macmillan*	8
1973 Dunrobin 6-11-5: 4/5	W. Crawford	*S. P. Taylor*	6
1974 Tamalin 7-11-9: 9/4	G. Richards	*J. J. O'Neill*	7
1975 Davy Lad 5-11-7: 2/5	M. O'Toole (Ir)	*D. T. Hughes*	5
1976 Set Point 8-11-9: 20/1 ⎫ dh	Lady Herries	*T. Stack*	6
Current Gold 5-11-7: 4/1 ⎭	G. Richards	*D. Goulding*	
1977 Goolagong 7-11-9: 8/1	N. Crump	*Mr H. Orde-Powlett*	8
1978 Fighting Fit 6-11-9: 6/5	K. Oliver	*R. Lamb*	5
1979 Sparkie's Choice 6-11-9: 9/2	N. Crump	*C. Hawkins*	8
1980 Manton Castle 6-11-9: 16/1	M. Camacho	*G. Holmes*	9
1981 Gay Return 6-11-10: 12/1	E. O'Grady (Ir)	*T. Ryan*	11
1982 Righthand Man 5-11-7: 11/10	M. Dickinson	*G. Bradley*	10
1983 Wayward Lad 8-11-10: 1/3	M. Dickinson	*R. Earnshaw*	3
1984 Burrough Hill Lad 8-11-9: 10/11	Mrs J. Pitman	*P. Tuck*	4
1985 Wayward Lad 10-11-6: 1/1	Mrs M. Dickinson	*G. Bradley*	4
1986 Forgive'N Forget 9-11-10: 5/2	J. FitzGerald	*M. Dwyer*	6
1987 Cybrandian 9-11-2: 7/4	M. H. Easterby	*C. Grant*	4
1988 High Edge Grey 7-11-2: 13/2	K. Oliver	*T. Reed*	10
1989 Durham Edition 11-11-2: 33/1	W. A. Stephenson	*A. Merrigan*	7
1990 Celtic Shot 8-11-2: 7/4	C. Brooks	*P. Scudamore*	7

124

| 1991 | Celtic Shot 9-11-10: 4/5 | C. Brooks | *G. Bradley* | 6 |
| 1992 | Tipping Tim 7-11-2: 11/4 | N. Twiston-Davies | *C. Llewellyn* | 7 |

PLYMOUTH GIN HALDON GOLD CUP CHASE (Devon & Exeter 2¼m)

1986	Kathies Lad 8-11-8: 4/5	A. Jarvis	*S. Smith Eccles*	8
1987	Admirals Cup 8-11-8: 11/4	F. Winter	*P. Scudamore*	4
1988	Barnbrook Again 7-11-0: 4/6	D. Elsworth	*S. Sherwood*	4
1989	Panto Prince 8-11-0: 4/11	C. Popham	*B. Powell*	5
1990	Sabin du Loir 11-11-0: 7/2	M. Pipe	*P. Scudamore*	5
1991	Sabin du Loir 12-11-6: 5/4	M. Pipe	*P. Scudamore*	6
1992	Waterloo Boy 9-11-6: 11/4	D. Nicholson	*R. Dunwoody*	5

BADGER BEER CHASE (LIMITED HANDICAP)
(Wincanton 3m 1f 110yds)

1983	Half Free 7-10-11: 9/4	F. Winter	*R. Linley*	8
1984	Beau Ranger 6-9-8: 11/4	J. Thorne	*J. Hurst*	9
1985	Oyster Pond 8-11-4: 20/1	M. McCourt	*G. McCourt*	7
1986	Von Trappe 9-11-7: 11/2	Mrs J. Pitman	*B. de Haan*	6
1987	Sun Rising 9-10-13: 7/4	F. Walwyn	*K. Mooney*	8
1988	Farmlea Boy 8-10-0: 3/1	G. Balding	*R. Guest*	8
1989	Tonights The Night 8-10-13: 11/8	O. Sherwood	*J. Osborne*	5
1990	Panto Prince 9-11-10: 40/95	C. Popham	*B. Powell*	2
1991	Foyle Fisherman 12-10-7: 4/1	J. Gifford	*E. Murphy*	4
1992	Captain Dibble 7-11-8: 7/4	N. Twiston-Davies	*C. Llewellyn*	7

STEEL PLATE AND SECTIONS YOUNG CHASERS
CHAMPIONSHIP FINAL (Cheltenham 3m 1f)

1980	Drusus 6-11-11: 10/11	F. Rimell	*J. King*	8
1981	Sea Captain 7-12-0: 9/4	R. Head	*H. Davies*	6
1982	Masterson 7-11-7: 6/1	Mrs M. Rimell	*P. Scudamore*	7
1983	Abandoned because course waterlogged			
1984	Gambir 6-11-8: 1/1	D. Nicholson	*P. Scudamore*	5
1985	Clutterbuck 7-11-8: 6/4 } dh	F. Winter	*R. Linley*	6
	Connaught River 6-11-4: 6/1 } dh	D. Nicholson	*P. Scudamore*	
1986	Arctic Stream 7-11-11: 6/4	F. Walwyn	*K. Mooney*	5
1987	Summons 8-12-0: 4/1	J. Gifford	*R. Rowe*	8
1988	Private Views 7-11-11: 8/13	N. Gaselee	*K. Mooney*	6
1989	Pin's Pride 7-11-4: 14/1	J. Gifford	*E. McKinley*	6
1990	Elfast 7-11-4: 11/10	J. Webber	*M. Lynch*	3
1991	Tipping Tim 6-10-5: 2/1	N. Twiston-Davies	*C. Llewellyn*	8
1992	Bradbury Star 7-11-12: 1/2	J. Gifford	*D. Murphy*	6

WHITBREAD WHITE LABEL HANDICAP HURDLE
(Cheltenham 2m 110yds)

1984	Robin Wonder 6-11-4: 7/4	D. Elsworth	*R. Arnott*	9
1985	Jim Thorpe 4-10-0: 8/1	G. Richards	*D. Coakley*	12
1986	Robin Wonder 8-11-10: 9/1	D. Elsworth	*G. Bradley*	9
1987	Celtic Shot 5-10-6: 9/4	F. Winter	*P. Scudamore*	9
1988	South Parade 4-11-0: 9/2	G. Balding	*G. Bradley*	10
1989	Highland Bounty 5-10-4: 14/1	S. Dow	*S. Turner*	10
1990	Liadett 5-11-10: 9/2	M. Pipe	*M. Perrett*	8
1991	Shu Fly 7-11-1: 10/1	Mrs S. Oliver	*S. Smith Eccles*	12
1992	Valfinet 5-10-9: 7/2	M. Pipe	*P. Scudamore*	9

MACKESON GOLD CUP HANDICAP CHASE (Cheltenham 2½m 110yds)

1960	Fortria 8-12-0: 8/1	T. Dreaper (Ir)	*P. Taaffe*	19
1961	Scottish Memories 7-10-12: 9/2	A. Thomas	*C. Finnegan*	17
1962	Fortria 10-12-0: 5/1	T. Dreaper (Ir)	*P. Taaffe*	25
1963	Richard of Bordeaux 8-10-5: 20/1	F. Walwyn	*H. Beasley*	20
1964	Super Flash 9-10-5	F. Cundell	*S. Mellor*	9
1965	Dunkirk 8-12-7: 11/10	P. Cazalet	*W. Rees*	8
1966	Pawnbroker 8-11-9: 7/2	W. A. Stephenson	*P. Broderick*	5
1967	Charlie Worcester 10-10-11: 7/1	R. Price	*J. Gifford*	13
1968	Jupiter Boy 7-10-3: 9/1	F. Rimell	*E. P. Harty*	13
1969	Gay Trip 7-11-5: 8/1	F. Rimell	*T. Biddlecombe*	14
1970	Chatham 6-10-3: 33/1	F. Rimell	*K. White*	17
1971	Gay Trip 9-11-3: 8/1	F. Rimell	*T. Biddlecombe*	10
1972	Red Candle 8-10-0: 20/1	G. Vallance	*J. Fox*	11

125

1973	Skymas 8-10-5: 7/1	B. Lusk (Ir)	*T. S. Murphy*	15
1974	Bruslee 8-10-7: 2/1	M. Scudamore	*A. Turnell*	11
1975	Clear Cut 11-10-9: 13/2	M. Camacho	*D. Greaves*	13
1976	Cancello 7-11-1: 4/1	N. Crump	*D. Atkins*	13
1977	Bachelor's Hall 7-10-6: 11/2	P. Cundell	*M. O'Halloran*	16
1978	Bawnogues 7-10-7: 5/1	M. Tate	*C. Smith*	11
1979	Man Alive 8-10-9: 6/1	G. Richards	*R. Barry*	11
1980	Bright Highway 6-11-1: 5/1	M. J. O'Brien (Ir)	*G. Newman*	15
1981	Henry Kissinger 7-10-13: 5/1	D. Gandolfo	*P. Barton*	11
1982	Fifty Dollars More 7-11-0: 11/1	F. Winter	*R. Linley*	11
1983	Pounentes 6-10-6: 7/1	W. McGhie	*N. Doughty*	9
1984	Half Free 8-11-10: 5/2	F. Winter	*R. Linley*	10
1985	Half Free 9-11-10: 9/2	F. Winter	*R. Linley*	10
1986	Very Promising 8-11-13: 7/1	D. Nicholson	*R. Dunwoody*	11
1987	Beau Ranger 9-10-2: 13/2	M. Pipe	*M. Perrett*	14
1988	Pegwell Bay 7-11-2: 6/1	T. Forster	*P. Scudamore*	13
1989	Joint Sovereignty 9-10-4: 10/1	P. Hobbs	*G. McCourt*	15
1990	Multum In Parvo 7-10-2: 12/1	J. Edwards	*N. Williamson*	13
1991	Another Coral 8-10-1: 15/2	D. Nicholson	*R. Dunwoody*	15
1992	Tipping Tim 7-10-10: 11/2	N. Twiston-Davies	*C. Llewellyn*	16

BELLWAY HOMES FIGHTING FIFTH HURDLE (Newcastle 2m 110yds)

1969	Mugatpura 6-11-7: 1/1	F. Walwyn	*G. W. Robinson*	7
1970	Inishmaan 4-11-2: 5/1	F. Rimell	*T. Biddlecombe*	11
1971	Dondieu 6-11-7: 4/5	Denys Smith	*B. Fletcher*	11
1972	Comedy of Errors 5-11-7: 11/8	F. Rimell	*W. Smith*	8
1973	Comedy of Errors 6-12-0: 8/11	F. Rimell	*W. Smith*	7
1974	Comedy of Errors 7-11-10: 8/13	F. Rimell	*K. White*	5
1975	Night Nurse 4-11-5: 6/4	M. H. Easterby	*P. Broderick*	4
1976	Bird's Nest 6-11-10: 4/1	R. Turnell	*S. C. Knight*	6
1977	Bird's Nest 7-11-10: 5/2	R. Turnell	*A. Turnell*	5
1978	Sea Pigeon 8-11-10: 4/6	M. H. Easterby	*I. Watkinson*	4
1979	Bird's Nest 9-11-9: 5/4	R. Turnell	*A. Turnell*	5
1980	Sea Pigeon 10-12-0: 7/4	M. H. Easterby	*A. Brown*	7
1981	Ekbalco 5-11-5: 7/2	R. Fisher	*D. Goulding*	7
1982	Donegal Prince 6-11-5: 10/1	P. Kelleway	*P. Tuck*	6
1983	Gaye Brief 6-12-0: 4/9	Mrs M. Rimell	*S. Morshead*	5
1984	Browne's Gazette 6-11-9: 1/2	Mrs M. Dickinson	*D. Browne*	8
1985	Out of The Gloom 4-11-6: 9/1	R. Hollinshead	*J. J. O'Neill*	9
1986	Tom Sharp 6-11-0: 7/2	W. Wharton	*S. J. O'Neill*	10
1987	Floyd 7-11-6: 5/6	D. Elsworth	*C. Brown*	7
1988	Floyd 8-11-6: 9/4	D. Elsworth	*S. Sherwood*	6
1989	Kribensis 5-11-9: 4/7	M. Stoute	*M. Dwyer*	5
1990	Beech Road 8-11-4: 4/6	G. Balding	*R. Guest*	5
1991	Royal Derbi 6-11-4: 7/2	N. Callaghan	*C. Grant*	4
1992	Halkopous 6-11-0: 7/4	M. Tompkins	*S. Smith Eccles*	6

RACECALL ASCOT HURDLE (Ascot 2½m)

1972	Bula 7-11-8: 4/5	F. Winter	*P. Kelleway*	6
1973	Moyne Royal 8-11-8: 13/8	A. Pitt	*D. Mould*	6
1974	Lanzarote 6-11-8: 8/15	F. Winter	*R. Pitman*	4
1975	Lanzarote 7-11-8: 6/4	F. Winter	*J. Francome*	4
1976	Dramatist 5-11-8: 6/4	F. Walwyn	*W. Smith*	6
1977	Dramatist 6-11-4: 1/3	F. Walwyn	*W. Smith*	5
1978	Kybo 5-11-8: 2/9	J. Gifford	*G. Enright*	4
1979	Connaught Ranger 5-11-8: 8/11	F. Rimell	*C. Tinkler*	10
1980	Connaught Ranger 6-11-8: 11/4	F. Rimell	*J. Burke*	8
1981	Lumen 6-10-13: 14/1	J. Gifford	*R. Rowe*	7
1982	Al Kuwait 6-10-13: 1/1	F. Winter	*J. Francome*	4
1983	Dawn Run 5-10-13: 1/3	P. Mullins (Ir)	*J. J. O'Neill*	7
1984	Gaye Brief 7-10-11: 4/6	Mrs M. Rimell	*R. Linley*	5
1985	Gaye Brief 8-10-11: 13/8	Mrs M. Rimell	*R. Linley*	9
1986	Ibn Majed 4-10-11: 9/2	C. Spares	*J. McLaughlin*	5
1987	Sabin du Loir 8-10-11: 5/2	M. Pipe	*P. Scudamore*	7
1988	Sabin du Loir 9-10-11: 1/2	M. Pipe	*P. Scudamore*	6
1989	Nodform 5-10-11: 12/1	J. Gifford	*R. Rowe*	5
1990	Morley Street 6-11-10: 4/5	G. Balding	*J. Frost*	5
1991	Morley Street 7-11-10: 4/9	G. Balding	*J. Frost*	6

1992 Muse 5-11-0: 9/1   D. Elsworth   *P. Holley*   7

HURST PARK NOVICES' CHASE (Ascot 2m)
1965 Stalbridge Colonist 6-11-4: 6/1	K. Cundell	*W. Rees*	9
1966 Sir Thopas 5-11-6: 1/1	R. Turnell	*J. King*	7
1967 Get Stepping 6-11-4: 4/1	R. Turnell	*J. King*	9
1968 Rehearsed 6-11-4: 15/2	R. Turnell	*W. Rees*	10
1969 Louis Napoleon 6-11-4: 11/4	F. Cundell	*S. Mellor*	8
1970 Table Mountain 5-11-1: 7/2	F. Rimell	*K. White*	9
1971 Shell Streak 4-10-6: 9/2	S. Pattemore	*R. Champion*	7
1972 Killiney 6-11-4: 11/8	F. Winter	*R. Pitman*	3
1973 Cool Million 5-11-1: 11/2	F. Walwyn	*A. Branford*	8
1974 Isle of Man 7-11-9: 4/9	F. Walwyn	*W. Smith*	4
1975 Hardier 7-11-9: 1/6	H. T. Jones	*I. Watkinson*	2
1976 Supreme Halo 6-11-4: 4/6	R. Smyth	*C. Read*	7
1977 Pavement Artist 5-11-8: 9/4	H. T. Jones	*S. Smith Eccles*	4
1978 Ramblix 6-11-4: 11/10	F. Winter	*J. Francome*	3
1979 Kybo 6-11-4: 5/4	J. Gifford	*R. Rowe*	3
1980 Little Bay 5-11-4: 4/6	G. Richards	*R. Barry*	4
1981 Run With Pride 6-11-7: 100/30	M. O'Toole (Ir)	*N. Madden*	7
1982 Jubilee Medal 5-11-1: 7/1	N. Henderson	*J. Francome*	6
1983 Monza 5-10-10: 6/4	P. Cundell	*R. Rowe*	3
1984 Townley Stone 5-11-8: 9/4	J. Webber	*G. McCourt*	7
1985 Desert Orchid 6-11-4: 4/9	D. Elsworth	*C. Brown*	4
1986 Ten of Spades 6-11-4: 8/1	S. Mellor	*G. Charles Jones*	8
1987 Barnbrook Again 6-11-8: 5/6	D. Elsworth	*S. Sherwood*	5
1988 Fred The Tread 6-11-4: 8/1	T. Casey	*R. Dunwoody*	5
1989 Young Snugfit 5-11-8: 11/8	O. Sherwood	*J. Osborne*	5
1990 African Safari 6-11-0: 7/2	Mrs S. Smith	*R. Stronge*	3
1991 Poetic Gem 6-11-0: 4/1	Mrs S. Smith	*R. Guest*	4
1992 Sybillin 6-11-0: 11/8	J. FitzGerald	*M. Dwyer*	5

H & T WALKER GOLD CUP HANDICAP CHASE (Ascot 2m 3f 110yds)
1981 Wayward Lad 6-11-10: 9/4	M. Dickinson	*R. Earnshaw*	8
1982 Pay Related 8-11-2: 7/1	M. H. Easterby	*J. J. O'Neill*	6
1983 The Tsarevich 7-11-6: 9/2	N. Henderson	*Mr J. White*	6
1984 Cybrandian 6-10-9: 6/4	M. H. Easterby	*A. Brown*	6
1985 Very Promising 7-11-7: 6/1	D. Nicholson	*P. Scudamore*	7
1986 Church Warden 7-10-7: 12/1	D. Murray-Smith	*R. Dunwoody*	6
1987 Weather The Storm 7-11-10: 6/1	A. Moore (Ir)	*T. Taaffe*	11
1988 Saffron Lord 6-11-3: 8/11	J. Gifford	*R. Rowe*	5
1989 Man O'Magic 8-11-5: 9/1	K. Bailey	*M. Perrett*	11
1990 Blazing Walker 6-11-6: 7/2	W. A. Stephenson	*C. Grant*	5
1991 Kings Fountain 8-11-1: 7/2	K. Bailey	*A. Tory*	8
1992 Deep Sensation 7-11-2: 11/2	J. Gifford	*D. Murphy*	10

PETERBOROUGH CHASE (Huntingdon 2½m 110yds)
1986 Western Sunset 10-11-1: 7/2	T. Forster	*H. Davies*	3
1987 Very Promising 9-11-9: 2/7	D. Nicholson	*R. Dunwoody*	3
1988 Townley Stone 9-11-1: 4/5	J. Webber	*G. Mernagh*	3
1989 Clever Folly 9-11-1: 5/4	G. Richards	*N. Doughty*	4
1990 Pegwell Bay 9-11-1: 11/10	T. Forster	*J. Railton*	5
1991 Sabin du Loir 12-11-9: 4/7	M. Pipe	*P. Scudamore*	4
1992 Remittance Man 8-11-9: 1/5	N. Henderson	*R. Dunwoody*	4

AKZO LONG DISTANCE HURDLE (Newbury 3m 110yds)
1990 Trapper John 6-11-7: 10/11	M. Morris (Ir)	*C. Swan*	3
1991 Cab On Target 5-11-4: 5/4	Mrs M. Reveley	*P. Niven*	11
1992 Tyrone Bridge 6-11-0: 6/1	M. Pipe	*R. Dunwoody*	9

HENNESSY COGNAC GOLD CUP HANDICAP CHASE
(Newbury 3m 2f 110yds)
1957 Mandarin 6-11-0: 8/1	F. Walwyn	*P. Madden*	19
1958 Taxidermist 6-11-1: 10/1	F. Walwyn	*Mr J. Lawrence*	13
1959 Kerstin 9-11-10: 4/1	C. Bewicke	*S. Hayhurst*	26
1960 Knucklecracker 7-11-1: 100/7	D. Ancil	*D. Ancil*	20
1961 Mandarin 10-11-5: 7/1	F. Walwyn	*G. W. Robinson*	22
1962 Springbok 8-10-8: 15/2	N. Crump	*G. Scott*	27

127

1963	Mill House 6-12-0: 15/8	F. Walwyn	G. W. Robinson	10
1964	Arkle 7-12-7: 5/4	T. Dreaper (Ir)	P. Taaffe	9
1965	Arkle 8-12-7: 1/6	T. Dreaper (Ir)	P. Taaffe	8
1966	Stalbridge Colonist 7-10-0: 25/1	K. Cundell	S. Mellor	6
1967	Rondetto 11-10-1: 100/8	R. Turnell	J. King	13
1968	Man of The West 7-10-0: 20/1	F. Walwyn	G. W. Robinson	11
1969	Spanish Steps 6-11-8: 7/1	E. Courage	J. Cook	15
1970	Border Mask 8-11-1: 7/1	P. Cazalet	D. Mould	12
1971	Bighorn 7-10-11: 7/1	C. V. Miller	D. Cartwright	13
1972	Charlie Potheen 7-11-4: 10/1	F. Walwyn	R. Pitman	13
1973	Red Candle 9-10-4: 12/1	G. Vallance	J. Fox	11
1974	Royal Marshal II 7-10-0: 11/2	T. Forster	G. Thorner	13
1975	April Seventh 9-11-2: 11/1	R. Turnell	A. Turnell	13
1976	Zeta's Son 7-10-9: 12/1	P. Bailey	I. Watkinson	21
1977	Bachelor's Hall 7-10-10: 11/2	P. Cundell	M. O'Halloran	14
1978	Approaching 7-10-6: 3/1	J. Gifford	R. Champion	8
1979	Fighting Fit 7-11-7: 15/2	K. Oliver	R. Linley	15
1980	Bright Highway 6-11-6: 2/1	M. J. O'Brien (Ir)	G. Newman	14
1981	Diamond Edge 10-11-10: 9/2	F. Walwyn	W. Smith	14
1982	Bregawn 8-11-10: 9/4	M. Dickinson	G. Bradley	11
1983	Brown Chamberlin 8-11-8: 7/2	F. Winter	J. Francome	12
1984	Burrough Hill Lad 8-12-0: 100/30	Mrs J. Pitman	J. Francome	13
1985	Galway Blaze 9-10-0: 11/2	J. FitzGerald	M. Dwyer	15
1986	Broadheath 9-10-5: 6/1	D. Barons	P. Nicholls	15
1987	Playschool 9-10-8: 6/1	D. Barons	P. Nicholls	12
1988	Strands of Gold 9-10-0: 10/1	M. Pipe	P. Scudamore	12
1989	Ghofar 6-10-2: 5/1	D. Elsworth	H. Davies	8
1990	Arctic Call 7-11-0: 5/1	O. Sherwood	J. Osborne	13
1991	Chatam 7-10-6: 10/1	M. Pipe	P. Scudamore	15
1992	Sibton Abbey 7-10-0: 40/1	F. Murphy	A. Maguire	13

BONUSPRINT GERRY FEILDEN HURDLE (Newbury 2m 110yds)

1951	Campari 4-11-0: 100/7	R. Price	F. Winter	11
1952	Pont Cordonnier 5-10-2: 13/8	V. Smyth	F. Crouch	9
1953	Straight Cut 4-10-1: 7/1	T. R. Rimell	K. Mullins	9
1954	Syrte 4-12-2: 7/2	R. Price	F. Winter	11
1955	Punjab 4-10-1: 9/4	T. Farmer	H. Sprague	6
1956	Hilarion 8-11-4: 9/1	W. Wightman	M. Scudamore	10
1957	Fare Time 4-10-12: 4/1	R. Price	J. Gilbert	13
1958	Retour de Flamme 5-12-4: 9/2	S. Warren	D. Dick	12
1959	Langton Heath 5-11-4: 100/8	T. Griffiths	R. Martin	16
1960	Rough Tweed 6-10-4: 7/1	N. Crump	H. East	15
1961	Anzio 4-11-1: 11/4	F. Walwyn	H. Beasley	14
1962	White Park Bay 7-11-4: 2/1	P. P-Gallwey	J. Gifford	14
1963	Salmon Spray 5-10-8: 5/4	R. Turnell	J. Haine	11
1964	Golden Sailor 5-10-4: 100/8	G. Vergette	D. Nicholson	22
1965	Lanconello 6-10-5: 5/2	K. Piggott	J. Haine	11
1966	Hanassi 6-10-6: 9/1	J. Goldsmith	A. Turnell	19
1967	Secret Agent II 5-10-10: 11/2	J. Benstead	J. Gifford	16
1968	Bric-Brac 9-11-6: 5/1	H. Hannon	J. Guest	9
1969	Viroy 5-11-6: 8/1	R. Price	J. Gifford	14
1970	Coral Diver 5-12-0: 1/1	F. Rimell	K. White	12
1971	Eric 4-10-8: 25/1	V. Cross	J. Nolan	11
1972	Comedy of Errors 5-12-0: 8/11	F. Rimell	W. Smith	10
1973	Lanzarote 5-11-10: 1/3	F. Winter	R. Pitman	7
1974	Flash Imp 5-11-6: 11/2	R. Smyth	J. King	5
1975	Dramatist 4-11-1: 10/1	F. Walwyn	W. Smith	9
1976	Beacon Light 5-12-0: 6/1	R. Turnell	A. Turnell	9
1977	Decent Fellow 4-11-9: 1/1	G. Balding	R. Linley	5
1978	Connaught Ranger 4-11-9: 6/1	F. Rimell	J. Burke	7
1979	Celtic Ryde 4-11-5: 5/4	P. Cundell	M. O'Halloran	7
1980	Pollardstown 5-11-8	S. Mellor	P. Blacker	8
1981	Heighlin 5-11-8: 4/1	D. Elsworth	S. Jobar	6
1982	Royal Vulcan 4-11-0: 4/6	N. Callaghan	J. J. O'Neill	8
1983	Buck House 5-11-8: 4/1	M. Morris (Ir)	T. Carmody	7
1984	Ra Nova 5-11-3: 11/8	Mrs N. Kennedy	M. Perrett	7
1985	Gala's Image 5-11-0: 9/2	Mrs M. Rimell	R. Linley	8

1986	Barnbrook Again 5-11-0: 7/2	D. Elsworth	*R. Arnott*	7
1987	Celtic Chief 4-11-0: 8/11	Mrs M. Rimell	*P. Scudamore*	9
1988	Kribensis 4-11-6: 8/11	M. Stoute	*R. Dunwoody*	5
1989	Cruising Altitude 6-11-3: 6/5	O. Sherwood	*J. Osborne*	8
1990	Fidway 5-11-6: 7/2	T. Thomson Jones	*S. Smith Eccles*	5
1991	Gran Alba 5-11-0: 5/4	R. Hannon	*G. McCourt*	6
1992	Mighty Mogul 5-11-3: 11/8	D. Nicholson	*R. Dunwoody*	6

EDWARD HANMER MEMORIAL CHASE (Haydock 3m)

1959	John Jacques 10-12-0: 5/1	N. Crump	*G. Scott*	11
1960	Badanloch 9-11-11: 11/8	G. Owen	*S. Mellor*	4
1961	Loch Sloy 7-11-7: 5/4	T. Robson	*M. Batchelor*	5
1962	Dancing Rain 7-10-4: 20/1	P. Upton	*E. Kelly*	11
1963	Prudent Barney 9-10-12: 5/1	R. Renton	*J. Gifford*	7
1964	Bodger 9-10-0: 100/30	G. Owen	*R. Langley*	3
1965	Forest Prince 7-11-7: 11/10	N. Crump	*G. Scott*	7
1966	Falls of Cruachan 10-12-0: 6/4	N. Crump	*P. Buckley*	5
1967	Abandoned because of foot and mouth epidemic			
1968	Two Springs 6-10-8: 4/5	G. Owen	*R. Edwards*	3
1969	Fearless Fred 7-11-10: 5/2	F. Rimell	*T. Biddlecombe*	5
1970	Supermaster 7-11-4: 5/1	W. A. Stephenson	*J. Enright*	9
1971	Red Sweeney 7-10-8: 5/1	G. Richards	*E. Fenwick*	10
1972	L'Escargot 9-11-7: 10/11	D. L. Moore (Ir)	*T. Carberry*	4
1973	Abandoned because of frost			
1974	Pendil 9-11-12: 1/3	F. Winter	*R. Pitman*	3
1975	Bula 10-12-0: 10/11	F. Winter	*J. Francome*	4
1976	Bula 11-12-0: 8/13	F. Winter	*J. Francome*	3
1977	Abandoned because of frost			
1978	Bawnogues 7-10-7: 9/4	M. Tate	*C. Smith*	8
1979	Silver Buck 7-11-6: 20/21	A. Dickinson	*T. Carmody*	3
1980	Silver Buck 8-12-0: 8/15	M. Dickinson	*T. Carmody*	4
1981	Silver Buck 9-11-12: 5/2	M. Dickinson	*J. Francome*	5
1982	Silver Buck 10-12-0: 8/11	M. Dickinson	*R. Earnshaw*	5
1983	Abandoned because of frost			
1984	Wayward Lad 9-12-0: 8/15	Mrs M. Dickinson	*R. Earnshaw*	5
1985	Forgive'N Forget 8-12-0: 2/1	J. FitzGerald	*M. Dwyer*	3
1986	Forgive'N Forget 9-12-0; 10/11	J. FitzGerald	*M. Dwyer*	3
1987	Beau Ranger 9-10-12: 6/4	M. Pipe	*P. Scudamore*	3
1988	Beau Ranger 10-11-13: 13/8	M. Pipe	*P. Scudamore*	8
1989	Golden Friend 11-10-10: 9/2	J. McConnochie	*G. McCourt*	5
1990	Celtic Shot 8-11-9: 11/10	C. Brooks	*G. McCourt*	6
1991	Auntie Dot 10-10-7: 8/1	J. Webber	*M. Lynch*	5
1992	Run For Free 8-11-0: 11/8	M. Pipe	*P. Scudamore*	4

MITSUBISHI SHOGUN TINGLE CREEK TROPHY
(LIMITED HANDICAP CHASE) (Sandown 2m)

1969	Spanish Steps 6-11-13: 5/2	E. Courage	*J. Cook*	11
1970	Even Keel 8-12-3: 7/1	K. Oliver	*B. Brogan*	10
1971	Happy Medium 9-10-2: 33/1	R. Armytage	*Lord Oaksey*	8
1972	Pendil 7-12-3: 5/4	F. Winter	*R. Pitman*	8
1973	Tingle Creek 7-12-5: 5/2	H. T. Jones	*D. Mould*	6
1974	Dorlesa 6-10-4: 8/1	A. Dickinson	*M. Dickinson*	10
1975	Easby Abbey 8-10-10: 6/4	M. H. Easterby	*R. Barry*	6
1976	No Race			
1977	Tree Tangle 8-11-5: 2/1	R. Turnell	*A. Turnell*	4
1978	Abandoned because of frost			
1979	Artifice 8-11-11: 7/4	J. Thorne	*R. Hoare*	5
1980	Stopped 8-11-10: 7/4	F. Winter	*B. de Haan*	5
1981	News King 7-10-13: 11/8	F. Winter	*J. Francome*	6
	(at Kempton)			
1982	News King 8-11-11: 9/4	F. Winter	*J. Francome*	3
1983	Abandoned because of frost			
1984	Far Bridge 8-10-0: 11/2	G. Balding	*B. Reilly*	4
1985	Lefrak City 8-10-1: 2/1	T. Forster	*R. Dunwoody*	5
1986	Berlin 7-11-2: 11/8	N. Gaselee	*D. Browne*	7
1987	Long Engagement 6-10-2: 3/1	D. Nicholson	*R. Dunwoody*	5
1988	Desert Orchid 9-12-0: 5/2	D. Elsworth	*S. Sherwood*	5
1989	Long Engagement 8-10-0: 9/2	D. Nicholson	*B. Powell*	4

129

1990	Young Snugfit 6-10-7: 7/2	O. Sherwood	*J. Osborne*	5
1991	Waterloo Boy 8-11-13: 7/4	D. Nicholson	*R. Dunwoody*	6
1992	Waterloo Boy 9-12-0: 11/4	D. Nicholson	*R. Dunwoody*	5

WILLIAM HILL HANDICAP HURDLE (Sandown 2m 110yds)

1970	Bula 5-12-1: 3/1	F. Winter	*P. Kelleway*	18
1971	Churchwood 7-11-9: 13/2	M. Goswell	*D. Barrott*	13
1972	True Luck 5-10-13: 11/1	F. Rimell	*T. Biddlecombe*	15
1973	St Columbus 6-11-9: 13/2	W. Marshall	*A. Turnell*	16
1974	Supreme Halo 4-10-10: 6/1	R. Smyth	*J. King*	21
1975	Fighting Taffy 8-11-6: 25/1	P. Upton	*M. Gifford*	16
1976	No Race			
1977	Narribinni 5-9-9: 14/1	D. Kent	*A. Webb*	13
1978	Abandoned because of frost			
1979	Golden Vow 5-10-0: 7/1	R. Hartop	*A. Webber*	12
1980	Ekbalco 4-10-0: 4/1	R. Fisher	*D. Goulding*	17
1981	Celtic Ryde 6-11-13: 9/2	P. Cundell	*J. Francome*	15
	(at Kempton)			
1982	Allten Glazed 5-10-2: 5/1	M. Naughton	*Mr D. Browne*	16
1983	Abandoned because of frost			
1984	Prideaux Boy 6-10-3: 6/1	G. Roach	*R. Dunwoody*	14
1985	Chrysaor 7-10-8: 16/1	S. Christian	*R. Beggan*	12
1986	Aonoch 7-11-7: 16/1	Mrs S. Oliver	*Jacqui Oliver*	17
1987	Celtic Shot 5-10-6: 6/4	F. Winter	*P. Scudamore*	12
1988	Corporal Clinger 9-10-7: 9/2	M. Pipe	*M. Perrett*	13
1989	Liadett 4-10-0: 12/1	M. Pipe	*J. Lower*	6
1990	Wonder Man 5-10-12: 11/4	Mrs J. Pitman	*M. Pitman*	13
1991	Balasani 5-10-0: 7/1	M. Pipe	*M. Perrett*	20
1992	Valfinet 5-10-2: 5/4	M. Pipe	*J. Lower*	10

REHEARSAL CHASE (LIMITED HANDICAP) (Chepstow 3m)

1988	Ten Plus 8-10-12: 4/5	F. Walwyn	*K. Mooney*	5
1989	Bonanza Boy 8-11-10: 4/1	M. Pipe	*P. Scudamore*	6
1990	Boraceva 7-10-7: 9/2	G. Balding	*J. Frost*	6
1991	Carvill's Hill 9-11-12: 7/4	M. Pipe	*P. Scudamore*	6
1992	Run For Free 8-10-7: 3/1	M. Pipe	*M. Perrett*	4

TRIPLEPRINT GOLD CUP HANDICAP CHASE (Cheltenham 2m 5f)

1963	Limeking 6-10-12: 100/9	D. Morgan (Ir)	*T. Taaffe*	14
1964	Flying Wild 8-10-6: 100/8	D. L. Moore (Ir)	*T. Carberry*	7
1965	Flyingbolt 6-12-6: 5/2	T. Dreaper (Ir)	*P. Taaffe*	11
1966	The Laird 5-10-9: 13/2	R. Turnell	*J. King*	8
1967	Abandoned because of foot and mouth epidemic			
1968	Tassilo 10-10-1: 8/1	F. Walwyn	*A. Branford*	14
1969	Titus Oates 7-11-13: 9/4	G. Richards	*R. Barry*	11
1970	Simian 8-11-8: 4/1	Miss A. Sinclair	*D. Moore*	7
1971	Leap Frog 7-12-1: 3/1	T. Dreaper (Ir)	*V. O'Brien*	12
1972	Arctic Bow 7-10-12: 9/2	R. Turnell	*A. Turnell*	11
1973	Pendil 8-12-7: 8/11	F. Winter	*R. Pitman*	8
1974	Garnishee 10-10-6: 12/1	H. T. Jones	*D. Mould*	9
1975	Easby Abbey 8-11-10: 5/1	M. H. Easterby	*R. Barry*	9
1976	Abandoned because of frost			
1977	Even Melody 8-11-2: 8/1	N. Crump	*C. Hawkins*	11
1978	The Snipe 8-10-0: 20/1	J. Webber	*A. Webber*	14
1979	Father Delaney 7-10-10: 12/1	M. H. Easterby	*A. Brown*	12
1980	Bueche Giorod 9-10-0: 14/1	Mrs J. Pitman	*B. Smart*	15
1981	Abandoned because of snow			
1982	Observe 6-10-11: 11/2	F. Winter	*J. Francome*	15
1983	Fifty Dollars More 8-11-10	F. Winter	*R. Linley*	13
1984	Beau Ranger 6-9-10: 8/1	J. Thorne	*J. Hurst*	10
1985	Combs Ditch 9-11-9: 13/2	D. Elsworth	*C. Brown*	7
1986	Oregon Trail 6-10-7: 3/1	S. Christian	*R. Beggan*	6
1987	Bishops Yarn 8-10-7: 100/30	G. Balding	*R. Guest*	5
1988	Pegwell Bay 7-10-13: 7/2	T. Forster	*B. Powell*	10
1989	Clever Folly 9-10-4: 4/1	G. Richards	*N. Doughty*	6
1990	Abandoned because of snow			
1991	Kings Fountain 8-11-10: 7/4	K. Bailey	*A. Tory*	8
1992	Another Coral 9-11-4: 11/2	D. Nicholson	*R. Dunwoody*	10

ARLINGTON BULA HURDLE (Cheltenham 2m 1f)

1963	Scottish Memories 9-11-11: 6/4	A. Thomas	C. Finnegan	7
1964	Magic Court 6-12-1: 4/7	T. Robson	P. McCarron	6
1965	Salmon Spray 7-12-1: 3/1	R. Turnell	J. Haine	5
1966	Sempervivum 8-11-11: 8/11	F. Walwyn	G. W. Robinson	4
1967	Abandoned because of foot and mouth epidemic			
1968	Solway Sands 4-11-6: 33/1	J. McMurchie	B. Fletcher	7
1969	Celtic Gold 7-12-1: 9/2	W. A. Stephenson	T. S. Murphy	7
1970	Pendil 5-11-8: 7/2	F. Winter	P. Kelleway	6
1971	Canasta Lad 5-11-8: 5/1	P. Bailey	J. King	8
1972	Bula 7-11-12: 8/13	F. Winter	P. Kelleway	8
1973	Comedy of Errors 6-11-12: 2/5	F. Rimell	W. Smith	5
1974	Comedy of Errors 7-11-10: 6/4	F. Rimell	K. White	4
1975	Sea Pigeon 5-11-2: 5/1	G. Richards	J. J. O'Neill	7
1976	Abandoned because of frost			
1977	Bird's Nest 7-11-6: 11/4	R. Turnell	A. Turnell	10
1978	Bird's Nest 8-11-6: 1/1	R. Turnell	A. Turnell	5
1979	Celtic Ryde 4-11-3: 11/4	P. Cundell	M. O'Halloran	5
1980	Bird's Nest 10-11-6: 5/2	R. Turnell	A. Turnell	7
1981	Abandoned because of snow			
1982	Ekbalco 6-11-10: 2/1	R. Fisher	J. J. O'Neill	5
1983	Amarach 5-11-6: 7/2	R. Fisher	J. Duggan	9
1984	Browne's Gazette 6-11-4: 7/2	Mrs M. Dickinson	Mr R. Beggan	5
1985	Corporal Clinger 6-11-2: 20/1	M. Pipe	P. Leach	9
1986	Floyd 6-11-2: 7/2	D. Elsworth	C. Brown	8
1987	Pat's Jester 4-11-2: 11/2	R. Allan	P. Niven	8
1988	Condor Pan 5-11-2: 12/1	J. Bolger (Ir)	C. Swan	8
1989	Cruising Altitude 6-11-4: 8/11	O. Sherwood	J. Osborne	8
1990	Abandoned because of snow			
1991	Royal Derbi 6-11-8: 9/2	N. Callaghan	D. Murphy	5
1992	Halkopous 6-11-2: 8/1	M. Tompkins	A. Maguire	6

LOWNDES LAMBERT DECEMBER NOVICES' CHASE
(Lingfield 3m)

1990	Sparkling Flame 6-11-0: 6/1	N. Henderson	J. White	6
1991	River Bounty 5-10-13: 9/2	J. Upson	R. Supple	3
1992	Midnight Caller 6-11-0: 9/2	S. Sherwood	M. Richards	10

TOMMY WHITTLE CHASE (Haydock 3m)

1982	Little Owl 8-11-2: 9/4	M. H. Easterby	Mr A. J. Wilson	2
1983	Prince Rowan 7-10-12: 12/1	M. Dickinson	Mr D. Browne	7
1984	Gaye Chance 9-10-12: 7/4	Mrs M. Rimell	S. Morshead	6
1985	Earls Brig 10-10-12: 3/1	W. Hamilton	P. Tuck	4
1986	Forgive'N Forget 9-11-2: 1/3	J. FitzGerald	M. Dwyer	3
1987	Abandoned because of frost			
1988	The Thinker 10-11-2: 4/6	W. A. Stephenson	A. Merrigan	3
1989	Baies 7-10-12: 20/1	C. Brooks	P. Scudamore	9
1990	Celtic Shot 8-11-2: 1/2	C. Brooks	G. McCourt	6
1991	Abandoned because of frost			
1992	Twin Oaks 12-11-2: 5/4	G. Richards	R. Dunwoody	5

WATERLOO HURDLE (Haydock 2½m)

1990	Run For Free 6-11-2: 11/1	M. Pipe	J. Lower	9
1991	Abandoned because of frost			
1992	Mighty Mogul 5-11-2: 3/10	D. Nicholson	R. Dunwoody	4

ROVACABIN NOEL NOVICES CHASE (Ascot 2m 3f 110yds)

1973	Paddy's Road House 5-10-13: 7/2	F. Winter	R. Pitman	9
1974	Broncho II 5-11-9: 7/2	A. Dickinson	M. Dickinson	9
1975	Ghost Writer 8-11-11: 3/1	F. Walwyn	W. Smith	7
1976	Abandoned because of frost			
1977	Artifice 6-11-11: 5/2	J. Thorne	P. Hobbs	4
1978	Night Nurse 7-11-11: 4/5	M. H. Easterby	I. Watkinson	9
1979	Venture To Cognac 6-11-1: 4/6	F. Winter	Mr O. Sherwood	7
1980	Acrow Lad 6-10-12: 20/1	D. Elsworth	S. Jobar	9
1981	Abandoned because of snow			
1982	Half Free 6-11-1: 7/2	F. Winter	R. Linley	10
1983	Aces Wild 5-10-13: 7/2	F. Winter	J. Francome	7

1984	Buckbe 5-10-8: 4/1	D. Elsworth	*C. Brown*	6
1985	Desert Orchid 6-11-11: 5/4	D. Elsworth	*C. Brown*	6
1986	Cavvies Clown 6-10-12: 11/2	D. Elsworth	*R. Arnott*	5
1987	Bonanza Boy 6-11-8: 6/4	P. Hobbs	*P. Hobbs*	7
1988	Larchwood 7-10-10: 7/2	S. Christian	*K. Mooney*	8
1989	The Proclamation 6-10-2: 5/2	N. Henderson	*R. Dunwoody*	7
1990	Remittance Man 6-11-7: 2/1	N. Henderson	*R. Dunwoody*	5
1991	Abandoned because of frost			
1992	Retail Runner 7-11-3: 9/2	J. Gifford	*D. Murphy*	7

S.G.B. HANDICAP CHASE (Ascot 3m 110yds)

1965	Vultrix 7-12-1: 6/4	F. Cundell	*S. Mellor*	7
1966	Arkle 9-12-7: 1/3	T. Dreaper (Ir)	*P. Taaffe*	5
1967	Abandoned because of foot and mouth epidemic			
1968	Abandoned because of waterlogged state of course			
1969	Straight Fort 6-12-0: 7/2	T. Dreaper (Ir)	*P. Taaffe*	7
1970	Glencaraig Lady 6-11-13: 4/1	F. Flood (Ir)	*R. Coonan*	10
1971	Spanish Steps 8-12-1: 4/1	E. Courage	*W. Smith*	12
1972	Soloning 7-10-12: 6/1	F. Winter	*R. Pitman*	16
1973	Mocharabuice 10-10-6: 7/1	T. Forster	*G. Thorner*	9
1974	Rough House 8-10-7: 11/1	F. Rimell	*J. Burke*	14
1975	What A Buck 8-10-4: 9/2	D. Nicholson	*J. King*	9
1976	Abandoned because of frost			
1977	Midnight Court 6-12-0: 6/5	F. Winter	*J. Francome*	8
1978	Grand Canyon 8-11-1: 15/8	D. Kent	*R. Barry*	10
1979	Raffi Nelson 6-10-1: 5/2	N. Henderson	*S. Smith Eccles*	6
1980	Henry Bishop 7-11-0: 7/1	J. Gifford	*R. Champion*	4
1981	Abandoned because of snow			
1982	Captain John 8-11-13: 11/8	M. Dickinson	*R. Earnshaw*	8
1983	The Mighty Mac 8-11-10: 13/8	M. Dickinson	*Mr D. Browne*	7
1984	Canny Danny 8-11-8: 6/4	J. FitzGerald	*M. Dwyer*	7
1985	Door Latch 7-10-2: 11/4	J. Gifford	*R. Rowe*	8
1986	Door Latch 8-11-1: 6/1	J. Gifford	*R. Rowe*	12
1987	Cavvies Clown 7-10-11: 10/1	D. Elsworth	*R. Arnott*	12
1988	Ballyhane 7-10-4: 13/8	J. Gifford	*P. Hobbs*	5
1989	Solidasarock 7-10-0: 33/1	R. Akehurst	*L. Harvey*	12
1990	Man O' Magic 9-11-10: 5/1	K. Bailey	*M. Perrett*	6
1991	Abandoned because of frost			
1992	Captain Dibble 7-10-1: 7/1	N. Twiston-Davies	*C. Llewellyn*	8

H.S.S. HIRE SHOPS HURDLE (Ascot 2m 110yds)

1965	Compton Martin 6-11-4: 5/2	G. Todd	*S. Mellor*	5
1966	Abandoned because of waterlogged state of course			
1967	Abandoned because of foot and mouth epidemic			
1968	Abandoned because of waterlogged state of course			
1969	Moyne Royal 4-10-5: 10/1	R. Akehurst	*B. Leyman*	12
1970	Bowie's Brig 4-10-8: 5/2	A. Pitt	*B. Brogan*	7
1971	Flower Picker 5-11-6: 100/30	F. Walwyn	*A. Branford*	7
1972	Ruisselet 5-11-6: 4/1	R. Price	*P. Kelleway*	22
1973	Lanzarote 5-11-13: 4/11	F. Winter	*R. Pitman*	7
1974	Tree Tangle 5-11-13: 11/10	R. Turnell	*A. Turnell*	9
1975	Grand Canyon 5-11-9: 8/1	D. Kent	*P. Haynes*	10
1976	Abandoned because of frost			
1977	Kybo 4-11-8: 13/2	J. Gifford	*G. Enright*	12
1978	Kybo 5-11-13: 11/4	J. Gifford	*R. Champion*	10
1979	Walnut Wonder 4-10-8: 33/1	L. Kennard	*L. Vincent*	8
1980	Heighlin 4-11-8: 6/4	D. Elsworth	*S. Jobar*	11
1981	Abandoned because of snow			
1982	Carved Opal 4-10-11: 7/1	F. Winter	*C. Brown*	6
1983	Admiral's Cup 5-11-6: 9/4	F. Winter	*J. Francome*	11
1984	See You Then 4-11-8: 11/10	N. Henderson	*J. Francome*	5
1985	First Bout 4-11-8: 5/1	N. Henderson	*S. Smith Eccles*	7
1986	Nohalmdun 5-11-4: 13/8	M. H. Easterby	*P. Scudamore*	5
1987	Osric 4-10-8: 11/4	M. Ryan	*G. McCourt*	7
1988	Celtic Chief 5-11-8: 2/5	Mrs M. Rimell	*R. Dunwoody*	7
1989	Forest Sun 4-10-8: 7/2	G. Balding	*J. Frost*	7
1990	Wonder Man 5-11-8: 7/2	Mrs J. Pitman	*M. Pitman*	6
1991	Abandoned because of frost			

| 1992 | Baydon Star 5-11-8: 8/15 | D. Nicholson | *R. Dunwoody* | 5 |

YOUNGMANS LONG WALK HURDLE (Ascot 3m 1f 110yds)

1965	Minute Gun 8-10-11: 100/8	W. Shand-Kydd	*R. Pitman*	26
1966	Sir Edward 6-10-9: 7/2	R. Price	*J. Gifford*	18
1967	Abandoned because of foot and mouth epidemic			
1968	Abandoned because of waterlogged state of course			
1969	Candid Camera 6-10-6: 100/8	E. Goddard	*J. Guest*	22
1970	Rouge Autumn 6-10-5: 9/2	F. Rimell	*K. White*	20
1971	St Patrick's Blue 6-11-12: 7/2	D. Tatlow	*W. Smith*	12
1972	Highland Abbe 6-11-12: 11/1	L. Kennard	*Mr R. Smith*	8
1973	Soloning 8-11-8: 9/2	F. Winter	*R. Pitman*	10
1974	Go Bingo 5-11-12: 9/4	S. Hall	*D. Munro*	6
1975	Lanzarote 7-12-5: 4/9	F. Winter	*J. Francome*	7
1976	Abandoned because of frost			
1977	John Cherry 6-10-11: 11/8	H. T. Jones	*S. Smith Eccles*	10
1978	Kelso Chant 6-11-7: 10/1	B. Wilkinson	*S. Charlton*	14
1979	John Cherry 8-10-11: 6/1	H. T. Jones	*S. Smith Eccles*	12
1980	Derring Rose 5-11-11: 7/1	F. Winter	*J. Francome*	9
1981	Abandoned because of snow			
1982	Mayotte 7-10-11: 15/8	R. Holder	*P. Richards*	11
1983	Crimson Embers 8-10-11: 14/1	F. Walwyn	*S. Shilston*	11
1984	Kristenson 7-10-8: 7/2	R. Fisher	*M. Williams*	11
1985	Misty Dale 7-10-8: 9/4	Mrs J. Pitman	*P. Tuck*	8
1986	Out of The Gloom 5-10-8: 4/1	R. Hollinshead	*P. Scudamore*	5
1987	Bluff Cove 5-10-8: 14/1	R. Hollinshead	*R. Dunwoody*	10
1988	French Goblin 5-11-1: 3/1	J. Gifford	*P. Hobbs*	10
1989	Royal Athlete 6-10-8: 33/1	Mrs J. Pitman	*D. Gallagher*	11
1990	Floyd 10-11-7: 10/1	D. Elsworth	*G. Bradley*	8
1991	Abandoned because of frost			
1992	Vagog 7-11-7: 15/2	M. Pipe	*M. Foster*	9

CORAL WELSH NATIONAL HANDICAP CHASE
(Chepstow 3m 5f 110yds)

1948	Bora's Cottage 10-10-2: 100/8	R. Price	*E. Reavey*	16
1949	Fighting Line 10-10-9: 7/1	K. Cundell	*R. Francis*	15
1950	Gallery 12-10-8: 7/2	W. Bissill	*A. Mullins*	12
1951	Skyreholme 8-10-13: 7/2	N. Crump	*A. Thompson*	16
1952	Dinton Lass 10-10-0: 10/1	J. Roberts	*A. Mullins*	16
1953	Stalbridge Rock 10-11-3: 6/1	H. Dufosee	*R. McCreery*	15
1954	Blow Horn 10-10-6: 100/8	T. Jarvis	*J. Hunter*	17
1955	Monaleen 10-9-7: 20/1	H. T. Smith	*P. Fitzgerald*	17
1956	Crudwell 10-11-6: 100/9	F. Cundell	*R. Francis*	16
1957	Creeola II 9-10-5: 3/1	F. Rimell	*M. Scudamore*	11
1958	Oscar Wilde 8-9-13: 20/1	W. Wightman	*B. Lawrence*	14
1959	Limonali 8-10-2: 100/8	E. C. Morel	*D. Nicholson*	10
1960	Clover Bud 10-10-10: 7/1	G. Llewellin	*D. Nicholson*	14
1961	Limonali 10-11-12: 7/4	I. Lewis	*D. Nicholson*	9
1962	Forty Secrets 8-10-11: 6/1	E. Jones	*J. Gifford*	15
1963	Motel 9-10-6: 7/1	W. Lowe	*P. Cowley*	10
1964	Rainbow Battle 8-10-0: 3/1	W. A. Stephenson	*P. Broderick*	11
1965	Norther 8-11-0: 9/2	D. Jenkins	*T. Biddlecombe*	11
1966	Kilburn 8-11-2: 11/4	C. Nesfield	*T. Norman*	11
1967	Happy Spring 11-10-4: 6/1	J. S. Wright	*K. White*	6
1968	Glenn 7-10-4: 11/2	F. Rimell	*E. P. Harty*	8
1969	Abandoned because of snow			
1970	French Excuse 8-10-9: 3/1	F. Rimell	*T. Biddlecombe*	11
1971	Royal Toss 9-10-12: 15/8	H. Handel	*P. Cowley*	13
1972	Charlie H 10-11-3: 11/2	R. Turnell	*J. Haine*	9
1973	Deblin's Green 10-9-12: 20/1	G. Yardley	*N. Wakley*	16
1974	Pattered 8-10-2: 25/1	E. Jones	*K. White*	24
1975	Abandoned because of waterlogged state of course			
1976	Rag Trade 10-11-2: 17/2	F. Rimell	*J. Burke*	17
1977	Abandoned because of waterlogged state of course			
1978	Abandoned because of frost			
1979	Abandoned because of snow			
1979	(Dec 22) Peter Scot 8-10-2: 8/1	D. Gandolfo	*P. Barton*	15
1980	Narvik 7-10-11: 15/1	N. Crump	*J. Francome*	18

1981	Peaty Sandy 7-10-3: 3/1	Miss H. Hamilton	*Mr G. Dun*	23
1982	Corbiere 7-10-10: 12/1	Mrs J. Pitman	*B. de Haan*	10
1983	Burrough Hill Lad 7-10-9: 100/30	Mrs J. Pitman	*J. Francome*	18
1984	Righthand Man 7-11-5: 6/1	Mrs M. Dickinson	*G. Bradley*	18
1985	Run And Skip 7-10-8: 13/1	J. Spearing	*P. Scudamore*	18
1986	Stearsby 7-11-5: 8/1	Mrs J. Pitman	*G. Bradley*	17
1987	Playschool 9-10-11: 5/1	D. Barons	*P. Nicholls*	13
1988	Bonanza Boy 7-10-1: 9/4	M. Pipe	*P. Scudamore*	12
1989	Bonanza Boy 8-11-11: 15/8	M. Pipe	*P. Scudamore*	12
1990	Cool Ground 8-10-0: 9/2	R. Akehurst	*L. Harvey*	14
1991	Carvill's Hill 9-11-12: 9/4	M. Pipe	*P. Scudamore*	17
1992	Run For Free 8-10-9: 11/4	M. Pipe	*M. Perrett*	11

FINALE JUNIOR HURDLE (3-y-o) (Chepstow 2m 110yds)

1971	Ballytruckle 11-0: 15/2	D. Gandolfo	*G. Thorner*	8
1972	Lightning Trial 11-0: 7/1	F. Rimell	*W. Smith*	16
1973	Fighting Kate 10-7: 12/1	H. Nicholson	*R. Dickin*	19
1974	Philominsky 11-0: 6/1	W. Marshall	*M. Wagner*	21
1975	Tiepolino 11-3: 4/1	J. Gifford	*R. Champion*	23
1976	Decent Fellow 11-0: 20/1	G. Balding	*R. Linley*	18
1977	Rodman 11-3: 2/11	F. Winter	*J. Francome*	12
1978	Abandoned because of snow			
1979	Good Ruler 11-0: 10/1	G. Beeson	*R. Goldstein*	14
1980	Broadsword 11-3: 15/8	D Nicholson	*P. Scudamore*	16
1981	Brave Hussar 11-0: 6/5	R. Turnell	*A. Turnell*	15
1982	Primrolla 11-0: 3/1	D. Nicholson	*H. Davies*	14
1983	Dodgy Future 11-0: 2/1	S. Mellor	*M. Perrett*	14
1984	Out of The Gloom 11-0: 7/1	R. Hollinshead	*J. J. O'Neill*	13
1985	The Footman 11-0: 11/1	D. Elsworth	*G. Bradley*	12
1986	High Knowl 11-0: 4/5	M. Pipe	*P. Scudamore*	9
1987	South Parade 11-3: 15/8	G. Balding	*G. Bradley*	7
1988	Enemy Action 11-3: 8/15	M. Pipe	*P. Scudamore*	9
1989	Crystal Heights 11-0: 33/1	J. G. Retter	*B. Powell*	10
1990	Hopscotch 10-9: 9/4	M. Pipe	*J. Lower*	13
1991	Good Profile 11-0: 7/1	G. Moore	*L. Wyer*	18
1992	Dare To Dream 11-0: 9/2	R. Akehurst	*D. Bridgwater*	11

TRIPLEPRINT FELTHAM NOVICES' CHASE (Kempton 3m)

1975	Nagari 6-11-4: 4/1	P. Cundell	*J. Francome*	16
1976	Never Rock 7-11-4: 5/1	F. Walwyn	*W. Smith*	12
1977	The Dealer 7-11-9: 11/8	F. Winter	*J. Francome*	7
1978	Jack Madness 6-11-0: 11/4	J. Gifford	*Mr G. Sloan*	9
1979	Sugarally 6-11-4: 5/1	G. Fairbairn	*D. Goulding*	9
1980	Two Swallows 7-11-8: 7/2	R. Armytage	*B. R. Davies*	11
1981	Abandoned because of frost			
1982	Gallaher 6-11-4: 10/11	F. Walwyn	*W. Smith*	5
1983	Duke of Milan 6-11-4: 9/4	N. Gaselee	*P. Scudamore*	6
1984	Catch Phrase 6-11-0: 9/2	J. Gifford	*R. Rowe*	3
1985	Von Trappe 8-11-4: 13/8	M. Oliver	*R. Dunwoody*	7
1986	Aherlow 6-11-0: 13/8	S. Christian	*R. Beggan*	6
1987	Twin Oaks 7-11-4: 9/4	D. Murray-Smith	*P. Croucher*	6
1988	Sir Blake 7-11-4: 8/11	D. Elsworth	*B. Powell*	4
1989	French Goblin 6-10-11: 15/8	J. Gifford	*P. Hobbs*	7
1990	Sparkling Flame 6-11-7: 7/2	N. Henderson	*R. Dunwoody*	7
1991	Mutare 6-11-7: 11/8	N. Henderson	*R. Dunwoody*	9
1992	Dakyns Boy 7-11-7: 9/2	N. Twiston-Davies	*P. Scudamore*	5

KING GEORGE VI CHASE (Kempton 3m)

1947	Rowland Roy 8-11-13: 5/1	F. Walwyn	*B. Marshall*	10
1948	Cottage Rake 9-12-6: 13/8	M. V. O'Brien (Ir)	*A. Brabazon*	9
1949	Finnure 8-11-10: 9/2	G. Beeby	*R. Francis*	4
1950	Manicou 5-11-8: 5/1	P. Cazalet	*B. Marshall*	7
1951	Statecraft 6-11-11: 100/6	P. Cazalet	*A. Grantham*	6
1952	Halloween 7-11-13: 7/4	W. Wightman	*F. Winter*	6
1953	Galloway Braes 8-12-6: 9/4	A. Kilpatrick	*R. Morrow*	7
1954	Halloween 9-11-10: 9/2	W. Wightman	*F. Winter*	8
1955	Limber Hill 8-11-13: 3/1	W. Dutton	*J. Power*	8

1956	Rose Park 10-11-7: 100/6	P. Cazalet	M. Scudamore	6
1957	Mandarin 6-12-0: 7/1	F. Walwyn	P. Madden	9
1958	Lochroe 10-11-7: 7/2	P. Cazalet	A. Freeman	7
1959	Mandarin 8-11-5: 5/2	F. Walwyn	P. Madden	9
1960	Saffron Tartan 9-11-7: 5/2	D. Butchers	F. Winter	10
1961	Abandoned because of frost			
1962	Abandoned because of frost			
1963	Mill House 6-12-0: 2/7	F. Walwyn	G. W. Robinson	3
1964	Frenchman's Cove 9-11-7: 4/11	H. T. Jones	S. Mellor	2
1965	Arkle 8-12-0: 1/7	T. Dreaper (Ir)	P. Taaffe	4
1966	Dormant 9-11-0: 10/1	J. Wells-Kendrew	J. King	7
1967	Abandoned because of foot and mouth epidemic			
1968	Abandoned because of waterlogged state of course			
1969	Titus Oates 7-11-10: 100/30	G. Richards	S. Mellor	5
1970	Abandoned because of snow			
1971	The Dikler 8-11-7: 11/2	F. Walwyn	B. Brogan	10
1972	Pendil 7-12-0: 4/5	F. Winter	R. Pitman	6
1973	Pendil 8-12-0: 30/100	F. Winter	R. Pitman	4
1974	Captain Christy 7-12-0: 5/1	P. Taaffe (Ir)	R. Coonan	6
1975	Captain Christy 8-12-0: 11/10	P. Taaffe (Ir)	G. Newman	7
1976	Royal Marshal II 9-11-7: 16/1	T. Forster	G. Thorner	10
1977	Bachelor's Hall 7-11-7: 9/2	P. Cundell	M. O'Halloran	9
1978	Gay Spartan 7-11-10: 3/1	A Dickinson	T. Carmody	16
1979	Silver Buck 7-11-10: 3/1	A. Dickinson	T. Carmody	11
1980	Silver Buck 8-11-10: 9/4	M. Dickinson	T. Carmody	8
1981	Abandoned because of frost			
1982	Wayward Lad 7-11-10: 7/2	M. Dickinson	J. Francome	6
1983	Wayward Lad 8-11-10: 11/8	M. Dickinson	R. Earnshaw	5
1984	Burrough Hill Lad 8-11-10: 1/2	Mrs J. Pitman	J. Francome	3
1985	Wayward Lad 10-11-10: 12/1	Mrs M. Dickinson	G. Bradley	5
1986	Desert Orchid 7-11-10: 16/1	D. Elsworth	S. Sherwood	9
1987	Nupsala 8-11-10: 25/1	F. Doumen (Fr)	A. Pommier	9
1988	Desert Orchid 9-11-10: 1/2	D. Elsworth	S. Sherwood	5
1989	Desert Orchid 10-11-10: 4/6	D. Elsworth	R. Dunwoody	6
1990	Desert Orchid 11-11-10: 9/4	D. Elsworth	R. Dunwoody	9
1991	The Fellow 6-11-10: 10/1	F. Doumen (Fr)	A. Kondrat	8
1992	The Fellow 7-11-10: 1/1	F. Doumen (Fr)	A. Kondrat	8

BONUSPRINT CHRISTMAS HURDLE (Kempton 2m)

1969	Coral Diver 4-12-0: 9/4	F. Rimell	T. Biddlecombe	6
1970	Abandoned because of snow			
1971	Coral Diver 6-12-5: 7/4	F. Rimell	T. Biddlecombe	4
1972	Canasta Lad 6-12-1: 4/7	P. Bailey	J. King	6
1973	Lanzarote 5-12-1: 1/6	F. Winter	R. Pitman	4
1974	Tree Tangle 5-12-1: 30/100	R. Turnell	A. Turnell	5
1975	Lanzarote 7-11-13: 1/1	F. Winter	J. Francome	5
1976	Dramatist 5-11-10: 9/1	F. Walwyn	W. Smith	6
1977	Beacon Light 6-11-10: 5/2	R. Turnell	A. Turnell	3
1978	Kybo 5-11-7: 5/4	J. Gifford	R. Champion	6
1979	Bird's Nest 9-11-10: 6/4	R. Turnell	A. Turnell	5
1980	Celtic Ryde 5-11-6: 2/1	P. Cundell	J. Francome	7
1981	Abandoned because of frost			
1982	Ekbalco 6-11-13: 1/2	R. Fisher	J. J. O'Neill	4
1983	Dawn Run 5-10-12: 9/4	P. Mullins (Ir)	J. J. O'Neill	4
1984	Browne's Gazette 6-11-3: 11/8	Mrs M. Dickinson	D. Browne	7
1985	Aonoch 6-11-3: 14/1	Mrs S. Oliver	J. Duggan	9
1986	Nohalmdun 5-11-3: 15/8	M. H. Easterby	P. Scudamore	7
1987	Osric 4-11-3: 12/1	M. Ryan	G. McCourt	8
1988	Kribensis 4-11-3: 4/9	M. Stoute	R. Dunwoody	7
1989	Kribensis 5-11-3: 4/6	M. Stoute	R. Dunwoody	8
1990	Fidway 5-11-7: 100/30	T. Thomson Jones	S. Smith Eccles	8
1991	Gran Alba 5-11-7: 3/1	R. Hannon	G. McCourt	7
1992	Mighty Mogul 5-11-7: 3/1	D. Nicholson	R. Dunwoody	8

ROWLAND MEYRICK HANDICAP CHASE (Wetherby 3m 110yds)

1957	Symaethis Nephew 7-10-0: 100/8	R. Renton	B. Wilkinson	6
1958	Dondrosa 6-10-9: 10/1	F. Taylor	T. Kellett	6

1959	Pendle Lady 9-10-6: 10/1	A. Watson	*M. Towers*	10
1960	Merryman II 9-12-6: 3/1	N. Crump	*G. Scott*	5
1961, 1962, 1963, 1964 and 1965 Abandoned because of frost				
1966	Tudor Fort 6-10-4: 7/1	N. Crump	*P. Buckley*	9
1967	Abandoned because of foot and mouth epidemic			
1968	Chancer 6-9-13: 10/1	W. Hall	*P. Vaughan*	6
1969	Chesapeake Bay 6-10-13: 4/1	N. Crump	*P. Buckley*	6
1970	Excess 8-10-9: 6/5	H. T. Jones	*S. Mellor*	6
1971	Great Noise 7-9-7: 7/2	W. Hall	*D. Taylor*	7
1972	Jomon 6-11-6: 9/2	H. T. Jones	*T. Stack*	8
1973	Tartan Ace 6-10-5: 6/4	W. A. Stephenson	*T. Stack*	7
1974	Glen Owen 7-10-2: 10/1	N. Crump	*P. Buckley*	6
1975	The Gent 7-10-9: 6/1	W. A. Stephenson	*T. Stack*	6
1976	Irish Tony 8-10-9: 9/2	N. Crump	*D. Atkins*	8
1977	Set Point 9-11-5: 5/2	Lady Herries	*D. Munro*	5
1978	Rambling Artist 8-10-11: 6/1	A. Gillam	*D. Goulding*	7
1979	Ballet Lord 8-11-10: 7/1	N. Crump	*C. Hawkins*	7
1980	Sunset Cristo 6-10-11: 9/4	R. Hawkey	*C. Grant*	6
1981	Abandoned because of snow and frost			
1982	Richdee 6-10-6: 5/1	N. Crump	*C. Hawkins*	8
1983	Phil The Fluter 8-10-0: 12/1	H. Wharton	*S. Keightley*	7
1984	Forgive' N Forget 7-11-7: 4/6	J. FitzGerald	*M. Dwyer*	4
1985	Fortina's Express 11-10-6: 14/1	W. A. Stephenson	*C. Hawkins*	5
1986	The Thinker 8-11-6: 12/1	W. A. Stephenson	*R. Dunwoody*	8
1987	Yahoo 6-10-4: 11/8	J. Edwards	*T. Morgan*	5
1988	Whats What 9-10-1: 3/1	B. Bousfield	*P. Niven*	5
1989	Durham Edition 11-10-6: 5/1	W. A. Stephenson	*A. Merrigan*	7
1990	Bluff Knoll 7-10-0: 2/1	R. Brewis	*G. Harker*	7
1991	Stay On Tracks 9-10-0: 6/1	W. A. Stephenson	*C. Grant*	5
1992	Abandoned because of frost			

CASTLEFORD CHASE (Wetherby 2m)
1975	Tingle Creek 9-12-0: 4/9	H. T. Jones	*I. Watkinson*	3
1976	Skryne 6-11-7: 2/1	P. Bailey	*R. Barry*	6
1977	Crofton Hall 8-11-0: 6/5	J. Dixon	*J. J. O'Neill*	6
1978	Lord Greystoke 7-10-11: 9/2	G. Richards	*R. Barry*	4
1979	Rathgorman 7-11-2: 6/4	A. Dickinson	*K. Whyte*	7
1980	Rathgorman 8-11-10: 13/8	M. Dickinson	*K. Whyte*	5
1981	Abandoned because of snow and frost			
1982	Little Bay 7-10-8: 9/2	G. Richards	*R. Barry*	6
1983	Badsworth Boy 8-12-0: 10/11	M. Dickinson	*G. Bradley*	5
1984	Ryeman 7-11-10: 5/2	Mrs M. Dickinson	*G. Bradley*	5
1985	Our Fun 8-10-11: 9/4	J. Gifford	*R. Rowe*	4
1986	Little Bay 11-11-7: 9/1	G. Richards	*P. Tuck*	8
1987	Pearlyman 8-12-7: 1/1	J. Edwards	*T. Morgan*	5
1988	Midnight Count 8-12-2: 15/8	J. Gifford	*P. Hobbs*	4
1989	Ida's Delight 10-10-7: 17/2	J. Charlton	*B. Storey*	5
1990	Waterloo Boy 7-11-10: 6/4	D. Nicholson	*R. Dunwoody*	5
1991	Waterloo Boy 8-11-10: 4/11	D. Nicholson	*R. Dunwoody*	4
1992	Katabatic 9-11-10: 1/1	A. Turnell	*S. McNeill*	3

BOOKMAKERS HURDLE (Leopardstown 2m)
1986	Derrymore Boy 4-11-3: 8/1	P. Mullins	*A. Mullins*	10
1987	Cloughtaney 6-12-0: 3/1	P. Mullins	*A. Mullins*	7
1988	Grabel 5-11-9: 7/1	P. Mullins	*Mr W. Mullins*	5
1989	Grabel 6-11-9: 8/11	P. Mullins	*A. Mullins*	5
1990	Grabel 7-11-9: 2/7	P. Mullins	*A. Mullins*	4
1991	Galevilla Express 4-10-11: 7/1	V. Bowens	*C. Bowens*	6
1992	Novello Allegro 4-11-2: 6/1	N. Meade	*C. Swan*	7

MANDARIN HANDICAP CHASE (Newbury 3m 2f 110yds)
1963	Mill House 6-12-5: 5/6	F. Walwyn	*G. W. Robinson*	6
1964	Out And About 9-10-5: 7/1	K. Cundell	*B. Gregory*	6
1965	Mill House 8-12-7: 6/4	F. Walwyn	*G. W. Robinson*	7
1966	Abandoned because of snow and frost			
1967	What A Myth 10-11-9: 5/2	R. Price	*P. Kelleway*	11
1968	Abandoned because of snow and frost			
1969	The Otter 8-10-11: 100/8	R. Denning	*B. Scott*	12

136

1970	Lord Jim 9-10-0: 4/1	F. Walwyn	*G. W. Robinson*	12
1971	The Pantheon 8-11-6: 6/1	F. Rimell	*T. Biddlecombe*	6
1972	Royal Toss 10-11-1: 3/1	H. Handel	*N. Wakley*	9
1973	Abandoned because of fog			
1974	Midnight Fury 7-10-3: 4/1	F. Winter	*V. Soane*	7
1975	Moonlight Escapade 8-10-5: 9/2	C. V. Miller	*D. Cartwright*	6
1976	Roman Holiday 12-10-6: 11/1	C. Bewicke	*V. Soane*	7
1977	Abandoned because of frost			
1977	(Dec 31) Master Spy 8-11-7: 2/1	T. Forster	*G. Thorner*	6
1978	Tommy Joe 8-11-4: 2/1	A. Dickinson	*T. Carmody*	8
1979	Zongalero 9-10-6: 5/2	N. Henderson	*B. R. Davies*	6
1981	Master Smudge 9-11-7: 9/1	A. Barrow	*R. Linley*	7
1982	Night Nurse 11-11-12: 11/2	M. H. Easterby	*J. J. O'Neill*	8
1983	Earthstopper 9-11-1: 9/2	J. Gifford	*Mr G. Sloan*	7
1983	(Dec 31) Observe 7-11-7: 8/13	F. Winter	*J. Francome*	6
1984	Maori Venture 8-11-5: 4/1	A. Turnell	*S. C. Knight*	5
1985	Abandoned because of frost			
1987	Maori Venture 11-11-3: 4/1	A. Turnell	*S. C. Knight*	6
1988	Contradeal 11-11-10: 9/4	F. Walwyn	*K. Mooney*	6
1988	(Dec 31) Ten Plus 8-11-10: 11/10	F. Walwyn	*K. Mooney*	4
1989	Polyfemus 7-10-5: 3/1	M. Robinson	*J. White*	7
1990	Party Politics 6-11-2: 4/5	N. Gaselee	*A. Adams*	4
1991	Chatam 7-11-10: 1/2	M. Pipe	*P. Scudamore*	3
1993	Jodami 8-12-0: 9/4	P. Beaumont	*M. Dwyer*	13

CHALLOW HURDLE (Newbury 2m 5f)

1982	Right Regent 4-10-7: 15/2	D. Elsworth	*C. Brown*	10
1983	Ambiance 4-10-12: 7/4	P. Bailey	*P. Scudamore*	3
1983	(Dec 31) Catch Phrase 5-11-5: 11/4	J. Gifford	*P. Double*	8
1984	The Breener 5-11-5: 15/8	O. Sherwood	*Mr S. Sherwood*	9
1985	Abandoned because of frost			
1987	Bonanza Boy 6-11-12: 4/1	P. Hobbs	*P. Hobbs*	8
1988	Slalom 7-11-12: 8/11	M. Robinson	*J. White*	4
1988	(Dec 30) Green Willow 6-11-13: 13/8	J. Gifford	*P. Hobbs*	4
1989	Forest Sun 4-11-13: 6/4	G. Balding	*J. Frost*	8
1990	Tyrone Bridge 4-11-8: 2/5	M. Pipe	*R. Dunwoody*	4
1991	Lift And Load 4-11-8: 5/4	R. Hannon	*G. McCourt*	6
1993	Lord Relic 7-11-7: 15/8	M. Pipe	*P. Scudamore*	7

LADBROKE RACING WELFARE HANDICAP HURDLE
(Newbury 2m 110yds)

1971	Broken Melody 7-10-3: 8/1	D. Gandolfo	*J. Haine*	16
1972	Dan'l Widden 6-10-2: 20/1	S. Morant	*A. Branford*	19
1973	Abandoned because of fog			
1974	Sycamore 4-10-9: 11/2	J. Gifford	*R. Pitman*	8
1975	Fighting Taffy 7-11-1: 11/2	P. Upton	*P. Blacker*	11
1976	Fighting Kate 6-10-12: 5/2	H. Nicholson	*R. Dickin*	17
1977	No Race			
1977	(Dec 31) Pinchow 6-10-3: 11/2	D. Kent	*P. Haynes*	13
1978	Western Rose 6-11-4: 100/30	F. Rimell	*J. Burke*	12
1979	Jack O'Lantern 4-10-4: 3/1	P. Cundell	*M. O'Halloran*	12
1981	News King 7-11-9: 7/1	F. Winter	*Mr O. Sherwood*	16
1982	Mr Moonraker 5-10-0: 9/2	Miss S. Morris	*M. O'Halloran*	15
1982	Great Light 5-10-12: 6/1	J. Jenkins	*J. J. O'Neill*	12
1983	Cool Decision 6-11-7: 11/2	Miss S. Hall	*R. Earnshaw*	16
1984	Flarey Sark 7-10-8: 7/1	R. Fisher	*J. Doyle*	11
1985	Abandoned because of frost			
1987	Juven Light 6-10-9: 2/1	R. Akehurst	*S. Smith Eccles*	10
1988	Tivian 8-11-0: 10/1	I. Matthews	*G. McCourt*	7
1988	(Dec 31) Afaristoun 4-10-10: 2/1	J. Edwards	*T. Morgan*	5
1989	Fragrant Dawn 5-11-0: 5/2	J. FitzGerald	*M. Dwyer*	16
1990	Honest Word 5-11-3: 9/4	M. Pipe	*J. Lower*	10
1991	Barge Boy 7-10-0: 20/1	J. Old	*T. Grantham*	11
1993	Martha's Son 6-10-13: 13/2	T. Forster	*C. Llewellyn*	14

NORTHUMBERLAND GOLD CUP NOVICES' CHASE
(Newcastle 2m 110yds)

1990 Moment of Truth 6-11-7: 9/2	P. Monteith	L. O'Hara	11
1991 Clay County 6-11-7: 6/4	R. Allan	B. Storey	10
1992 Sybillin 6-11-7: 15/8	J. FitzGerald	C. Grant	7

CHEVELEY PARK STUD NEW YEAR'S DAY HURDLE
(LIMITED HANDICAP) (Windsor 2m)

1975 Flash Imp 6-12-3: 6/4	R. Smyth	P. Beasant	5
1976 Comedy of Errors 9-12-1: 10/11	F. Rimell	K. White	8
1977 Strombolus 6-11-9: 12/1	P. Bailey	R. Barry	6
1978 Beacon Light 7-12-1: 4/5	R. Turnell	A. Turnell	6
1979 Abandoned because of snow			
1980 Abandoned because of frost			
1981 Celtic Ryde 6-11-8: 4/9	P. Cundell	H. Davies	9
1982 Celtic Ryde 7-11-8: 1/5	P. Cundell	H. Davies	5
1983 Sula Bula 5-11-0: 10/11	M. H. Easterby	Mr T. Easterby	6
1984 Secret Ballot 9-11-4: 14/1	A. Turnell	E. Waite	6
1985 Ra Nova 6-11-10: 11/8	Mrs N. Kennedy	R. Dunwoody	8
1986 Southernair 6-11-4: 9/2	P. Haynes	A. Webb	5
1987 Ra Nova 8-11-4: 9/2	I. Matthews	M. Perrett	7
1988 Celtic Shot 6-11-4: 5/2	F. Winter	P. Scudamore	10
1989 Wishlon 6-11-4: 9/2	R. Smyth	I. Shoemark	5
1990 Aldino 7-11-7: 3/1	O. Sherwood	J. Osborne	5
1991 Royal Derbi 6-11-7: 9/2	N. Callaghan	D. Murphy	8
1992 Shu Fly 8-11-4: 4/1	Mrs S. Oliver	A. Jones	4
1993 Muse 6-11-5: 13/2	D. Elsworth	A. Procter	9

MITSUBISHI SHOGUN NEWTON CHASE (Haydock 2½m)

1991 Sabin du Loir 12-11-10: 1/2	M. Pipe	M. Perrett	4
1992 Pat's Jester 9-11-10: 7/1	G. Richards	N. Doughty	6
1993 Gold Options 11-11-10: 14/1	J. FitzGerald	L. Wyer	6

BARING SECURITIES TOLWORTH HURDLE (Sandown 2m 110yds)

1976 Grand Canyon 6-12-0: 4/7	D. Kent	P. Haynes	4
1977 Levaramoss 4-10-1: 9/2	S. Ingham	A. Gonsalves	6
1978 Western Rose 6-11-7: 4/7	F. Rimell	J. Burke	6
1979 Abandoned because of snow			
1980 Esparto 5-11-9: 9/2	F. Winter	Mr O. Sherwood	10
1981 Broadsword 4-10-11: 4/7	D. Nicholson	P. Scudamore	8
1982 Abandoned because of frost and snow			
1983 Hawkbarrow 5-11-5: 13/2	D. Gandolfo	P. Barton	4
1984 Desert Orchid 5-11-11: 5/6	D. Elsworth	C. Brown	6
1985 Wing And A Prayer 4-10-13: 5/4	J. Jenkins	J. Francome	6
1986 Midnight Count 6-11-7: 9/4	J. Gifford	R. Rowe	7
1987 Mister Point 5-11-7: 5/1	C. Tinkler	G. McCourt	9
1988 Away We Go 6-11-11: 4/6	J. Jenkins	S. Smith Eccles	11
1989 Wishlon 6-12-0: 4/6	R. Smyth	I. Shoemark	4
1990 Forest Sun 5-11-12: 8/11	G. Balding	J. Frost	7
1991 Change The Act 6-11-7: 9/1	O. Sherwood	J. Osborne	6
1992 New York Rainbow 7-11-7: 5/1	N. Henderson	J. Kavanagh	7
1993 Sun Surfer 5-11-7: 7/1	T. Forster	C. Llewellyn	7

ANTHONY MILDMAY, PETER CAZALET MEMORIAL TROPHY
HANDICAP CHASE (Sandown 3m 5f 110yds)

1952 Cromwell 11-11-10: 9/2	P. Cazalet	B. Marshall	12
1953 Whispering Steel 8-11-3: 7/1	A. Kilpatrick	R. Emery	16
1954 Domata 8-10-12: 6/1	F. Cundell	A. Corbett	10
1955 Abandoned because of snow and frost			
1956 Linwell 8-9-9: 4/1	C. Mallon	R. Hamey	10
1957 Much Obliged 9-10-12: 100/8	N. Crump	H. East	20
1958 Polar Flight 8-10-7: 11/2	G. Spann	G. Slack	14
1959 Abandoned because of snow and frost			
1960 Team Spirit 8-9-10: 10/1	D. L. Moore (Ir)	G. W. Robinson	12
1961 Mac Joy 9-10-7: 25/1	K. Bailey	M. Scudamore	13
1962 Duke of York 7-10-12: 6/1	J. Tilling	Mr D. Scott	18
1963 Abandoned because of snow and frost			
1964 Dormant 7-10-12: 11/4	N. Crump	P. Buckley	9

138

1965	Freddie 8-10-5: 2/1	R. Tweedie	*P. McCarron*	12
1966	What A Myth 9-12-0: 4/1	R. Price	*P. Kelleway*	5
1967	Abandoned because of frost			
1968	Stalbridge Colonist 9-12-0: 7/1	K. Cundell	*S. Mellor*	18
1969	Abandoned because of fog			
1970	Larbawn 11-11-13: 9/1	M. L. Marsh	*J. Gifford*	8
1971	Abandoned because of frost			
1972	Royal Toss 10-11-4: 5/2	H. Handel	*N. Wakley*	9
1973	Midnight Fury 7-10-0: 12/1	F. Winter	*V. Soane*	9
1974	High Ken 8-10-4: 16/1	J. Edwards	*B. R. Davies*	10
1975	Money Market 8-10-11: 6/1	C. Bewicke	*J. King*	11
1976	Money Market 9-11-0: 3/1	C. Bewicke	*R. Barry*	9
1977	Zeta's Son 8-11-7: 11/2	P. Bailey	*R. Barry*	12
1978	Shifting Gold 9-11-4: 11/8	K. Bailey	*J. Francome*	5
1979	Abandoned because of snow and frost			
1980	Modesty Forbids 8-10-2: 9/1	J. Gifford	*R. Rowe*	13
1981	Peter Scot 10-10-9: 6/1	D. Gandolfo	*P. Barton*	9
1982	Abandoned because of frost and snow			
1983	Fifty Dollars More 8-11-5: 4/6	F. Winter	*R. Linley*	5
1984	Burrough Hill Lad 8-10-9: 11/8	Mrs J. Pitman	*J. Francome*	9
1985	West Tip 8-10-1: 11/4	M. Oliver	*R. Dunwoody*	5
1986	Run And Skip 8-11-1: 7/2	J. Spearing	*P. Scudamore*	8
1987	Stearsby 8-11-5: 11/8	Mrs J. Pitman	*G. McCourt*	7
1988	Rhyme 'N' Reason 9-10-7: 11/8	D. Elsworth	*C. Brown*	6
1989	Mr Frisk 10-10-13: 3/1	K. Bailey	*R. Dunwoody*	7
1990	Cool Ground 8-10-5: 6/1	N. Mitchell	*A. Tory*	12
1991	Cool Ground 9-10-11: 6/4	R. Akehurst	*L. Harvey*	8
1992	Arctic Call 9-11-6: 4/1	O. Sherwood	*J. Osborne*	6
1993	Rushing Wild 8-10-1: 1/1	M. Pipe	*P. Scudamore*	11

DIPPER NOVICES' CHASE (Newcastle 2½m)

1980	Little Owl 6-11-5: 9/4	M. H. Easterby	*J. J. O'Neill*	13
1981	Abandoned because of frost			
1982	Rosewell Riever 9-11-6: 16/1	P. Monteith	*D. Nolan*	9
1983	Lettoch 6-11-10: 4/5	M. Dickinson	*G. Bradley*	6
1984	Jimbrook 7-11-6: 11/4	M. H. Easterby	*A. Brown*	6
1985	Abandoned because of snow			
1986	Joint Sovereignty 6-11-10: 4/5	J. FitzGerald	*M. Dwyer*	4
1987	Jim Thorpe 6-11-13: 15/8	G. Richards	*P. Tuck*	6
1988	Cool Strike 7-11-6: 9/2	G. Moore	*B. Storey*	6
1989	Blazing Walker 5-11-9: 8/11	W. A. Stephenson	*C. Grant*	6
1991	(Jan.) Meritmoore 8-11-5: 11/8	G. Moore	*J. Callaghan*	5
1992	Gale Again 5-10-8: 7/2	W. A. Stephenson	*C. Grant*	6
1993	Dawson City 6-11-9: 1/2	M. H. Easterby	*L. Wyer*	6

P.M.L. LIGHTNING NOVICES' CHASE (Ascot 2m)

1979	Dramatist 8-11-11: 1/1	F. Walwyn	*W. Smith*	4
1980	Beacon Light 9-12-0: 8/11	R. Turnell	*A. Turnell*	6
1981	Double Bluff 8-11-4: 9/2	F. Winter	*J. Francome*	7
1982	Abandoned because of snow			
1983	Starfen 7-11-4: 9/4	M. H. Easterby	*Mr T. Easterby*	8
1984	Norton Cross 6-11-4: 5/2	M. H. Easterby	*A. Brown*	6
1985	Abandoned because of snow and frost			
1986	Pearlyman 7-11-4: 5/1	J. Edwards	*P. Barton*	3
1987	Abandoned because of snow and frost			
1988	Saffron Lord 6-11-5: 100/30	J. Gifford	*R. Rowe*	6
1989	Sabin du Loir 10-11-5: 6/5	M. Pipe	*P. Scudamore*	4
1990	Cashew King 7-11-5: 12/1	B. McMahon	*T. Wall*	3
1991	Uncle Ernie 6-11-8: 2/1	J. FitzGerald	*M. Dwyer*	6
1992	Deep Sensation 7-11-4: 7/4	J. Gifford	*D. Murphy*	4
1993	Valiant Boy 7-11-4: 7/4	S. Kettlewell	*R. Garritty*	3

FIRST NATIONAL CHASE (HANDICAP) (Ascot 3m 110yds)

1990	Zuko 9-10-0: 6/1	S. Mellor	*M. Perrett*	11
1991	Arctic Call 8-11-10: 2/1	O. Sherwood	*J. Osborne*	6
1992	Kildimo 12-10-10: 12/1	Mrs S. Smith	*R. Guest*	7
1993	Very Very Ordinary 7-10-1: 2/1	J. Upson	*R. Supple*	6

139

ROSLING KING HURDLE (HANDICAP) (Ascot 3m)

1988 Ruby Flight 6-9-9: 20/1	R. Eckley	*D. Tegg*	17
1989 Mrs Muck 8-11-13: 16/1	N. Twiston-Davies	*S. Sherwood*	12
1990 Calabrese 5-10-5: 4/5	N. Henderson	*R. Dunwoody*	10
1991 King's Curate 7-11-3: 8/1	S. Mellor	*Mr D. Gray*	16
1992 Sweet Glow 5-11-8: 7/4	M. Pipe	*P. Scudamore*	6
1993 Sweet Glow 6-10-12: 16/1	M. Pipe	*D. Richmond*	14

VICTOR CHANDLER HANDICAP CHASE (Ascot 2m)

1987 Abandoned because of snow and frost			
1988 Abandoned because of fog			
1989 Desert Orchid 10-12-0: 6/4	D. Elsworth	*S. Sherwood*	5
1990 Meikleour 11-10-10: 10/1	J. FitzGerald	*D. Byrne*	10
1991 Blitzkreig 8-10-4: 11/4	E. O'Grady (Ir)	*T. Carmody*	5
1992 Waterloo Boy 9-11-10: 6/4	D. Nicholson	*R. Dunwoody*	5
1993 Sybillin 7-10-10: 9/2	J. FitzGerald	*M. Dwyer*	11

THE LADBROKE (Leopardstown 2m)

1969 Normandy 4-11-2: 15/2	F. Rimell	*T. Biddlecombe*	15
1970 Persian War 7-12-0: 5/4	A. Pitt	*J. Uttley*	11
1971 Kelanne 7-11-6: 20/1	W. Marshall	*W. Smith*	16
1972 Captain Christy 5-11-6: 15/2	P. Taaffe (Ir)	*H. Beasley*	13
1973 Comedy of Errors 6-12-0: 4/5	F. Rimell	*W. Smith*	9
1974 Comedy of Errors 7-12-0: 11/10	F. Rimell	*K. White*	8
1975 Night Nurse 4-11-5: 6/4	M. H. Easterby	*P. Broderick*	9
1976 Master Monday 6-10-2: 25/1	L. Quirke (Ir)	*J. P. Harty*	19
1977 Decent Fellow 4-11-4: 4/1	G. Balding	*R. Linley*	18
1978 Chinrullah 6-10-6: 8/1	M. O'Toole (Ir)	*G. Newman*	12
1979 Irian 5-10-0: 25/1	A. Moore (Ir)	*Mrs A. Ferris*	20
1980 Carrig Willy 5-10-0: 33/1	M. O'Toole (Ir)	*T. Quinn*	26
1981 No Race			
1982 For Auction 6-10-10: 9/1	M. Cunningham (Ir)	*Mr C. Magnier*	20
1983 Fredcoteri 7-10-0: 10/1	A. Moore (Ir)	*T. Taaffe*	15
1984 Fredcoteri 8-10-4: 8/1	A. Moore (Ir)	*T. Taaffe*	18
1985 Hansel Rag 5-10-0: 14/1	A. Redmond (Ir)	*A. Powell*	20
1986 Bonalma 6-10-13: 5/1	A. Moore (Ir)	*T. Taaffe*	23
1987 Barnbrook Again 6-11-8: 5/2	D. Elsworth	*C. Brown*	22
1988 Roark 6-11-1: 5/1	A. Moore (Ir)	*T. Taaffe*	15
1989 Redundant Pal 6-10-0: 16/1	P. Mullins (Ir)	*P. Kavanagh*	17
1990 Redundant Pal 7-11-5: 20/1	P. Mullins (Ir)	*C. O'Dwyer*	27
1991 The Illiad 10-10-13: 7/1	A. Geraghty (Ir)	*P. McWilliams*	17
1992 How's The Boss 6-10-2: 20/1	J. Brassil (Ir)	*J. Titley*	20
1993 Glencloud 5-10-3: 20/1	N. Meade (Ir)	*G. O'Neill*	25

BIC RAZOR LANZAROTE HANDICAP HURDLE (Kempton 2m)

1978 Nougat 8-11-11: 8/1	J. Gifford	*G. Enright*	13
1979 Love From Verona 5-10-1: 12/1	R. Sheather	*R. Cochrane*	14
1980 Danish King 6-10-3: 4/1	R. Turnell	*A. Turnell*	10
1981 Walnut Wonder 6-10-6: 7/1	L. Kennard	*A. Webber*	12
1982 Knighthood 7-10-0: 10/1	R. Turnell	*S. C. Knight*	14
1983 Brave Hussar 5-10-7: 16/1	J. Gifford	*R. Rowe*	16
1984 Janus 6-11-1: 5/1	Mrs N. Smith	*C. Brown*	10
1985 Abandoned because of snow and frost			
1986 Prideaux Boy 8-11-10: 11/1	G. Roach	*M. Bowlby*	14
1987 Stray Shot 9-9-10: 16/1	G. Hubbard	*Miss G. Armytage*	9
1988 Fredcoteri 12-11-4: 15/2	G. Moore	*M. Hammond*	11
1989 Grey Salute 6-10-7: 9/4	J. Jenkins	*R. Dunwoody*	8
1990 Atlaal 5-10-3: 10/1	J. Jenkins	*R. Dunwoody*	13
1991 Star Season 7-10-3: 9/2	R. Holder	*N. Mann*	11
1992 Egypt Mill Prince 6-10-13: 11/2	Mrs J. Pitman	*M. Pitman*	7
1993 Tomahawk 6-10-0: 12/1	P. Murphy	*D. Murphy*	10

JIM ENNIS CONSTRUCTION PREMIER LONG DISTANCE
HURDLE (Haydock 2m 7f 110yds)

1970 Clever Scot 5-10-9: 4/1	C. Davies	*B. R. Davies*	8
1971 Colonel Imp 9-11-9: 3/1	D. Smith	*B. Fletcher*	7
1972 Notification 7-11-9: 8/1	F. Rimell	*K. White*	8
1973 Be My Guest 5-11-10: 5/2	B. Wilkinson	*B. Fletcher*	7

1974	Abandoned because of waterlogged state of course		
1975	Moyne Royal 10-11-9: 4/6	A. Pitt	*J. King*	7
1976	Abandoned because of waterlogged state of course		
1977	Abandoned because of waterlogged state of course		
1978	Abandoned because of frost		
1979	Abandoned because of frost		
1980	Abandoned because of waterlogged state of course		
1981	Richdee 5-11-5: 11/2	N. Crump	*C. Hawkins*	10
1982	Shell Burst 7-11-5: 4/1	L. Kennard	*H. Davies*	12
1983	Here's Why 6-11-13: 5/1	J. Gifford	*J. J. O'Neill*	9
1984	Abandoned because of frost		
1985	Abandoned because of frost		
1986	Sheer Gold 6-11-6: 7/2	G. Balding	*G. Bradley*	10
1987	Aonoch 8-12-0: 2/1	Mrs S. Oliver	*J. Duggan*	5
1988	Abandoned because of snow		
1989	Out of The Gloom 8-11-7: 3/1	M. Pipe	*P. Scudamore*	10
1990	Mrs Muck 9-11-2: 13/8	N. Twiston-Davies	*G. Bradley*	7
1991	Abandoned because of frost		
1992	Trapper John 8-11-10: 13/8	M. Morris (Ir)	*C. Swan*	9
1993	Pragada 10-11-10: 13/2	M. Pipe	*P. Scudamore*	7

HAYDOCK PARK CHAMPION HURDLE TRIAL (Haydock 2m)

1981	Starfen 5-11-12: 5/2	M. H. Easterby	*Mr T. Easterby*	6
1982	Gaye Chance 7-12-0: 7/2	Mrs M. Rimell	*S. Morshead*	7
1983	Ekbalco 7-12-0: 8/13	R. Fisher	*J. J. O'Neill*	3
1984	Abandoned because of frost		
1985	Abandoned because of frost		
1986	Humberside Lady 5-11-6: 4/1	G. Huffer	*M. Dwyer*	7
1987	Nohalmdun 6-12-0: 2/5	M. H. Easterby	*L. Wyer*	5
1988	Abandoned because of snow		
1989	Vicario di Bray 6-11-8: 11/1	J. J. O'Neill	*M. Dwyer*	6
1990	Bank View 5-11-8: 33/1	N. Tinkler	*G. Bradley*	7
1991	Abandoned because of frost		
1992	Granville Again 6-11-10: 1/2	M. Pipe	*P. Scudamore*	5
1993	Jinxy Jack 9-11-7: 9/4	G. Richards	*N. Doughty*	5

PETER MARSH CHASE (LIMITED HANDICAP) (Haydock 3m)

1981	Little Owl 7-11-3: 4/6	M. H. Easterby	*Mr A. J. Wilson*	6
1982	Bregawn 8-10-7: 11/2	M. Dickinson	*R. Earnshaw*	8
1983	Ashley House 9-10-7: 11/8	M. Dickinson	*R. Earnshaw*	7
1984	Abandoned because of frost		
1985	Abandoned because of frost		
1986	Combs Ditch 10-11-8: 3/1	D. Elsworth	*C. Brown*	7
1987	The Thinker 9-11-10: 9/2	W. A. Stephenson	*R. Lamb*	6
1988	Abandoned because of snow		
1989	Bishops Yarn 10-10-12: 13/2	G. Balding	*R. Guest*	4
1990	Nick The Brief 8-10-9: 15/8	J. Upson	*M. Lynch*	6
1991	Abandoned because of frost		
1992	Twin Oaks 12-11-10: 5/4	G. Richards	*N. Doughty*	8
1993	Jodami 8-11-2: 5/4	P. Beaumont	*M. Dwyer*	6

FOOD BROKERS FINESSE HURDLE (4-y-o) (Cheltenham 2m 1f)

1985	Out of The Gloom 11-7: 11/4	R. Hollinshead	*J. J. O'Neill*	10
1986	Tangognat 11-7: 7/4	R. Simpson	*P. Scudamore*	11
1987	Abandoned because of frost		
1988	Jason's Quest 11-0: 16/1	J. Baker	*M. Williams*	9
1989	Highland Bud 11-3: 4/1	D. Nicholson	*R. Dunwoody*	6
1990	Sayyure 11-8: 3/1	N. Tinkler	*G. McCourt*	4
1991	Hopscotch 11-2: 8/11	M. Pipe	*P. Scudamore*	7
1992	Abandoned because of frost		
1993	Major Bugler 11-0: 13/2	G. Balding	*A. Maguire*	6

WYKO POWER TRANSMISSION HURDLE (Cheltenham 2m 5f 110yds)

1983	Al Kuwait 7-11-10: 3/1	F. Winter	*J. Francome*	5
1984	Buckbe 5-11-5: 6/4	D. Elsworth	*C. Brown*	10
1985	Rose Ravine 6-11-5: 100/30	F. Walwyn	*R. Pusey*	9
1986	Stans Pride 9-11-5: 17/2	G. Price	*R. Beggan*	8
1987	Abandoned because of frost		

1988	Cloughtaney 7-12-0: 5/2	P. Mullins (Ir)	*A. Mullins*	11
1989	Calapaez 5-11-10: 6/4	Miss B. Sanders	*S. Sherwood*	4
1990	Beech Road 8-12-0: 1/3	G. Balding	*R. Guest*	5
1991	Crystal Spirit 4-10-9: 4/1	I. Balding	*J. Frost*	9
1992	Abandoned because of frost			
1993	Muse 6-11-8: 11/4	D. Elsworth	*P. Holley*	4

TIMEFORM HALL OF FAME CHASE (Cheltenham 3m 1f 110yds)

1980	Raffi Nelson 7-11-6: 5/2	N. Henderson	*S. Smith Eccles*	7
1981	Little Owl 7-11-12: 8/11	M. H. Easterby	*Mr A. J. Wilson*	6
1982	Lesley Ann 8-11-12: 5/2	D. Elsworth	*C. Brown*	3
1983	Combs Ditch 7-11-9: 6/1	D. Elsworth	*C. Brown*	6
1984	Everett 9-11-8: 15/8	F. Walwyn	*S. Shilston*	6
1985	West Tip 8-11-6: 5/2	M. Oliver	*R. Dunwoody*	4
1986	Misty Spirit 6-11-6: 9/1	D. Lee	*S. Smith Eccles*	6
1987	Abandoned because of frost			
1988	Twin Oaks 8-11-6: 6/1	D. Murray-Smith	*P. Croucher*	3
1989	Deep Moment 7-11-3: 12/1	Mrs M. Rimell	*D. Browne*	4
1990	Toby Tobias 8-11-6: 5/4	Mrs J. Pitman	*M. Pitman*	4
1991	Celtic Shot 9-11-12: 11/4	C. Brooks	*P. Scudamore*	4
1992	Abandoned because of frost			
1993	Sibton Abbey 8-11-12: 16/1	F. Murphy	*S. Smith Eccles*	7

ROSSINGTON MAIN NOVICES' HURDLE (Doncaster 2m 110yds)

1971	Pry 5-11-2: 7/1	G. Balding	*E. Harty*	6
1972	The Bugler 4-10-5: 10/1	J. Astor	*R. Griffin*	10
1973	Dark Sultan 5-11-7: 5/1	P. Chisman	*R. Barry*	18
1974	Charlie Mouse 5-11-2: 14/1	T. Forster	*G. Thorner*	22
1975	Sea Pigeon 5-11-12: 13/8	G. Richards	*R. Barry*	13
1976	Grand Canyon 6-12-0: 1/2	D. Kent	*P. Haynes*	6
1977	French Hollow 5-11-12	A. Dickinson	*M. Dickinson*	12
1978	Newgate 5-11-12: 5/1	A. Scott	*R. Lamb*	11
1979	No Bombs 4-10-8: 3/1	M. H. Easterby	*N. Tinkler*	11
1980	Pulse Rate 4-10-8: 21/20	M. H. Easterby	*A. Brown*	8
1981	Hard About 5-11-7: 3/1	E. O'Grady (Ir)	*T. Ryan*	8
1982	Gaye Brief 5-11-7: 3/1	Mrs M. Rimell	*S. Morshead*	16
1983	Cardinal Flower 6-11-4: 7/4	A. Scott	*J. J. O'Neill*	8
1984	Abandoned because of snow			
1985	Abandoned because of snow and frost			
1986	Shean Lad 6-11-7: 50/1	Miss L. Siddall	*P. Tuck*	15
1987	Abandoned because of frost			
1988	Drumlin Hill 5-11-0: 15/2	F. Winter	*P. Scudamore*	9
1989	Cruising Altitude 6-11-7: 5/4	O. Sherwood	*S. Sherwood*	5
1990	Peanuts Pet 5-11-0: 4/5	B. McMahon	*T. Wall*	6
1991	Ruling 5-11-0: 11/8	F. J. Houghton	*P. Niven*	7
1992	Abandoned because of frost			
1993	Frickley 7-11-9: 11/10	G. Richards	*N. Doughty*	5

GREAT YORKSHIRE HANDICAP CHASE (Doncaster 3m)

1948	Cool Customer 9-12-7: 4/1	J. Fawcus	*P. Murphy*	17
1949	Old Morality 7-10-1: 33/1	F. Rimell	*R. Turnell*	11
1950	Freebooter 9-11-11: 5/2	R. Renton	*J. Power*	14
1951	Arctic Gold 6-11-0: 5/1	G. Balding	*T. Molony*	10
1952	No Race			
1953	Knock Hard 9-11-7: 5/1	M. V. O'Brien (Ir)	*T. Molony*	9
1954	Abandoned because of frost			
1955	Bramble Tudor 7-11-3: 6/1	J. Wight	*R. Curran*	14
1956	Abandoned because of snow and frost			
1957	E.S.B. 11-11-10: 10/1	F. Rimell	*T. Molony*	13
1958	Hall Weir 8-10-10: 11/4	F. Cundell	*W. Rees*	17
1959	Abandoned because of frost			
1960	Knightsbrook 8-11-1: 11/4	W. Hall	*G. Slack*	10
1961	Chavara 8-10-7: 10/1	G. Owen	*S. Mellor*	13
1962	Nicolaus Silver 10-11-9: 100/8	F. Rimell	*H. Beasley*	15
1963	Abandoned because of frost			
1964	King's Nephew 10-11-10: 7/4	F. Cundell	*S. Mellor*	9
1965	King of Diamonds 7-10-4: 20/1	G. Vergette	*J. Kenneally*	12
1966	Freddie 9-11-7: 2/1	R. Tweedie	*P. McCarron*	12

1967	Spear Fir 8-10-6: 100/6	R. Fairbairn	*J. Leech*	12
1968	Sixty Nine 8-12-0: 7/1	Denys Smith	*B. Fletcher*	16
1969	Playlord 8-11-6: 100/8	G. Richards	*R. Barry*	15
1970	Freddie Boy 9-11-3: 100/9	F. Winter	*R. Pitman*	11
1971	Two Springs 9-10-10: 11/1	G. Owen	*R. Edwards*	14
1972	Slaves Dream 8-10-6: 8/1	R. Hall	*M. Dickinson*	9
1973	Charlie Potheen 8-11-10: 9/2	F. Walwyn	*T. Biddlecombe*	10
1974	Cuckolder 9-10-1: 15/2	R. Turnell	*A. Turnell*	11
1975	Rough House 9-10-5: 9/2	F. Rimell	*J. Burke*	9
1976	Abandoned because of frost			
1977	Abandoned because of frost			
1978	Autumn Rain 7-10-2: 12/1	A. Dickinson	*C. Tinkler*	7
1979	Abandoned because of snow			
1980	Jer 9-10-0: 9/2	P. Bevan	*P. Tuck*	8
1981	Tragus 9-10-13: 6/1	D. Morley	*B. R. Davies*	10
1982	Bregawn 8-11-6: 11/8	M. Dickinson	*J. Francome*	9
1983	Get Out of Me Way 8-10-0: 7/2	G. Thorner	*P. Barton*	9
1984	Abandoned because of snow			
1985	Abandoned because of snow and frost			
1986	Abandoned because of frost			
1987	Abandoned because of frost			
1988	Bob Tisdall 9-12-5: 16/1	J. Edwards	*T. Morgan*	21
1989	Proverity 8-11-8: 100/30	J. Edwards	*T. Morgan*	11
1990	Man O'Magic 9-11-0: 7/2	K. Bailey	*M. Perrett*	11
1991	Dalkey Sound 8-10-9: 9/1	Mrs M. Reveley	*P. Niven*	19
1992	Abandoned because of frost			
1993	Young Hustler 6-10-0: 9/2	N. Twiston-Davies	*D. Bridgwater*	14

WEST OF SCOTLAND PATTERN NOVICES' CHASE (Ayr 3m 1f)

1976	Stay-Bell 7-11-4: 2/1	Mrs S. Chesmore	*R. Barry*	5
1977	Zarib 9-11-5: 13/8	F. Rimell	*R. Evans*	11
1978	Ballet Lord 7-11-0: 5/2	N. Crump	*C. Hawkins*	7
1979	Abandoned because of frost and snow			
1980	Little Owl 6-11-10: 8/11	M. H. Easterby	*J. J. O'Neill*	7
1981	Wayward Lad 6-11-0: 9/4	M. Dickinson	*T. Carmody*	8
1982	Seamus O'Flynn 7-11-0: 2/1	M. Dickinson	*G. Bradley*	6
1983	Branding Iron 6-11-0: 15/8	M. Dickinson	*R. Earnshaw*	8
1984	Abandoned because of snow and frost			
1985	Abandoned because of frost			
1986	Abandoned because of frost			
1987	Abandoned because of frost			
1988	Randolph Place 7-11-7: 13/8	G. Richards	*P. Tuck*	7
1989	Southern Minstrel 6-11-7: 7/2	W. A. Stephenson	*A. Merrigan*	3
1990	Carrick Hill Lad 7-11-11: 11/10	G. Richards	*N. Doughty*	4
1991	Over The Deel 5-10-7: 8/1	W. A. Stephenson	*Mr K. Johnson*	9
1992	Jodami 7-11-5: 11/8	P. Beaumont	*P. Farrell*	8
1993	Whispering Steel 7-11-9: 8/11	G. Richards	*N. Doughty*	7

AGFA DIAMOND CHASE (LIMITED HANDICAP) (Sandown 3m 110yds)

1954	Shaef 10-11-7: 5/4	J. Gosden	*B. Marshall*	3
1955	Abandoned because of snow			
1956	Abandoned because of frost			
1957	Rose Park 11-12-5: 8/13	P. Cazalet	*G. Nicholls*	7
1958	Pelopidas 8-11-11: 7/2	H. Nicholson	*D. Dick*	5
1959	Saffron Tartan 8-11-11: 2/5	M. V. O'Brien (Ir)	*T. Taaffe*	3
1960	Double Star 8-11-11: 4/9	P. Cazalet	*A. Freeman*	3
1961	Carraroe 9-11-7: 5/1	C. Mitchell	*R. Jenkins*	4
1962	Blue Dolphin 9-11-5: 10/11	P. Cazalet	*W. Rees*	5
1963	Abandoned because of snow and frost			
1964	Mill House 7-12-5: 1/7	F. Walwyn	*G. W. Robinson*	5
1965	Mill House 8-12-5: 8/13	F. Walwyn	*G. W. Robinson*	4
1966	What A Myth 9-11-9: 10/11	R. Price	*P. Kelleway*	6
1967	Mill House 10-11-9: 6/5	F. Walwyn	*G. W. Robinson*	4
1968	The Laird 7-11-9: 5/1	R. Turnell	*J. King*	3
1969	Stalbridge Colonist 10-11-9: 2/1	K. Cundell	*S. Mellor*	3
1970	Spanish Steps 7-12-0: 10/11	E. Courage	*J. Cook*	3
1971	Titus Oates 9-12-0: 10/1	G. Richards	*R. Barry*	3
1972	Crisp 9-12-0: 11/10	F. Winter	*R. Pitman*	3

1973 Royal Toss 11-11-9: 2/1	H. Handel	*N. Wakley*	3
1974 Kilvulgan 7-10-9: 5/2	R. Turnell	*A. Turnell*	6
1975 Abandoned because of waterlogged state of course			
1976 Bula 11-12-0: 1/3	F. Winter	*J. Francome*	3
1977 Master H 8-10-8: 11/1	M. Oliver	*Mr J. Weston*	7
1978 Master H 9-11-3: 4/1	M. Oliver	*J. Francome*	6
1979 Diamond Edge 8-11-3: 11/4	F. Walwyn	*W. Smith*	11
1980 Diamond Edge 9-12-0: 11/4	F. Walwyn	*W. Smith*	7
1981 Tragus 9-10-7: 9/2	D. Morley	*B. R. Davies*	8
1982 Bregawn 8-10-7: 3/1	M. Dickinson	*R. Earnshaw*	9
(at Kempton)			
1983 Observe 7-11-3: 11/8	F. Winter	*J. Francome*	5
1984 Burrough Hill Lad 8-11-10: 11/8	Mrs J. Pitman	*J. Francome*	5
1985 Burrough Hill Lad 9-12-0: —	Mrs J. Pitman	*J. Francome*	w.o.
1986 Burrough Hill Lad 10-12-0: 100/30	Mrs J. Pitman	*P. Scudamore*	6
1987 Desert Orchid 8-11-10: 11/4	D. Elsworth	*C. Brown*	6
1988 Charter Party 10-10-11: 100/30	D. Nicholson	*R. Dunwoody*	11
1989 Desert Orchid 10-12-0: 6/5	D. Elsworth	*S. Sherwood*	4
1990 Abandoned because of waterlogged state of course			
1991 Desert Orchid 12-12-0: 4/6	D. Elsworth	*R. Dunwoody*	4
1992 Espy 9-10-7: 11/1	C. Brooks	*G. Bradley*	9
1993 Country Member 8-10-7: 10/3	A. Turnell	*L. Harvey*	3

SCILLY ISLES NOVICES' CHASE (Sandown 2½m 110yds)

1964 Buona notte 7-12-1: 2/5	R. Turnell	*J. Haine*	6
1965 The Braggart 7-10-12: 100/7	H. T. Jones	*T. Biddlecombe*	13
1966 Abandoned because of waterlogged state of course			
1967 Bowgeeno 7-11-11: 2/1	R. Turnell	*J. King*	9
1968 Aurelius 10-11-8: 4/6	K. Cundell	*S. Mellor*	6
1969 Abandoned because of snow			
1970 Royal Relief 6-12-0: 13/8	E. Courage	*J. Cook*	6
1971 Black Magic 7-12-0: 6/4	P. Cazalet	*R. Dennard*	8
1972 Potentate 7-11-8: 7/4	J. Gifford	*D. Barrott*	6
1973 Killiney 7-12-0: 1/10	F. Winter	*R. Pitman*	3
1974 Even Up 7-11-8: 100/30	Mrs D. Oughton	*G. Thorner*	8
1975 Abandoned because of waterlogged state of course			
1976 Skryne 6-11-9: 2/1	P. Bailey	*R. Barry*	5
1977 Flitgrove 6-11-4: 10/1	D. Nicholson	*J. King*	5
1978 Space Project 8-11-9: 7/1	R. Brown	*R. Hyett*	6
1979 Abandoned because of frost			
1980 Beacon Light 9-11-12: 1/2	R. Turnell	*A. Turnell*	6
1981 Clayside 7-11-9: 13/8	M. H. Easterby	*A. Brown*	7
1982 Sea Image 7-11-8: 11/4	F. Winter	*J. Francome*	8
(at Kempton)			
1983 Kilbrittain Castle 7-11-0: 6/4	F. Walwyn	*W. Smith*	5
1984 Norton Cross 6-11-10: 2/1	M. H. Easterby	*A. Brown*	6
1985 Karenomore 7-11-5: 9/4	M. H. Easterby	*J. J. O'Neill*	5
1986 Berlin 7-11-10: 5/2	N. Gaselee	*D. Browne*	6
1987 First Bout 6-11-5: 11/10	N. Henderson	*S. Smith Eccles*	6
1988 Yeoman Broker 7-11-0: 7/4	J. Gifford	*R. Rowe*	5
1989 The Bakewell Boy 7-11-6: 6/1	R. Frost	*J. Frost*	4
1990 Abandoned because of waterlogged state of course			
1991 Tildarg 7-11-6: 11/2	O. Sherwood	*J. Osborne*	6
1992 Bradbury Star 7-11-6: 6/5	J. Gifford	*D. Murphy*	9
1993 Young Hustler 6-11-6: 5/2	N. Twiston-Davies	*C. Llewellyn*	11

TOTE JACKPOT HANDICAP HURDLE (Sandown 2¾m)

1986 Hoorah Henry 6-10-5: 8/1	B. Sayers	*H. Davies*	19
1987 Taberna Lord 6-9-10: 8/1	A. J. Wilson	*L. Harvey*	14
1988 Hill-Street-Blues 10-10-2: 25/1	J. Fox	*S. Moore*	17
1989 Special Vintage 9-10-12: 20/1	J. FitzGerald	*M. Dwyer*	15
1990 Abandoned because of waterlogged state of course			
1991 Rouyan 5-10-0: 8/1	R. Simpson	*W. Morris*	15
1992 Black Sapphire 5-10-0: 33/1	M. Tompkins	*B. Powell*	12
1993 Trainglot 6-10-2: 7/2	J. FitzGerald	*M. Dwyer*	15

AGFA HURDLE (Sandown 2m 110yds)

1949	National Spirit 8-12-5: 1/3	V. Smyth	*B. Marshall*	5
1950	National Spirit 9-12-7: 1/4	V. Smyth	*D. Dillon*	5
1951	Abandoned because of waterlogged state of course			
1952	Telegram II 5-11-5: 3/1	F. Walwyn	*D. Dick*	8
1953	Abandoned because of snow			
1954	Fastnet Rock 7-11-9: 7/4	C. Jellis	*A. Freeman*	6
1955	Abandoned because of snow			
1956	Abandoned because of frost			
1957	Vermillion 9-12-5: 10/11	R. Price	*F. Winter*	6
1958	Retour de Flamme 5-11-13: 4/1	S. Warren	*J. Lindley*	8
1959	Fare Time 6-12-3: 1/3	R. Price	*F. Winter*	6
1960	Fare Time 7-12-3: 1/1	R. Price	*F. Winter*	7
1961	Eborneezer 6-12-3: 6/1	R. Price	*F. Winter*	5
1962	Snuff Box 5-10-10: 9/2	J. Benstead	*J. Gilbert*	9
1963	Abandoned because of snow and frost			
1964	Kirriemuir 4-10-12: 8/15	F. Walwyn	*D. Mould*	7
1965	Magic Court 7-12-5: 6/4	T. Robson	*P. McCarron*	12
1966	Abandoned because of waterlogged state of course			
1967	Chenonceaux 6-10-7: 100/6	K. Cundell	*D. Briscoe*	11
1968	Into View 5-10-8: 50/1	F. Winter	*E. P. Harty*	15
1969	Abandoned because of snow			
1970	Major Rose 8-10-10: 1/1	R. Price	*J. Gifford*	7
1971	Major Rose 9-11-4: 15/8	R. Price	*P. Kelleway*	5
1972	Phaestus 6-11-4: 5/2	F. Rimell	*K. White*	9
1973	Lanzarote 5-11-2: 15/8	F. Winter	*R. Pitman*	4
1974	Lanzarote 6-11-12: 1/6	F. Winter	*R. Pitman*	3
1975	Abandoned because of waterlogged state of course			
1976	Sea Pigeon 6-11-12: 2/1	G. Richards	*J. J. O'Neill*	8
1977	Bird's Nest 7-12-2: 30/100	R. Turnell	*A. Turnell*	4
1978	Sea Pigeon 8-11-12: 2/1	M. H. Easterby	*J. J. O'Neill*	5
1979	Abandoned because of frost			
1980	Pollardstown 5-12-2: 9/4	S. Mellor	*P. Blacker*	4
1981	Celtic Ryde 6-11-12: 1/6	P. Cundell	*J. Francome*	4
1982	Heighlin 6-11-4: 8/11	D. Elsworth	*S. Jobar*	8
	(at Kempton)			
1983	Cima 5-11-4: 8/1	J. Old	*S. Morshead*	5
1984	Sula Bula 6-11-5: 5/1	M. H. Easterby	*Mr T. Easterby*	8
1985	Desert Orchid 6-11-5: 2/1	D. Elsworth	*C. Brown*	8
1986	See You Then 6-11-12: 3/1	N. Henderson	*S. Smith Eccles*	9
1987	Prideaux Boy 9-11-0: 9/4	G. Roach	*M. Bowlby*	7
1988	Celtic Chief 5-11-2: 4/1	Mrs M. Rimell	*R. Dunwoody*	7
1989	Aldino 6-10-7: 4/1	O. Sherwood	*S. Sherwood*	6
1990	Abandoned because of waterlogged state of course			
1991	Voyage Sans Retour 6-11-0: 8/1	M. Pipe	*P. Scudamore*	5
1992	Fidway 7-11-10: 9/2	T. Thomson Jones	*P. Scudamore*	6
1993	Mole Board 11-10-9: 33/1	J. Old	*C. Llewellyn*	5

MARSTON MOOR CHASE (LIMITED HANDICAP) (Wetherby 2m 5f)

1991	Katabatic 8-11-3: 4/1	A. Turnell	*S. McNeill*	8
1992	Abandoned because of frost			
1993	Armagret 8-10-7: 25/1	B. Wilkinson	*D. Byrne*	8

PHILIP CORNES SADDLE OF GOLD STAYERS' NOVICES' HURDLE FINAL (Chepstow 3m)

1977	Kas 5-10-12: 9/4	P. Ashworth	*K. Gray*	14
1978	Lighter 5-10-12: 1/1	J. Edwards	*P. Blacker*	8
1979	Quarry Stone 6-11-0: 4/1	J. Cox (Ir)	*T. McGivern*	12
1980	Woodford Prince 7-11-0: 11/2	P. Cundell	*J. Francome*	10
1981	Gaye Chance 6-11-5: 11/1	F. Rimell	*S. Morshead*	15
1982	Angelo Salvini 6-11-5: 4/1	M. H. Easterby	*S. C. Knight*	10
1983	Inish Glora 7-11-5: 5/2	G. Thorner	*R. Kington*	14
1984	Bucko 7-11-0: 7/1	J. FitzGerald	*R. O'Leary*	13
1985	Lonach 7-11-5: 7/2	G. Balding	*R. Linley*	8
1986	Pike's Peak 5-11-5: 11/8	N. Henderson	*S. Smith Eccles*	16
1987	Abandoned because of snow			
1988	Crumpet Delite 8-11-5: 4/1	Mrs J. Pitman	*M. Pitman*	13
1989	Pertemps Network 5-11-5: 4/5	M. Pipe	*P. Scudamore*	5

145

1990	Miinnehoma 7-11-5: 1/1	M. Pipe	*P. Scudamore*	6
1991	Smith's Cracker 5-11-0: 16/1	Mrs J. Pitman	*M. Pitman*	14
1992	Rothko 11-11-0: 20/1	Mrs S. Smith	*R. Guest*	10
1993	Brackenfield 7-11-5: 10/3	Mrs M. Reveley	*P. Niven*	10

BAILEYS ARKLE PERPETUAL CUP CHASE (Leopardstown 2m 3f)

1969	King's Sprite 7-11-9: 100/7	G. Wells	*P. Black*	8
1970	Not run			
1971	Dim Wit 6-11-9: 3/1	P. Mullins	*M. Curran*	7
1972	Ormond King 7-11-9: 11/5	C. Powell	*B. Hannon*	12
1973	Good Review 7-12-0: 4/9	J. Dreaper	*V. O'Brien*	4
1974	Ten Up 7-12-0: 4/7	J. Dreaper	*T. Carberry*	6
1975	Spanish Tan 7-11-6: 12/1	F. Flood	*F. Berry*	13
1976	Troubled Times 7-11-2: 6/1	P. McCreery	*D. Hughes*	6
1977	Siberian Sun 6-11-9: 9/2	F. Flood	*F. Berry*	8
1978	Kilmakillogue 9-11-2: 4/6	E. O'Grady	*Mr W. Madden*	7
1979	Chinrullah 7-11-2: 5/4	M. O'Toole	*D. Hughes*	13
1980	Anaglogs Daughter 7-10-12: 7/1	W. Durkan	*M. Mulligan*	11
1981	Light The Wad 8-11-7: 5/4	D. Hughes	*F. Leavy*	6
1982	Sean Ogue 6-11-5: 1/2	M. O'Brien	*P. Walsh*	4
1983	Pearlstone 7-10-11: 4/1	P. Mullins	*A. Mullins*	14
1984	Bobsline 8-11-9: 4/5	F. Flood	*F. Berry*	10
1985	Buck House 7-11-9: 7/4	M. Morris	*T. Carmody*	6
1986	Passage Creeper 9-10-13: 3/1	J. Dreaper	*K. Morgan*	7
1987	Barrow Line 10-12-0: 4/5	P. Hughes	*F. Berry*	10
1988	Wolf of Badenoch 7-11-6: 11/10	J. Mulhern	*T. Carmody*	5
1989	Abbenoir 7-11-6: 10/1	F. Flood	*R. Byrne*	5
1990	On The Other Hand 7-11-6: 5/2	J. Mulhern	*T. Carmody*	8
1991	Garamycin 9-11-10: 100/30	W. Deacon	*B. Sheridan*	6
1992	General Idea 7-12-0: 7/2	D. K. Weld	*B. Sheridan*	6
1993	Soft Day 8-12-0: 6/4	A. Moore	*T. Taaffe*	6

AIG EUROPE CHAMPION HURDLE (Leopardstown 2m)

1977	Master Monday 7-12-0: 20/1	L. Quirke (Ir)	*J. P. Harty*	16
1978	Prominent King 6-11-4: 6/1	K. Prendergast (Ir)	*R. Coonan*	16
1979	Connaught Ranger 5-11-5: 5/1	F. Rimell	*C. Tinkler*	12
1980	Twinburn 5-11-5: 7/4	A. Redmond (Ir)	*T. Quinn*	13
1981	Daring Run 6-11-8: 13/8	P. McCreery (Ir)	*Mr T. M. Walsh*	13
1982	Daring Run 7-12-0: 9/4	P. McCreery (Ir)	*Mr T. M. Walsh*	13
1983	Royal Vulcan 5-11-5: 2/1	N. Callaghan	*J. J. O'Neill*	7
1984	Dawn Run 6-11-9: 4/5	P. Mullins (Ir)	*J. J. O'Neill*	8
1985	Fredcoteri 9-11-4: 5/1	A. Moore (Ir)	*T. Taaffe*	8
1986	Herbert United 7-11-4: 8/1	D. McDonogh (Ir)	*H. Rogers*	11
1987	Deep Idol 7-11-9: 12/1	P. Osborne (Ir)	*B. Sheridan*	7
1988	Classical Charm 5-11-3: 9/1	J. O'Connell (Ir)	*K. Morgan*	8
1989	Kingsmill 6-11-7: 8/1	T. Stack (Ir)	*D. Murphy*	12
1990	Nomadic Way 5-11-4: 3/1	B. Hills	*B. Powell*	8
1991	Nordic Surprise 4-10-9: 10/1	J. Bolger (Ir)	*C. Swan*	6
1992	Chirkpar 5-11-7: 20/1	J. Bolger (Ir)	*L. Cusack*	9
1993	Royal Derbi 8-11-10: 14/1	N. Callaghan	*D. Murphy*	11

GAME SPIRIT CHASE (Newbury 2m 1f)

1953	Marcianus 7-11-7: 13/2	G. Beeby	*R. Francis*	8
1954	Big Bill 8-11-12: 6/4	P. P-Gallwey	*E. Fisher*	6
1955	Belliquex 6-9-12: 20/1	C. Cooper	*E. Kelly*	9
1956	Abandoned because of frost			
1957	Buttercleugh 6-11-6: 11/10	C Bewicke	*G. Milburn*	3
1958	Highland Bard 7-10-10: 9/2	C. Bewicke	*G. Milburn*	13
1959	Chatelet 7-10-0: 100/7	R. Renton	*B. Wilkinson*	13
1960	Threepwood 7-10-9: 8/1	C. Bewicke	*G. Milburn*	8
1961	Richard of Bordeaux 6-10-7: 1/1	F. Walwyn	*F. Winter*	5
1962	Sea Horse 8-11-5: 4/1	W. Marshall	*P. Jones*	10
1963	Abandoned because of snow and frost			
1964	Irish Imp 7-12-7: 4/9	F. Walwyn	*G. W. Robinson*	7
1965	Dunkirk 8-11-10: 9/2	P. Cazalet	*D. Dick*	9
1966	Flash Bulb 9-11-9: 9/2	R. Turnell	*J. Haine*	14
1967	Vulmidas 10-10-9: 6/1	J. Barclay	*Mr T. Pinner*	7
1968	Stonehaven 8-12-3: 4/1	R. Armytage	*S. Mellor*	6

146

1969	Abandoned because of frost			
1970	Abandoned because of snow and frost			
1971	Royal Relief 7-12-1: 11/4	E. Courage	*J. Cook*	6
1972	Straight Fort 9-11-3: 4/6	J. Dreaper (Ir)	*E. Wright*	3
1973	Pendil 8-12-0: 4/7	F. Winter	*R. Pitman*	8
1974	Abandoned because of waterlogged state of course			
1975	Shock Result 9-10-1: 25/1	R. Turnell	*A. Turnell*	5
1976	Uncle Bing 7-10-0: 16/1	G. Doidge	*J. Burke*	8
1977	Isle of Man 10-11-7: 5/2	F. Walwyn	*W. Smith*	6
1978	Abandoned because of frost			
1979	Casbah 12-10-5: 20/1	T. Forster	*G. Thorner*	5
1980	Gambling Prince 7-10-1: 100/30	Mrs G. Jones	*J. Suthern*	7
1981	Abandoned because of frost			
1982	News King 8-11-7: 7/4	F. Winter	*J. Francome*	5
1983	Abandoned because of snow and frost			
1984	Ragafan 7-10-7: 6/1	R. Smyth	*R. Hughes*	5
1985	Abandoned because of snow			
1986	Abandoned because of snow			
1987	Pearlyman 8-11-7: 3/1	J. Edwards	*P. Scudamore*	6
1988	Very Promising 10-11-6: 5/4	D. Nicholson	*R. Dunwoody*	5
1989	Mr Key 8-10-7: 14/1	D. Murray-Smith	*S. Sherwood*	6
1990	Feroda 9-11-2: 10/11	A. Moore (Ir)	*T. Taaffe*	4
1991	Abandoned because of frost			
1992	Waterloo Boy 9-11-10: 10/11	D. Nicholson	*R. Dunwoody*	6
1993	Waterloo Boy 10-11-7: 9/4	D. Nicholson	*R. Dunwoody*	5

ARLINGTON PREMIER SERIES CHASE FINAL (Newbury 2½m)

1989	Barnbrook Again 8-11-7: 5/2	D. Elsworth	*S. Sherwood*	4
1990	Sabin du Loir 11-11-7: 9/4	M. Pipe	*G. McCourt*	4
1991	Al Hashimi 7-11-7: 4/1	D. Nicholson	*G. McCourt*	5
1992	Remittance Man 8-11-7: 2/7	N. Henderson	*R. Dunwoody*	5
1993	Young Hustler 6-11-10: 2/1	N. Twiston-Davies	*C. Llewellyn*	9

TOTE GOLD TROPHY HANDICAP HURDLE (Newbury 2m 110yds)

1963	Rosyth 5-10-0: 20/1	R. Price	*J. Gifford*	41
1964	Rosyth 6-10-2: 10/1	R. Price	*J. Gifford*	24
1965	Elan 6-10-7: 9/2	J. Sutcliffe, jnr	*D. Nicholson*	21
1966	Le Vermontois 5-11-3: 15/2	R. Price	*J. Gifford*	28
1967	Hill House 7-10-10: 9/1	R. Price	*J. Gifford*	28
1968	Persian War 5-11-13: 9/2	C. Davies	*J. Uttley*	33
1969	Abandoned because of frost			
1970	Abandoned because of snow and frost			
1971	Cala Mesquida 7-10-9: 33/1	J. E. Sutcliffe	*J. Cook*	23
1972	Good Review 6-10-9: 8/1	J. Dreaper (Ir)	*V. O'Brien*	26
1973	Indianapolis 6-10-6: 15/2	J. E. Sutcliffe	*J. King*	26
1974	Abandoned because of waterlogged state of course			
1975	Tammuz 7-10-13: 18/1	F. Walwyn	*W. Smith*	28
1976	Irish Fashion 5-10-4: 16/1	M. Cunningham (Ir)	*R. Barry*	29
1977	True Lad 7-10-4: 14/1	W. Swainson	*T. Stack*	27
1978	Abandoned because of frost			
1979	Within The Law 5-11-4: 25/1	M. H. Easterby	*A. Brown*	28
1980	Bootlaces 6-10-9: 20/1	D. Barons	*P. Leach*	21
1981	Abandoned because of frost			
1982	Donegal Prince 6-10-8: 13/1	P. Kelleway	*J. Francome*	27
1983	Abandoned because of snow and frost			
1984	Ra Nova 5-10-6: 16/1	Mrs N. Kennedy	*P. Farrell*	26
1985	Abandoned because of snow			
1986	Abandoned because of snow			
1987	Neblin 8-10-0: 10/1	G. Balding	*S. Moore*	21
1988	Jamesmead 7-10-0: 11/1	D. Elsworth	*B. Powell*	19
1989	Grey Salute 6-11-5: 8/1	J. Jenkins	*R. Dunwoody*	10
1990	Deep Sensation 5-11-3: 7/1	J. Gifford	*R. Rowe*	17
1991	Abandoned because of frost			
1992	Rodeo Star 6-10-10: 15/2	N. Tinkler	*G. McCourt*	15
1993	King Credo 8-10-0: 10/1	S. Woodman	*A. Maguire*	16

SIDNEY BANKS MEMORIAL NOVICES HURDLE
(Huntingdon 2m 5f 110yds)

1976	Grand Canyon 6-12-0: 1/1	D. Kent	*P. Haynes*	6
1977	Abandoned because of waterlogged state of course			
1978	Abandoned because of frost			
1979	Abandoned because of waterlogged state of course			
1980	Abandoned because of flooding			
1981	Glamour Show 5-11-2: 6/1	J. Gifford	*R. Champion*	8
1982	Angelo Salvini 6-11-4: 7/1	M. H. Easterby	*A. Brown*	18
1983	Abandoned because of snow			
1984	The Pawn 5-11-2: 9/2	M. Ryan	*H. Davies*	15
1985	Sheer Gold 5-10-11: 7/4	G. Balding	*B. Reilly*	11
1986	Abandoned because of snow and frost			
1987	Robin Goodfellow 6-11-4: 7/1	G. Balding	*G. Bradley*	8
1988	Nick The Brief 6-11-4: 9/2	T. Casey	*E. Buckley*	16
1989	Celtic Barle 5-11-2: 12/1	T. Casey	*M. Lynch*	7
1990	Abandoned because of waterlogged state of course			
1991	Abandoned because of frost			
1992	Sendai 6-10-13: 11/2	J. Gifford	*D. Murphy*	9
1993	Hebridean 6-11-4: 7/2	D. Nicholson	*R. Dunwoody*	7

DAILY TELEGRAPH HURDLE (Ascot 3m)

1971	Bannon's Star 9-10-12: 12/1	J. Gifford	*D. Barrott*	8
1972	Highland Seal 9-10-12: 11/2	R. Dening	*T. Jones*	9
1973	True Luck 6-12-2: 11/10	F. Rimell	*K. White*	6
1974	Abandoned because of waterlogged state of course			
1975	Adulation 9-10-10: 7/1	D. Kent	*P. Haynes*	13
1976	Sunyboy 6-12-5: 9/4	F. Walwyn	*W. Smith*	5
1977	Garliestown 10-11-5: 14/1	M. Tate	*C. Smith*	6
1978	Abandoned because of frost			
1979	Abandoned because of frost			
1980	Ross du Vin 9-11-5: 15/2	J. Gifford	*C. Kinane*	9
1981	Richdee 5-11-12: 9/1	N. Crump	*C. Hawkins*	10
1982	Crimson Embers 7-11-5: 7/4	F. Walwyn	*S. Shilston*	8
1983	Abandoned because of frost			
1984	Mayotte 9-11-13: 11/2	R. Holder	*P. Richards*	8
1985	Rose Ravine 6-11-9: 100/30	F. Walwyn	*R. Pusey*	10
1986	King's College Boy 8-11-9: 6/1	N. Vigors	*D. Browne*	4
1987	Model Pupil 7-11-9: 9/2	O. O'Neill	*G. Bradley*	8
1988	Miss Nero 7-11-3: 7/1	R. Lee	*B. Dowling*	11
1989	Calapaez 5-11-13: 6/5	Miss B. Sanders	*S. Sherwood*	6
1990	Ryde Again 7-11-0: 11/4	P. Cundell	*G. McCourt*	11
1991	Abandoned because of frost			
1992	Floyd 12-11-10: 4/1	D. Elsworth	*G. Bradley*	4
1993	Sweet Glow 6-11-0: 4/6	M. Pipe	*P. Scudamore*	4

REYNOLDSTOWN NOVICES CHASE (Ascot 3m 110yds)

1971	Orient War 8-12-0: 6/5	F. Walwyn	*S. Mellor*	4
1972	Colebridge 8-11-11: 10/11	J. Dreaper (Ir)	*E. Wright*	5
1973	Killiney 7-12-0: 1/4	F. Winter	*R. Pitman*	3
1974	Abandoned because of waterlogged state of course			
1975	Brown Lad 9-11-9: 10/11	J. Dreaper (Ir)	*T. Carberry*	5
1976	Ghost Writer 9-12-0: 7/4	F. Walwyn	*W. Smith*	7
1977	Lanzarote 9-12-0: 4/9	F. Winter	*J. Francome*	6
1978	Abandoned because of frost			
1979	Abandoned because of snow			
1980	Little Owl 6-12-0: 11/10	M. H. Easterby	*J. J. O'Neill*	9
1981	Easter Eel 10-12-0: 8/11	F. Winter	*J. Francome*	7
1982	Richdee 6-11-10: 3/1	N. Crump	*C. Hawkins*	12
1983	Abandoned because of frost			
1984	Duke of Milan 7-11-12: 11/4	N. Gaselee	*S. Smith Eccles*	5
1985	Drumadowney 7-11-8: 3/1	T. Forster	*H. Davies*	8
1986	Bolands Cross 7-11-8: 2/1	N. Gaselee	*P. Scudamore*	7
1987	Tawridge 7-11-12: 2/1	A. Turnell	*S. C. Knight*	5
1988	Kissane 7-11-8: 4/1	J. Edwards	*T. Morgan*	6
1989	Vulgan Warrior 8-11-8: 8/1	S. Christian	*J. Osborne*	6
1990	Royal Athlete 7-11-8: 11/4	Mrs J. Pitman	*M. Pitman*	7
1991	Abandoned because of frost			

| 1992 | Danny Harrold 8-11-5: 2/1 | Mrs J. Pitman | *M. Pitman* | 3 |
| 1993 | Capability Brown 6-11-5: 11/8 | M. Pipe | *P. Scudamore* | 4 |

CRISPIN HANDICAP CHASE (Ascot 3m 110yds)

1966	Highland Wedding 9-10-12: 4/1	G. Balding	*O. McNally*	12
1967	No Race			
1968	Regal John 10-10-11: 6/1	R. Price	*J. Gifford*	7
1969	Abandoned because of frost			
1970	French Tan 8-11-9: 4/1	A. Watson (Ir)	*P. Taaffe*	8
1971	The Laird 10-11-10: 6/1	R. Turnell	*J. King*	8
1972	Prairie Dog 8-10-1: 5/1	F. Walwyn	*B. Brogan*	6
1973	Balinese 8-11-1: 5/2	R. Turnell	*A. Turnell*	6
1974	Abandoned because of waterlogged state of course			
1975	Ten Up 8-11-6: 7/4	J. Dreaper (Ir)	*T. Carberry*	8
1976	April Seventh 10-11-7: 15/8	R. Turnell	*A. Turnell*	6
1977	Ghost Writer 10-11-5: 3/1	F. Walwyn	*W. Smith*	8
1978	Abandoned because of frost			
1979	Abandoned because of snow			
1980	Master Spy 11-10-11: 9/1	T. Forster	*Mr T. Thomson Jones*	7
1981	Aldaniti 11-11-7: 14/1	J. Gifford	*R. Champion*	8
1982	Cavity Hunter 9-10-3: 5/1	M. Dickinson	*R. Earnshaw*	9
1983	Abandoned because of frost			
1984	Tracys Special 7-10-5: 100/30	A. Turnell	*S. C. Knight*	5
1985	Greenwood Lad 8-10-6: 10/1	J. Gifford	*R. Rowe*	7
1986	Brunton Park 8-10-4: 14/1	Mrs M. Dickinson	*G. Bradley*	8
1987	Castle Warden 10-9-12: 10/1	J. Edwards	*Mr M. Richards*	10
1988	Aquilifer 8-10-1: 5/2	D. Murray-Smith	*P. Croucher*	8
1989	Proud Pilgrim 10-10-9: 6/1	J. FitzGerald	*M. Dwyer*	10
1990	Ten of Spades 10-10-0: 11/2	F. Walwyn	*K. Mooney*	7
1991	Abandoned because of frost			
1992	Combermere 8-10-10: 11/4	R. Frost	*P. Scudamore*	6
1993	Very Very Ordinary 7-11-3: 15/8	J. Upson	*A. Maguire*	7

TOTE EIDER HANDICAP CHASE (Newcastle 4m 1f)

1952	Witty 7-9-8: 100/8	W. Hall	*G. Slack*	11
1953	Gigolo 8-11-7: 10/11	J. Wight	*Mr A Moralee*	7
1954	Gentle Moya 8-9-10: 7/2	C. Bewicke	*Mr J. Straker*	13
1955	Abandoned because of snow			
1956	Abandoned because of snow and frost			
1957	Wyndburgh 7-10-4: 100/8	P. Wilkinson	*M. Batchelor*	15
1958	Wyndburgh 8-11-1: 9/4	P. Wilkinson	*M. Batchelor*	10
1959	Turmoil 9-10-0: 7/1	T. Hudson	*J. Hudson*	14
1960	Abandoned because of snow and frost			
1961	Carmen IV 9-11-3: 5/1	R. Brewis	*Mr R. Brewis*	13
1962	Ballydar 9-10-10: 13/2	N. Crump	*P. Buckley*	11
1963	Abandoned because of snow and frost			
1964	Vice Regent 7-9-12: 6/1	T. Scott	*S. Hayhurst*	5
1965	Pontin-Go 13-9-9: 10/1	W. Marshall	*J. Lehane*	16
1966	Highland Wedding 9-10-11: 6/1	G. Balding	*O. McNally*	10
1967	Highland Wedding 10-12-0: 1/1	G. Balding	*O. McNally*	7
1968	Abandoned because of snow and frost			
1969	Highland Wedding 12-11-11: 7/4	G. Balding	*R. Champion*	10
1970	China Cloed 7-9-10: 7/2	K. Oliver	*P. Ennis*	8
1971	Abandoned because of waterlogged state of course			
1972	Fair Vulgan 8-9-7: 6/1	H. Bell	*M. Barnes*	8
1973	Abandoned because of snow and frost			
1974	Scarlet Letch 9-10-4: 4/1	R. Brewis	*P. Mangan*	11
1975	Abandoned because of waterlogged state of course			
1976	Forest King 7-10-0: 11/10	K. Hogg	*D. Munro*	12
1977	Set Point 9-11-11: 6/4	Lady Herries	*D. Munro*	6
1978	Abandoned because of snow			
1979	Abandoned because of frost and snow			
1980	Abandoned because of waterlogged state of course			
1981	Waggoners Walk 12-10-2: 6/1	Miss C. Mason	*R. Earnshaw*	12
1982	Lasobany 9-10-0: 5/1	H. Bell	*P. Tuck*	14
1983	Abandoned because of frost			
1984	Lucky Vane 9-10-11: 11/4	G. Balding	*J. Burke*	14
1985	Abandoned because of snow and frost			

1986	Abandoned because of snow and frost			
1987	Peaty Sandy 13-11-11: 11/4	Mrs H. Hamilton	*Mr A. Dudgeon*	9
1988	Star of Screen 8-10-7: 5/2	J. Edwards	*T. Morgan*	8
1989	Polar Nomad 8-9-11: 11/2	W. A. Stephenson	*J. O'Gorman*	10
1990	Jelupe 8-10-0: 13/2	R. Sandys-Clarke	*R. Sandys-Clarke*	13
1991	Abandoned because of snow			
1992	David's Duky 10-9-7: 16/1	A. Reid	*K. Hartnett*	13
1993	Into The Red 9-10-0: 3/1	J. White	*N. Williamson*	14

PERSIAN WAR PREMIER NOVICE HURDLE (Chepstow 2½m 110yds)

1977	The Dealer 7-12-0: 15/8	F. Winter	*J. Francome*	14
1978	Ballyfin Lake 7-11-10: 15/2	F. Winter	*J. Francome*	12
1979	Abandoned because of snow and frost			
1980	Broadleas 6-11-10: 11/4	J. Gifford	*R. Rowe*	14
1981	Abandoned because of waterlogged state of course			
1982	Arabian Music 7-11-10: 10/1	J. Gifford	*R. Rowe*	10
1983	Abandoned because of frost			
1984	Brown Trix 6-11-7: 7/1	F. Winter	*J. Francome*	10
1985	Abandoned because of snow and frost			
1986	Abandoned because of frost			
1987	Bonanza Boy 6-11-3: 11/4	P. Hobbs	*P. Hobbs*	13
1988	Sir Blake 7-11-10: 10/1	D. Elsworth	*C. Brown*	8
1989	Abandoned because of waterlogged state of course			
1990	Abandoned because of waterlogged state of course			
1991	Abandoned because of snow			
1992	Mighty Mogul 5-11-7: 11/8	Mrs J. Pitman	*M. Pitman*	6
1993	High Alltitude 5-11-9: 11/4	G. Moore	*N. Bentley*	5

TOTE CITY TRIAL HURDLE (LIMITED HANDICAP) (Nottingham 2m)

1982	Broadsword 5-11-13: 4/6	D. Nicholson	*P. Scudamore*	12
1983	Gaye Brief 6-11-7: 4/7	Mrs M. Rimell	*R. Linley*	6
1984	Desert Hero 10-11-0: 9/1	F. Walwyn	*K. Mooney*	5
1985	Abandoned because of snow			
1986	Abandoned because of snow and frost			
1987	Stepaside Lord 5-10-7: 13/2	D. Nicholson	*R. Dunwoody*	6
1988	Nos Na Gaoithe 5-11-1: 7/2	M. H. Easterby	*P. Tuck*	8
1989	Chatam 5-10-11: 6/1	M. Pipe	*J. Lower*	7
1990	Royal Derbi 5-10-7: 7/4	N. Callaghan	*H. Davies*	8
1991	Abandoned because of snow			
1992	Royal Gait 9-10-7: 10/11	J. Fanshawe	*G. McCourt*	9
1993	Coulton 6-12-0: 4/7	M. W. Easterby	*M. Dwyer*	5

NOTTINGHAMSHIRE NOVICES CHASE (Nottingham 2m)

1974	The Sundance Kid 7-11-9: 4/1	H. T. Jones	*Mr C. T. Jones*	10
1975	Traite de Paix 7-11-13: 6/1	A. Jarvis	*S. Taylor*	7
1976	Sycamore 7-11-1: 6/1	J. Gifford	*P. Blacker*	6
1977	Abandoned because of waterlogged state of course			
1978	Abandoned because of frost			
1979	Abandoned because of snow			
1980	Beacon Light 9-11-11: 4/9	R. Turnell	*A. Turnell*	5
1981	Palace Dan 5-10-7: 2/1	F. Rimell	*S. Morshead*	7
1982	Sailor's Return 6-11-11: 4/1	D. Nicholson	*P. Scudamore*	10
1983	Bold Yeoman 7-11-1: 25/1	J. Gifford	*H. Davies*	7
1984	Noddy's Ryde 7-11-10: 8/11	G. Richards	*N. Doughty*	5
1985	Abandoned because of snow			
1986	Abandoned because of snow and frost			
1987	Kouros 8-11-5: 20/1	O. Brennan	*M. Brennan*	6
1988	Danish Flight 9-11-5: 5/1	J. FitzGerald	*M. Dwyer*	4
1989	Phoenix Gold 9-11-5: 15/8	J. FitzGerald	*P. Scudamore*	6
1990	Cashew King 7-11-10: 7/4	B. McMahon	*T. Wall*	6
1991	Abandoned because of snow			
1992	Deep Sensation 7-11-12: 13/8	J. Gifford	*D. Murphy*	5
1993	Sybillin 7-11-12: 2/5	J. FitzGerald	*M. Dwyer*	5

HENNESSY COGNAC GOLD CUP CHASE (Leopardstown 3m)

1987	Forgive'N Forget 10-12-0: 5/4	J. FitzGerald	*M. Dwyer*	9
1988	Playschool 10-12-0: 2/1	D. Barons	*P. Nicholls*	5
1989	Carvill's Hill 7-12-0: 9/4	J. Dreaper (Ir)	*K. Morgan*	9

150

1990	Nick The Brief 8-12-0: 5/1	J. Upson	*M. Lynch*	6
1991	Nick The Brief 9-12-0: 11/8	J. Upson	*R. Supple*	6
1992	Carvill's Hill 10-12-0: 4/9	M. Pipe	*P. Scudamore*	10
1993	Jodami 8-12-0: 11/8	P. Beaumont	*M. Dwyer*	7

FAIRLAWNE CHASE (Windsor 3m)

1962	Hedgelands 9-11-7: 4/1	C. Mitchell	*J. Gifford*	9
1963	Certain Justice 10-11-1: 4/1	A. Neaves	*T. Baldwin*	4
1964	Sir Daniel 8-11-4: 11/10	P. Cazalet	*W. Rees*	6
1965	Anglo 7-11-2: 8/11	F. Winter	*T. Norman*	6
1966	No Race			
1967	Abandoned because of frost			
1968	Bassnet 9-11-4: 6/1	A. Kilpatrick	*D. Nicholson*	6
1969	The Laird 8-11-7: 4/5	R. Turnell	*J. King*	4
1970	Specify 8-11-4: 100/8	D. Weeden	*T. Biddlecombe*	5
1971	Into View 8-12-0: 4/9	F. Winter	*P. Kelleway*	2
1972	Cardinal Error 8-11-0: 8/1	F. Winter	*J. Francome*	5
1973	Spanish Steps 10-12-0: 7/4	E. Courage	*B. R. Davies*	3
1974	Game Spirit 8-11-4: 1/3	F. Walwyn	*T. Biddlecombe*	5
1975	Bula 10-12-0: 8/13	F. Winter	*J. Francome*	5
1976	Bula 11-12-0: —	F. Winter	*J. Francome*	2
1977	Abandoned because of waterlogged state of course			
1978	Abandoned because of frost			
1979	Joint Venture 10-11-8: 33/1	J. Old	*J. Francome*	4
1980	Border Incident 10-12-0: 4/11	R. Head	*J. Francome*	3
1981	Abandoned because of frost			
1982	Venture To Cognac 9-11-12: 11/10	F. Winter	*Mr O. Sherwood*	4
1983	Abandoned because of snow			
1984	Everett 9-11-12: 4/5	F. Walwyn	*S. Shilston*	4
1985	Abandoned because of snow and frost			
1986	Abandoned because of snow and frost			
1987	Western Sunset 11-11-12: 5/4	T. Forster	*H. Davies*	5
1988	Rhyme 'N' Reason 9-11-4: 15/8	D. Elsworth	*B. Powell*	5
1989	Bartres 10-11-8: 1/1	D. Murray-Smith	*G. Bradley*	5
1990	Abandoned because of flooding			
1991	Espy 8-11-8: 10/11	C. Brooks	*P. Scudamore*	3
1992	Toby Tobias 10-11-12: 1/2	Mrs J. Pitman	*M. Pitman*	4
1993	Zeta's Lad 10-11-4: 7/4	J. Upson	*J. Kavanagh*	5

KINGWELL HURDLE (Wincanton 2m)

1971	Bula 6-11-13: 2/5	F. Winter	*R. Pitman*	7
1972	Bula 7-12-3: 11/10	F. Winter	*P. Kelleway*	9
1973	Bula 8-12-3: 2/7	F. Winter	*P. Kelleway*	3
1974	Lanzarote 6-12-3: 1/3	F. Winter	*R. Pitman*	7
1975	Lanzarote 7-12-3: 1/4	F. Winter	*R. Pitman*	12
1976	Lanzarote 8-12-0: 1/3	F. Winter	*J. Francome*	7
1977	Dramatist 6-11-7: 4/9	F. Walwyn	*W. Smith*	7
1978	Abandoned because of snow			
1979	Western Rose 7-12-0: 11/8	F. Rimell	*C. Tinkler*	9
1980	Random Leg 5-11-5: 4/1	J. Gifford	*R. Rowe*	7
1981	Jugador 6-11-7: 15/2	D. Kent	*P. Haynes*	11
1982	Walnut Wonder 7-11-7: 4/1	D. Elsworth	*C. Brown*	6
1983	Migrator 7-11-7: 8/1	L. Kennard	*R. Linley*	14
1984	Desert Orchid 5-11-2: 2/1	D. Elsworth	*C. Brown*	9
1985	Abandoned because of snow and frost			
1986	Abandoned because of frost			
1987	Hypnosis 8-11-2: 25/1	D. Elsworth	*P. Scudamore*	6
1988	Floyd 8-11-8: 9/2	D. Elsworth	*C. Brown*	8
1989	Floyd 9-11-8: 10/11	D. Elsworth	*R. Dunwoody*	5
1990	Kribensis 6-11-12: 4/6	M. Stoute	*R. Dunwoody*	8
1991	Welsh Bard 7-11-2: 11/1	C. Brooks	*P. Scudamore*	7
1992	Fidway 7-11-10: 11/4	T. Thomson Jones	*P. Scudamore*	6
1993	Valfinet 6-11-2: 4/5	M. Pipe	*P. Scudamore*	6

REGENCY HURDLE (Warwick 2½m 110yds)

| 1991 | Run For Free 7-11-12: 6/5 | M. Pipe | *P. Scudamore* | 9 |
| 1992 | Don Valentino 7-11-5: 33/1 | Mrs J. Pitman | *M. Pitman* | 10 |

| 1993 | Flakey Dove 7-11-0: 6/5 | R. J. Price | *D. Tegg* | 4 |

COVENTRY CITY NOVICES' TRIAL HURDLE (Warwick 2½m 110yds)

1987	Wild Flyer 6-11-8: 20/1	R. Lee	*B. Dowling*	24
1988	Rebel Song 6-11-9: 5/2	O. Sherwood	*S. Sherwood*	9
1989	Sayfar's Lad 5-11-9: 9/4	M. Pipe	*P. Scudamore*	7
1990	Run For Free 6-11-12: 5/2	M. Pipe	*P. Scudamore*	8
1991	Better Times Ahead 5-11-6: 12/1	G. Richards	*G. McCourt*	11
1992	Thetford Forest 5-12-0: 7/4	D. Nicholson	*R. Dunwoody*	8
1993	Trainglot 6-11-2: 2/7	J. FitzGerald	*M. Dwyer*	3

MITSUBISHI SHOGUN 'PENDIL' TROPHY (NOVICES' CHASE)
(Kempton 2½m 110yds)

1965	Solbina 8-12-7: 1/1	F. Winter	*E. Harty*	3
1966	Stalbridge Colonist 7-12-0: 11/10	K. Cundell	*S. Mellor*	4
1967	China 6-11-5: 11/2	H. Nicholson	*D. Nicholson*	6
1968	Vital Moment 5-11-10: 9/2	F. Winter	*E. Harty*	6
1969	Charter Flight 7-11-5: 6/1	R. Turnell	*J. King*	9
1970	Into View 7-11-8: 11/10	F. Winter	*P. Kelleway*	3
1971	Stradivarius 7-11-3: 6/1	L. Kennard	*W. Smith*	5
1972	Pendil 7-11-12: 8/11	F. Winter	*R. Pitman*	6
1973	Cinvultrist 7-10-11: 7/2	G. Bach	*G. McNally*	6
1974	(D.1) Merry Maker 9-11-0: 7/1	G. Doidge	*Mr A. Mildmay-White*	8
	(D.2) Remigio 6-10-9: 10/1	J. O'Donoghue	*C. Goldsworthy*	9
1975	Uncle Byng 6-11-5: 5/2	G. Doidge	*S. May*	14
1976	Brawny Scot 6-11-0: 1/1	F. Winter	*J. Francome*	2
1977	Young Arthur 8-11-0: 5/1	D. Kent	*W. Smith*	14
1978	Dyscole 6-11-10: 7/4	D. Kent	*P. Haynes*	7
1979	Dramatist 8-11-10: 8/13	F. Walwyn	*W. Smith*	14
1980	Doddington Park 7-11-7: 15/8	N. Gaselee	*J. King*	5
1981	Balmers Coombe 9-11-0: 66/1	N. Mitchell	*Mr O. Sherwood*	8
1982	Water Rock 7-11-0: 9/1	J. Thorne	*R. Hoare*	8
1983	Branding Iron 6-11-7: 4/5	M. Dickinson	*R. Earnshaw*	13
1984	Mossy Moore 8-11-7: 4/1	B. Chinn	*J. Francome*	15
1985	Abandoned because of frost			
1986	Abandoned because of frost			
1987	Panto Prince 6-11-7: 10/11	L. Kennard	*B. Powell*	7
1988	Saffron Lord 6-11-9: 13/8	J. Gifford	*R. Rowe*	5
1989	Brookmount 7-11-9: 2/1	J. Gifford	*P. Hobbs*	8
1990	Combermere 6-11-4: 4/7	R Frost	*J. Frost*	3
1991	Remittance Man 7-11-7: 100/30	N. Henderson	*R. Dunwoody*	8
1992	Tinryland 8-11-3: 15/8	N. Henderson	*J. Osborne*	7
1993	Snitton Lane 7-10-12: 15/8	J. Edwards	*R. Dunwoody*	4

RACING POST HANDICAP CHASE (Kempton 3m)

1949	Royal Mount 10-11-5: 15/8	J. Powell	*P. Doyle*	5
1950	Printers Pie 6-11-2: 4/1	G. Wilson	*I. Stephens*	7
1951	Cadamstown 11-10-9: 6/1	V. Brunt	*J. Dowdeswell*	7
1952	Mont Tremblant 6-11-5: 6/4	F. Walwyn	*D. Dick*	7
1953	Wigby 7-11-0: 5/2	F. Cundell	*R. Francis*	4
1954	Claude Duval 9-10-13: 7/2	P. Thrale	*J. Beasty*	5
1955	Halloween 10-12-6: 11/10	W. Wightman	*F. Winter*	5
1956	Abandoned because of snow and frost			
1957	Pointsman 9-12-1: 3/1	A. Kilpatrick	*R. Morrow*	7
1958	Lochroe 10-11-13: 9/4	P. Cazalet	*Mr E. Cazalet*	5
1959	Stanton Johnie 9-9-12: 20/1	D. Ancil	*R. Hirons*	3
1960	Dandy Scot 10-11-4: 4/11	R. Price	*F. Winter*	4
1961	Pouding 8-10-8: 7/4	F. Walwyn	*F. Winter*	6
1962	Frenchman's Cove 7-11-13: 4/5	H. T. Jones	*S. Mellor*	4
1963	Dark Venetian 8-10-10: 6/1	R. Bassett	*D. Bassett*	7
1964	Abandoned because of frost			
1965	The Rip 10-12-0: 7/4	P. Cazalet	*D. Dick*	6
1966	Kapeno 9-11-1: 100/30	P. Cazalet	*D. Mould*	9
1967	Maigret 10-10-4: 9/1	I. Herbert	*J. Haine*	5
1968	Different Class 8-11-9: 30/100	P. Cazalet	*D. Mould*	2
1969	Bassnet 10-11-9: 3/1	R. Price	*J. Gifford*	8
1970	Titus Oates 8-11-12: 3/1	G. Richards	*S. Mellor*	9
1971	The Laird 10-11-0: 11/8	R. Turnell	*J. King*	3

1972 Crisp 9-12-0: 9/4	F. Winter	*R. Pitman*	5
1973 Pendil 8-12-0: 1/7	F. Winter	*R. Pitman*	3
1974 Pendil 9-12-0: 1/6	F. Winter	*R. Pitman*	3
1975 Cuckolder 10-10-0: 6/1	R. Turnell	*A. Turnell*	5
1976 Canadius 7-10-9: 4/1	G. Richards	*J. J. O'Neill*	4
1977 Don't Hesitate 7-9-9: 20/1	P. Cundell	*M. O'Halloran*	7
1978 Fort Devon 12-12-0: 10/11	F. Walwyn	*W. Smith*	5
1979 Strombolus 8-10-10: 16/1	P. Bailey	*R. Champion*	14
1980 Father Delaney 8-10-11: 9/1	M. H. Easterby	*A. Brown*	10
1981 Sugarally 8-10-0: 9/2	G. Fairbairn	*P. Scudamore*	8
1982 Two Swallows 9-10-9: 6/1	R. Armytage	*A. Webber*	7
1983 Manton Castle 9-11-7: 15/2	J. Gifford	*H. Davies*	10
1984 Tom's Little Al 8-10-3: 6/1	W. R. Williams	*C. Brown*	10
1985 Abandoned because of frost			
1986 Abandoned because of frost			
1987 Combs Ditch 11-11-7: 11/10	D. Elsworth	*C. Brown*	4
1988 Rhyme 'N' Reason 9-10-11: 7/2	D. Elsworth	*B. Powell*	12
1989 Bonanza Boy 8-11-1: 5/1	M. Pipe	*P. Scudamore*	11
1990 Desert Orchid 11-12-3: 8/11	D. Elsworth	*R. Dunwoody*	8
1991 Docklands Express 9-10-7: 7/2	K. Bailey	*A. Tory*	9
1992 Docklands Express 10-11-10: 6/1	K. Bailey	*A. Tory*	11
1993 Zeta's Lad 10-10-10: 11/1	J. Upson	*J. White*	12

TOTE PLACEPOT HURDLE (4-y-o) (Kempton 2m)

1965 Bronzino 10-10: 11/2	G. Todd	*R. Broadway*	10
1966 Harwell 11-10: 11/10	A. Thomas	*H. Beasley*	12
1967 Acrania 11-1: 20/1	G. Harwood	*H. Beasley*	16
1968 St Cuthbert 11-3: 9/4	F. Rimell	*T. Biddlecombe*	12
1969 Rabble Rouser 10-10: 25/1	R. Akehurst	*R. Atkins*	25
1970 Frozen Alive 11-5: 7/2	H. T. Jones	*S. Mellor*	15
1971 Melody Rock 11-3: 11/8	R. Price	*T. Biddlecombe*	7
1972 Official 11-8: 4/1	G. Balding	*R. Bailey*	12
1973 Padlocked 11-8: 6/4	R. Price	*P. Kelleway*	10
1974 Supreme Halo 11-8: 6/1	R. Smyth	*J. King*	26
1975 Wovoka 11-1: 14/1	I. Dudgeon	*R. Floyd*	14
1976 Soldier Rose 10-13: 2/1	R. Price	*P. Kelleway*	14
1977 Rathconrath 10-10: 3/1	F. Winter	*J. Francome*	13
1978 Bootlaces 10-10: 10/1	D. Barons	*P. Leach*	16
1979 Pollardstown 11-3: 13/8	S. Mellor	*P. Blacker*	11
1980 Hill of Slane 11-3: 2/1	A. Jarvis	*A. Turnell*	7
1981 Ra Tapu 10-10: 12/1	P. Mitchell	*R. Hughes*	12
1982 Morice 10-10: 4/1	R. Hannon	*A. Turnell*	8
1983 Jorge Miguel 10-0: 10/1	G. Pritchard-Gordon	*R. Earnshaw*	15
1984 Clarinbridge 10-10: 11/4	J. Bolger (Ir)	*B. Nolan*	11
1985 Abandoned because of frost			
1986 Abandoned because of frost			
1987 Framlington Court 10-10: 6/1	P. Walwyn	*D. Browne*	10
1988 Russian Affair 11-0: 7/1	R. Akehurst	*D. McKeown*	12
1989 Royal Derbi 11-3: 10/1	N. Callaghan	*H. Davies*	6
1990 Philosophos 11-0: 33/1	J. Baker	*W. McFarland*	11
1991 Marlingford 10-12: 20/1	Mrs J. Jordan	*D. Morris*	7
1992 Qualitair Sound 10-12: 11/1	J. Bottomley	*J. Quinn*	8
1993 Amazon Express 10-12: 12/1	R. Akehurst	*J. Osborne*	12

RENDLESHAM HURDLE (Kempton 3m 110yds)

1980 Derring Rose 5-10-11: 50/1	A. Jarvis	*A. Turnell*	6
1981 Derring Rose 6-11-6: 11/10	F. Winter	*J. Francome*	7
1982 Hill of Slane 6-11-3: 7/2	A. Jarvis	*A. Turnell*	10
1983 Mellie 8-11-7: 33/1	R. Blakeney	*S. Morshead*	15
1984 Gaye Chance 9-11-5: 4/6	Mrs M. Rimell	*S. Morshead*	6
1985 Abandoned because of frost			
1986 Abandoned because of frost			
1987 Aonoch 8-12-0: 6/4	Mrs S. Oliver	*J. Duggan*	9
1988 King's College Boy 10-11-5: 15/8	Mrs M. Dickinson	*G. Bradley*	8
1989 Cliffalda 6-11-9: 11/4	J. Edwards	*T. Morgan*	5
1990 Old Dundalk 6-11-3: 33/1	D. Murray-Smith	*M. Bowlby*	7
1991 Floyd 11-11-12: 11/2	D. Elsworth	*G. Bradley*	10
1992 Forest Sun 7-11-5: 6/1	G. Balding	*J. Frost*	6

153

1993 Baydon Star 6-11-9: 10/11   D. Nicholson   *R. Dunwoody*   4

CAVALIER CHASE (Worcester 2½m 110yds)

1991 Sabin du Loir 12-11-10: 4/6	M. Pipe	*P. Scudamore*	8
1992 Star's Delight 10-11-3: 2/1	M. Pipe	*P. Scudamore*	3
1993 The Illywhacker 8-11-10: 5/2	Mrs J. Pitman	*M. Pitman*	4

VICTOR LUDORUM HURDLE (4-y-o) (Haydock 2m)

1962 Pillock's Green 10-13: 5/1	F. Rimell	*H. Beasley*	9
1963 Abandoned because of frost			
1964 Makaldar 11-3: 8/11	P. Cazalet	*D. Mould*	11
1965 Anselmo 11-3: 13/8	K. Piggott	*T. Carberry*	15
1966 Harwell 11-3: 4/9	A. Thomas	*H. Beasley*	9
1967 Persian War 11-3: 5/4	B. Swift	*J. Uttley*	9
1968 Wing Master 11-3: 8/1	J. Bower	*R. Reid*	6
1969 Coral Diver 11-0: 7/2	F. Rimell	*T. Biddlecombe*	11
1970 Abandoned because of snow and frost			
1971 Nerak 11-0: 3/1	S. Norton	*S. A. Taylor*	13
1972 North Pole 11-0: 100/30	F. Rimell	*K. White*	7
1973 Mythical King 11-4: 5/1	J. Gifford	*D. Barrott*	13
1974 Relevant 11-4: 10/1	R. Edwards	*G. Griffin*	15
1975 Zip Fastener 11-4: 5/1	F. Rimell	*J. King*	11
1976 Sweet Joe 11-9: 5/1	H. T. Jones	*I. Watkinson*	11
1977 Rathconrath 11-9: 7/2	F. Winter	*J. Francome*	12
1978 Mixed Melody 11-4: 12/1	G. Richards	*D. Goulding*	13
1979 Exalted 11-4: 5/2	J. Bolger (Ir)	*J. P. Harty*	13
1980 Jubilee Saint 11-4: 6/1	Miss S. Hall	*D. Goulding*	8
1981 Abandoned because of waterlogged state of course			
1982 Azaam 11-4: 14/1	R. Fisher	*D. Goulding*	11
1983 Wollow Will 11-9: 8/13	F. Winter	*J. Francome*	8
1984 Childown 11-9: 9/4	N. Henderson	*S. Smith Eccles*	11
1985 Wing And A Prayer 11-10: 4/7	J. Jenkins	*J. Francome*	8
1986 Abandoned because of frost			
1987 Cashew King 11-4: 10/1	B. McMahon	*T. Wall*	6
1988 Royal Illusion 11-10: 20/1	G. Moore	*M. Hammond*	13
1989 Liadett 11-10: 7/4	M. Pipe	*J. Lower*	7
1990 Ninja 11-4: 5/1	D. Nicholson	*R. Dunwoody*	5
1991 Reve de Valse 11-4: 2/1	D. Smith	*G. Moore*	8
1992 Snowy Lane 11-4: 8/1	M. Pipe	*P. Scudamore*	6
1993 Bold Boss 11-10: 7/2	G. Moore	*M. Dwyer*	7

EAST LANCS CHASE (Haydock 2½m)

1981 Little Owl 7-11-10: 4/5	M. H. Easterby	*Mr A. J. Wilson*	4
1982 Wayward Lad 7-11-12: 2/5	M. Dickinson	*R. Earnshaw*	4
1983 Fifty Dollars More 8-11-8: 13/8	F. Winter	*R. Linley*	4
1984 Forgive'N Forget 7-11-0: 5/2	J. FitzGerald	*M. Dwyer*	6
1985 Forgive'N Forget 8-11-8: 4/7	J. FitzGerald	*M. Dwyer*	7
1986 Abandoned because of frost			
1987 Abandoned because of snow			
1988 Raise An Argument 9-11-4: 7/2	Mrs M. Dickinson	*J. Osborne*	7
1989 Southern Minstrel 6-11-0: 1/1	W. A. Stephenson	*A. Merrigan*	3
1990 Tartan Takeover 8-11-0: 2/1	G. Richards	*M. Dwyer*	5
1991 Carrick Hill Lad 8-11-6: 4/6	G. Richards	*N. Doughty*	4
1992 Last 'o' The Bunch 8-11-4: 5/1	G. Richards	*N. Doughty*	5
1993 Gale Again 6-11-4: 9/4	P. Cheesborough	*K. Johnson*	5

GREENALLS GOLD CUP (HANDICAP CHASE) (Haydock 3½m 110yds)

1968 Half Awake 8-10-13: 7/2	D. Thomson	*T. Stack*	9
1969 Two Springs 7-10-4: 5/1	G. Owen	*R. Edwards*	6
1970 Abandoned because of snow and frost			
1971 Rainbow Valley 8-10-13: 7/2	A. Dickinson	*M. Dickinson*	6
1972 Young Ash Leaf 8-11-8: 6/1	K. Oliver	*T. Stack*	9
1973 Tregarron 6-10-6: 7/1	K. Oliver	*C. Tinkler*	11
1974 Glanford Brigg 8-10-7: 4/1	J. Hardy	*S. Holland*	12
1975 The Benign Bishop 8-11-8: 4/1	K. Oliver	*R. Barry*	6
1976 Royal Frolic 7-10-12: 3/1	F. Rimell	*Mr S. Morshead*	7
1977 General Moselle 8-10-3: 15/2	H. Wharton	*I. Watkinson*	10
1978 Rambling Artist 8-10-6: 3/1	T. Gillam	*J. J. O'Neill*	8

1979	Alverton 9-11-5: 2/1	M. H. Easterby	*J. J. O'Neill*	13
1980	Cavity Hunter 7-11-1: 4/1	A. Dickinson	*R. Lamb*	9
1981	Sunset Cristo 7-11-7: 5/1	R. Hawkey	*C. Grant*	8
1982	Scot Lane 9-10-0: 14/1	M. Tate	*C. Smith*	12
1983	Righthand Man 6-10-9: 9/4	M. Dickinson	*R. Earnshaw*	10
1984	Midnight Love 9-10-3: 14/1	D. Smith	*C. Grant*	10
1985	Earls Brig 10-10-6: 3/1	W. Hamilton	*P. Tuck*	9
1986	Abandoned because of frost			
1987	Abandoned because of snow			
1988	Yahoo 7-10-10: 11/4	J. Edwards	*T. Morgan*	8
1989	Eton Rouge 10-10-1: 11/2	Mrs M. Rimell	*J. Bryan*	4
1990	Rinus 9-10-4: 11/2	G. Richards	*R. Dunwoody*	11
1991	Twin Oaks 11-11-0: 7/4	G. Richards	*N. Doughty*	15
1992	Cool Ground 10-11-3: 12/1	G. Balding	*A. Maguire*	11
1993	Party Politics 9-11-7: 16/1	N. Gaselee	*C. Llewellyn*	9

BERKSHIRE HURDLE (Newbury 2m 5f)

1991	Morley Street 7-11-12: 8/11	G. Balding	*J. Frost*	6
1992	Crystal Spirit 5-11-12: 11/10	I. Balding	*J. Frost*	8
1993	Lift And Load 6-11-12: 9/2	R. Hannon	*D. Murphy*	5

SUNDERLANDS IMPERIAL CUP HANDICAP HURDLE
(Sandown 2m 110yds)

1947	Tant Pis 5-9-10: 20/1	J. Goldsmith	*H. Nicholson*	33
1948	Anglesey 6-11-8: 4/1	S. Ingham	*J. Gilbert*	12
1949	Secret Service 6-11-11: 20/1	F. Walwyn	*J. Gilbert*	17
1950	Secret Service 7-11-10: 100/8	F. Walwyn	*T. Cusack*	13
1951	Master Bidar 6-10-11: 100/7	R. Smyth	*R. Emery*	21
1952	High Point 6-10-4: 10/1	J. Dennistoun	*H. Sprague*	19
1953	High Point 7-10-7: 10/1	J. Dennistoun	*H. Sprague*	19
1954	The Pills 6-10-5: 20/1	P. Rice-Stringer	*J. Dowdeswell*	26
1955	Bon Mot II 6-10-11: 11/2	S. Wootton	*M. Haynes*	32
1956	Peggy Jones 6-10-10: 100/9	S. Palmer	*A. Oughton*	22
1957	Camugliano 7-10-10: 20/1	H. T. Smith	*R. Emery*	29
1958	Flaming East 9-10-5: 100/9	G. Vallance	*Mr J. Lawrence*	23
1959	Langton Heath 5-10-9: 100/6	T. Griffiths	*R. Martin*	21
1960	Farmer's Boy 7-11-7: 25/1	W. Stephenson	*D. Nicholson*	20
1961	Fidus Achates 6-10-4: 25/1	M. James	*C. Chapman*	23
1962	Irish Imp 5-10-12: 10/1	R. Smyth	*G. Ramshaw*	26
1963	Antiar 5-11-2: 7/1	P. Cazalet	*D. Mould*	21
1964	Invader 6-11-4: 6/1	L. Dale	*T. M. Jones*	15
1965	Kildavin 7-10-7: 100/7	J. Sutcliffe, jnr	*J. King*	19
1966	Royal Sanction 7-10-1: 10/1	F. Winter	*R. Pitman*	18
1967	Sir Thopas 6-11-8: 100/9	R. Turnell	*J. Haine*	20
1968	Persian Empire 5-11-4: 4/1	C. Davies	*B. Scott*	18
1969	Abandoned because of waterlogged state of course			
1970	Solomon II 6-11-1: 11/2	D. Barons	*B. R. Davies*	17
1971	Churchwood 7-11-3: 10/1	M. Goswell	*D. Barrott*	12
1972	Spy Net 5-10-0: 15/1	L. Dale	*G. Lawson*	18
1973	Lanzarote 5-12-4: 5/2	F. Winter	*R. Pitman*	14
1974	Flash Imp 5-10-9: 5/1	R. Smyth	*J. King*	17
1975	Abandoned because of waterlogged state of course			
1976	Nougat 6-10-6: 7/1	J. Gifford	*G. Enright*	11
1977	Acquaint 6-11-2: 16/1	F. Winter	*Mr N. Henderson*	20
1978	Winter Melody 7-11-3: 12/1	J. Hanson	*W. Smith*	15
1979	Flying Diplomat 8-10-6: 5/1	A. Smith	*Mr T. Thomson Jones*	9
1980	Prayukta 5-11-0: 14/1	F. Winter	*J. Francome*	16
1981	Ekbalco 5-11-3: 8/1	R. Fisher	*D. Goulding*	14
1982	Holemoor Star 5-11-7: 2/1	Miss S. Morris	*M. O'Halloran*	7
	(at Kempton)			
1983	Desert Hero 9-9-8: 20/1	F. Walwyn	*R. Chapman*	16
1984	Dalbury 6-9-12: 9/2	P. Haynes	*P. Corrigan*	13
1985	Floyd 5-10-3: 13/8	D. Elsworth	*C. Brown*	16
1986	Insular 6-9-10: 14/1	I. Balding	*E. Murphy*	19
1987	Inlander 6-10-3: 10/1	R. Akehurst	*S. Smith Eccles*	23
1988	Sprowston Boy 5-10-11: 10/1	P. Kelleway	*S. McCrystal*	15
1989	Travel Mystery 6-10-0: 3/1	M. Pipe	*P. Scudamore*	8
1990	Moody Man 5-10-13: 20/1	P. J. Hobbs	*P. Hobbs*	15

1991	Precious Boy 5-10-6: 16/1	M. O'Neill	*L. Wyer*	13
1992	King Credo 7-10-4: 9/2	S. Woodman	*A. Maguire*	10
1993	Olympian 6-10-0: 6/4	M. Pipe	*P. Scudamore*	15

BEAUFORT HURDLE (5-y-o) (Chepstow 2m 110yds)

1971	Killiney 11-0: 5/2	F. Winter	*E. P. Harty*	8
1972	Celtic Cone 11-0: 4/6	F. Cundell	*A. Turnell*	13
1973	Dark Sultan 11-0: 5/4	P. Chisman	*R. Barry*	8
1974	True Song 11-0: 7/1	D. Underwood	*G. Old*	13
1975	Border Incident 11-0: 7/4	R. Head	*J. Francome*	10
1976	Winter Melody 11-0: 15/2	J. Hanson	*A. Bowker*	15
1977	French Hollow 11-0: 6/4	A. Dickinson	*M. Dickinson*	17
1978	Gruffandgrim 11-0: 5/1	F. Winter	*J. Guest*	9
1979	Applalto 11-0: 10/1	R. Armytage	*H. J. Davies*	8
1980	Run Hard 11-0: 7/2	R. Turnell	*S. C. Knight*	9
1981	Passing Parade 11-0: 5/2	M. O'Toole (Ir)	*P. Scudamore*	11
1982	Gaye Brief 11-0: 1/1	Mrs M. Rimell	*P. Scudamore*	8
1983	Very Promising 11-0: 100/30	Mrs M. Rimell	*S. Morshead*	12
1984	Aonoch 11-0: 4/5	R. Fisher	*J. Duggan*	10
1985	Maganyos 11-0: 17/2	N. Henderson	*S. SmithEccles*	8
1986	Canute Express 11-5: 5/4	H. Scott (Ir)	*Mr L. Wyer*	12
1987	Positive 11-5: 8/1	K. Bailey	*P. Croucher*	7
1988	Rymster 11-5: 9/4	N. Henderson	*G. McCourt*	12
1989	Dis Train 11-5: 4/1	Mrs J. Pitman	*M. Pitman*	6
1990	Sacre d'Or 11-5: 14/1	J. Mackie	*S. O'Neill*	12
1991	Mudahim 11-5: 40/1	C. Broad	*D. Tegg*	11
1992	Carobee 11-5: 6/4	D. Nicholson	*R. Dunwoody*	6
1993	Winter Squall 5-11-5: 5/4	D. Nicholson	*R. Dunwoody*	8

TRAFALGAR HOUSE SUPREME NOVICES' HURDLE

(Cheltenham 2m 110yds)

1948	(D.1) Vulgan 5-10-10: 9/2	J. de Moraville	*R. Black*	13
	(D.2) Jean's Last 6-11-0: 7/4	F. Walwyn	*B. Marshall*	21
1949	(D.1) French Wedding 4-10-7: 11/2	G. Wilson	*J. Brogan*	14
	(D.2) Tough Guy 4-10-0: 4/1	I. Anthony	*D. Dillon*	18
1950	(D.1) Tsaoko 5-11-8 4/9	F. Armstrong	*M. Molony*	9
	(D.2) Sir Charles 4-10-4: 25/1	J. Scudamore	*Mr M. Scudamore*	15
1951	(D.1) Red Stanger 4-10-12: 100/8	R. Smyth	*D. Dillon*	20
	(D.2) Oukilele II 4-10-12: 6/1	G. Archibald	*F. Winter*	13
1952	(D.1) Cockatoo 6-11-3: 4/1	M. V. O'Brien (Ir)	*Mr A. O'Brien*	13
	(D.2) Evian 4-10-7: 10/1	G. Archibald	*F. Winter*	14
1953	(D.1) Assynt 5-11-1: 9/4	D. Morgan (Ir)	*E. Newman*	18
	(D.2) Dessin 7-11-8: 100/9	F. Hudson	*J. Gilbert*	17
1954	(D.1) Stroller 6-11-8: 13/8	M. V. O'Brien (Ir)	*P. Taaffe*	18
	(D.2) Tasmin 4-10-7: 5/1	M. Count (Fr)	*R. Emery*	18
1955	(D.1) Vindore 6-11-12: 1/1	M. V. O'Brien (Ir)	*Mr A. O'Brien*	19
	(D.2) Illyric 6-11-8: 3/1	M. V. O'Brien (Ir)	*T. P. Burns*	23
1956	(D.1) Boy's Hurrah 8-11-8: 9/4	M. V. O'Brien (Ir)	*T. P. Burns*	17
	(D.2) Pelargos 5-11-6: 6/4	M. V. O'Brien (Ir)	*T. P. Burns*	22
1957	(D.1) Tokoroa 6-12-1: 5/4	F. Rimell	*D. Dick*	10
	(D.2) Saffron Tartan 6-11-8: 10/11	M. V. O'Brien (Ir)	*T. P. Burns*	12
1958	(D.1) Admiral Stuart 7-11-12: 6/5	M. V. O'Brien (Ir)	*T. P. Burns*	19
	(D.2) Prudent King 6-11-8: 3/1	M. V. O'Brien (Ir)	*T. P. Burns*	19
1959	(D.1) York Fair 5-11-10: 4/5	M. V. O'Brien (Ir)	*T. P. Burns*	16
	(D.2) Albergo 5-11-6: 9/1	C. Magnier (Ir)	*D. Page*	19
1960	(D.1) Blue Mountain 6-11-8: 5/1	G. Todd	*R. Broadway*	20
	(D.2) Bastille 5-11-6: 33/1	T. Masson	*W. Woods*	18
1961	(D.1) Beau Normand 5-11-6: 5/1	R. Turnell	*W. Rees*	18
	(D.2) Greektown 5-12-2: 100/8	W. Stephenson	*M. Scudamore*	15
1962	(D.1) Tripacer 4-10-12 : 20/1	D. L. Moore (Ir)	*T. Carberry*	18
	(D.2) Clerical Grey 4-11-12: 100/8	P. Murphy (Ir)	*G. W. Robinson*	18
1963	(D.1) Honour Bound 5-11-10: 3/1	F. Rimell	*T. Biddlecombe*	18
	(D.2) Buona notte 6-11-8: 7/2	R. Turnell	*J. Haine*	15
	(D.3) Deetease 5-12-2: 9/1	B. Foster	*C. Chapman*	18
1964	(D.1) Flyingbolt 5-12-2: 4/9	T. Dreaper (Ir)	*P. Taaffe*	11

156

(D.2) Elan 5-12-2: 9/2	J. Sutcliffe, jnr	*D. Dick*	18
1965 (D.1) Red Tears 5-11-6: 7/1	H. T. Jones	*S. Mellor*	19
(D.2) Havago 6-12-4: 11/8	P. Sleator (Ir)	*H. Beasley*	15
1966 (D.1) Beau Caprice 12-12-2: 6/1	F. Walwyn	*T. Jennings*	14
(D.2) Fosco 5-11-6: 7/2	M. Goswell	*D. Moore*	19
1967 (D.1) Chorus 6-11-12: 15/2	H. T. Jones	*J. Haine*	20
(D.2) Early To Rise 7-11-12: 11/2	R. Turnell	*J. King*	14
1968 (D.1) King Cutler 5-12-0: 85/40	Denys Smith	*B. Fletcher*	12
(D.2) L'Escargot 5-12-4: 13/2	D. L. Moore (Ir)	*T. Carberry*	11
1969 (D.1) Normandy 4-11-2: 10/1	F. Rimell	*T. Biddlecombe*	28
(D.2) Private Room 5-11-10: 10/1	F. Walwyn	*G. W. Robinson*	20
1970 (D.1) Ballywilliam Boy 5-12-0: 4/1	P. Sleator (Ir)	*R. Coonan*	20
(D.2) Bula 5-12-0: 3/1	F. Winter	*P. Kelleway*	21
1971 (D.1) Persian Majesty 4-10-13: 13/2	R. Price	*T. Biddlecombe*	10
(D.2) Barnard 7-12-0: 4/1	F. Walwyn	*J. Haine*	13
1972 Noble Life 5-11-6: 16/1	C. Grassick (Ir)	*T. Murphy*	18
1973 King Pele 4-10-10: 13/2	G. P-Gordon	*D. Nicholson*	20
1974 Avec Moi 5-11-6: 5/4	Miss A. Sinclair	*R. Rowell*	16
1975 Bannow Rambler 6-11-8: 9/2	P. Berry (Ir)	*F. Berry*	18
1976 Beacon Light 5-11-8: 14/1	R. Turnell	*A. Turnell*	11
1977 Mac's Chariot 6-11-8: 7/1	M. O'Toole (Ir)	*D. T. Hughes*	16
1978 Golden Cygnet 6-11-8: 4/5	E. O'Grady (Ir)	*Mr N. Madden*	18
1979 Stranfield 6-11-8: 16/1	D. McDonogh (Ir)	*T. Kinane*	16
1980 Slaney Idol 5-11-8: 9/1	L. Browne (Ir)	*T. Carmody*	27
1981 Hartstown 6-11-8: 2/1	M. O'Toole (Ir)	*N. Madden*	16
1982 Miller Hill 6-11-8: 20/1	D. Hughes (Ir)	*T. Morgan*	19
1983 Buck House 5-11-8: 8/1	M. Morris (Ir)	*T. Carmody*	22
1984 Browne's Gazette 6-11-8: 11/2	M. Dickinson	*Mr D. Browne*	18
1985 Harry Hastings 6-11-8: 14/1	J. S. Wilson	*C. Grant*	30
1986 River Ceiriog 5-11-8: 40/1	N. Henderson	*S. Smith Eccles*	29
1987 Tartan Tailor 6-11-8: 14/1	G. Richards	*P. Tuck*	20
1988 Vagador 5-11-8: 4/1	G. Harwood	*M. Perrett*	26
1989 Sondrio 8-11-8: 25/1	M. Pipe	*J. Lower*	21
1990 Forest Sun 5-11-8: 7/4	G. Balding	*J. Frost*	18
1991 Destriero 5-11-8: 6/1	A. Geraghty (Ir)	*P. McWilliams*	21
1992 Flown 5-11-8: 13/2	N. Henderson	*J. Osborne*	17
1993 Montelado 6-11-8: 5/1	P. Flynn (Ir)	*C. Swan*	15

WATERFORD CASTLE ARKLE CHALLENGE TROPHY CHASE

(Cheltenham 2m)

1969 Chatham 5-11-0: 10/1	F. Rimell	*T. Biddlecombe*	10
1970 Soloning 5-11-0: 4/1	F. Winter	*P. Kelleway*	13
1971 Alpheus 6-11-8: 15/1	T. Dreaper (Ir)	*E. Wright*	11
1972 Pendil 7-12-1: 10/11	F. Winter	*R. Pitman*	10
1973 Denys Adventure 8-12-1: 8/1	T. Forster	*G. Thorner*	10
1974 Canasta Lad 8-11-11: 2/1	P. Bailey	*J. King*	10
1975 Broncho 6-11-11: 8/1	A. Dickinson	*C. Tinkler*	12
1976 Roaring Wind 8-11-8: 11/1	R. Cambidge	*R. Crank*	16
1977 Tip the Wink 7-11-8: 15/2	P. Taylor	*D. T. Hughes*	10
1978 Alverton 8-11-8: 5/2	M. H. Easterby	*G. Thorner*	12
1979 Chinrullah 7-11-8: 10/11	M. O'Toole (Ir)	*D. T. Hughes*	8
1980 Anaglogs Daughter 7-11-8: 9/4	W. Durkan (Ir)	*T. Carberry*	9
1981 Clayside 7-11-8: 5/2	M. H. Easterby	*A. Brown*	13
1982 The Brockshee 7-11-8: 12/1	A. Moore (Ir)	*T. Carberry*	19
1983 Ryeman 6-11-8: 16/1	M. H. Easterby	*A. Brown*	16
1984 Bobsline 8-11-8: 5/4	F. Flood (Ir)	*F. Berry*	8
1985 Boreen Prince 8-11-8: 15/2	A. McNamara (Ir)	*N. Madden*	16
1986 Oregon Trail 6-11-8: 14/1	S. Christian	*R. Beggan*	14
1987 Gala's Image 7-11-8: 25/1	Mrs M. Rimell	*R. Linley*	19
1988 Danish Flight 9-11-8: 11/2	J. FitzGerald	*M. Dwyer*	12
1989 Waterloo Boy 6-11-8: 20/1	D. Nicholson	*R. Dunwoody*	14
1990 Comandante 8-11-8: 9/2	J. Gifford	*P. Hobbs*	14
1991 Remittance Man 7-11-8: 85/40	N. Henderson	*R. Dunwoody*	14
1992 Young Pokey 7-11-8: 4/1	O. Sherwood	*J. Osborne*	11
1993 Travado 7-11-8: 5/1	N. Henderson	*J. Osborne*	8

RITZ CLUB NATIONAL HUNT HANDICAP CHASE

(Cheltenham 3m 1f)

1948 Cavaliero 7-11-10: 7/1	F. Rimell	E. Vinall	21
1949 Frere Jacques II 7-10-6: 20/1	F. Rimell	E. Vinall	13
1950 Silver Fame 11-12-7: 5/4	G. Beeby	M. Molony	11
1951 Land Fort 7-11-8: 8/1	F. Rimell	J. Bullock	14
1952 Royal Tan 8-11-8: 7/2	M. V. O'Brien (Ir)	Mr A. O'Brien	11
1953 Four Ten 7-10-7: 4/1	J. Roberts	T. Cusack	12
1954 Holly Bank 7-10-13: 7/2	F. Rimell	Mr P. Brookshaw	12
1955 Limber Hill 8-11-2: 7/1	W. Dutton	T. Molony	19
1956 Kerstin 6-10-5: 100/9	C. Bewicke	G. Milburn	14
1957 Sentina 7-10-4: 3/1	T. Dreaper (Ir)	P. Taaffe	12
1958 Sentina 8-11-7: 7/1	T. Dreaper (Ir)	T. Taaffe	14
1959 Winning Coin 7-11-4: 100/9	G. Beeby	D. Dick	14
1960 Isle of Syke 9-10-5: 100/8	A. Kilpatrick	A. Keen	12
1961 Ravencroft 8-10-3: 9/2	F. Walwyn	F. Winter	10
1962 Longtail 7-11-0: 100/7	R. Curran	S. Mellor	18
1963 Team Spirit 11-11-4: 100/8	F. Walwyn	G. W. Robinson	24
1964 Prudent Barney 10-10-11: 10/1	R. Renton	T. Biddlecombe	10
1965 Rondetto 9-11-10: 11/2	R. Turnell	J. Haine	20
1966 Arkloin 7-12-5: 5/2	T. Dreaper (Ir)	P. Taaffe	12
1967 Different Class 7-11-13: 13/2	P. Cazalet	D. Mould	16
1968 Battledore 7-10-10: 3/1	W. A. Stephenson	C. Stobbs	8
1969 Chancer 7-11-0: 6/1	W. Hall	P. McCarron	13
1970 Charter Flight 8-11-9: 100/8	R. Turnell	A. Turnell	16
1971 Lord Jim 10-10-8: 8/1	F. Walwyn	J. Haine	10
1972 Jomon 6-10-12: 8/1	H. T. Jones	D. Mould	15
1973 The Chisler 7-10-10: 6/1	A. Dickinson	M. Dickinson	13
1974 Cuckolder 9-10-13: 6/1	R. Turnell	A. Turnell	11
1975 King Flame 9-10-6: 12/1	R. Head	J. Francome	14
1976 Barmer 8-10-3: 20/1	R. Blakeney	J. McNaught	14
1977 Gay Vulgan 9-11-4: 4/1	F. Walwyn	W. Smith	12
1978 Abandoned because of snow			
1979 Fair View 9-10-4: 12/1	G. Fairbairn	R. Lamb	13
1980 Again The Same 7-11-1: 10/1	J. Edwards	Mr A. J. Wilson	16
1981 Current Gold 10-10-7: 10/1	G. Richards	N. Doughty	16
1982 Scot Lane 9-10-12: 15/2	M. Tate	C. Smith	18
1983 Scot Lane 10-11-7: 20/1	M. Tate	C. Smith	19
1984 Tracys Special 7-11-1: 5/1	A. Turnell	S. C. Knight	12
1985 West Tip 8-10-13: 6/1	M. Oliver	R. Dunwoody	20
1986 Charter Party 8-10-10: 12/1	D. Nicholson	P. Scudamore	16
1987 Gainsay 8-10-5: 10/1	Mrs J. Pitman	B. de Haan	12
1988 Aquilifer 8-10-12: 9/2	D. Murray-Smith	P. Croucher	16
1989 Dixton House 10-11-0: 13/2	J. Edwards	T. Morgan	16
1990 Bigsun 9-10-11: 15/2	D. Nicholson	R. Dunwoody	14
1991 Seagram 11-10-11: 6/1	D. Barons	N. Hawke	14
1992 Tipping Tim 7-10-0: 20/1	N. Twiston-Davies	C. Llewellyn	17
1993 Givus A Buck 10-10-8: 11/2	D. Elsworth	P. Holley	7

FULKE WALWYN KIM MUIR CHALLENGE CUP
HANDICAP CHASE (Amateur Riders) (Cheltenham 3m 1f)

1946 Astrometer 8-10-13: 5/4	C. Rogers (Ir)	D. Baggallay	14
1947 Abandoned because of snow and frost			
1948 Double Bridge 7-10-10: 20/1	J. Powell	J. Gale	16
1949 Jack Tatters 11-12-2: 4/1	F. Walwyn	Lord Mildmay	11
1950 Morning Cover 9-10-10: 6/1	G. Wilson	A. Parker	6
1951 Mighty Fine 9-11-11: 2/1	F. Rimell	P. Chisman	9
1952 Menzies 10-10-11: 4/1	S. Mercer	P. Chisman	9
1953 Crudwell 7-11-11: 5/4	F. Cundell	A. Corbett	10
1954 Arctic Gold 9-12-3: 6/1	G. Balding	F. Greenway	11
1955 Gay Monarch II 9-11-3: 100/8	F. Rimell	R. Watson	15
1956 Filon d'Or 9-10-10: 20/1	H. Cousins	A. Moralee	11
1957 Mighty Apollo 8-10-13: 25/1	D. Machin	R. Brewis	16
1958 Lochroe 10-12-2: 10/11	P. Cazalet	E. Cazalet	11
1959 Irish Coffee 9-10-13: 100/30	C. McCartan (Ir)	G. Kindersley	12
1960 Solray 6-11-3: 7/1	F. Cliffe	N. Upton	9
1961 Nicolaus Silver 9-10-5: 10/1	F. Rimell	W. Tellwright	11
1962 Carrickbeg 6-9-12: 7/1	D. Butchers	G. Pitman	10

1963	Centre Circle 8-10-12: 6/1	D. Ancil	*B. Ancil*	18
1964	Jim's Tavern 7-10-4: 10/1	J. Hicks	*G. Pitman*	11
1965	Burton Tan 10-11-3: 10/1	R. Collie	*E. Collie*	15
1966	Jimmy Scot 10-10-9: 6/1	F. Walwyn	*J. Lawrence*	14
1967	Chu-Teh 8-10-8: 9/2	K. Cundell	*N. Gaselee*	11
1968	Chu-Teh 9-10-6: 3/1	K. Cundell	*D. Crossley-Cooke*	8
1969	Pride of Kentucky 7-10-4: 100/8	E. Courage	*R. Charlton*	13
1970	Rainbow Valley 7-10-12 : 10/1	A. Dickinson	*M. Dickinson*	20
1971	Black Baize 6-10-6: 13/8	W. Shand Kydd	*J. Lawrence*	9
1972	The Ghost 7-11-11: 5/2	V. Cross	*J. Mead*	15
1973	Hinterland 7-10-7: 5/2	T. Forster	*W. Foulkes*	22
1974	Castleruddery 8-10-5: 14/1	P. McCreery (Ir)	*T. Walsh*	19
1975	Quick Reply 10-11-1: 15/2	H. Bell	*R. Lamb*	17
1876	Prolan 7-11-7: 3/1	E. O'Grady (Ir)	*T. Walsh*	14
1977	Double Negative 7-10-9: 11/2	F. Rimell	*P. Brookshaw*	16
1978	Abandoned because of snow			
1979	Redundant Punter 9-9-12: 14/1	T. Forster	*D. Jackson*	20
1980	Good Prospect 11-10-12: 9/2	J. Edwards	*A. J. Wilson*	12
1981	Waggoners Walk 12-10-3: 7/1	Miss C. Mason	*C. Cundall*	20
1982	Political Pop 8-12-0: 15/2	M. Dickinson	*D. Browne*	18
1983	Greasepaint 8-11-5: 8/1	M. Cunningham (Ir)	*C. Magnier*	16
1984	Broomy Bank 9-11-4: 16/1	J. Edwards	*A. J. Wilson*	18
1985	Glyde Court 8-10-5: 11/1	F. Winter	*S. Sherwood*	18
1986	Glyde Court 9-11-0: 13/2	F. Winter	*J. Queally*	20
1987	The Ellier 11-10-5: 16/1	N. Tinkler	*Miss G. Armytage*	16
1988	Golden Minstrel 9-11-1: 7/1	J. Gifford	*T. Grantham*	13
1989	Cool Ground 7-10-0: 7/2	N. Mitchell	*A. Tory*	16
1990	Master Bob 10-10-1: 20/1	N. Henderson	*J. Berry*	17
1991	Omerta 11-9-13: 11/1	M. Pipe	*A. Maguire*	19
1992	Tug of Gold 7-10-2: 11/1	D. Nicholson	*M. Armytage*	19
1993	Strong Beau 8-9-8: 6/1	D. Nicholson	*T. Jenks*	12

AMERICAN EXPRESS GOLD CARD HANDICAP HURDLE FINAL

(Cheltenham 3¼m)

1974	Kastrup 7-10-3: 10/1	D. Barons	*G. Thorner*	22
1975	Saffron Cake 6-10-7: 13/1	L. Kennard	*E. Wright*	24
1976	Good Prospect 7-11-10: 10/1	J. Edwards	*R. R. Evans*	17
1977	Outpoint 7-11-3: 10/1	F. Winter	*P. O'Brien*	27
1978	Water Colour 9-10-1: 11/1	M. Tate	*K. Whyte*	23
1979	Willie Wumpkins 11-10-4: 25/1	Mrs T. Pilkington	*Mr A. J. Wilson*	22
1980	Willie Wumpkins 12-10-7: 10/1	Mrs T. Pilkington	*Mr A. J. Wilson*	19
1981	Willie Wumpkins 13-10-8: 13/1	Mrs T. Pilkington	*Mr A. J. Wilson*	20
1982	Tall Order 8-10-2: 15/1	L. Foster	*A. Stringer*	31
1983	Forgive'N Forget 6-11-6: 5/2	J. FitzGerald	*M. Dwyer*	23
1984	Canio 7-10-9: 20/1	R. Hodges	*J. Francome*	31
1985	Von Trappe 8-10-6: 12/1	M. Oliver	*R. Dunwoody*	30
1986	Motivator 6-10-7: 15/2	M. Ryan	*G. McCourt*	31
1987	Taberna Lord 6-11-5: 10/1	A. J. Wilson	*L. Harvey*	31
1988	Pragada 5-11-0: 16/1	J. Gifford	*R. Rowe*	29
1989	Rogers Princess 7-10-0: 8/1	M. Tate	*S. Keightley*	27
1990	Henry Mann 7-11-9: 20/1	S. Christian	*A. Mulholland*	27
1991	Danny Connors 7-10-12: 9/1	J. J. O'Neill	*M. Dwyer*	29
1992	My View 8-10-4: 33/1	M. Purcell (Ir)	*J. Titley*	31
1993	Fissure Seal 7-11-4: 14/1	H. de Bromhead (Ir)	*C. Swan*	22

SUN ALLIANCE NOVICES' HURDLE (Cheltenham 2m 5f)

1971	Midsprite 5-11-12: 7/1	H. T. Jones	*M. Gifford*	20
1972	Even Dawn 5-11-6: 40/1	Mrs E. Gaze	*R. Hyett*	17
1973	Willie Wumpkins 5-11-6: 11/1	A. Maxwell (Ir)	*P. Colville*	15
1974	Brown Lad 8-11-8: 2/1	P. Osborne (Ir)	*R. Barry*	25
1975	Davy Lad 5-11-7: 5/2	M. O'Toole (Ir)	*D. T. Hughes*	20
1976	Parkhill 5-11-7: 4/1	M. O'Toole (Ir)	*D. T. Hughes*	21
1977	Counsel Cottage 6-11-8: 6/1	P. Mullins (Ir)	*S. Treacy*	26
1978	Mr Kildare 5-11-7: 8/11	L. Browne (Ir)	*T. Carmody*	20
1979	Venture To Cognac 6-11-8: 4/1	F. Winter	*Mr O. Sherwood*	29
1980	Drumlargan 6-11-8: 5/2	E. O'Grady (Ir)	*T. Ryan*	27
1981	Gaye Chance 6-11-8: 7/1	F. Rimell	*S. Morshead*	21
1982	Mister Donovan 6-11-8: 9/2	E. O'Grady (Ir)	*T. Ryan*	21

159

1983	Sabin du Loir 4-10-8: 16/1	M. Dickinson	*G. Bradley*	27
1984	Fealty 4-10-12: 33/1	P. Brookshaw	*S. O'Neill*	29
1985	Asir 5-11-7: 9/1	P. Kelleway	*Mr R. Beggan*	27
1986	Ten Plus 6-11-7: 5/2	F. Walwyn	*K. Mooney*	28
1987	The West Awake 6-11-7: 16/1	O. Sherwood	*S. Sherwood*	28
1988	Rebel Song 6-11-7: 14/1	O. Sherwood	*S. Sherwood*	25
1989	Sayfar's Lad 5-11-7: 12/1	M. Pipe	*M. Perrett*	22
1990	Regal Ambition 6-11-7: 3/1	M. Pipe	*P. Scudamore*	22
1991	Crystal Spirit 4-10-12: 2/1	I. Balding	*J. Frost*	29
1992	Thetford Forest 5-11-7: 7/1	D. Nicholson	*R. Dunwoody*	27
1993	Gaelstrom 6-11-2: 16/1	N. Twiston-Davies	*C. Llewellyn*	19

SUN ALLIANCE CHASE (Cheltenham 3m 1f)

1964	Buona notte 7-12-4: 11/8	R. Turnell	*J. Haine*	16
1965	Arkloin 6-11-7: 100/7	T. Dreaper (Ir)	*L. McLoughlin*	17
1966	Different Class 6-11-12: 10/1	P. Cazalet	*D. Mould*	17
1967	Border Jet 7-11-0: 4/1	R. Price	*J. Gifford*	19
1968	Herring Gull 6-11-12: 9/1	P. Mullins (Ir)	*J. Crowley*	16
1969	Spanish Steps 6-11-12: 100/8	E. Courage	*J. Cook*	22
1970	Proud Tarquin 7-11-12: 100/7	T. Dreaper (Ir)	*P. Taaffe*	17
1971	Tantalum 7-11-7: 14/1	M. Pope	*D. Nicholson*	16
1972	Clever Scot 7-11-7: 11/1	H. T. Jones	*D. Mould*	18
1973	Killiney 7-11-3: 8/15	F. Winter	*R. Pitman*	9
1974	Ten Up 7-11-0: 7/2	J. Dreaper (Ir)	*T. Carberry*	12
1975	Pengrail 7-11-0: 12/1	F. Winter	*J. Francome*	11
1976	Tied Cottage 8-11-0: 12/1	D. L. Moore (Ir)	*T. Carberry*	15
1977	Gay Spartan 6-11-4: 13/2	A. Dickinson	*M. Dickinson*	15
1978	Sweet Joe 6-11-4: 12/1	H. T. Jones	*S. Smith Eccles*	17
1979	Master Smudge 7-11-4: 16/1	A. Barrow	*R. Hoare*	17
1980	Lacson 8-11-4: 16/1	R. Hawker	*S. C. Knight*	17
1981	Lesley Ann 7-11-4: 25/1	D. Elsworth	*C. Brown*	17
1982	Brown Chamberlin 7-11-4: 7/1	F. Winter	*J. Francome*	15
1983	Canny Danny 7-11-4: 33/1	J. FitzGerald	*N. Madden*	14
1984	A. Kinsman 8-11-4: 10/1	J. Brockbank	*T. G. Dun*	18
1985	Antarctic Bay 8-11-4: 6/4	P. Hughes (Ir)	*F. Berry*	11
1986	Cross Master 9-11-4: 16/1	T. Bill	*R. Crank*	30
1987	Kildimo 7-11-4: 13/2	G. Balding	*G. Bradley*	18
1988	The West Awake 7-11-4: 11/4	O. Sherwood	*S. Sherwood*	14
1989	Envopak Token 8-11-4: 16/1	J. Gifford	*P. Hobbs*	15
1990	Garrison Savannah 7-11-4: 12/1	Mrs J. Pitman	*B. de Haan*	9
1991	Rolling Ball 8-11-4: 7/2	M. Pipe	*P. Scudamore*	20
1992	Miinnehoma 9-11-4: 7/2	M. Pipe	*P. Scudamore*	18
1993	Young Hustler 6-11-4: 9/4	N. Twiston-Davies	*P. Scudamore*	8

CORAL CUP (HANDICAP HURDLE) (Cheltenham 2m 5f)

1993	Olympian 6-10-0: 4/1	M. Pipe	*P. Scudamore*	21

THE QUEEN MOTHER CHAMPION CHASE (Cheltenham 2m)

1959	Quita Que 10-12-0: 4/9	D. L. Moore (Ir)	*J. Cox*	9
1960	Fortria 8-12-0: 15/8	T. Dreaper (Ir)	*P. Taaffe*	7
1961	Fortria 9-12-0: 2/5	T. Dreaper (Ir)	*P. Taaffe*	5
1962	Piperton 8-12-0: 100/6	A. Thomlinson	*D. Dick*	7
1963	Sandy Abbot 8-12-0: 5/1	G. Owen	*S. Mellor*	5
1964	Ben Stack 7-12-0: 2/1	T. Dreaper (Ir)	*P. Taaffe*	5
1965	Dunkirk 8-12-0: 8/1	P. Cazalet	*D. Dick*	6
1966	Flyingbolt 7-12-0: 1/5	T. Dreaper (Ir)	*P. Taaffe*	6
1967	Drinny's Double 9-12-0: 7/2	R. Turnell	*F. Nash*	8
1968	Drinny's Double 10-12-0: 6/1	R. Turnell	*F. Nash*	5
1969	Muir 10-12-0: 15/2	T. Dreaper (Ir)	*B. Hannon*	11
1970	Straight Fort 7-12-0: 7/4	T. Dreaper (Ir)	*P. Taaffe*	6
1971	Crisp 8-12-0: 3/1	F. Winter	*P. Kelleway*	8
1972	Royal Relief 8-12-0: 15/8	E. Courage	*W. Smith*	5
1973	Inkslinger 6-12-0: 6/1	D. L. Moore (Ir)	*T. Carberry*	6
1974	Royal Relief 10-12-0: 6/1	E. Courage	*W. Smith*	6
1975	Lough Inagh 8-12-0: 100/30	J. Dreaper (Ir)	*S. Barker*	8
1976	Skymas 11-12-0: 8/1	B. Lusk (Ir)	*M. Morris*	7
1977	Skymas 12-12-0: 7/2	B. Lusk (Ir)	*M. Morris*	8
1978	Hilly Way 8-12-0: 7/1	P. McCreery (Ir)	*T. Carmody*	10

1979 Hilly Way 9-12-0: 7/1	P. McCreery (Ir)	*Mr T. Walsh*	9
1980 Another Dolly 10-12-0: 33/1	F. Rimell	*S. Morshead*	7
1981 Drumgora 9-12-0: 25/1	A. Moore (Ir)	*F. Berry*	9
1982 Rathgorman 10-12-0: 100/30	M. Dickinson	*K. Whyte*	9
1983 Badsworth Boy 8-12-0: 2/1	M. Dickinson	*R. Earnshaw*	6
1984 Badsworth Boy 9-12-0: 8/13	M. Dickinson	*R. Earnshaw*	10
1985 Badsworth Boy 10-12-0: 11/8	Mrs M. Dickinson	*R. Earnshaw*	5
1986 Buck House 8-12-0: 5/2	M. Morris (Ir)	*T. Carmody*	11
1987 Pearlyman 8-12-0: 13/8	J. Edwards	*P. Scudamore*	8
1988 Pearlyman 9-12-0: 15/8	J. Edwards	*T. Morgan*	8
1989 Barnbrook Again 8-12-0: 7/4	D. Elsworth	*S. Sherwood*	8
1990 Barnbrook Again 9-12-0: 11/10	D. Elsworth	*H. Davies*	9
1991 Katabatic 8-12-0: 9/1	A. Turnell	*S. McNeill*	7
1992 Remittance Man 8-12-0: 1/1	N. Henderson	*J. Osborne*	6
1993 Deep Sensation 8-12-0: 11/1	J. Gifford	*D. Murphy*	9

NATIONAL HUNT CHASE (Amateur Riders) (Cheltenham 4m)

1946 Prattler 11-12-3: 33/1	T. Yates	*Major D. Daly*	20
1947 Maltese Wanderer 8-12-3: 6/1	T. Yates	*Major D. Daly*	20
1948 Bruno II 8-12-3: 20/1	W. A-Gray	*Major G. Cunard*	37
1949 Castledermot 7-12-7: 6/4	M. V. O'Brien (Ir)	*Lord Mildmay*	17
1950 Ellesmere 7-12-7: 100/30	K. Cundell	*A. Corbett*	26
1951 Cushendun 6-12-4: 10/1	R. Renton	*P. Chisman*	18
1952 Frosty Knight 6-12-0: 15/2	I. Straker	*C. Straker*	19
1953 Pontage 7-12-4: 9/4	D. L. Moore (Ir)	*J. Cox*	22
1954 Quare Times 8-12-4: 5/2	M. V. O'Brien (Ir)	*J. Cox*	26
1955 Reverend Prince 9-12-0: 33/1	P. Dufosee	*C. Pocock*	26
1956 Rosana III 7-12-0: 9/1	J. Everitt	*J. Everitt*	22
1957 Kari Sou 8-12-0: 100/6	A. Thomlinson	*A. Lillingston*	24
1958 Spud Tamson 7-12-4: 13/2	T. Dun	*G. Dun*	28
1959 Sabaria 8-12-0: 5/2	R. Turnell	*J. Lawrence*	17
1960 Proud Socks 8-12-0: 100/6	V. Bishop	*H. Thompson*	22
1961 Superfine 8-12-4: 10/1	F. Cundell	*Sir W. P-Brown*	33
1962 Go Slow 7-12-7: 10/1	A. Piper	*G. Small*	26
1963 Time 8-12-0: 8/1	W. Stephenson	*I. Balding*	35
1964 Dorimont 10-12-1: 4/1	T. Taaffe (Ir)	*C. Vaughan*	30
1965 Red Vale II 11-12-0: 100/8	A. Piper	*G. Small*	26
1966 Polaris Missile 7-11-9: 100/6	H. Thorne	*M. Thorne*	29
1967 Master Tammy 9-11-7: 100/7	G. Guilding	*B. Fanshawe*	24
1968 Fascinating Forties 9-11-7: 9/1	G. Owen	*M. Dickinson*	22
1969 Lizzy The Lizard 10-12-0: 10/1	A. Hartnoll	*G. Cann*	35
1970 Domason 7-12-1: 10/1	H. Dufosee	*R. Alner*	18
1971 Deblin's Green 8-11-7: 9/2	G. Yardley	*J. Edmunds*	20
1972 Charley Winking 7-12-0: 20/1	I. Scott	*D. Scott*	23
1973 Foreman 7-12-1: 11/2	H. T. Jones	*W. Shand-Kydd*	25
1974 Mr Midland 7-12-4: 7/2	E. O'Grady (Ir)	*M. Morris*	17
1975 Abandoned because of waterlogged state of course			
1976 Sage Merlin 8-12-7: 5/2	J. Hardy	*P. Greenall*	22
1977 Alpenstock 10-12-4: 14/1	S. Mellor	*C. Saunders*	21
1978 Gay Tie 5-11-9: 10/1	M. O'Toole (Ir)	*J. Fowler*	17
1979 Artic Ale 8-12-0: 20/1	D. Moore (Ir)	*J. Fowler*	25
1980 Waggoners Walk 11-12-4: 10/1	Miss C. Mason	*A. Fowler*	23
1981 Lucky Vane 6-12-7: 13/1	G. Balding	*S. Bush*	21
1982 Hazy Dawn 7-12-7: 8/1	P. Mullins (Ir)	*W. Mullins*	26
1983 Bit Of A Skite 7-12-0: 5/1	E. O'Grady (Ir)	*F. Codd*	29
1984 Macks Friendly 7-12-7: 11/4	P. Mullins (Ir)	*W. Mullins*	18
1985 Northern Bay 9-12-4: 12/1	T. Bill	*A. Fowler*	20
1986 Omerta 6-12-7: 9/4	H. Scott (Ir)	*L. Wyer*	22
1987 Mighty Mark 8-12-7: 8/1	F. Walton	*J. Walton*	30
1988 Over The Road 7-12-4: 10/1	T. Casey	*T. Costello*	28
1989 Boraceva 6-12-7: 4/1	G. Balding	*S. Mullins*	21
1990 Topsham Bay 7-12-0: 40/1	D. Barons	*P. Hacking*	25
1991 Smooth Escort 7-12-0: 7/1	Mrs D. Haine	*A. Martin*	18
1992 Keep Talking 7-12-7: 5/2	T. Thomson Jones	*M. Armytage*	24
1993 Ushers Island 7-12-4: 15/2	H. Johnson	*N. Wilson*	13

MILDMAY OF FLETE CHALLENGE CUP HANDICAP CHASE

(Cheltenham 2½m 110yds)

1951	Slender 9-10-11: 7/1 ⎫ dh	R. Price	*F. Winter*	9
	Canford 9-12-2: 100/8 ⎭	I. Anthony	*G. Kelly*	
1952	Portarlington 7-10-8	W. Stephenson	*K. Mullins*	10
1953	Sy Oui 8-10-3: 100/8	R. Price	*F. Winter*	17
1954	Tudor Line 9-10-12: 11/4	R. Renton	*G. Slack*	11
1955	Mont Tremblant 9-12-7: 11/2	F. Walwyn	*D. Dick*	19
1956	Pondapatarri 7-11-0: 100/6	G. Beeby	*R. Emery*	21
1957	Madras 7-10-2: 100/7	M. L. Marsh	*J. Bullock*	12
1958	Caesar's Helm 7-11-6: 9/2	R. Renton	*F. Winter*	14
1959	Siracusa 6-10-12: 9/4	R. Renton	*B. Wilkinson*	12
1960	Devon Customer 8-10-4: 100/7	S. Bowler	*J. Guest*	12
1961	Malting Barley 6-10-4: 5/1	G. Balding	*O. McNally*	8
1962	Spring Greeting 7-10-6: 100/8	C. Bewicke	*J. Lehane*	19
1963	Milo 8-10-4: 11/2	H. Blagrave	*J. Gifford*	19
1964	Take Plenty 8-10-1: 100/9	T. Forster	*R. Vibert*	12
1965	Snaigow 6-10-3: 100/6	C. Bewicke	*J. Lehane*	15
1966	Tibidabo 6-10-4: 7/1	A. Freeman	*J. King*	12
1967	French March 7-9-9: 25/1	T. Hanbury	*Mr B. Hanbury*	14
1968	Merrycourt 7-10-3: 20/1	R. Renton	*J. Gifford*	14
1969	Specify 7-11-2: 5/1	D.Rayson	*B. R. Davies*	8
1970	Verona Forest 7-11-0: 25/1	N. Crump	*G. Scott*	19
1971	Hound Tor 7-10-2: 14/1	G. Harwood	*M. Gifford*	10
1972	Mocharabuice 9-10-7: 11/2	T. Forster	*G. Thorner*	17
1973	Vulgan Town 7-10-0: 9/2	G. Balding	*J. Haine*	15
1974	Garnishee 10-10-10: 9/2	H. T. Jones	*D. Mould*	7
1975	Summerville 9-10-13: 4/1	R. Turnell	*A. Turnell*	13
1976	Broncho II 7-11-1: 7/2	A. Dickinson	*M. Dickinson*	14
1977	Uncle Bing 8-12-5: 9/2	R. Head	*J. Francome*	7
1978	King Or Country 7-10-9: 7/1	D. Barons	*P. Leach*	16
1979	Brawny Scot 9-10-0: 10/1	G. Fairbairn	*R. Lamb*	15
1980	Snowshill Sailor 8-10-4: 8/1	R. Turnell	*A. Turnell*	14
1981	Political Pop 7-10-0: 15/8	M. Dickinson	*R. Earnshaw*	12
1982	Doubleuagain 8-10-0: 11/1	A. Geraghty (Ir)	*F. Berry*	13
1983	Mr Peapock 7-9-7: 20/1	T. Hallett	*L. Bloomfield*	15
1984	Half Free 8-11-6: 16/1	F. Winter	*R. Linley*	16
1985	The Tsarevich 9-11-7: 5/1	N. Henderson	*J. White*	16
1986	The Tsarevich 10-11-5: 8/1	H. Henderson	*J. White*	16
1987	Gee-A 8-9-10: 33/1	G. Hubbard	*Miss G. Armytage*	18
1988	Smart Tar 7-10-2: 11/1	M. Wilkinson	*C. Llewellyn*	15
1989	Paddyboro 11-10-7: 9/2	J. Gifford	*R. Rowe*	10
1990	New Halen 9-9-7: 66/1	P. James	*E. Tierney*	14
1991	Foyle Fisherman 12-11-0: 33/1	J. Gifford	*E. Murphy*	15
1992	Elfast 9-11-0: 10/1	J. Webber	*M. Lynch*	19
1993	Sacre d'Or 8-11-0: 7/1	N. Tinkler	*G. McCourt*	11

FESTIVAL BUMPER (NATIONAL HUNT FLAT) (Cheltenham 2m 110yds)

1992	Montelado 5-11-13: 8/1	P. Flynn (Ir)	*R. Dunwoody*	23
1993	Rhythm Section 4-10-11: 16/1	H. Scott (Ir)	*P. Carberry*	24

DAILY EXPRESS TRIUMPH HURDLE (4-y-o) (Cheltenham 2m 1f)

1950	Abrupto 11-6: 9/2	E. Diggle (Fr)	*R. Mantelin*	19
1951	Blue Song II 10-7: 6/1	G. Pelat (Fr)	*F. Thirion*	12
1952	Hoggar 10-10: 13/2	J. Cunnington (Fr)	*R. Triboit*	15
1953	Clair Soleil 11/4: 8/1	F. Mathet (Fr)	*F. Winter*	13
1954	Prince Charlemagne 10-10: 11/4	T. Carey	*L. Piggott*	12
1955	Kwannin 10-10: 2/1	A. Head (Fr)	*P. Delfarguiel*	12
1956	Square Dance 10-12: 13/2	F. Walwyn	*M. Scudamore*	11
1057	Meritorious 10-12: 20/1	P. Thrale	*D. Dillon*	14
1958	Pundit 11-4: 5/2	S. Ingham	*H. Sprague*	14
1959	Amazons Choice 10-10: 7/1	P. Thrale	*J. Gilbert*	13
1960	Turpial 10-10: 7/1	P. Cazalet	*A. Freeman*	13
1961	Cantab 10-10: 4/1	R. Price	*F. Winter*	15
1962	Beaver II 10-10: 100/6	R. Price	*J. Gifford*	11
1963	No Race			
1964	No Race			
1965	Blarney Beacon 11-4: 8/1	R. Smyth	*G. Ramshaw*	7

162

1966	Black Ice 11-4: 9/2	A. Thomas	*H. Beasley*	11
1967	Persian War 11-8: 4/1	B. Swift	*J. Uttley*	13
1968	England's Glory 10-10: 9/2	S. Ingham	*J. Uttley*	16
1969	Coral Diver 11-4: 3/1	F. Rimell	*T. Biddlecombe*	26
1970	Varma 11-4: 100/7	M. Masson	*B. Barker*	31
1971	Boxer 11-3: 100/30	R. Smyth	*J. Uttley*	18
1972	Zarib 11-0: 16/1	F. Rimell	*W. Smith*	16
1973	Moonlight Bay 11-0: 85/40	R. Price	*J. Haine*	18
1974	Attivo 11-0: 4/5	C. Mitchell	*R. G. Hughes*	21
1975	Royal Epic 11-0: 20/1	V. Cross	*F. McKenna*	28
1976	Peterhof 11-0: 10/1	M. W. Easterby	*J. J. O'Neill*	23
1977	Meladon 11-0: 6/1	A. Maxwell (Ir)	*T. Carberry*	30
1978	Connaught Ranger 11-0: 25/1	F. Rimell	*J. Burke*	14
1979	Pollardstown: 12/1	S. Mellor	*P. Blacker*	28
1980	Heighlin 11-0: 40/1	D. Elsworth	*S. Jobar*	26
1981	Baron Blakeney 11-0: 66/1	M. Pipe	*P. Leach*	29
1982	Shiny Copper 11-0: 66/1	Mrs N. Smith	*A. Webb*	29
1983	Saxon Farm 11-0: 12/1	S. Mellor	*M. Perrett*	30
1984	Northern Game 11-0: 20/1	E. O'Grady (Ir)	*T. Ryan*	30
1985	First Bout 11-0: 5/1	N. Henderson	*S. Smith Eccles*	27
1986	Solar Cloud 11-0: 40/1	D. Nicholson	*P. Scudamore*	28
1987	Alone Success 11-0: 11/1	N. Henderson	*S. Smith Eccles*	29
1988	Kribensis 11-0: 6/1	M. Stoute	*R. Dunwoody*	26
1989	Ikdam 11-0: 66/1	R. Holder	*N. Coleman*	27
1990	Rare Holiday 11-0: 25/1	D. K. Weld (Ir)	*B. Sheridan*	30
1991	Oh So Risky 11-0: 14/1	D. Elsworth	*P.Holley*	27
1992	Duke of Monmouth 11-0: 33/1	S. Sherwood	*M. Richards*	30
1993	Shawiya 10-9: 12/1	M. O'Brien (Ir)	*C. Swan*	25

BONUSPRINT STAYERS' HURDLE (Cheltenham 3m 110ys)

1972	Parlour Moor 8-11-12: 13/2	H. T. Jones	*M. Gifford*	11
1973	Moyne Royal 8-11-12: 10/1	A. Pitt	*D. Mould*	8
1974	Highland Abbe 8-11-12: 15/2	L. Kennard	*R. Smith*	15
1975	Brown Lad 9-11-12: 7/2	J. Dreaper (Ir)	*T. Carberry*	12
1976	Bit of a Jig 8-11-12: 2/1	M. O'Toole (Ir)	*D. T. Hughes*	12
1977	Town Ship 6-11-12: 5/2	M. H. Easterby	*T. Carberry*	11
1978	Flame Gun 6-11-12: 14/1	E. O'Grady (Ir)	*Mr N. Madden*	13
1979	Lighter 6-11-12: 14/1	J. Edwards	*P. Blacker*	14
1980	Mountrivers 6-11-12: 7/1	E. O'Grady (Ir)	*T. Ryan*	19
1981	Derring Rose 6-11-12: 3/1	F. Winter	*J. Francome*	14
1982	Crimson Embers 7-11-12: 12/1	F. Walwyn	*S. Shilston*	11
1983	A Kinsman 7-11-12: 50/1	J. Brockbank	*T. G. Dun*	21
1984	Gaye Chance 9-11-10: 5/1	Mrs M. Rimell	*S. Morshead*	14
1985	Rose Ravine 6-11-5: 5/1	F. Walwyn	*R. Pusey*	22
1986	Crimson Embers 11-11-10: 12/1	F. Walwyn	*S. Shilston*	19
1987	Galmoy 8-11-10: 9/2	J. Mulhern (Ir)	*T. Carmody*	14
1988	Galmoy 9-11-10: 2/1	J. Mulhern (Ir)	*T. Carmody*	16
1989	Rustle 7-11-10: 4/1	N. Henderson	*M. Bowlby*	21
1990	Trapper John 6-11-10: 15/2	M. Morris (Ir)	*C. Swan*	22
1991	King's Curate 7-11-10: 5/2	S. Mellor	*M. Perrett*	15
1992	Nomadic Way 7-11-10: 15/2	B. Hills	*J. Osborne*	17
1993	Shuil Ar Aghaidh 7-11-5: 20/1	P. Kiely	*C. Swan*	12

CHRISTIES FOXHUNTER CHALLENGE CUP (Hunter Chase)
(Cheltenham 3¼m 110yds)

1946	Koilo 9-12-0: 6/1	H. Jackson	*H. Jackson*	16
1947	Lucky Purchase 9-12-0: 7/1	S. Banks	*J. Nichols*	26
1948	State Control 8-12-0: 7/2	H. Llewellyn	*H. Llewellyn*	38
1949	Abandoned because of frost			
1950	Greenwood 13-12-0: 100/7	J. Evans	*J. Stuart-Evans*	25
1951	Halloween 6-12-0: 11/8	W. Wightman	*R. Smalley*	26
1952	Parasol II 7-12-0: 8/1	A. Walton	*I. Kerwood*	19
1953	Dunboy II 9-12-0: 3/1 ⎱ dh	P. Bruce	*C. Scott*	22
	Merry 13-12-0: 100/7 ⎰	A. Kerr	*G. Kindersley*	
1954	Happymint 9-12-0: 7/1	J. Wight	*A. Moralee*	21
1955	Abandoned because of snow			
1956	The Callant 8-12-0: 11/8	J. Wight	*J. Scott-Aiton*	17
1957	The Callant 9-12-0: 10/11	J. Wight	*J. Scott-Aiton*	9

163

1958	Whinstone Hill 9-12-0: 7/1	R. Brewis	*R. Brewis*	16
1959	Some Baby 10-12-0: 100/8	T. Rootes	*J. Thorne*	15
1960	Whinstone Hill 11-12-0: 11/8	R. Brewis	*R. Brewis*	15
1961	Colledge Master 11-12-0: 7/2	L. Morgan	*L. Morgan*	17
1962	Colledge Master 12-12-0: 9/2	L. Morgan	*L. Morgan*	17
1963	Grand Morn II 9-12-0: 15/2	G. Shepheard	*R. Bloomfield*	20
1964	Freddie 7-11-7: 1/3	R. Tweedie	*A. Mactaggart*	10
1965	Woodside Terrace 12-11-7: 33/1	R. Woodhouse	*R. Woodhouse*	19
1966	Straight Lady 10-11-7: 100/8	W. Shepherd	*R. Shepherd*	21
1967	Mulbarton 11-12-0: 1/1	I. Pattullo	*N. Gaselee*	13
1968	Bright Beach 8-11-11: 5/1	G. Dun	*C. MacMillan*	12
1969	Queens Guide 8-11-7: 10/1	W. Wade	*G. Wade*	10
1970	Highworth 9-11-7: 15/2	R. Woodhouse	*R. Woodhouse*	13
1971	Hope Again 9-11-7: 16/1	D. Windell	*R. Smith*	18
1972	Credit Call 8-12-0: 7/4	W. A. Stephenson	*C. Collins*	9
1973	Bullock's Horn 10-12-0: 5/1	R. Turnell	*Lord Oaksey*	20
1974	Corrie Burn 8-12-0: 20/1	G. Fairbairn	*I. Williams*	16
1975	Real Rascal 12-11-10: 8/1	Mrs B. Surman	*G. Hyatt*	16
1976	False Note 10-11-9: 11/4	J. Horton	*B. Smart*	16
1977	Long Lane 9-11-11: 9/4	R. Shepherd	*R. Shepherd*	16
1978	Mountolive 8-12-0: 13/2	R. Shepherd	*R. Shepherd*	17
1979	Spartan Missile 7-12-0: 9/4	J. Thorne	*J. Thorne*	10
1980	Rolls Rambler 9-12-0: 9/4	F. Winter	*O. Sherwood*	7
1981	Grittar 8-12-0: 12/1	F. Gilman	*R. Saunders*	17
1982	The Drunken Duck 9-12-0: 12/1	B. Munro-Wilson	*B. Munro-Wilson*	19
1983	Eliogarty 8-12-0: 3/1	B. Kelly (Ir)	*Miss C. Beasley*	16
1984	Venture To Cognac 11-12-0: 7/1	F. Winter	*O. Sherwood*	21
1985	Elmboy 7-12-0: 10/1	W. Mawle	*A. Hill*	17
1986	Attitude Adjuster 6-12-0: 10/1	M. Morris (Ir)	*T. Walsh*	14
1987	Observe 11-12-0: 14/1	F. Winter	*C. Brooks*	14
1988	Certain Light 10-12-0: 10/1	Mrs A. Campbell	*P. Hacking*	9
1989	Three Counties 12-12-0: 6/1	Mrs M. Rimell	*Miss K. Rimell*	16
1990	Call Collect 9-12-0: 7/4	J. Parkes	*R. Martin*	15
1991	Lovely Citizen 8-12-0: 14/1	E. O'Sullivan (Ir)	*W. O'Sullivan*	18
1992	Rushing Wild 7-12-0: 9/1	R. Barber	*J. Farthing*	24
1993	Double Silk 9-12-0: 12/1	R. Wilkins	*R. Treloggen*	18

CHELTENHAM GRAND ANNUAL CHALLENGE CUP
HANDICAP CHASE (Cheltenham 2m 110yds)

1946	Loyal King 6-11-12: 7/2	C. Rogers (Ir)	*D. L. Moore*	11
1947	Rope Trick 6-10-8: 100/7	C. Bewicke	*D. Doyle*	12
1948	Clare Man 7-10-3: 20/1	W. Nightingall	*C. Hook*	20
1949	Abandoned because of frost			
1950	Norborne 6-11-4: 8/1	E. Champneys	*E. Reavey*	11
1951	Merry Court 6-10-11: 10/1	T. Yates	*T. Molony*	11
1952	Marcianus 6-11-2: 7/1	G. Beeby	*T. Molony*	12
1953	Rose & Crown 6-10-0: 33/1	F. Walwyn	*J. Bullock*	13
1954	Hipparchus 5-10-1: 100/1	P. Rice-Stringer	*J. Dowdeswell*	11
1955	Abandoned because of snow			
1956	Rosenkavalier 7-10-6: 8/1	R. Turnell	*H. Sprague*	11
1957	Sir Edmund 7-10-12: 6/1	A. Kilpatrick	*R. Morrow*	11
1958	Top Twenty 9-10-7: 10/1	C. Magnier (Ir)	*F. Shortt*	18
1959	Top Twenty 10-12-6: 9/2	C. Magnier (Ir)	*F. Winter*	12
1960	Monsieur Trois Etoiles 8-11-6: 3/1	J. Brogan (Ir)	*F. Carroll*	9
1961	Barberyn 6-11-0: 3/1	W. Stephenson	*M. Scudamore*	10
1962	Moretons 9-10-12: 100/8	P. Cazalet	*W. Rees*	14
1963	Anner Loch 8-10-6: 7/1	J. Hicks	*D. Nicholson*	13
1964	Richard of Bordeaux 9-11-3: 9/1	F. Walwyn	*G. W. Robinson*	14
1965	Fort Rouge 7-11-0: 13/2	K. Oliver	*G. Milburn*	10
1966	Well Packed 8-10-11: 100/7	R. Renton	*Mr T. Stack*	12
1967	San Angelo 7-11-1: 10/1	E. Courage	*J. Buckingham*	13
1968	Hal's Farewell 7-10-10: 5/1	P. Bailey	*J. King*	10
1969	All Glory 8-10-0: 10/1	J. Edwards	*Mr A. Robinson*	10
1970	Fortina's Palace 7-11-11: 10/1	M. Scudamore	*P. Jones*	18
1971	Khan 7-10-8: 2/1	M. Burke (Ir)	*F. Carroll*	8
1972	Tudor Dance 6-10-2: 4/1	R. Turnell	*J. King*	15
1973	Coolera Prince 8-10-10: 8/1	H. Handel	*N. Wakley*	15

1974	Dulwich 7-10-13: 100/30	C. Davies	*M. Salaman*	9
1975	Abandoned because of waterlogged state of course			
1976	Dulwich 9-11-7: 9/4	C. Davies	*B. R. Davies*	10
1977	Tom Morgan 8-11-6: 9/4	K. Oliver	*T. Stack*	9
1978	Young Arthur 9-11-4: 3/1	D. Kent	*A. Webb*	8
1979	Casbah 12-11-13: 5/1	T. Forster	*G. Thorner*	10
1980	Stopped 8-11-12: 7/2	F. Winter	*B. de Haan*	13
1981	Friendly Alliance 8-10-7: 11/2	F. Winter	*J. Francome*	11
1982	Reldis 8-10-0: 9/1	D. Gandolfo	*P. Barton*	16
1983	Churchfield Boy 7-10-0: 8/1	M. Cunningham (Ir)	*J. P. Byrne*	18
1984	Mossy Moore 8-10-0: 11/2	B. Chinn	*J. J. O'Neill*	13
1985	Kathies Lad 8-11-10: 7/1	A. Jarvis	*S. Smith Eccles*	19
1986	Pearlyman 7-11-5: 14/1	J. Edwards	*G. Bradley*	19
1987	French Union 9-11-3: 13/2	D. Nicholson	*R. Dunwoody*	16
1988	Vodkatini 9-10-13: 4/1	J. Gifford	*R. Rowe*	14
1989	Pukka Major 8-10-2: 4/1	T. T. Jones	*P. Scudamore*	17
1990	Katabatic 7-10-8: 11/4	A. Turnell	*H. Davies*	13
1991	Aldino 8-10-0: 15/2	O. Sherwood	*J. Osborne*	12
1992	My Young Man 7-11-10: 7/1	C. Brooks	*G. Bradley*	17
1993	Space Fair 10-11-1: 5/1	R. Lee	*A. Maguire*	12

CATHCART CHALLENGE CUP CHASE (Cheltenham 2m 5f)

1946	Leap Man 9-12-0: 100/7	F. Walwyn	*B. Marshall*	14
1947	Abandoned because of snow and frost			
1948	Jack Tatters 10-12-3: 9/2	F. Walwyn	*B. Marshall*	13
1949	Abandoned because of frost			
1950	River Trout 7-12-1: 8/13	J. Dennistoun	*M. Molony*	10
1951	Semeur 5-11-5: 11/8	F. Walwyn	*B. Marshall*	10
1952	Coolrock 7-11-13: 11/8	F. Walwyn	*B. Marshall*	5
1953	Arctic Gold 8-11-8: 4/1	G. Balding	*G. Kelly*	10
1954	Royal Approach 6-11-13: 10/11	T. Dreaper (Ir)	*P. Taaffe*	6
1955	Abandoned because of snow			
1956	Amber Wave 8-11-8: 6/1	E. Champneys	*M. Scudamore*	10
1957	Rose's Quarter 10-12-4: 3/1	G. Beeby	*D. Dick*	7
1958	Quita Que 9-11-8: 10/11	D. Moore (Ir)	*J. Cox*	7
1959	Gallery Goddess 8-11-3: 11/2	C. Mallon	*F. Winter*	7
1960	Dove Cote 10-11-8: 2/1	J. Wight	*M. Batchelor*	8
1961	Quita Que 12-11-3: 8/11	D. Moore (Ir)	*G. Robinson*	7
1962	Hoodwinked 7-12-1: 8/1	N. Crump	*D. Nicholson*	8
1963	Some Alibi 8-12-1: 9/4	F. Walwyn	*G. Robinson*	13
1964	Panisse 9-11-12: 7/2	W. Stephenson	*M. Scudamore*	10
1965	Scottish Memories 11-11-8: 4/9	P. Sleator (Ir)	*H. Beasley*	5
1966	Flying Wild 10-11-3: 5/4	D. Moore (Ir)	*T. Carberry*	6
1967	Prince Blarney 7-11-8: 100/8	J. Barclay	*R. Barry*	5
1968	Muir 9-11-12: 10/11	T. Dreaper (Ir)	*P. Taaffe*	8
1969	Kinloch Brae 6-12-4: 3/1	W. O'Grady (Ir)	*T. Hyde*	8
1970	Garrynagree 7-11-3: 2/1	T. Dreaper (Ir)	*P. Taaffe*	6
1971	The Laird 10-12-4: 2/1	R. Turnell	*J. King*	5
1972	Soloning 7-12-1: 6/5	F. Winter	*R. Pitman*	8
1973	Inkslinger 6-12-4: 21/20	D. Moore (Ir)	*T. Carberry*	4
1974	Soothsayer 7-11-3: 11/8	F. Winter	*R. Pitman*	7
1975	Abandoned because of waterlogged state of course			
1976	No Race			
1977	No Race			
1978	Abandoned because of snow			
1979	Roller-Coaster 6-11-9: 6/4	F. Winter	*J. Francome*	5
1980	King Weasel 8-11-9: 5/2	M. H. Easterby	*J. J. O'Neill*	6
1981	Lord Greystoke 10-11-6: 7/2	G. Richards	*N. Doughty*	8
1982	Dramatist 11-11-8: 15/8	F. Walwyn	*W. Smith*	6
1983	Observe 7-11-8: 1/2	F. Winter	*J. Francome*	7
1984	The Mighty Mac 9-11-8: 4/7	M. Dickinson	*Mr D. Browne*	7
1985	Straight Accord 10-11-8: 15/2	F. Walwyn	*S. Shilston*	8
1986	Half Free 10-11-8: 11/8	F. Winter	*S. Sherwood*	6
1987	Half Free 11-11-12: 5/4	F. Winter	*P. Scudamore*	4
1988	Private Views 7-11-0: 7/1	N. Gaselee	*B. Powell*	8
1989	Observer Corps 8-11-0: 66/1	J. Edwards	*T. Morgan*	9
1990	Brown Windsor 8-11-3: 13/8	N. Henderson	*J. White*	8
1991	Chatam 7-11-0: 3/1	M. Pipe	*P. Scudamore*	6

| 1992 | Repeat The Dose 7-11-10: 14/1 | T. Etherington | *M. Richards* | 7 |
| 1993 | Second Schedual 8-11-3: 6/1 | A. Moore (Ir) | *A. Maguire* | 7 |

COUNTY HANDICAP HURDLE (Cheltenham 2m 1f)

1946	Vidi 5-11-10: 6/1	R. Hobbs	*D. Butchers*	27
1947	Abandoned because of snow and frost			
1948	Cape Light 5-11-1: 2/1	I. Anthony	*J. Maguire*	21
1949	Abandoned because of frost			
1950	Blue Raleigh 7-10-0: 25/1	R. Renton	*J. Power*	19
1951	Southwick 7-10-3: 100/7	J. Whiting	*G. Spann*	21
1952	Ballymacan 5-10-12: 100/7	N. Crump	*B. Marshall*	21
1953	Teapot II 8-12-7: 4/1	C. Magnier (Ir)	*P. Taaffe*	16
1954	Bold Baby 8-12-0: 13/8	M. Dawson (Ir)	*P. Powell, jnr*	14
1955	Abandoned because of snow			
1956	Pommell 9-10-11: 100/7	J. C. Waugh	*S. Boddy*	18
1957	Flaming East 8-10-5: 100/6	G. Vallance	*P. Pickford*	19
1958	Friendly Boy 6-10-5: 3/1	J. Osborne (Ir)	*W. Brennan*	18
1959	Approval 13-11-2: 10/1	S. Mercer	*D. Leslie*	20
1960	Albergo 6-12-5: 7/4	C. Magnier (Ir)	*D. Page*	26
1961	Most Unusual 6-10-7: 100/7	W. Ransom	*J. Gifford*	23
1962	Sky Pink 5-10-11: 100/8	R. Price	*F. Winter*	20
1963	Bahrain 6-10-6: 11/2	D. L. Moore (Ir)	*T. Carberry*	19
1964	Icy Wonder 5-10-2: 11/2	V. Cross	*J. King*	17
1965	Mayfair Bill 6-10-4: 100/7	R. Turnell	*A. Turnell*	25
1966	Roaring Twenties 6-11-2: 10/1	K. Oliver	*G. Milburn*	16
1967	Cool Alibi 5-10-9: 20/1	J. Bower	*R. Reid*	28
1968	Jolly Signal 6-10-11: 6/1	E. Jones	*J. Uttley*	16
1969	Gay Knight 5-10-3: 100/7	L. Kennard	*A. Branford*	27
1970	Khan 6-9-11: 100/8	Miss D. Harty (Ir)	*Lord Petersham*	32
1971	Carry Off 7-10-1: 25/1	N. Angus	*D. Goulding*	24
1972	Cold Day 6-10-8: 15/1	Mrs E. Gaze	*R. Hyett*	25
1973	Current Romance 7-10-7: 20/1	H. Nicholson	*D. Nicholson*	31
1974	True Song 5-11-2: 14/1	D. Underwood	*G. Old*	20
1975	Abandoned because of waterlogged state of course			
1976	Java Fox 6-10-1: 16/1	R. Cambidge	*Mr G. Jones*	13
1977	Kilcoleman 5-10-7: 14/1	J. Boyers (Ir)	*T. Kinane*	26
1978	Abandoned because of snow			
1979	Monte Ceco 6-10-12: 6/1	F. Rimell	*C. Tinkler*	20
1980	Prince of Bermuda 5-10-0: 9/1	R. Turnell	*S. C. Knight*	18
1981	Staplestown 6-10-7: 11/2	E. O'Grady (Ir)	*T. Ryan*	25
1982	Path of Peace 6-10-6: 4/1	C. Thornton	*J. J. O'Neill*	23
1983	Robin Wonder 5-10-3: 10/1	D. Elsworth	*J. Davies*	29
1984	Hill's Guard 5-10-11: 6/1	A. Scott	*A. Stringer*	19
1985	Floyd 5-10-5: 5/2	D. Elsworth	*C. Brown*	27
1986	Jobroke 6-10-3: 6/1	M. H. Easterby	*J. J. O'Neill*	29
1987	Neblin 8-11-0: 14/1	G. Balding	*R. Guest*	24
1988	Cashew King 5-10-4: 9/1	B. McMahon	*T. Wall*	24
1989	Willsford 6-10-8: 11/1	Mrs J. Pitman	*M. Bowlby*	21
1990	Moody Man 5-11-2: 9/1	P. Hobbs	*P. Hobbs*	20
1991	Winnie The Witch 7-9-8: 33/1	K. Bridgwater	*D. Bridgwater*	26
1992	Dusty Miller 10-10-6: 9/1	S. Sherwood	*J. Osborne*	27
1993	Thumbs Up 7-10-2: 16/1	N. Henderson	*R. Dunwoody*	21

TETLEY BITTER MIDLANDS NATIONAL (HANDICAP CHASE)
(Uttoxeter 4¼m)

1969	Happy Spring 13-9-11: 10/1	J. Wright	*K. White*	7
1970	Two Springs 8-10-6: 9/2	G. Owen	*R. Edwards*	9
1971	Grey Sombrero 7-9-7: 13/1	D. Gandolfo	*G. Thorner*	14
1972	Proud Percy 9-10-0: 7/1	W. A. Stephenson	*G. Faulkner*	11
1973	Rip's Lyric 8-10-6: 13/2	W. Whiston	*K. White*	13
1974	Fighting Chance 6-9-8: 5/2	G. Kindersley	*W. Shoemark*	13
1975	Rag Trade 9-10-10: 9/2	A. Pitt	*J. Burke*	17
1976	Burrator 7-10-1: 11/1	A. Jarvis	*Mr J. Docker*	9
1977	Watafella 7-9-11: 25/1	Mrs J. Pitman	*B. Smart*	18
1978	Kick On 11-10-8: 16/1	K. Lewis	*R. Hyett*	22
1979	Jimmy Miff 7-9-10: 12/1	I. Wardle	*S. Kemble*	22
1980	Pacify 10-10-0: 7/2	S. Mellor	*S. Jobar*	9
1981	Master Brutus 9-10-2: 9/1	Mrs C. Mason	*J. Goulding*	22

1982	Bridge Ash 9-10-13: 10/1	J. Johnson	*Mr I. Johnson*	15
1983	Abandoned because of waterlogged state of course			
1984	Mr Mole 9-10-0: 18/1	J. Webber	*A. Webb*	16
1985	Northern Bay 9-11-0: 7/2	T. Bill	*P. Hobbs*	16
1986	The Thinker 8-11-6: 6/1	W. A. Stephenson	*R. Lamb*	16
1987	Midnight Madness 9-9-13: 6/1	D. Bloomfield	*D. Morris*	14
1988	Knock Hill 12-11-7: 20/1	J. Webber	*G. Mernagh*	18
1989	Gallic Prince 10-10-1: 12/1	P. J. Hobbs	*P. Hobbs*	18
1990	Willsford 7-11-0: 6/1	Mrs J. Pitman	*M. Pitman*	17
1991	Bonanza Boy 10-11-10: 15/8	M. Pipe	*P. Scudamore*	11
1992	Laura's Beau 8-10-8: 12/1	F. Berry (Ir)	*C. O'Dwyer*	17
1993	Mister Ed 10-10-3: 25/1	R. Curtis	*D. Morris*	17

SEAGRAM TOP NOVICES' HURDLE (Aintree 2m 110yds)

1976	Beacon Light 5-11-6: 4/1	R. Turnell	*A. Turnell*	13
1977	Irish Rambler 6-11-0: 3/1	J. Crowley (Ir)	*J. Crowley*	21
1978	Prousto 5-11-5: 4/1	A. Jarvis	*J. J. O'Neill*	13
1979	Rimondo 4-10-10: 8/1	E. Carter	*J. J. O'Neill*	20
1980	Jugador 5-11-5: 17/2	D. Kent	*B. R. Davies*	22
1981	Burns 5-11-5: 14/1	F. Walwyn	*W. Smith*	18
1982	Bright Oassis 6-11-5: 14/1	K. Bailey	*A. Webb*	17
1983	Very Promising 5-12-3: 7/4	Mrs M. Rimell	*S. Morshead*	13
1984	Browne's Gazette 6-11-11: 10/11	M. Dickinson	*Mr D. Browne*	14
1985	Sailor's Dance 5-11-0: 12/1	F. Winter	*J. Duggan*	18
1986	I Bin Zaidoon 5-11-0: 14/1	Mrs J. Pitman	*G. McCourt*	17
1987	Convinced 5-11-0: 100/30	M. Pipe	*P. Scudamore*	14
1988	Faraway Lad 5-11-0: 10/1	O. Sherwood	*S. Sherwood*	14
1989	Young Benz 5-11-0: 3/1	M. H. Easterby	*L. Wyer*	11
1990	Fidway 5-11-0: 16/1	T. Thomson Jones	*S. Smith Eccles*	15
1991	Granville Again 5-11-6: 5/4	M. Pipe	*P. Scudamore*	8
1992	Carobee 5-11-10: 2/1	D. Nicholson	*R. Dunwoody*	9
1993	Roll A Dollar 7-11-6: 9/4	D. Elsworth	*P. Holley*	9

SANDEMAN MAGHULL NOVICES' CHASE (Aintree 2m)

1954	Evian 6-11-4: 100/6	M. V. O'Brien (Ir)	*E. McKenzie*	11
1955	Wise Child 7-12-0: 11/4	C. Bewicke	*G. Milburn*	17
1956	Sir Ken 9-12-0: 1/1	W. Stephenson	*T. Molony*	7
1957	Northern King 6-11-4: 11/2	E. Cousins	*M. Pumfrey*	9
1958	Just Awake 6-12-0: 110/7	P. Cazalet	*A. Freeman*	14
1959	Liquidator 7-11-4: 100/7	W. Hall	*P. Farrell*	13
1960	Cupid's Charge 5-11-0: 100/6	P. Cazalet	*A. Freeman*	13
1961	Peacetown 7-11-11: 7/1	G. Owen	*S. Mellor*	8
1962	Rye Light 10-11-8: 5/1	W. Hall	*P. Farrell*	14
1963	Border Sparkle 7-11-8: 13/2	N. Robinson	*T. McGinley*	9
1964	Brand X 9-11-8: 11/2	F. Cundell	*R. Edwards*	6
1965	Oedipe 7-11-11: 5/2	P. Cazalet	*S. Mellor*	11
1966	Roe Gemmel 7-11-8: 100/7	R. Fairbairn	*Mr G. Macmillan*	20
1967	Glenn 6-11-11: 7/2	F. Rimell	*T. Biddlecombe*	11
1968	Brian's Best 8-11-11: 10/1	G. Owen	*R. Edwards*	13
1969	Rainbow Cottage 6-11-8: 100/8	W. A. Stephenson	*T. S. Murphy*	14
1970	Tenterclef 8-11-4: 5/1	P. Ransom	*B. Brogan*	6
1971	Vegeo 8-11-4: 16/1	W. Stephenson	*D. Nicholson*	12
1972	Explicit 8-12-0: 9/2	L. Shedden	*T. Stack*	11
1973	Line Regiment 9-11-4: 14/1	W. D. Francis	*J. Bourke*	6
1974	Winter Rain 6-12-0: 9/4	A. Dickinson	*M. Dickinson*	15
1975	Tom Morgan 6-12-0: 3/1	K. Oliver	*C. Tinkler*	9
1976	Vaguely Attractive 7-11-3: 15/1	S. Murphy (Ir)	*Mr J. Fowler*	11
1977	Siberian Sun 6-11-9: 11/2	F. Flood (Ir)	*F. Berry*	10
1978	Another Dolly 8-11-9: 11/4	F. Rimell	*J. Burke*	4
1979	Night Nurse 8-11-3: 1/1	M. H. Easterby	*J. J. O'Neill*	4
1980	Western Rose 8-11-3: 15/2	F. Rimell	*S. Morshead*	7
1981	Irian 7-11-3: 10/1	A. Moore (Ir)	*F. Berry*	10
1982	Brave Fellow 8-11-3: 9/2	J. FitzGerald	*P. Charlton*	11
1983	Ryeman 6-11-11: 10/11	M. H. Easterby	*A. Brown*	8
1984	Noddy's Ryde 7-11-10: 1/2	G. Richards	*N. Doughty*	12
1985	Pan Arctic 6-11-3: 100/1	T. Bill	*P. Hobbs*	10
1986	Pearlyman 7-11-13: 4/1	J. Edwards	*P. Barton*	10
1987	Dan The Millar 8-11-13: 5/2	Mrs M. Dickinson	*G. Bradley*	9

167

1988	Jim Thorpe 7-11-8: 11/4	G. Richards	*C. Grant*	7
1989	Feroda 8-11-8: 13/8	A. Moore (Ir)	*T. Taaffe*	6
1990	Boutzdaroff 8-11-1: 8/1	J. FitzGerald	*D. Byrne*	14
1991	Young Benz 7-11-3: 13/2	M. H. Easterby	*L. Wyer*	10
1992	Cyphrate 6-11-3: 8/1	M. Pipe	*P. Scudamore*	11
1993	Valiant Boy 7-11-10: 12/1	S. Kettlewell	*R. Garrity*	7

MARTELL CUP CHASE (Aintree 3m 1f)

1984	Royal Bond 11-11-5: 11/2	A. Moore (Ir)	*T. Taaffe*	4
1985	Wayward Lad 10-11-5: 6/1	Mrs M. Dickinson	*J. Francome*	6
1986	Beau Ranger 8-11-5: 40/1	J. Thorne	*H. Davies*	4
1987	Wayward Lad 12-11-5: 7/1	Mrs M. Dickinson	*G. McCourt*	6
1988	Desert Orchid 9-11-5: 3/1	D. Elsworth	*S. Sherwood*	4
1989	Yahoo 8-11-5: 5/1	J. Edwards	*T. Morgan*	8
1990	Toby Tobias 8-11-9: 1/1	Mrs J. Pitman	*M. Pitman*	5
1991	Aquilifer 11-11-5: 11/2	M. Pipe	*R. Dunwoody*	5
1992	Kings Fountain 9-11-9: 11/4	K. Bailey	*A. Tory*	8
1993	Docklands Express 11-11-5: 6/4	K. Bailey	*J. Osborne*	4

JOHN HUGHES MEMORIAL TROPHY HANDICAP CHASE
(Aintree 2¾m)

1949	Cadamstown 9-11-4: 20/1	J. Powell	*J. Brogan*	24
1950	Culworth 9-10-12: 7/1	W. Hall	*R. Curran*	16
1951	Culworth 10-11-6: 5/1	W. Hall	*R. Curran*	18
1952	Ballymagillan 6-10-9: 7/2	T. Dreaper (Ir)	*P. Taaffe*	15
1953	Irish Lizard 10-10-4: 100/8	H. Nicholson	*R. Francis*	17
1954	Little Yid 12-10-11: 3/1	R. Renton	*G. Slack*	17
1955	Stormhead 11-11-12: 10/1	W. Hall	*P. Farrell*	14
1956	John Jacques 7-11-4: 13/2	W. Wharton	*J. Power*	10
1957	Roughan 9-10-8: 100/7	N. Crump	*H. East*	14
1958	Roughan 10-11-0: 11/2	N. Crump	*F. Winter*	16
1959	Clanyon 11-11-2: 6/1	W. J-Powell	*G. Underwood*	19
1960	Fresh Winds 9-11-1: 100/7	R. Whiston	*S. Mellor*	21
1961	Cupid's Charge 6-11-3: 9/1	P. Cazalet	*W. Rees*	13
1962	Dagmar Gittell 7-10-11: 100/8	R. Renton	*J. Gifford*	22
1963	Barberyn 8-11-9: 7/1	W. Stephenson	*M. Scudamore*	20
1964	Red Tide 7-10-6: 10/1	R. Turnell	*J. King*	14
1965	Hopkiss 7-10-12: 11/2	A. Kilpatrick	*E. P. Harty*	13
1966	Walpole 10-11-5: 10/1	R. Price	*J. Gifford*	24
1967	Georgetown 7-10-7: 100/8	N. Kusbish	*P. Mahoney*	23
1968	Surcharge 10-10-8: 100/8	J. Barclay	*S. Davenport*	16
1969	Dozo 8-10-5: 10/1	G. Balding	*E. P. Harty*	20
1970	Charter Flight 8-11-12: 9/2	R. Turnell	*J. Haine*	23
1971	Rigton Prince 10-11-1: 8/1	W. A. Stephenson	*J. Enright*	15
1972	Sunny Lad 8-10-8: 8/1	F. Rimell	*K. White*	17
1973	Inch Arran 9-11-2: 8/1	P. Cazalet	*D. Mould*	14
1974	Clear Cut 10-11-8: 8/1	W. Hall	*J. J. O'Neill*	18
1975	Our Greenwood 7-12-0: 11/2	J. Dreaper (Ir)	*T. Carberry*	18
1976	Lictor 9-10-0: 20/1	E. Courage	*D. Sunderland*	12
1977	Churchtown Boy 10-10-0: 9/1	M. Salaman	*C. Read*	26
1978	Canit 8-10-0: 8/1	F. Rimell	*C. Tinkler*	15
1979	Artic Ale 8-10-8: 12/1	D. Moore (Ir)	*Mr J. Fowler*	23
1980	Uncle Bing 11-11-11: 17/2	R. Head	*J. Francome*	24
1981	Mr Marlsbridge 8-10-10: 10/1	D. Gandolfo	*P. Barton*	18
1982	Beacon Time 8-10-9: 13/2	F. Walwyn	*K. Mooney*	26
1983	Tiepolino 11-10-4: 16/1	K. Bishop	*H. Davies*	19
1984	Fabulous 11-10-0: 33/1	J. S. Wilson	*A. Stringer*	23
1985	Smith's Man 7-10-0: 10/1	Mrs J. Pitman	*M. Perrett*	21
1986	Glenrue 9-10-2: 20/1	T. Casey	*R. Dunwoody*	22
1987	Strath Leader 9-11-0: 12/1	J. Edwards	*T. Morgan*	15
1988	Wiggburn 9-10-2: 12/1	Mrs A. Hewitt	*M. Williams*	19
1989	Villierstown 10-11-10: 5/2	W. A. Stephenson	*S. Sherwood*	7
1990	Wont Be Gone Long 8-10-2: 25/1	N. Henderson	*R. Dunwoody*	30
1991	J-J-Henry 12-10-10: 11/1	P. Beaumont	*Mrs A. Farrell*	11
1992	The Antartex 9-10-2: 33/1	G. Richards	*R. Dunwoody*	26
1993	Sirrah Jay 13-10-0: 16/1	G. Balding	*A. Maguire*	23

GLENLIVET ANNIVERSARY HURDLE (4-y-o) (Aintree 2m 110yds)

1976	Cooch Behar 11-0: 4/1	C. Kinane (Ir)	*L. O'Donnell*	8
1977	Decent Fellow 11-3: 7/2	G. Balding	*R. Linley*	11
1978	Beparoejojo 11-0: 10/1	J. Bolger (Ir)	*D. T. Hughes*	11
1979	Pollardstown 11-7: 10/11	S. Mellor	*P. Blacker*	9
1980	Starfen 11-0: 3/1	M. H. Easterby	*J. J. O'Neill*	20
1981	Broadsword 11-3: 6/5	D. Nicholson	*P. Scudamore*	10
1982	Prince Bless 11-0: 12/1	Mrs N. Smith	*M. O'Halloran*	12
1983	Benfen 11-0: 16/1	M. H. Easterby	*A. Brown*	9
1984	Afzal 11-0: 9/1	R. Hollinshead	*G. McCourt*	17
1985	Humberside Lady 10-9: 15/2	G. Huffer	*M. Dwyer*	15
1986	Dark Raven 11-0: 7/2	D. Weld (Ir)	*T. Carmody*	16
1987	Aldino 11-0: 11/1	O. Sherwood	*S. Sherwood*	13
1988	Royal Illusion 11-0: 9/1	G. Moore	*M. Hammond*	14
1989	Vayrua 11-0: 12/1	G. Harwood	*M. Perrett*	9
1990	Sybillin 11-0: 25/1	J. FitzGerald	*D. Byrne*	18
1991	Montpelier Lad 11-0: 9/1	G. Richards	*N. Doughty*	14
1992	Salwan 11-0: 5/1	P. Bevan	*R. Stronge*	13
1993	Titled Dancer 10-9: 9/2	J. Coogan (Ir)	*J. Shortt*	8

100 PIPERS HANDICAP HURDLE (Aintree 3m 110yds)

1985	Gembridge Jupiter 7-10-3: 12/1	C. Trietline	*J. Suthern*	21
1986	Ishkomann 7-10-9: 11/1	J. Spearing	*G. McCourt*	14
1987	Mandavi 6-10-4: 12/1	N. Henderson	*M. Bowlby*	20
1988	Rapier Thrust 6-11-3: 8/1	J. FitzGerald	*M. Dwyer*	16
1989	Slalom 8-12-0: 9/1	M. Robinson	*J. White*	17
1990	Sip of Orange 8-10-3: 5/1	J. FitzGerald	*M. Dwyer*	21
1991	Merano 8-10-4: 9/2	M. W. Easterby	*G. McCourt*	15
1992	Threeoutoffour 7-10-0: 20/1	O. Brennan	*M. Brennan*	25
1993	Andrew's First 6-10-2: 100/30	M. Wilkinson	*C. Llewellyn*	13

PERRIER JOUET HANDICAP CHASE (Aintree 3m 1f)

1977	Our Edition 10-11-13: 7/2	S. Mellor	*S. Jobar*	12
1978	Mr Snowman 9-10-10: 5/1	T. Forster	*G. Thorner*	8
1979	Silent Valley 6-9-10: 16/1	I. Jordon	*J. Allen*	12
1980	New Colonist 8-10-3: 9/4	A. Dickinson	*T. Carmody*	10
1981	Megan's Boy 8-11-5: 11/2	E. Carter	*P. Charlton*	12
1982	Silent Valley 9-10-13: 16/1	I. Jordon	*P. Scudamore*	11
1983	Fauloon 8-10-7: 8/1	F. Walwyn	*W. Smith*	13
1984	Straight Accord 9-11-8: 9/2	F. Walwyn	*S. Shilston*	9
1985	Green Bramble 8-10-3: 5/2	N. Henderson	*S. Smith Eccles*	11
1986	Arctic Beau 8-10-1: 10/1	J. Thorne	*R. Dunwoody*	7
1987	Gainsay 8-10-11: 7/2	Mrs J. Pitman	*M. Pitman*	10
1988	Rinus 7-10-2: 7/2	G. Richards	*R. Dunwoody*	8
1989	Travel Over 8-10-1: 3/1	Mrs M. Dickinson	*M. Hammond*	6
1990	One More Knight 7-10-12: 10/1	Mrs I. McKie	*L. Harvey*	12
1991	Gold Options 9-11-10: 7/2	J. FitzGerald	*M. Dwyer*	7
1992	River Bounty 6-10-0: 12/1	J. Upson	*R. Supple*	14
1993	Black Humour 9-12-0: 9/2	C. Brooks	*G. Bradley*	11

MUMM MELLING CHASE (Aintree 2½m)

1991	Blazing Walker 7-11-10: 5/1	W. A. Stephenson	*C. Grant*	7
1992	Remittance Man 8-11-10: 4/9	N. Henderson	*R. Dunwoody*	4
1993	Deep Sensation 8-11-10: 7/4	J. Gifford	*D. Murphy*	4

MUMM MILDMAY NOVICES' CHASE (Aintree 3m 1f)

1981	Bregawn 7-11-8: 7/4	M. Dickinson	*R. Earnshaw*	8
1982	Burrough Hill Lad 6-11-5: 9/1	Mrs J. Pitman	*P. Tuck*	10
1983	Everett 8-11-9: 7/2	F. Walwyn	*S. Shilston*	5
1984	Baron Blakeney 7-11-6: 14/1	M. Pipe	*Mr O. Sherwood*	8
1985	Rhyme 'N' Reason 6-11-3: 11/8	D. Murray-Smith	*G. Bradley*	12
1986	Stearsby 7-11-6: 11/4	Mrs J. Pitman	*G. Bradley*	11
1987	Against The Grain 6-11-3: 8/1	D. Nicholson	*R. Dunwoody*	13
1988	Delius 10-11-3: 9/1	R. Lee	*B. Dowling*	13
1989	Swardean 7-11-3: 16/1	R. Lee	*B. Dowling*	13
1990	Royal Athlete 7-11-9: 5/2	Mrs J. Pitman	*M. Pitman*	11
1991	Sparkling Flame 7-11-9: 4/1	N. Henderson	*R. Dunwoody*	13
1992	Bradbury Star 7-11-9: 6/4	J. Gifford	*E. Murphy*	7

1993 Cab On Target 7-11-3: 15/8   Mrs M. Reveley   *P. Niven*   5

MARTELL FOX HUNTERS' CHASE (Aintree 2¾m)

Year	Horse	Trainer	Jockey	Ran
1947	Lucky Purchase 9-12-0: 100/30	S. Banks	*J. Nichols*	6
1948	San Michele 8-12-0: 7/1	G. Cunard	*G. Cunard*	12
1949	Ballyhartfield 10-12-0: 7/2	J. Makin	*J. Straker*	5
1950	Hilmere 17-12-0: 100/7	L. Dalton	*P. Brookshaw*	14
1951	Candy II 9-11-7: 10/1	R. Brewis	*R. Brewis*	17
1952	Pampeenne II 9-12-0: 7/2	H. Alexander	*H. Alexander*	11
1953	Solo Call 9-12-0: 6/1	M. Brewis	*M. Brewis*	7
1954	Dark Stranger 9-12-0: 10/1	L. Colville	*J. Bosley*	14
1955	Happymint 10-12-0: 9/2	J. Wight	*A. Moralee*	13
1956	Mr Shanks 9-12-0: 5/2	J. Keith	*J. Everitt*	8
1957	Colledge Master 7-12-0: 11/10	L. Morgan	*L. Morgan*	6
1958	Surprise Packet 9-12-0: 2/1	Mrs S. Richards	*T. Johnson*	13
1959	Merryman II 8-12-0: 5/2	N. Crump	*C. Scott*	10
1960	April Queen 9-12-0: 100/7	M. Fear	*J. Daniell*	8
1961	Colledge Master 11-12-0: 4/6	L. Morgan	*L. Morgan*	8
1962	Dominion 10-12-0: 8/1	K. Beeston	*C. Foulkes*	12
1963	Sea Knight 8-12-0: 13/2	W. A. Stephenson	*P. Nicholson*	15
1964	Aerial III 8-12-0: 5/2	R. Armytage	*J. Daniell*	8
1965	Sea Knight 10-11-9: 8/1	W. A. Stephenson	*P. Nicholson*	14
1966	Sulbaltern 12-12-0: 100/7	C Alexander	*J. Lawrence*	13
1967	Minto Burn 11-11-7: 5/1	Miss B. Johnson	*B. Surtees*	10
1968	Juan 12-11-7: 11/4	P. Wills	*P. Wills*	8
1969	Bitter Lemon 8-11-11: 7/1	V. Rowe	*V. Rowe*	15
1970	Lismateige 7-11-7: 6/1	P. Wates	*A. Wates*	5
1971	Bright Willow 10-11-11: 5/1	G. Cure	*R. Chugg*	15
1972	Credit Call 8-12-0: 8/13	W. A. Stephenson	*C. Collins*	8
1973	Bullock's Horn 10-12-0: 7/2	R. Turnell	*Lord Oaksey*	14
1974	Lord Fortune 11-11-9: 7/2	Mrs J. Brutton	*D. Edmunds*	10
1975	Credit Call 11-11-7: 6/1	W. A. Stephenson	*J. Newton*	10
1976	Credit Call 12-11-9: 5/4	Mrs R. Newton	*J. Newton*	9
1977	Happy Warrior 10-12-0: 6/1	F. Winter	*N. Henderson*	20
1978	Spartan Missile 6-12-0: 15/8	J. Thorne	*J. Thorne*	19
1979	Spartan Missile 7-12-7: 8/15	J. Thorne	*J. Thorne*	15
1980	Rolls Rambler 9-12-5: 100/30	F. Winter	*O. Sherwood*	24
1981	Grittar 8-12-5: 7/4	F. Gilman	*R. Saunders*	25
1982	Lone Soldier 10-12-0: 25/1	J. Docker	*P. Greenall*	12
1983	Atha Cliath 8-12-0: 5/1	P. Mullins (Ir)	*W. Mullins*	8
1984	Gayle Warning 10-12-0: 85/40	J. Dudgeon	*A. Dudgeon*	17
1985	City Boy 10-12-0: 4/1	Mrs J. Mann	*T. Thomson Jones*	18
1986	Eliogarty 11-12-0: 11/1	D. Murray Smith	*Miss C. Beasley*	20
1987	Border Burg 10-12-0: 7/2	J. Delahooke	*A. Hill*	25
1988	Newnham 11-12-0: 50/1	M. Johnson	*S. Andrews*	23
1989	Call Collect 8-12-0: 5/1	J. Parkes	*R. Martin*	16
1990	Lean Ar Aghaidh 13-12-0: 5/1	S. Mellor	*D. Gray*	25
1991	Double Turn 10-12-0: 100/1	J. Jenkins	*P. Harding-Jones*	27
1992	Gee-A 13-12-0: 66/1	G. Hubbard	*P. Murphy*	29
1993	Double Silk 9-12-0: 5/2	R. Wilkins	*R. Treloggen*	27

ODDBINS HANDICAP HURDLE (Aintree 2½m)

Year	Horse	Trainer	Jockey	Ran
1989	Hill Street 7-10-5: 10/1	J. FitzGerald	*M. Dwyer*	15
1990	Sayparee 5-11-3: 10/1	M. Pipe	*P. Scudamore*	14
1991	Trefelyn Cone 7-10-5: 9/1	M. Pipe	*P. Scudamore*	17
1992	Ninepins 5-10-4: 14/1	A. Moore (Ir)	*C. Swan*	16
1993	Gallateen 5-10-11: 12/1	G. Richards	*N. Doughty*	12

BELLE EPOQUE SEFTON NOVICES' HURDLE (Aintree 3m 110yds)

Year	Horse	Trainer	Jockey	Ran
1988	Rustle 6-11-7: 13/8	N. Henderson	*M. Bowlby*	12
1989	Boreen Belle 7-11-2: 10/1	W. Harney (Ir)	*C. Swan*	14
1990	Dwadme 5-11-4: 5/1	O. Sherwood	*J. Osborne*	10
1991	Derring Valley 6-11-4: 25/1	A. P. Jones	*G. McCourt*	16
1992	Barton Bank 6-11-4: 20/1	D. Nicholson	*C. Llewellyn*	15
1993	Cardinal Red 6-11-4: 4/1	Mrs F. Walwyn	*B. de Haan*	6

TOTE 7TH RACE HANDICAP CHASE (Aintree 2½m)

Year	Horse	Trainer	Jockey	Ran
1977	Batchelor's Hall 7-9-9: 18/1	P. Cundell	*M. O'Halloran*	18

170

1978	King Or Country 7-11-2: 11/2	D. Barons	*P. Leach*	15
1979	King Or Country 8-12-1: 7/2	D. Barons	*P. Leach*	11
1980	Carrow Boy 8-10-5: 12/1	W. Durkan (Ir)	*M. Mulligan*	10
1981	Swift Albany 7-10-3: 7/1	R. Robinson	*C. Pimlott*	16
1982	Polars Laddie 9-10-0: 33/1	R. Goldie	*A. Dickman*	10
1983	King Or Country 12-10-4: 9/1	D. Barons	*H. Davies*	12
1984	Gambling Prince 11-10-0: 20/1	Mrs G. Jones	*J. Burke*	12
1985	Beau Ranger 7-11-3: 5/2	J. Thorne	*J. Hurst*	8
1986	Fifty Dollars More 11-11-8: 7/1	F. Winter	*S. Sherwood*	9
1987	Gee-A 8-10-9: 13/2	G. Hubbard	*Miss G. Armytage*	13
1988	Worthy Knight 7-10-0: 14/1	B. McLean	*B. Storey*	8
1989	Golden Freeze 7-11-10: 4/1	Mrs J. Pitman	*M. Bowlby*	8
1990	Sure Metal 7-10-0: 100/1	D. McCain	*B. Storey*	13
1991	Guiburn's Nephew 9-10-1: 15/2	P. Hobbs	*C. Maude*	11
1992	Howe Street 9-10-7: 13/2	H. Johnson	*A. Orkney*	10
1993	Wind Force 8-11-6: 11/2	G. Richards	*N. Doughty*	8

CORDON BLEU HANDICAP HURDLE (Aintree 2m 110yds)
1990	Jubail 5-10-0: 11/4	K. Morgan	*R. Supple*	11
1991	Ivors Guest 5-10-0: 16/1	R. Lee	*C. Grant*	12
1992	Flakey Dove 6-10-0: 7/1	R. Price	*D. Tegg*	13
1993	Spinning 6-10-7: 13/8	I. Balding	*J. Frost*	10

MARTELL AINTREE CHASE (LIMITED HANDICAP)
(Aintree 2m)
1976	Menehall 9-10-0: 25/1	F. Walwyn	*M. Floyd*	10
1977	Skymas 12-12-0: 5/1	B. Lusk (Ir)	*M. Morris*	9
1978	Even Melody 9-11-6: 11/1	N. Crump	*C. Hawkins*	14
1979	Funny Baby 8-10-7: 9/1	G. Fairbairn	*R. Lamb*	8
1980	Drumgora 8-10-7: 8/1	A. Moore (Ir)	*T. McGivern*	10
1981	Western Rose 9-10-7: 8/1	F. Rimell	*S. Morshead*	11
1982	Little Bay 7-10-7: 14/1	G. Richards	*J. J. O'Neill*	12
1983	Artifice 12-11-0: 9/1	J. Thorne	*P. Scudamore*	9
1984	Little Bay 9-11-7: 11/4	G. Richards	*J. Francome*	7
1985	Kathies Lad 8-11-7: 6/5	A. Jarvis	*S. Smith Eccles*	8
1986	Kathies Lad 9-10-13: 11/8	A. Jarvis	*S. Smith Eccles*	6
1987	Sea Merchant 10-10-7: 9/1	W. A. Stephenson	*R. Lamb*	9
1988	Prideaux Boy 10-10-7: 25/1	G. Roach	*A. Webb*	13
1989	Feroda 8-10-7: 9/1	A. Moore (Ir)	*T. Taaffe*	9
1990	Nohalmdun 9-10-7: 11/1	M. H. Easterby	*L. Wyer*	12
1991	Blitzkreig 8-10-13: 4/1	E. O'Grady (Ir)	*T. Carmody*	11
1992	Katabatic 9-12-0: 6/5	A. Turnell	*S. McNeill*	4
1993	Boutzdaroff 11-10-7: 9/1	J. FitzGerald	*M. Dwyer*	6

MARTELL AINTREE HURDLE (Aintree 2½m)
1976	Comedy of Errors 9-11-9: 2/1	F. Rimell	*K. White*	10
1977	Night Nurse 6-11-11: 4/5 ⎫ dh	M. H. Easterby	*P. Broderick*	10
	Monksfield 5-11-5: 7/2 ⎭	D. McDonogh (Ir)	*D. T. Hughes*	
1978	Monksfield 6-11-11: 9/4	D. McDonogh (Ir)	*D. T. Hughes*	7
1979	Monksfield 7-11-11: 5/4	D. McDonogh (Ir)	*D. T. Hughes*	4
1980	Pollardstown 5-11-5: 2/1	S. Mellor	*P. Blacker*	3
1981	Daring Run 6-11-9: 9/4	P. McCreery (Ir)	*Mr T. Walsh*	7
1982	Daring Run 7-11-9: 2/1	P. McCreery (Ir)	*Mr T. Walsh*	5
1983	Gaye Brief 6-11-11: 11/8	Mrs M. Rimell	*R. Linley*	6
1984	Dawn Run 6-11-6: 4/6	P. Mullins (Ir)	*A. Mullins*	8
1985	Bajan Sunshine 6-11-6: 11/1	M. Tate	*P. Scudamore*	7
1986	Aonoch 7-11-9: 16/1	Mrs S. Oliver	*J. Duggan*	9
1987	Aonoch 8-11-9: 5/2	Mrs S. Oliver	*Jacqui Oliver*	7
1988	Celtic Chief 5-11-6: 4/5	Mrs M. Rimell	*R. Dunwoody*	9
1989	Beech Road 7-11-9: 10/1	G. Balding	*R. Guest*	12
1990	Morley Street 6-11-6: 4/5	G. Balding	*J. Frost*	6
1991	Morley Street 7-11-7: 11/8	G. Balding	*J. Frost*	9
1992	Morley Street 8-11-7: 4/5	G. Balding	*R. Dunwoody*	6
1993	Morley Street 9-11-7: 6/1	G. Balding	*G. Bradley*	6

MARTELL MERSEY NOVICES' HURDLE (Aintree 2½m)
| 1985 | Out of The Gloom 4-11-0: 11/4 | R. Hollinshead | *J. J. O'Neill* | 14 |
| 1986 | Canute Express 5-11-9: 3/1 | H. Scott (Ir) | *Mr L. Wyer* | 15 |

1987	The West Awake 6-11-9: 11/8	O. Sherwood	*S. Sherwood*	11
1988	Sir Blake 7-11-5: 2/1	D. Elsworth	*B. Powell*	13
1989	Morley Street 5-11-5: 7/2	G. Balding	*J. Frost*	10
1990	Vazon Bay 6-11-0: 33/1	Mrs J. Pitman	*M. Pitman*	10
1991	Shannon Glen 5-11-1: 8/1	Mrs J. Pitman	*M. Bowlby*	9
1992	Coulton 5-11-1: 9/1	M. W. Easterby	*G. McCourt*	12
1993	Lemon's Mill 4-10-3: 1/2	M. Pipe	*P. Scudamore*	3

SCOTTISH CHAMPION HURDLE (Ayr 2m)

1966	Blue Venom 7-11-1: 7/1	P. Adams	*Mr P. Adams*	5
1967	Originator 6-11-1: 13/2	J. Barclay	*E. Wilson*	13
1968	Al-'Alawi 5-10-8: 9/1	T. Robson	*P. McCarron*	19
1969	Mugatpura 6-11-3: 9/2	F. Walwyn	*T. Jennings*	13
1970	Easter Pirate 6-10-0: 100/6	R. Fairbairn	*S. Hayhurst*	17
1971	Dondieu 6-11-11: 3/1	Denys Smith	*B. Fletcher*	9
1972	Coral Diver 7-11-11: 3/1	F. Rimell	*K. White*	7
1973	Captain Christy 6-12-0: 2/1	P. Taaffe (Ir)	*H. Beasley*	5
1974	Santon Brig 5-11-3: 6/4	A. Dickinson	*M. Dickinson*	3
1975	Comedy of Errors 8-12-0: 1/5	F. Rimell	*K. White*	5
1976	Night Nurse 5-12-0: 1/4	M. H. Easterby	*P. Broderick*	2
1977	Sea Pigeon 7-11-4: 4/9	M. H. Easterby	*J. J. O'Neill*	3
1978	Sea Pigeon 8-12-0: 7/4	M. H. Easterby	*J. J. O'Neill*	7
1979	Bird's Nest 9-11-8: 100/30	R. Turnell	*A. Turnell*	5
1980	Secret Ballot 6-10-7: 11/2	R. Turnell	*A. Turnell*	7
1981	Bird's Nest 11-11-6: 6/1	R. Turnell	*A. Turnell*	5
1982	Gay George 6-11-7: 4/6	F. Walwyn	*W. Smith*	5
1983	Royal Vulcan 5-11-13: 7/2	N. Callaghan	*P. Scudamore*	6
1984	Rushmoor 6-10-13: 3/1	R. Peacock	*P. Scudamore*	8
1985	Sailor's Dance 5-11-1: 5/2	F. Winter	*J. Duggan*	4
1986	River Ceiriog 5-10-9: 4/1	N. Henderson	*S. Smith Eccles*	7
1987	Positive 5-10-8: 11/2	K. Bailey	*P. Croucher*	6
1988	Pat's Jester 5-11-1: 5/1	R. Allan	*B. Storey*	8
1989	Aldino 6-12-0: 13/2	O. Sherwood	*S. Sherwood*	6
1990	Sayparee 5-10-7: 11/2	M. Pipe	*J. Lower*	13
1991	Precious Boy 5-11-2: 9/2	M. O'Neill	*L. Wyer*	5
1992	Granville Again 6-11-10: 4/7	M. Pipe	*P. Scudamore*	5
1993	Staunch Friend 5-11-10: 5/1	M. Tompkins	*A. Maguire*	6

EDINBURGH WOOLLEN MILL FUTURE CHAMPIONS NOVICES CHASE (Ayr 2½m)

1971	Chorus 10-11-7: 11/2	H. T. Jones	*S. Mellor*	11
1972	Avondhu 9-11-7: 8/1	P. Chesmore	*P. Brogan*	11
1973	The Benign Bishop 6-12-1: 11/4	K. Oliver	*R. Barry*	13
1974	Winter Rain 6-12-1: 4/7	A. Dickinson	*M. Dickinson*	6
1975	Easby Abbey 8-11-7: 5/4	M. H. Easterby	*R. Barry*	6
1976	Cromwell Road 6-12-1: 5/2	G. Richards	*D. Goulding*	11
1977	Crofton Hall 8-11-8: 5/1	J. Dixon	*J. J. O'Neill*	5
1978	King Weasel 6-11-1: 1/2	M. H. Easterby	*J. J. O'Neill*	4
1979	Night Nurse 8-12-0: 5/6	M. H. Easterby	*J. J. O'Neill*	6
1980	Don't Forget 6-11-3: 8/1	W. A. Stephenson	*R. Lamb*	6
1981	Little Bay 6-11-11: 5/2	G. Richards	*R. Barry*	9
1982	Full Sutton 9-11-3: 5/1	D. Kent	*B. R. Davies*	6
1983	Mountain Hays 8-11-8: 11/10	M. H. Easterby	*A. Brown*	5
1984	Noddy's Ryde 7-11-11: 4/11	G. Richards	*N. Doughty*	8
1985	Buck House 7-11-10: 4/6	M. Morris (Ir)	*T. Carmody*	10
1986	Amber Rambler 7-11-3: 5/1	H. Wharton	*S. Youlden*	5
1987	General Chandos 6-11-3: 8/1	J. Bradburne	*Mr J. Bradburne*	6
1988	Jim Thorpe 7-11-10: 9/4	G. Richards	*M. Dwyer*	6
1989	Southern Minstrel 6-11-13: 5/4	W. A. Stephenson	*C. Grant*	7
1990	Celtic Shot 8-11-13: 5/2	C. Brooks	*G. McCourt*	12
1991	High Knowl 8-11-8: 15/2	M. Pipe	*G. McCourt*	6
1992	The Illywhacker 7-11-8: 6/1	Mrs J. Pitman	*M. Pitman*	10
1993	Cab On Target 7-11-8: 4/9	Mrs M. Reveley	*P. Niven*	7

WILLIAM HILL SCOTTISH NATIONAL (HANDICAP CHASE)
(Ayr 4m 1f)

1947	Rowland Roy 8-11-2: 6/1	F. Walwyn	*Mr R. Black*	15
1948	Magnetic Fin 9-10-5: 100/8	W. Hall	*L. Vick*	12

1949	Wot No Sun 7-11-5: 2/1	N. Crump	*A. Thompson*	10
1950	Sanvina 10-12-2: 25/1	J. Wight	*Mr K. Oliver*	19
1951	Court Painter 11-9-7: 20/1	C. Bewicke	*F. Carroll*	13
1952	Flagrant Mac 8-11-12: 100/8	R. Renton	*J. Power*	17
1953	Queen's Taste 7-10-2: 100/6	H. Clarkson	*Mr T. Robson*	21
1954	Queen's Taste 8-10-9: 10/1	H. Clarkson	*G. Slack*	15
1955	Bar Point 8-10-2: 20/1	R. Renton	*D. Ancil*	18
1956	Queen's Taste 10-11-0: 8/1	H. Clarkson	*R. Curran*	14
1957	Bremontier 10-10-12: 10/1	P. Taylor	*A. Rossio*	13
1958	Game Field 8-11-10: 9/1	J. Fawcus	*J. Boddy*	14
1959	Merryman II 8-10-12: 100/8	N. Crump	*G. Scott*	18
1960	Fincham 8-10-0: 9/4	J. White	*M. Batchelor*	8
1961	Kinmont Wullie 7-10-7: 8/1	W. A. Stephenson	*C. Stobbs*	18
1962	Sham Fight 10-10-10: 100/6	T. Robson	*T. Robson*	18
1963	Pappageno's Cottage 8-10-9: 100/8	K. Oliver	*T. Brookshaw*	18
1964	Popham Down 7-10-0: 8/1	F. Walwyn	*J. Haine*	14
1965	Brasher 9-10-5: 4/1	T. Robson	*J. FitzGerald*	9
1966	African Patrol 7-10-7: 10/1	R. Fairbairn	*J. Leech*	17
1967	The Fossa 10-9-12: 8/1	F. Rimell	*A. Turnell*	18
1968	Arcturus 7-10-4: 4/1	N. Crump	*P. Buckley*	10
1969	Playlord 8-12-0: 9/1	G. Richards	*R. Barry*	17
1970	The Spaniard 8-10-0: 8/1	K. Oliver	*B. Brogan*	10
1971	Young Ash Leaf 7-10-2: 12/1	K. Oliver	*P. Ennis*	21
1972	Quick Reply 7-9-9: 11/1	H. Bell	*M. Barnes*	17
1973	Esban 9-9-11: 16/1	R. Clay	*J. Bourke*	21
1974	Red Rum 9-11-13: 11/8	D. McCain	*B. Fletcher*	17
1975	Barona 9-10-0: 33/1	R. Armytage	*P. Kelleway*	17
1976	Barona 10-10-2: 12/1	R. Armytage	*P. Kelleway*	23
1977	Sebastian V 9-10-2: 9/2	H. Bell	*R. Lamb*	18
1978	King Con 9-9-13: 33/1	G. Renilson	*Mr P. Craggs*	21
1979	Fighting Fit 7-10-10: 9/1	K. Oliver	*C. Hawkins*	19
1980	Salkeld 8-10-0: 14/1	N. Crump	*D. Atkins*	23
1981	Astral Charmer 8-9-10: 66/1	H. Bell	*J. Goulding*	21
1982	Cockle Strand 9-9-11: 9/1	K. Oliver	*D. Dutton*	15
1983	Canton 9-10-2: 16/1	N. Crump	*K. Whyte*	22
1984	Androma 7-10-0: 7/1	J. FitzGerald	*M. Dwyer*	19
1985	Androma 8-10-0: 11/1	J. FitzGerald	*M. Dwyer*	18
1986	Hardy Lad 9-10-0: 28/1	B. Wilkinson	*M. Hammond*	24
1987	Little Polveir 10-10-0: 12/1	J. Edwards	*P. Scudamore*	11
1988	Mighty Mark 9-10-5: 9/1	F. Walton	*B. Storey*	17
1989	Roll-A-Joint 11-10-0: 4/1	C. Popham	*B. Powell*	11
1990	Four Trix 9-10-0: 25/1	G. Richards	*D. Byrne*	28
1991	Killone Abbey 8-10-0: 40/1	W. A. Stephenson	*C. Grant*	18
1992	Captain Dibble 7-11-0: 9/1	N. Twiston-Davies	*P. Scudamore*	21
1993	Run For Free 9-11-10: 6/1	M. Pipe	*M. Perrett*	21

GOLDEN EAGLE NOVICES CHASE (Ascot 2m 3f 110yds)

1974	Colondine 7-11-3: 7/1	I. Dudgeon	*D. O'Donovan*	13
1975	Galloway Edition 6-11-3: 100/30	G. Balding	*J. Fox*	8
1976	The Snipe 6-11-3: 85/40	J. Webber	*A. Webber*	5
1977	Autumn Rain 6-11-3: 7/4	A. Dickinson	*M. Dickinson*	6
1978	Valiant Charger 7-11-3: 100/30	F. Winter	*J. Francome*	12
1979	Sweet September 7-11-3: 8/13	R. Turnell	*A. Turnell*	12
1980	O'er The Border 6-11-3: 7/1	P. Calver	*P. Haynes*	16
1981	Spring Chancellor 6-11-3: 33/1	W. A. Stephenson	*P. Scudamore*	14
1982	New Lyric 7-11-3: 13/2	D. Nicholson	*P. Scudamore*	9
1983	Gallaher 7-11-3: 100/30	F. Walwyn	*W. Smith*	7
1984	Just For The Crack 6-11-3: 20/1	K Bailey	*A. Webber*	3
1985	Townley Stone 6-11-7: 8/1	J. Webber	*G. McCourt*	7
1986	Oregon Trail 6-11-10: 2/1	S. Christian	*K Mooney*	5
1987	Foyle Fisherman 8-11-3: 9/1	J. Gifford	*R. Rowe*	8
1988	Saffron Lord 6-11-8: 2/1	J. Gifford	*R. Rowe*	3
1989	Abandoned because of snow			
1990	Okeetee 7-11-4: 40/85	C. Brooks	*B. de Haan*	3
1991	Southerly Buster 8-11-4: 9/2	O. Sherwood	*J. Osborne*	7
1992	Hey Cottage 7-11-4: 33/1	D. McCain	*G. McCourt*	6
1993	Antonin 5-10-10: 11/2	Mrs S. Bramall	*J. Burke*	7

173

LETHEBY & CHRISTOPHER LONG-DISTANCE HURDLE (Ascot 3m)

1974 Moyne Royal 9-12-3: 11/2	A. Pitt	*J. King*	20
1975 Lanzarote 7-11-12: 5/2	F. Winter	*R. Pitman*	10
1976 Good Prospect 7-11-3: 5/2	J. Edwards	*A. Turnell*	7
1977 Mark Henry 6-11-3: 7/1	W. Elsey	*T. Stack*	12
1978 Flame Gun 6-11-12: 11/2	E. O'Grady (Ir)	*Mr N. Madden*	11
1979 Prominent King 7-11-12: 13/8	M. H. Easterby	*J. J. O'Neill*	9
1980 Derring Rose 5-11-12: 4/1	A. Jarvis	*A. Turnell*	9
1981 Shell Burst 6-11-0: 20/1	L. Kennard	*H. Davies*	13
1982 Gaye Chance 7-11-12: 7/4	Mrs M. Rimell	*P. Scudamore*	7
1983 Sandalay 5-11-3: 8/1	P. Cundell	*P. Charlton*	11
1984 Alastor O Mavros 5-11-3: 9/1	J. Gifford	*H. Davies*	6
1985 Bajan Sunshine 6-12-2: 4/1	M. Tate	*P. Scudamore*	9
1986 Gaye Brief 9-12-2: 4/1	Mrs M. Rimell	*P. Scudamore*	11
1987 Mrs Muck 6-11-2: 9/4	N. Twiston-Davies	*P. Scudamore*	10
1988 Gaye Brief 11-12-2: 14/1	Mrs M. Rimell	*D. Browne*	6
1989 Abandoned because of snow			
1990 Battalion 6-11-7: 100/30	C. Brooks	*B. de Haan*	8
1991 Mole Board 9-11-3: 6/1	J. Old	*J. Osborne*	7
1992 Pragada 9-11-3: 5/1	M. Pipe	*P. Scudamore*	12
1993 Sweet Duke 6-11-3: 5/1	N. Twiston-Davies	*C. Llewellyn*	7

PEREGRINE HANDICAP CHASE (Ascot 2m 3f 110yds)

1976 Game Spirit 10-11-12: 7/4	F. Walwyn	*W. Smith*	5
1977 Cloud Park 8-10-0: 8/1	M. Tate	*J. J. O'Neill*	8
1978 Royal Epic 7-11-3: 8/1	V. Cross	*J. King*	6
1979 Breemount Don 6-11-8: 3/1	F. Winter	*J. Francome*	10
1980 Tiepolino 8-12-4: 9/2	P. Cundell	*H. Davies*	6
1981 Fairy King 8-10-2: 3/1	J. FitzGerald	*A. Brown*	16
1982 Shady Deal 9-10-3: 3/1	J. Gifford	*R. Rowe*	5
1983 Richdee 7-11-7: 3/1	N. Crump	*C. Hawkins*	6
1984 Tom's Little Al 8-10-9: 4/1	W. Williams	*P. Scudamore*	6
1985 Restless Shot 10-10-2: 12/1	J. Webber	*J. Burke*	9
1986 Ryeman 9-11-3: 7/1	M. H. Easterby	*J. J. O'Neill*	9
1987 Desert Orchid 8-12-4: 7/4	D. Elsworth	*C. Brown*	7
1988 Dunkirk 12-10-2: 8/1	M. Francis	*M. Richards*	6
1989 Abandoned because of snow			
1990 Ida's Delight 11-11-2: 11/4	J. Charlton	*B. Storey*	6
1991 John O'Dee 8-9-11: 25/1	F. Murphy	*J. Kavanagh*	8
1992 Monumental Lad 9-10-4: 13/2	Mrs H. Parrott	*D. Leahy*	7
1993 Calapaez 9-11-10: 9/2	Miss B. Sanders	*S. McNeill*	6

JAMESON IRISH GRAND NATIONAL HANDICAP CHASE

(Fairyhouse 3m 5f)

1946 Golden View II 11-12-7: 7/1	R. O'Connell	*M. Molony*	11
1947 Revelry 7-11-5: 6/1	J. Doyle	*D. L. Moore*	17
1948 Hamstar 8-9-7: 6/1	W O'Grady	*E. Kennedy*	17
1949 Shagreen 8-10-0: 5/1	T. Dreaper	*E. Newman*	20
1950 Dominick's Bar 6-10-6: 8/1	T. Hyde	*M. Molony*	12
1951 Icy Calm 8-10-3: 100/6	W. O'Grady	*P. Doyle*	19
1952 Alberoni 9-10-1: 6/1	M. V. O'Brien	*L. Stephens*	11
1953 Overshadow 13-10-4: 20/1	C. Magnier	*A. Power*	15
1954 Royal Approach 6-12-0: 1/1	T. Dreaper	*P. Taaffe*	11
1955 Umm 8-10-5: 100/7	G. Wells	*P. Taaffe*	16
1956 Air Prince 12-10-0: 20/1	J. McClintock	*T. O'Brien*	19
1957 Kilballyown 10-9-10: 10/1	P. Norris	*G. W. Robinson*	26
1958 Gold Legend 8-9-7: 100/8	J. Brogan	*J. Lehane*	21
1959 Zonda 8-10-6: 5/1	M. Geraghty	*P. Taaffe*	15
1960 Olympia 6-9-11: 6/1	T. Dreaper	*T. Taaffe*	16
1961 Fortria 9-12-0: 17/2	T. Dreaper	*P. Taaffe*	14
1962 Kerforo 8-10-3: 9/1	T. Dreaper	*L. McLoughlin*	11
1963 Last Link 7-9-7: 7/1	T. Dreaper	*P. Woods*	10
1964 Arkle 7-12-0: 1/2	T. Dreaper	*P. Taaffe*	4
1965 Splash 7-10-13: 6/4	T. Dreaper	*P. Woods*	4
1966 Flyingbolt 7-12-7: 8/11	T. Dreaper	*P. Taaffe*	6
1967 Vulpine 6-11-6: 7/1	P. Mullins	*M. Curran*	12
1968 Herring Gull 6-11-13: 5/2	P. Mullins	*J. Crowley*	12
1969 Sweet Dreams 8-9-10: 10/1	K. Bell	*R. Coonan*	18

1970	Garoupe 6-9-9: 10/1	F. Flood	*C. Finnegan*	13
1971	King's Sprite 9-9-13: 7/1	G. Wells	*A. Moore*	19
1972	Dim Wit 7-10-13: 15/2	P. Mullins	*M. Curran*	14
1973	Tartan Ace 6-9-7: 10/1	T. Costello	*J. Cullen*	14
1974	Colebridge 10-11-2: 11/5	J. Dreaper	*F. Wright*	10
1975	Brown Lad 9-10-5: 6/4	J. Dreaper	*T. Carberry*	8
1976	Brown Lad 10-12-0: 7/2	J. Dreaper	*T. Carberry*	15
1977	Billycan 7-10-0: 8/1	A. Maxwell	*M. Morris*	20
1978	Brown Lad 12-12-2: 5/1	J. Dreaper	*G. Dowd*	19
1979	Tied Cottage 11-10-2: 13/2	D. Moore	*Mr A. Robinson*	20
1980	Daletta 7-11-4: 11/1	G. St J. Williams	*J. P. Harty*	25
1981	Luska 7-9-9: 11/1	P. Mullins	*T. Finn*	20
1982	King Spruce 8-10-2: 20/1	M. O'Brien	*G. Newman*	25
1983	Bit Of A Skite 7-9-7: 7/1	E. O'Grady	*T. Ryan*	27
1984	Bentom Boy 9-9-9: 33/1	W. Rooney	*Mrs A. Ferris*	29
1985	Rhyme 'N' Reason 6-10-6: 6/1	D. Murray-Smith (Eng)	*G. Bradley*	23
1986	Insure 8-9-7: 16/1	P. Hughes	*M. Flynn*	15
1987	Brittany Boy 8-10-0: 14/1	K. Hitchmough	*T. Taaffe*	26
1988	Perris Valley 7-10-0: 12/1	D. Weld	*B. Sheridan*	18
1989	Maid of Money 7-11-6: 10/1	J. Fowler	*A. Powell*	22
1990	Desert Orchid 11-12-0: 1/1	D. Elsworth (Eng)	*R. Dunwoody*	14
1991	Omerta 11-10-9: 6/1	M. Pipe (Eng)	*Mr A. Maguire*	22
1992	Vanton 8-10-11: 13/2	M. O'Brien	*J. Titley*	23
1993	Ebony Jane 8-10-7: 6/1	F. Flood	*C. Swan*	27

MITSUBISHI SHOGUN GOLDEN MILLER HANDICAP CHASE
(Cheltenham 3m 2f 110yds)

1980	Lacson 8-10-11: 13/2	R. Hawker	*S. C. Knight*	10
1981	Master Smudge 9-10-13: 5/2	A. Barrow	*R. Linley*	6
1982	Scot Lane 9-11-7: 10/1	M. Tate	*C. Smith*	13
1983	Abandoned because course waterlogged			
1984	Plundering 7-10-0: 5/1	F. Winter	*B. de Haan*	10
1985	Aces Wild 7-10-5: 4/1	F. Winter	*J. Duggan*	10
1986	Charter Party 8-11-9: 11/4	D. Nicholson	*P. Scudamore*	9
1987	Golden Friend 9-11-4: 15/8	Mrs M. Rimell	*D. Browne*	5
1988	Ten of Spades 8-11-3: 11/8	Mrs M. Rimell	*P. Scudamore*	5
1989	Smart Tar 8-10-5: 9/2	M. Wilkinson	*C. Llewellyn*	9
1990	Royal Cedar 9-10-13: 3/1	J. McConnochie	*R. Dunwoody*	7
1991	Gala's Image 11-10-5: 14/1	J. McConnochie	*J. Shortt*	15
1992	Topsham Bay 9-11-5: 11/2	D. Barons	*H. Davies*	6
1993	Le Piccolage 9-10-1: 11/8	N. Henderson	*R. Dunwoody*	12

SOUTH WALES SHOWERS SILVER TROPHY CHASE
(Cheltenham 2m 5f)

1986	Mr Moonraker 9-11-2: 7/2	L. Kennard	*B. Powell*	7
1987	Duke of Milan 10-10-2: 11/2	N. Gaselee	*S. Sherwood*	5
1988	Beau Ranger 10-11-0: 11/10	M. Pipe	*P. Scudamore*	5
1989	Norton's Coin 8-11-0: 20/1	S. Griffiths	*R. Dunwoody*	8
1990	Barnbrook Again 9-11-10: 6/4	D. Elsworth	*H. Davies*	5
1991	Norton's Coin 10-11-4: 9/4	S. Griffiths	*G. McCourt*	4
1992	Katabatic 9-11-4: 8/13	A. Turnell	*L. Harvey*	4
1993	Beech Road 11-11-0: 5/1	G. Balding	*R. Dunwoody*	4

EBF 'NATIONAL HUNT' NOVICES' HURDLE FINAL
(HANDICAP) (Cheltenham 2m 1f)

1981	Mr Foodbroker 6-9-7: 4/1	D. Kent	*J. Lovejoy*	14
1982	Allten Glazed 5-10-10: 14/1	M. Naughton	*G. Bradley*	16
1983	Talkabout 6-10-10: 12/1	G. Fletcher	*J. J. O'Neill*	17
1984	Golden Fancy 7-10-6: 25/1	I. Vickers	*R. Lamb*	9
1985	Cats Eyes 5-11-10: 10/1	M. Pipe	*P. Leach*	17
1986	Atrabates 6-11-7: 7/1	O. Sherwood	*S. Sherwood*	19
1987	Teletrader 6-11-9: 6/1	R. Hodges	*H. Davies*	14
1988	Western Dandy 5-9-7: 33/1	N. Gaselee	*A. Adams*	24
1989	For The Grain 5-11-10: 14/1	J. Wilson	*L. Wyer*	18
1990	Vazon Bay 6-12-0: 7/1	Mrs J. Pitman	*M. Pitman*	12
1991	Poetic Gem 6-10-0: 9/2	G. Balding	*R. Guest*	8
1992	Current Express 5-12-0: 6/1	N. Henderson	*R. Dunwoody*	13
1993	Country Lad 5-10-7: 33/1	Mrs S. Williams	*S. McNeill*	18

BOLLINGER CHAMPAGNE NOVICES HANDICAP CHASE

(Ascot 2m 3f 110yds)

Year	Horse	Jockey	Trainer	Runners
1967	Three No Trumps 8-10-7: 2/1	P. Cazalet	*D. Mould*	10
1968	Gay Trip 6-11-7: 100/30	F. Rimell	*T. Biddlecombe*	7
1969	Beau Champ 7-12-0: 6/1	F. Winter	*H. Beasley*	9
1970	Into View 7-12-0: 11/8	F. Winter	*P. Kelleway*	6
1971	Bobby Corbett 6-10-10: 14/1	K. Oliver	*P. McCarron*	10
1972	Balinese 7-11-7: 10/1	R. Turnell	*D. R. Hughes*	8
1973	Proper Charlie 8-11-7: 20/1	C. V. Miller	*D. Cartwright*	4
1974	Winter Rain 6-10-4: 15/8	A. Dickinson	*M. Dickinson*	12
1975	Floating Proud 6-10-6: 9/2	F. Winter	*R. Pitman*	11
1976	Grangewood Girl 7-10-10: 11/2	Mrs A. Finch	*J. Fox*	14
1977	Commandant 5-10-5: 14/1	G. Balding	*S. McNally*	12
1978	Race abandoned			
1979	Bennachie 6-10-8: 9/1	A. Scott	*R. Lamb*	7
1980	Mister Bosun 7-10-6: 9/1	J. Thorne	*R. Hoare*	15
1981	Prayukta 6-11-10: 8/1	F. Winter	*J. Francome*	12
1982	Masterson 7-10-12: 4/1	Mrs M. Rimell	*R. Linley*	12
1983	Another Breeze 8-11-3: 7/2	N. Gaselee	*Mr A. J. Wilson*	7
1984	The Thatcher 6-10-4: 4/1	J. Gifford	*P. Hobbs*	9
1985	Townley Stone 6-12-2: 4/1	J. Webber	*G. McCourt*	8
1986	Repington 8-10-3: 9/1	N. Crump	*C. Hawkins*	13
1987	Barryphilips Disco 10-10-0: 7/1	R. Whitaker	*R. Beggan*	10
1988	Ballyhane 7-11-10: 11/2	J. Gifford	*R. Rowe*	6
1989	Man O'Magic 8-10-0: 14/1	K. Bailey	*M. Perrett*	17
1990	Sword Beach 6-10-1: 6/4	M. H. Easterby	*L. Wyer*	6
1991	Kings Fountain 8-10-3: 8/1	K. Bailey	*A. Tory*	11
1992	Very Very Ordinary 6-10-7: 12/1	J. Upson	*R. Supple*	17
1993	Grange Brake 7-10-8: 11/1	N. Twiston-Davies	*C. Llewellyn*	13

WHITBREAD GOLD CUP HANDICAP CHASE (Sandown 3m 5f 110yds)

Year	Horse	Jockey	Trainer	Runners
1957	Much Obliged 9-10-12: 10/1	N. Crump	*H. East*	24
1958	Taxidermist 6-10-8: 100/6	F. Walwyn	*Mr J. Lawrence*	31
1959	Done Up 9-10-13: 100/6	R. Price	*H. Sprague*	23
1960	Plummers Plain 7-10-0: 20/1	L. Dale	*R. Harrison*	21
1961	Pas Seul 8-12-0: 8/1	R. Turnell	*D. Dick*	23
1962	Frenchman's Cove 7-11-3: 7/2	H. T. Jones	*S. Mellor*	22
1963	Hoodwinked 8-10-9: 100/7	N. Crump	*P. Buckley*	32
1964	Dormant 7-9-7: 11/4	N. Crump	*P. Buckley*	11
1965	Arkle 8-12-7: 4/9	T. Dreaper (Ir)	*P. Taaffe*	7
1966	What a Myth 9-9-8: 5/4	R. Price	*P. Kelleway*	8
1967	Mill House 10-11-11: 9/2	F. Walwyn	*D. Nicholson*	13
1968	Larbawn 9-10-9: 8/1	M. L. Marsh	*M. Gifford*	16
1969	Larbawn 10-11-4: 9/2	M. L. Marsh	*J. Gifford*	18
1970	Royal Toss 8-10-0: 20/1	H. Handel	*R. Pitman*	17
1971	Titus Oates 9-11-13: 11/1	G. Richards	*R. Barry*	18
1972	Grey Sombrero 8-9-10: 16/1	D. Gandolfo	*W. Shoemark*	28
1973	Charlie Potheen 8-12-0: 11/4	F. Walwyn	*R. Barry*	21
1974	The Dikler 11-11-13: 5/1	F. Walwyn	*R. Barry*	16
1975	April Seventh 9-9-13: 16/1	R. Turnell	*S. C. Knight*	12
1976	Otter Way 8-10-10: 15/2	O. Carter	*J. King*	14
1977	Andy Pandy 8-10-12: 4/1	F. Rimell	*J. Burke*	15
1978	Strombolus 7-10-0: 7/1	P. Bailey	*T. Stack*	15
1979	Diamond Edge 8-11-11: 7/1	F. Walwyn	*W. Smith*	14
1980	Royal Mail 10-11-5: 8/1	S. Mellor	*P. Blacker*	12
1981	Diamond Edge 10-11-7: 5/1	F. Walwyn	*W. Smith*	18
1982	Shady Deal 9-10-0: 4/1	J. Gifford	*R. Rowe*	9
1983	Drumlargan 8-10-10: 11/1	E. O'Grady (Ir)	*Mr F. Codd*	15
1984	Special Cargo 11-11-2: 8/1	F. Walwyn	*K. Mooney*	13
1985	By The Way 7-10-0: 11/2	Mrs M. Dickinson	*R. Earnshaw*	20
1986	Plundering 9-10-6: 14/1	F. Winter	*S. Sherwood*	16
1987	Lean Ar Aghaidh 10-9-4: 6/1	S. Mellor	*G. Landau*	9
1988	Desert Orchid 9-11-11: 6/1	D. Elsworth	*S. Sherwood*	12
1989	Brown Windsor 7-10-0: 12/1	N. Henderson	*M. Bowlby*	18
1990	Mr Frisk 11-10-5: 9/2	K. Bailey	*Mr M. Armytage*	13
1991	Docklands Express 9-10-3: 4/1	K. Bailey	*A. Tory*	10
1992	Topsham Bay 9-10-1: 9/2	D. Barons	*H. Davies*	11
1993	Topsham Bay 10-10-1: 10/1	D. Barons	*R. Dunwoody*	13

COUNTRY PRIDE CHAMPION NOVICE HURDLE (Punchestown 2m)

1976	Hilly Way 6-12-0: 11/10	P. McCreery	*T. Carberry*	6
1977	Drumgora 5-11-1: 4/1	M. Cunningham	*T. McGivern*	13
1978	Settle It 7-12-0: 12/1	E. O'Grady	*F. Berry*	12
1979	Light The Wad 6-11-4: 20/1	R. Hoey	*M. Cummins*	9
1980	Deep Gale 7-11-8: 7/1	E. O'Grady	*Mr F. Codd*	12
1981	Tie Anchor 4-10-9: 2/1	P. Prendergast	*T. McGivern*	11
1982	Bustineto 4-10-5: 5/2	M. O'Toole	*N. Madden*	7
1983	Dawn Run 5-11-7: 5/2	P. Mullins	*A. Mullins*	14
1984	Gav's Delight 6-11-7: 2/5	M. Cunningham	*K. Morgan*	4
1985	Hungary Hur 6-11-6: 5/1	P. Mullins	*A. Mullins*	10
1986	Barney Burnett 6-11-9: 1/1	R. Walsh	*B. Sheridan*	12
1987	High Plains 5-11-5: 8/1	D. Nicholson (Eng)	*R. Dunwoody*	9
1988	El-Sid Senor 5-11-7: 9/4	F. Flood	*F. Berry*	11
1989	The Proclamation 6-10-13: 9/2	P. Prendergast	*R. Dunwoody*	12
1990	Vestris Abu 4-10-5: 5/2	J. Bolger	*C. Swan*	8
1991	Young Pokey 6-12-0: 5/2	O. Sherwood (Eng)	*J. Osborne*	6
1992	Fortune And Fame 5-11-13: 11/4	D. K. Weld	*B. Sheridan*	10
1993	Bayrouge 5-11-8: 7/2	Mrs A. O'Brien	*R. Dunwoody*	8

MURPHYS IRISH STOUT CHAMPION 4-Y-O HURDLE
(Punchestown 2m)

1976	Mwanadike 11-8: 6/4	J. Bryce-Smith	*T. Carberry*	8
1977	Almond Green 11-8: 16/1	P. McCreery	*T. Carmody*	8
1978	Fast Score 11-8: 6/4	J. Maxwell	*T. Stack*	8
1979	Seldom Dry 11-4: 8/1	P. Prendergast	*T. Carmody*	12
1980	Pearlstone 10-13: 11/2	P. Mullins	*S. Treacy*	13
1981	Tie Anchor 11-1: 3/1	P. Prendergast	*T. Morgan*	16
1982	Bustineto 11-8: 4/6	M. O'Toole	*N. Madden*	6
1983	Grateful Heir 11-0: 20/1	L. Browne	*Mr D. Browne*	19
1984	Clarinbridge 11-6: 9/2	J. Bolger	*B. Nolan*	12
1985	Atherstone 11-3: 25/1	N. Meade	*P. Leech*	17
1986	Derrymore Boy 11-3: 9/2	P. Mullins	*A. Mullins*	7
1987	Grabel 11-0: 8/1	P. Mullins	*A. Mullins*	10
1988	Allen's Mistake 11-3: 5/2	D. K. Weld	*B. Sheridan*	9
1989	Royal Derbi 11-9: 7/1	N. Callaghan (Eng)	*G. McCourt*	11
1990	Orbis 11-6: 7/4	J. Bolger	*T. Carmody*	8
1991	Mounamara 11-4: 6/1	P. Mullins	*T. Carmody*	12
1992	Staunch Friend 11-9: 6/1	M. Tompkins (Eng)	*S. Smith Eccles*	14
1993	Shawiya 10-9: 11/4	M. O'Brien	*C. Swan*	13

BANK OF IRELAND COLLIERS NOVICE CHASE (Punchestown 2m)

1992	Classical Charm 9-11-8: 8/1	J. O'Connell	*K. Morgan*	8
1993	Viking Flagship 6-12-0: 4/1	D. Nicholson	*R. Dunwoody*	8

SWINTON HANDICAP HURDLE (Haydock 2m)

1978	Royal Gaye 5-10-0: 20/1	F. Rimell	*C. Tinkler*	20
1979	Beacon Light 8-11-1: 12/1	R. Turnell	*A. Turnell*	17
1980	No Bombs 5-10-9: 7/1	M. H. Easterby	*J. J. O'Neill*	14
1981	Gaye Chance 6-10-10: 13/2	F. Rimell	*S. Morshead*	18
1982	Secret Ballot 8-10-3: 10/1	R. Turnell	*A. Turnell*	17
1983	Abandoned because course waterlogged			
1984	Bajan Sunshine 5-10-13: 6/1	M. Tate	*P. Scudamore*	15
1985	Corporal Clinger 6-10-3: 11/2	M. Pipe	*P. Leach*	21
1986	Prideaux Boy 8-11-2: 15/2	G. Roach	*M. Bowlby*	20
1987	Inlander 6-10-8: 4/1	R. Akehurst	*S. Smith Eccles*	8
1988	Past Glories 5-11-9: 16/1	W. Elsey	*P. Farrell*	23
1989	State Jester 6-10-0: 14/1	W. Elsey	*J. Quinn*	18
1990	Sybillin 4-10-1: 8/1	J. FitzGerald	*D. Byrne*	14
1991	Winnie The Witch 7-10-2: 8/1	K. Bridgwater	*D. Bridgwater*	12
1992	Bitofabanter 5-11-1: 14/1	A. Moore (Ir)	*T. Taaffe*	22
1993	Spinning 6-11-0: 3/1	I. Balding	*J. Frost*	17

HORSE AND HOUND CUP FINAL CHAMPION HUNTERS CHASE
(Stratford 3¼m)

1959	Speylove 10-11-12: 25/1	V. Bishop	*J. Jackson*	15
1960	Bantry Bay 9-12-3: 6/1	H. Dufosee	*M. Tory*	17
1961	Bantry Bay 10-12-0: 8/1	H. Dufosee	*M. Tory*	8

1962	Baulking Green 9-12-0: 11/2	J. Reade	R. Willis	16
1963	Baulking Green 10-12-0: 7/4	T. Forster	A. Frank	17
1964	Royal Phoebe 8-11-7: 100/7	R. Whiston	M. Gifford	13
1965	Baulking Green 12-12-0: 4/7	T. Forster	G. Small	8
1966	Santa Grand 7-11-11: 7/1	W. A. Stephenson	C. Collins	10
1967	Cham 10-12-0: 3/1	F. Cundell	J. Lawrence	16
1968	Green Plover 8-11-9: 33/1	J. Ford	A. Maxwell	8
1969	Touch of Tammy 9-11-12: 11/4	G. Guilding	R. Guilding	14
1970	Some Man 8-12-0: 8/1	H. Poole	R. Knipe	15
1971	Credit Call 7-12-0: 4/1	W. A. Stephenson	G. Macmillan	10
1972	Credit Call 8-12-0: 1/1	W. A. Stephenson	C. Collins	11
1973	Credit Call 9-12-0: 4/7	W. A. Stephenson	C. Collins	5
1974	Stanhope Street 8-11-7: 2/1	H. Counsell	B. Venn	12
1975	Credit Call 11-12-0: 11/2	W. A. Stephenson	J. Newton	12
1976	Otter Way 8-12-0: 7/4	O. Carter	G. Cann	10
1977	Devil's Walk 9-12-0: 50/1	M. Bishop	T. Rooney	16
1978	Rolls Rambler 7-12-0: 8/11	F. Winter	N. Henderson	9
1979	Spartan Missile 7-12-0: 4/7	J. Thorne	J. Thorne	8
1980	Rolls Rambler 9-12-0: 13/8	F. Winter	O. Sherwood	16
1981	Ottery News 8-12-0: 7/4	O. Carter	A. J. Wilson	12
1982	Loyal Partner 8-12-0: 7/1	T. Clay	T. Clay	10
1983	Otter Way 15-12-0: 20/1	O. Carter	A. J. Wilson	17
1984	Prominent King 12-12-0: 7/1	M. H. Easterby	T. Easterby	20
1985	Flying Ace 9-12-0: 5/1	A. Calder	Miss D. Calder	10
1986	The Pain Barrier 7-12-0: 12/1	O. Sherwood	Miss A. Langton	10
1987	Three Counties 10-12-0: 9/4	Mrs M. Rimell	Miss K. Rimell	11
1988	Three Counties 11-12-0: 5/2	Mrs M. Rimell	Miss K. Rimell	14
1989	Mystic Music 10-11-9: 2/1	Miss H. Wilson	K. Anderson	16
1990	Mystic Music 11-11-9: 8/11	Miss H. Wilson	K. Anderson	9
1991	Federal Trooper 10-12-0: 14/1	P. Bonner	T. McCarthy	16
1992	Abandoned because of waterlogging			
1993	Generals Boy 11-12-0: 11/2	P. Craggs	P. Craggs	6

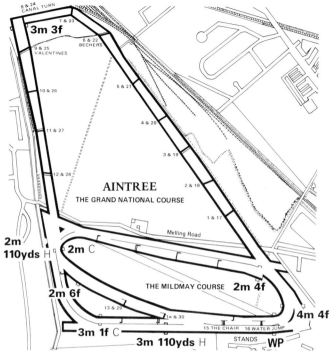

The Grand National course is triangular with its apex (at the Canal Turn) the furthest point from the stands. It covers two and a quarter miles and is perfectly flat throughout. Inside is the easier Mildmay course, providing a circuit of one and a half miles, which has birch fences. Despite re-alignment of the last two bends in 1989, a major feature of the Mildmay course remains its sharpness.

The Grand National is run over two complete circuits taking in sixteen spruce fences first time round and fourteen the second, and, in spite of welcome modifications to the fences in recent years (which has reduced the chances of a surprise result), the race still provides one of the toughest tests ever devised for horse and rider. The run from the final fence to the winning post is 494 yards long and includes an elbow.

Most winners: G. Balding 9 J. FitzGerald 8 M. Pipe 7 D. Nicholson 5
  Mrs J. Pitman 5
Notable % of winners: M. W. Easterby J. FitzGerald M. H. Easterby

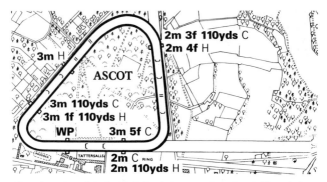

The triangular, right-handed circuit is approximately a mile and three quarters round. The turns are easy and in spite of the downhill run to the water jump in Swinley Bottom the course is galloping in nature. The sides of the triangle away from the stands have four fences each, and the circuit is completed by two plain fences in the straight of two furlongs. The finish is uphill and the course is a real test of stamina when the ground is heavy. The fences are stiff, and good jumping is essential.

Most winners: M. Pipe 28 J. Gifford 19 G. Balding 13 Mrs J. Pitman 12
Notable % of winners: J. FitzGerald J. Upson Mrs J. Pitman M. Pipe

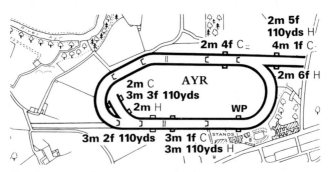

The Ayr course is a left-handed circuit of one and a half miles comprising nine fences, with well-graduated turns. There is a steady downhill run to the home turn and a gentle rise to the finish. There is a run-in of 210 yards. When the going is firm the course is quite sharp.

Most winners: G. Richards 57 Mrs M. Reveley 24 G. Moore 24
Mrs S. Bradburne 15
Notable % of winners: Mrs M. Reveley C. Thornton M. Jefferson S. Mellor

FIXTURES 1994

AYR

SCOTLAND'S PREMIER COURSE

JANUARY	Monday 3rd	N.H.
	Thursday 20th	N.H.
	Saturday 29th	N.H.
FEBRUARY	Saturday 12th	N.H.
MARCH	Friday 11th	N.H.
	Saturday 12th	N.H.
APRIL	Thursday 14th	N.H.
	Friday 15th	N.H.
	Saturday 16th	N.H.
MAY	Saturday 21st	FLAT
	Monday 23rd	FLAT
JUNE	Friday 17th	FLAT
	Saturday 18th	FLAT
JULY	Friday 8th (EVE)	FLAT
	Saturday 16th (EVE)	FLAT
	Monday 18th	FLAT
	Saturday 23rd	FLAT
AUGUST	Saturday 6th	FLAT
	Thursday 18th	FLAT
SEPTEMBER	Thursday 15th	FLAT
	Friday 16th	FLAT
	Saturday 17th	FLAT
OCTOBER	Saturday 8th	N.H.
NOVEMBER	Friday 11th	N.H.
	Saturday 12th	N.H.
DECEMBER	Monday 26th	N.H.

How to get there

Glasgow Airport *1 Hour by Car*
Prestwick Airport *10 Minutes by Car*
Racecourse Landing Ground *Helicopters Only*
Train Service *Every 30 Minutes from Glasgow*

**All Enquiries to The Racecourse Office
2 Whitletts Road, Ayr.
Telephone Ayr (0292) 264179**

2m 4f 110yds C

4m 1f C

2m 4f H

River Dee

2m 1f 110yds C

3m 6f C

2m 1f H

BANGOR-ON-DEE

2m 7f 110yds H

WP

3m

110yds C

3m 2f

Bangor has a left-handed circuit of approximately one and a half miles. Nine fences are jumped in a circuit and the run-in is about a furlong. The track is fairly sharp because of its many bends, and the paddock bend is very tight.

Most winners: G. Richards 34 M. Pipe 26 F. Jordan 13 J Edwards 11
Notable % of winners: M. Hammond M. Pipe K. Bailey D. Barons

182

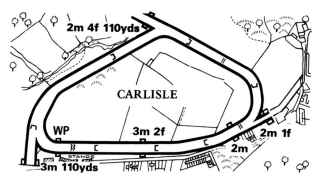

The course is right-handed, pear-shaped and undulating, a mile and five furlongs in extent. The track is a particularly stiff one and the uphill home stretch is very severe. The three-mile start on the chase course is on a spur at the first bend, the horses taking the first fence only once. Normally there are nine fences to a circuit but on the final one the water jump is omitted, making a run-in of 300 yards. A long-striding galloper suited by a real test of stamina is an ideal type for Carlisle.

Most winners: G. Richards 33 J. J. O'Neill 18 M. Hammond 14 G. Moore 13
C. Parker 13

Notable % of winners: R. Armytage W. Bentley R. Beever J. Edwards

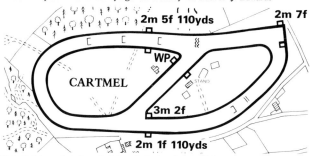

This tight, undulating, left-handed circuit is a little over a mile round. There are six fences to a circuit and the winning post is a little over a furlong from the turn into the finishing straight, which bisects the course and which the horses enter after two circuits for races of seventeen furlongs or three circuits for three and a quarter miles. The fences are stiff for a minor track; the run of half a mile from the last fence is the longest in the country.

Most winners: G. Richards 17 M. Chapman 13 G. Moore 8 M. Pipe 7
D. Moffatt 6 D. Smith 6

Notable % of winners: R. Armytage D. Eddy L. Lungo G. Richards N. Tinkler
D. Burchell

183

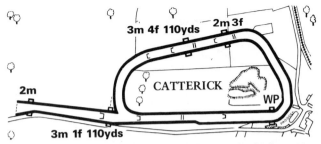

The Catterick course is a left-handed, oval-shaped circuit of around a
mile and a quarter, with eight fences and a run-in of about 280 yards.
Races over two miles and three miles one and a half furlongs start on an
extension to the straight and over two miles the first fence is jumped
before joining the round course. Catterick's undulations and sharp turns
make it unsuitable for the long-striding galloper and ideal for the nippy,
front-running type of horse.

Most winners: J. FitzGerald 23 Mrs M. Reveley 23 G. Richards 19 N. Tinkler 14
G. Moore 11 M. H. Easterby 10

Notable % of winners: Mrs P. Sly K. Morgan F. Walton Mrs M. Reveley
N. Tinkler

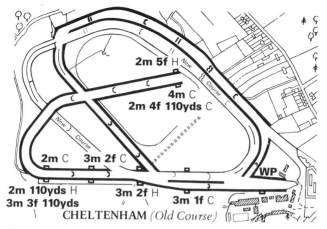

CHELTENHAM *(Old Course)*

2m 5f H
4m C
2m 4f 110yds C
2m C 3m 2f C
2m 110yds H 3m 2f H 3m 1f C
3m 3f 110yds

There are three left-handed courses at Cheltenham, the Old Course, the New Course, and the Park Course. The Old Course is oval in shape and about one and a half miles in extent. There are nine fences to a circuit, only one of which is jumped in the final straight.

The New Course leaves the old track at the furthest point from the stands and runs parallel to it before rejoining at the entrance to the finishing straight. This circuit is a little longer than the Old Course and has ten fences, two of which are jumped in the final straight.

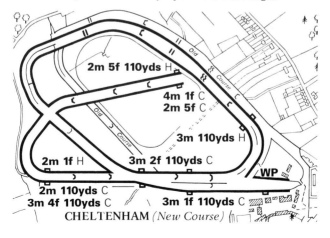

CHELTENHAM *(New Course)*

2m 5f 110yds H
4m 1f C
2m 5f C
3m 110yds H
2m 1f H 3m 2f 110yds C
2m 110yds C 3m 1f 110yds C
3m 4f 110yds C

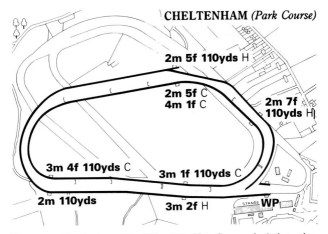

CHELTENHAM *(Park Course)*

2m 5f 110yds H

2m 5f C
4m 1f C

2m 7f 110yds H

3m 4f 110yds C

3m 1f 110yds C

2m 110yds

3m 2f H

STANDS WP

The most telling feature of the Old and the New Courses is their testing nature. The fences are stiff and the last half mile is uphill, with a run-in of just over a furlong. The four-mile and two-and-a-half-mile starts are on an extension, with five fences, which bisects both courses almost at right angles. The two-mile start is also on this extension, and two fences are jumped before reaching the main circuit.

The Park Course, which was used for the first time in 1991, links the two-and-a-half-mile extension with the round course, turning left before the water jump on the back stretch. It has been introduced in order to give horses the chance to race on watered ground in the autumn on a less undulating and less testing circuit than the other two. There are nine fences and six hurdles to a circuit, four fences (including a portable ditch) and three hurdles in the long finishing straight which switches to the Old Course in the closing stages.

Most winners: M. Pipe 60 D. Nicholson 37 J. Gifford 31 G. Balding 24
N. Henderson 20

Notable % of winners: I. Balding N. Tinkler K. Bailey T. T. Jones D. Nicholson
M. Pipe

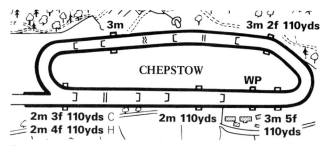

Chepstow is a left-handed, undulating, oval course, nearly two miles round with eleven fences to a circuit, a five-furlong home straight, and a run-in of 250 yards. With five fences (four hurdles) in the straight, the first part of which is downhill, front runners do well here.

Most winners: M. Pipe 69 Mrs J. Pitman 18 D. Barons 13 G. Balding 12
J. Gifford 12 D. Nicholson 12

Notable % of winners: M. Pipe R. Alner D. Nicholson

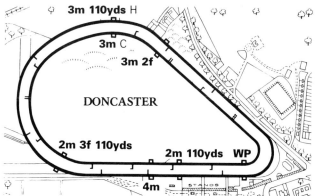

The Doncaster course is a left-handed pear-shaped circuit of approximately two miles, and has eleven fences—including four in the home straight—with a run-in of 240 yards. Only one fence is jumped twice in races over two miles. The course is flat apart from one slight hill about one and a quarter miles from the finish. The track is well drained and often produces a sound surface, even in winter, conditions which naturally favour horses with more speed than stamina.

Most winners: J. Edwards 11 Mrs M. Reveley 11 J. FitzGerald 9 R. Lee 8
O. Sherwood 8

Notable % of winners: P. Cheesbrough Mrs J. Ramsden D. Smith R. Lee
O. Sherwood

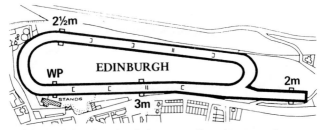

A right-handed oval track a little over a mile and a quarter in extent, almost flat with sharp bends, favouring the handy type of animal and also front runners. There are eight fences (four in each straight) or six flights of hurdles (four in the back straight, two in the home straight) to a circuit. The two-mile start is on a spur on the last bend.

Most winners: Mrs M. Reveley 18 J. FitzGerald 15 N. Tinkler 14 D. Smith 11

Notable % of winners: D. Barron N. Tinkler J. Hellens Mrs M. Reveley
J. FitzGerald

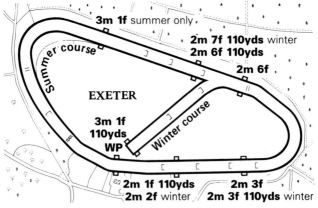

This is a tricky, hilly course. Its right-handed two-mile circuit is laid out in a long oval, with eleven fences and a run-in of over 300 yards. Only one fence is jumped twice in races of two and a quarter miles. The winter course uses a slightly longer bend than the summer course and its three-and-a-quarter-mile chases start on an inside spur with two fences. The half-mile home straight is on the rise all the way to the finish.

Most winners: M. Pipe 109 G. Balding 24 P. Hobbs 23 R. Frost 14
Mrs J. Retter 10

Notable % of winners: M. Pipe T. T. Jones A. Dunn M. McCormack J. Gifford

2m 5f 110yds C

2m 5f H

FAKENHAM

2m 110yds C

3m C   **WP**

2m 110yds H

3m 110yds H

STANDS

Fakenham is an undulating, sharp track, ideal for the handy, front-running type and unsuitable for the long-striding animal. The left-handed, square-shaped track has a circuit of a mile, six fences to each circuit and a run-in of 250 yards.

Most winners: J. Jenkins 11 C. Brooks 8 M. Ryan 7 M. Tompkins 6
Notable % of winners: C. Brooks O. Sherwood J. Upson M. Tompkins

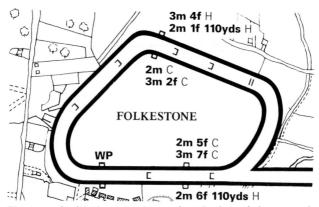

3m 4f H
2m 1f 110yds H
2m C
3m 2f C

FOLKESTONE

2m 5f C
3m 7f C

WP

2m 6f 110yds H

The course is right-handed and approximately eleven furlongs round. The turns are easy, but the undulations can put a long-striding horse off balance. There are seven fences to a circuit, the fences relatively easy, and a run-in of about a furlong.

Most winners: J. Gifford 16 D. Grissell 12 R. Akehurst 8
Notable % of winners: M. Pipe Miss H. Knight J. Upson R. Rowe R. O'Sullivan

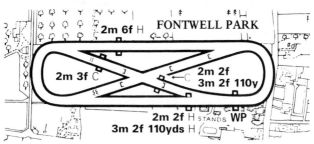

2m 6f H   **FONTWELL PARK**

2m 3f C   **2m 2f**
3m 2f 110y

2m 2f H STANDS **WP**
3m 2f 110yds H

There are two very different types of track at Fontwell, the hurdle course being left-handed, an oval about a mile in circumference with four flights, and the chase course a figure of eight with seven fences which are all in the two straight intersections linked with the hurdle course. Fontwell is not a course for the big, long-striding chaser, and despite the easy fences it can cause problems for inexperienced chasers. The unusual demands made by its layout have produced a number of track specialists over the years.

Most winners: M. Pipe 39 J. Gifford 38 G. Balding 18 P. Hobbs 16 R. Curtis 15
D. Grissell 15
Notable % of winners: Mrs J. Pitman M. Pipe G. Harwood Miss S. Wilton
Miss H. Knight

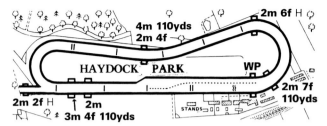

The left-handed oval-shaped circuit of a mile and five furlongs has ten fences which are spaced evenly along the back and home stretches. The fences are stiff. The last open ditch and water jump are omitted on the final circuit leaving a run-in of 440 yards. The course is flat and for chasers is of a galloping nature; the hurdles course, inside the chase course, is sharp and has tight bends.

Most winners: M. Pipe 57 G. Richards 35 J. FitzGerald 13 D. McCain 11
Notable % of winners: M. Pipe P. Cheesbrough T. Tate G. Richards C. Brooks

191

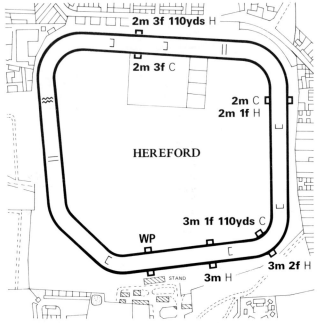

2m 3f 110yds H

2m 3f C

2m C
2m 1f H

HEREFORD

3m 1f 110yds C

WP

3m 2f H

STAND   3m H

Hereford's right-handed circuit of about a mile and a half is almost square and has nine fences, of which the first after the winning post has to be taken on a turn. The home turn, which is on falling ground, is pretty sharp but the other bends are easy. The fences are fairly stiff.

Most winners: M. Pipe 44 K. Bailey 16 D. Nicholson 15 D. Burchell 13
          J. Edwards 13

Notable % of winners: O. Sherwood S. Christian C. Brooks M. Pipe
          N. Henderson

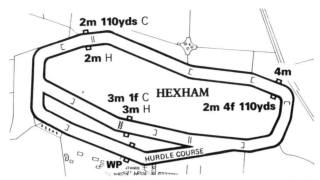

Hexham has an undulating left-handed circuit of a mile and a half with ten fences. Although the fences are easy the course is very testing: the long back straight runs steeply downhill for most of the way but there is a steep climb from the end of the back straight to the home straight, which levels out in front of the stands. The finish is on a spur, the spur having one fence and a run-in of about a furlong.

Most winners: G. Richards 34 G. Moore 29 M. Hammond 16 Mrs M. Reveley 16
P. Monteith 12

Notable % of winners: J. Edwards W. Bentley L. Lungo G. Moore P. Monteith

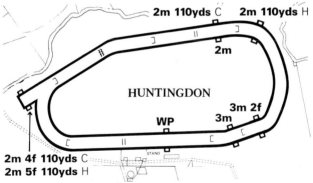

The course is right-handed, oval with easy bends, and is a flat, fast track about one and a half miles in length with nine fences to a circuit, some of them rather tricky.

Most winners: F. Murphy 20 J. Gifford 18 D. Nicholson 16 Mrs J. Pitman 16
M. Ryan 10

Notable % of winners: M. Pipe G. Harwood Mrs M. Reveley Mrs J. Pitman
T. Etherington

193

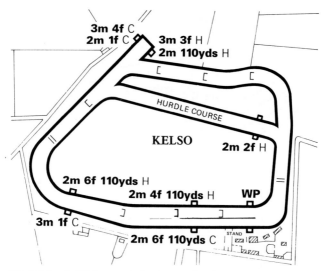

The left-handed Kelso course has two tracks, the oval hurdle course of approximately a mile and a quarter and the chase course of approximately eleven furlongs. There are nine fences to be jumped in a complete circuit of the chase course. The run-in, which is on an elbow, is a tiring one of 440 yards. The hurdle track is very sharp, with a particularly sharp bend after the stands.

Most winners: G. Richards 43 Mrs M. Reveley 30 P. Monteith 16 G. Moore 16
M. Hammond 12

Notable % of winners: Mrs M. Reveley G. Richards T. Tate Mrs D. Goodfellow
J. FitzGerald

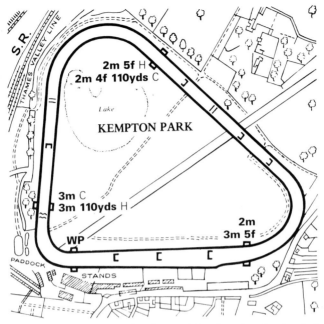

Kempton is a very fair test for a jumper; it is a flat, triangular circuit of one mile five furlongs, right-handed with a run-in from the last fence of about 175 yards. There are ten fences to a circuit.

Most winners: N. Henderson 17 O. Sherwood 17 M. Pipe 15 J. Gifford 14
D. Elsworth 13

Notable % of winners: P. Harris J. FitzGerald T. T. Jones N. Tinkler
O. Sherwood

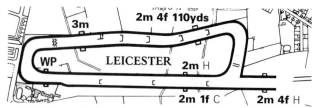

The right-handed course is rectangular in shape, a mile and three quarters in extent and has ten fences. Leicester is a stiff test and the last three furlongs are uphill. The run-in of 250 yards has a slight elbow on the chase course 150 yards from the winning post. The runners in three-mile chases miss out the first open ditch.

Most winners: M. Pipe 30 Mrs J. Pitman 28 R. Lee 7 D. Nicholson 7
Notable % of winners: M. Pipe Mrs J. Pitman M. Tompkins

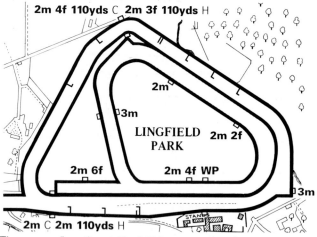

The new configuration at Lingfield incorporates a mile-and-a-quarter all-weather track. The original turf course, which encloses the all-weather, has been re-aligned so that the turn out of the home straight is much more gradual, but most of its characteristics remain. It is about a mile and a half in length, triangular and taken left-handed, sharp, has several gradients and a tight downhill turn into the straight. Nine fences have to be jumped in a complete circuit, while the run-in is comparatively short. The all-weather surface is Equitrack, whereas Southwell's is Fibresand.

Most winners: Miss B. Sanders 28 R. Akehurst 21 J. Jenkins 20 S. Dow 19
Notable % of winners: P. Kelleway R. Simpson C. Benstead S. Dow
Miss B. Sanders

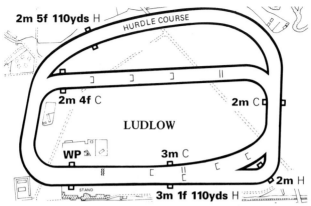

Ludlow is a sharp, right-handed track in the shape of an oval, with a nine-fence chase circuit about a mile and a half and a run-in of 450 yards. The hurdle course, which runs on the outside of the chase course, has easier turns. Whereas the chase course is flat, the hurdle course has slight undulations but they rarely provide difficulties for a long-striding horse.

Most winners: M. Pipe 22 J. Edwards 17 D. Nicholson 15 R. Lee 10
Notable % of winners: N. Henderson D. Murray Smith P. J. Jones M. Pipe

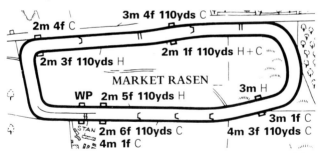

There is a right-handed, oval circuit of a mile and a quarter, eight relatively easy fences and a run-in of 250 yards at Market Rasen. The track is sharp, covered with minor undulations, and favours the handy, nippy type of horse.

Most winners: J. FitzGerald 31 N. Tinkler 24 M. H. Easterby 23
Mrs M. Reveley 22 M. Pipe 20
Notable % of winners: M. Pipe C. Thornton Mrs M. Reveley M. H. Easterby
N. Tinkler

197

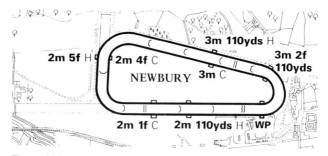

The oval Newbury course, with eleven fences to the circuit, is about a mile and three quarters in circumference and is set inside the Flat track, following a left-handed line. It is one of the fairest courses in the country. The home straight is five furlongs with three plain fences, an open ditch (the water jump being omitted on the final circuit) and a run-in of 255 yards. The course is galloping in nature, with easy bends, plenty of room and few significant undulations.

Most winners: N. Henderson 27 M. Pipe 27 D. Elsworth 24 D. Nicholson 24
O. Sherwood 23

Notable % of winners: M. Tompkins M. Pipe G. Harwood O. Sherwood
T. T. Jones

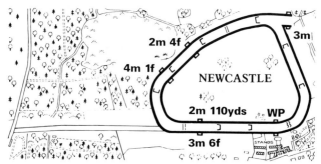

The Newcastle track is laid out inside the Flat racecourse, its left-handed circuit of one and three quarter miles containing eleven fences. There is a steady rise from the fourth last to the winning post and the course puts a premium on stamina, with the fences being on the stiff side. The ground is often testing here, too.

Most winners: M. H. Easterby 21 G. Moore 18 H. Johnson 16 Mrs M. Reveley 14
G. Richards 12

Notable % of winners: M. Camacho M. H. Easterby G. Moore N. Tinkler

198

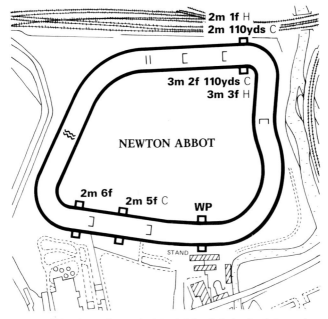

Newton Abbot has a flat, oval, tight, left-handed circuit of about nine furlongs that favours the handy sort of horse. There are seven fences to a circuit, and a very short run-in.

Most winners: M. Pipe 125 P. Hobbs 26 D. Barons 18

Notable % of winners: M. Pipe R. O'Sullivan N. Twiston-Davies J. Edwards

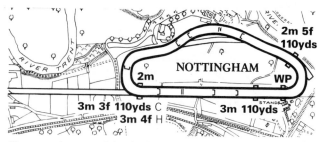

The course has an oval circuit of about a mile and a half. The left-handed turns are easy and the home straight is over four and a half furlongs with lengthy run-ins on both hurdle and chase courses, making the track a galloping one. In races over two miles thirteen fences have to be taken.

Most winners: M. Pipe 13 J. FitzGerald 12 N. Henderson 11 O. Brennan 8
D. Nicholson 8

Notable % of winners: C. Egerton Mrs I. McKie J. Gifford N. Callaghan
B. Curley N. Henderson

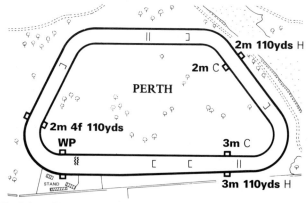

Perth is a right-handed circuit of one and a quarter miles, with eight fences to the circuit. The course has sweeping turns and a flat running surface. The water jump is in front of the stands and is left out on the run-in, leaving a long run from last fence to winning post.

Most winners: G. Richards 33 P. Monteith 13 G. Moore 13 M. Hammond 12
Mrs M. Reveley 12

Notable % of winners: N. Twiston-Davies C. Weedon N. Tinkler M. H. Easterby
S. Kettlewell

200

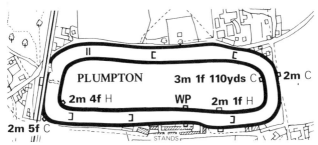

The oblong-shaped course is only nine furlongs in circumference and has tight, left-handed bends, steep undulations, and an uphill home straight. The climb becomes pretty steep near the finish but the course is not a particularly stiff one; it favours the handy and quick-jumping types. There are seven fences to a circuit and the run-in is 200 yards.

Most winners: R. Akehurst 23 J. Ffitch-Heyes 21 Mrs J. Pitman 16 D. Grissell 15
J. Jenkins 15

Notable % of winners: Lady Herries C. Egerton D. Murray Smith Mrs J. Pitman
R. Akehurst

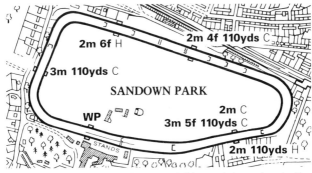

Sandown's right-handed oval course of thirteen furlongs is a testing and, for the steeplechasers, a tricky one. Of the eleven fences on a circuit seven are on the back straight, with the water jump in the middle of the line. The three fences after the water come in very quick succession and many races are won and lost here. From the home turn to 100 yards from the finish the climb is severe; there are two fences in the straight and a run-in of 220 yards. The hurdles course uses the Flat racing circuit.

Most winners: J. Gifford 27 D. Nicholson 19 M. Pipe 19 C. Brooks 15

Notable % of winners: J. FitzGerald G. Harwood D. Nicholson C. Brooks
D. Grissell M. Pipe

201

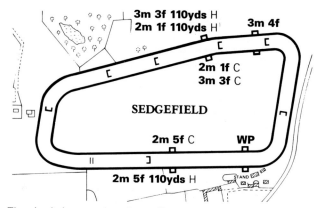

3m 3f 110yds H
2m 1f 110yds H
3m 4f

2m 1f C
3m 3f C

SEDGEFIELD

2m 5f C   **WP**

2m 5f 110yds H

The circuit is approximately a mile and a quarter, oval, and taken left-handed. It is essentially sharp in character and the eight fences are fairly easy, though some uphill sections of the undulating ground, notably the final 150 yards, are punishing and three-mile-plus chases are a thorough test of stamina. The run-in is 200 yards.

Most winners: Mrs M. Reveley 54 M. H. Easterby 27 G. Moore 27
J. FitzGerald 24 D. Smith 19

Notable % of winners: T. Tate J. FitzGerald N. Tinkler C. Thornton
M. H. Easterby Mrs M. Reveley

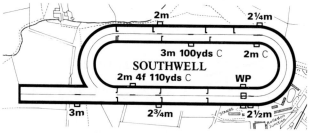

2m   **2¼m**

3m 100yds C   **2m C**
SOUTHWELL
2m 4f 110yds C   **WP**

3m   **2¾m**   **2½m**

The new track is laid out in a tight, level, mile-and-a-quarter oval, a spur to the three-furlong run-in providing a three-mile start. The runners go left-handed. There are two types of surface, all-weather and turf, the all-weather track being on the outside of the turf track which has three fences in each straight. The all-weather surface is Fibresand whereas Lingfield's is Equitrack.

Most winners: R. Hollinshead 32 M. Pipe 28 W. Clay 19 J. Harris 18
Notable % of winners: O. Sherwood Mrs D. Haine J. Upson M. Pipe G. Moore

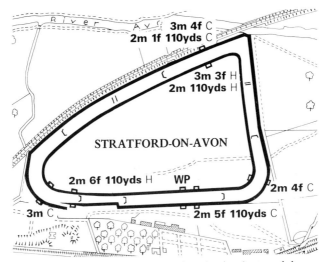

3m 4f C
2m 1f 110yds C

3m 3f H
2m 110yds H

STRATFORD-ON-AVON

2m 6f 110yds H   **WP**

2m 4f C

3m C   **2m 5f 110yds** C

The sharp Stratford track is flat, triangular in shape and has a left-handed circuit of a mile and a quarter, taking in eight fences of which two are in the short straight before the winning post.

Most winners: M. Pipe 19 T. Forster 17 G. Richards 12 D. Nicholson 10
Mrs J. Pitman 10

Notable % of winners: J. FitzGerald G. Richards Mrs J. Retter T. Forster
C. Brooks

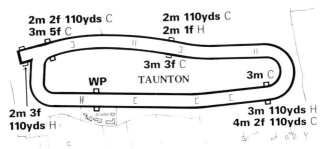

2m 2f 110yds C   **2m 110yds** C
3m 5f C   **2m 1f** H

3m 3f C

WP   TAUNTON   **3m** C

2m 3f
110yds H   **3m 110yds** H
4m 2f 110yds C

The right-handed course is a long oval, about a mile and a quarter round, and has eight fences, four in each straight. The bend after the winning post is tight and the chase run-in short.

Most winners: M. Pipe 59 R. Hodges 21 C. Popham 14 P. Hobbs 11
Notable % of winners: S. Mellor M. Pipe J. Old

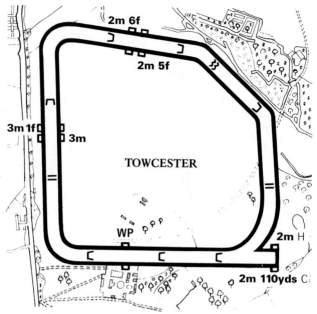

Towcester is a right-handed course, a mile and three quarters round, and is generally against the collar. The last mile or so is very punishing with a steep climb to the home turn and a continuing rise past the winning post. Of the ten fences on the circuit, two are in the finishing straight. The run-in is 200 yards.

Most winners: O. Brennan 18 Mrs I. McKie 15 Mrs J. Pitman 14
N. Henderson 13 O. Sherwood 13

Notable % of winners: Miss C. Saunders R. Hodges O. Brennan O. Sherwood

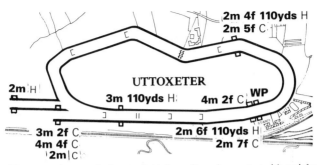

The course is an oval of approximately a mile and a quarter with mainly easy, sweeping, left-handed bends, and is essentially of a galloping nature, although there are minor undulations and the back stretch has slight bends. There are eight fences, with a run-in of around 170 yards. Races of two miles and three and a quarter miles are started on a spur on the last bend.

Most winners: M. Pipe 39 J. Edwards 17 G. Richards 17 J. Mackie 12
Notable % of winners: M. Tompkins M. Pipe T. Forster C. Brooks
                N. Twiston-Davies

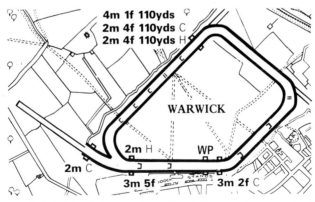

Warwick's left-handed course is a mile and three quarters round and there are ten fences to a circuit. The bends are rather tight and the track is a sharp one, favouring the handy horse. There is a run-in of 250 yards, the finishing straight is short and has only two fences.

Most winners: M. Pipe 39 D. Nicholson 17 Mrs J. Pitman 17
Notable % of winners: W. G. M. Turner M. Tompkins N. Gaselee M. Pipe

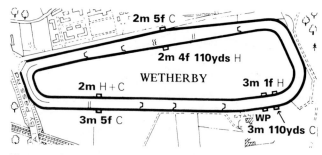

2m 5f C

2m 4f 110yds H

WETHERBY

2m H + C **3m 1f** H

3m 5f C

WP

3m 110yds C

The course is left-handed, with easy turns and follows a long oval circuit of a mile and a half. There are nine fences, and in races over three miles all the fences are jumped twice. The slightly uphill run-in is comparatively short for the chasers. The Wetherby track provides a very fair test for any horse, but is ideal for the free-running, long-striding individual with plenty of jumping ability. The old hurdle course is much sharper in character, having a circuit of one and a quarter miles with only two hurdles in the straight.

Most winners: G. Richards 30 M. H. Easterby 25 Mrs M. Reveley 24
　　　　　　　J. FitzGerald 22

Notable % of winners: M. Tompkins D. Nicholson J. Gifford Mrs M. Reveley

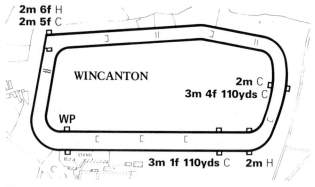

2m 6f H
2m 5f C

WINCANTON

2m C

3m 4f 110yds C

WP

3m 1f 110yds C **2m** H

Wincanton is a level course with an oval, right-handed circuit of around a mile and a half containing nine fences. The run from the last fence is only about 200 yards.

Most winners: M. Pipe 37 Mrs J. Pitman 26 D. Elsworth 22 R. Hodges 14
　　　　　　　D. Nicholson 14

Notable % of winners: Mrs J. Pitman M. Pipe D. Murray Smith
　　　　　　　N. Twiston-Davies

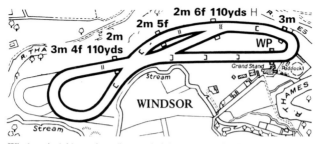

Windsor is laid out in a figure-of-eight pattern, the larger upper loop containing seven fences and the lower loop two fences. Three-mile chases take in almost two circuits. The track is flat, and sharp in nature.

Most winners: N. Henderson 11 Mrs J. Pitman 11 R. Akehurst 9 P. Hobbs 9
  O. Sherwood 9

Notable % of winners: J. Upson N. Henderson P. Hedger S. Sherwood

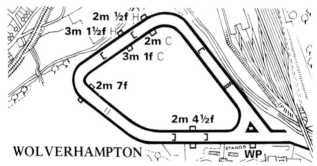

The course in use at Wolverhampton in 1992/93 was much sharper than the previous one, with seven fences to the left-handed circuit of about a mile and a quarter. The track, level throughout, had a two-furlong straight with a 230-yard run-in. There will be an entirely new course in use there in 1993/94 (all-weather).

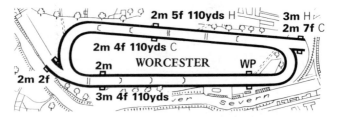

The course is laid out in the shape of a long oval of thirteen furlongs, flat throughout with easy, left-handed turns. There are nine well-sited fences, five in the back straight, four in the home straight, and a run-in of 220 yards. Worcester is regarded as one of the best and fairest courses for introducing a horse to steeplechasing.

Most winners: M. Pipe 54   O. Sherwood 25   P. Hobbs 17   T. Forster 16
               D. Nicholson 16

Notable % of winners: G. Harwood   M. Pipe   O. Sherwood   Miss H. Knight
                    N. Tinkler

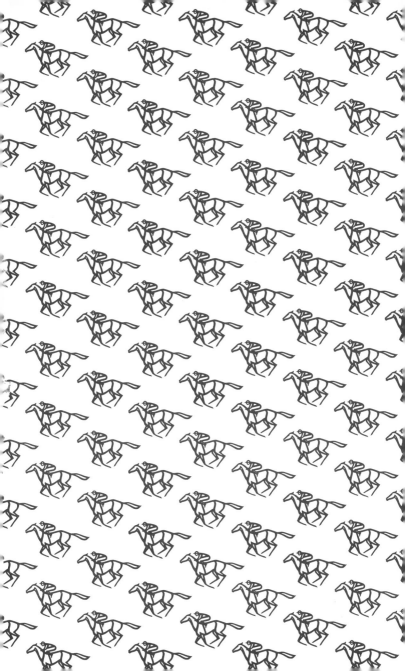